D1606050

JOURNAL FOR THE STUDY OF THE NEW TESTAMENT
SUPPLEMENT SERIES

291

Editor
Mark Goodacre

Editorial Board
John M.G. Barclay, Craig Blomberg, Elizabeth A.
Castelli, Kathleen E. Corley, R. Alan Culpepper,
James D.G. Dunn, Craig A. Evans, Stephen Fowl,
Robert Fowler, Simon J. Gathercole, Michael Labahn,
Robert Wall, Robert L. Webb, Catrin H. Williams

Looking for Life

The Role of 'Theo-Ethical Reasoning' in Paul's Religion

John G. Lewis

T & T CLARK INTERNATIONAL
A Continuum imprint
LONDON • NEW YORK

BS
2651
.L48
2005

For Pat

Copyright © 2005 John G. Lewis
A Continuum imprint

Published by T&T Clark International
The Tower Building, 11 York Road, London SE1 7NX
15 East 26th Street, Suite 1703, New York, NY 10010

www.tandtclark.com

All rights reserved. No part of this publication may be reproduced or transmitted in any form or by any means, electronic or mechanical, including photocopying, recording or any information storage or retrieval system, without permission in writing from the publishers.

British Library Cataloguing-in-Publication Data
A catalogue record for this book is available from the British Library

Library of Congress Cataloging-in-Publication Data
A catalogue record for this book is available from the Library of Congress

ISBN 0-5670-4272-3 (hardback)

Typeset by CA Typesetting, www.sheffieldtypesetting.com
Printed on acid-free paper in Great Britain by MPG Books Ltd, Bodmin, Cornwall.

CONTENTS

ACKNOWLEDGMENTS

This is a slightly revised version of my Oxford D.Phil. dissertation supervised by Robert Morgan, submitted in September 2003 and defended in March 2004. There are many people who have participated in this project and to whom thanks are owed. First, I am grateful to the Episcopal Church Foundation and Bell-Woolfall Foundation for awarding Fellowships that have provided generous funding during our residency in Oxford from 1997–2001. Dean Martha Horne and the faculty of Virginia Theological Seminary in Alexandria, Virginia were instrumental in supporting my applications for these fellowships. I am also grateful to Keble College, Oxford, and its Chaplains, the Rev. John Davies and his successor, the Rev. Mark Butchers, for naming me as the Water-Newton Graduate Student at Keble. This not only provided additional funding for our residency, but gave me the opportunity to serve for two years as Assistant Chaplain in the Keble Chapel under Mark Butchers, whose friendship buoyed me in the good and bad times. More recently, thanks to Mark Goodacre, Editor of the JSNT Supplement Series, for reviewing my dissertation manuscript and recommending its publication, and to Sarah Norman and Slav Todorov of T&T Clark for their editorial work on the manuscript.

Our four years in Oxford were life-transforming in many ways. Four people in particular are owed a special debt of gratitude. First, thanks to Dr Kevin Sullivan for many enjoyable and deep discussions about scripture, theology, angels, revelation, and St Paul. Thanks also to Kevin for his close reading of major portions of this manuscript and offering very helpful insights. Thanks also to the Rev. Professor Christopher Rowland for generously offering his valuable time to meet and discuss this project at a number of critical junctures in the development of the thesis. His grace, expertise and candor have shaped my thinking in this final work product in more ways than I can name. I am also indebted to my two examiners – Professor Rowland and Professor John M.G. Barclay of Durham – whose challenges to certain aspects of the original dissertation have resulted in some modifications reflected in the present text. Finally, I give great thanks for and to my supervisor, the Rev. Robert Morgan. Bob's gracious hospitality was instrumental in convincing us to move to England in 1997. A doctoral student could never ask or expect the extraordinary support, enthusiasm, time, expertise, and patience that Bob has offered over the last seven years. In so many ways, his selfless dedication to his students presents a vivid model of Christ's pattern of self-giving love for others. Bob's ministry has certainly shaped this project. Thanks to Bob for being a fine mentor, tutor, and friend throughout this project.

Thanks also to my friends at St Mark's Episcopal Church, San Antonio, Texas and to its Rector, the Rev. Michael Chalk. Their support and encouragement for the past two-and-a-half years have sustained us through some difficult and challenging times. I am especially grateful to the members of our spiritual discernment groups at St Mark's Center for Faith in the WorkPlace, whose weekly practice of this discipline has surely affirmed the fruitfulness of the thesis presented in this book. And thanks also to my St Mark's friend Kate Crone, whose proofreading skills have made this manuscript easier reading for everyone.

Finally, I thank my wife Pat for her love, support, kindness, patience and long-suffering during our journey together, especially over the last seven years. Her willingness to give up her successful law career, family, friends, and security to move 5,000 miles from home has illuminated for me what Christ-like self-emptying looks like. She has shown me regularly what it means to die daily to the standards and expectations of the world and to live to God in Christ. As a result, we have experienced the life-giving, community-building power of God throughout the last seven years of our journey together. To her this dissertation is dedicated with love and heartfelt thanks.

John G. Lewis
Holy Cross Day 2004
San Antonio, Texas

ABBREVIATIONS

AB	Anchor Bible
ABD	David Noel Feedman (ed.), *The Anchor Bible Dictionary* (New York: Doubleday, 1992)
AGJU	Arbeiten zur Geschichte des antiken Judentums und des Urchristentums
AnBib	Analecta biblica
ATR	*Anglican Theological Review*
AusBR	*Australian Biblical Review*
BAGD	Walter Bauer, William F. Arndt, F. William Gingrich, and Frederick W. Danker, *A Greek-English Lexicon of the New Testament and Other Early Christian Literature* (Chicago: University of Chicago Press, 2nd edn, 1958)
BHTh	Bieträge zur historischen Theologie
Bib	*Biblica*
BJRL	*Bulletin of the John Rylands University Library of Manchester*
BNTC	Black's New Testament Commentaries
BR	*Bible Review*
BZ	*Biblische Zeitschrift*
BZNW	Beihefte zur *ZNW*
CBQ	*Catholic Biblical Quarterly*
EvQ	*Evangelical Quarterly*
ExpTim	*Expository Times*
FRLANT	Forschungen zur Religion und Literatur des Alten und Neuen Testaments
HBT	*Horizons in Biblical Theology*
HDR	Harvard Dissertations in Religion
HTR	*Harvard Theological Review*
IBS	*Irish Biblical Studies*
ICC	International Critical Commentary
IDB	George Arthur Buttrick (ed.), *The Interpreter's Dictionary of the Bible* (4 vols.; Nashville: Abingdon Press, 1962)
IDBSup	*IDB*, Supplementary Volume
Int	*Interpretation*
ISBE	Geoffrey Bromily (ed.), *The International Standard Bible Encyclopedia* (4 vols.; Grand Rapids: Eerdmans, rev. edn, 1979–88)
JAAR	*Journal of the American Academy of Religion*
JBL	*Journal of Biblical Literature*
JETS	*Journal of the Evangelical Theological Society*
JJS	*Journal of Jewish Studies*
JR	*Journal of Religion*
JSNT	*Journal for the Study of the New Testament*
JSNTSup	*Journal for the Study of the New Testament*, Supplement Series
JSPSup	*Journal for the Study of the Pseudepigrapha*, Supplement Series
JTS	*Journal of Theological Studies*

KJV	King James Version
LCL	Loeb Classical Library
LSJ	H.G. Liddell, Robert Scott and H. Stuart Jones, *Greek-English Lexicon* (Oxford: Clarendon Press, 9th edn, 1968)
NAB	*New American Bible*
NCBC	New Century Bible Commentary
NedTTs	*Nederlands theologisch tijdschrift*
Neot	*Neotestamentica*
NICNT	New International Commentary on the New Testament
NIGTC	The New International Greek Testament Commentary
NIV	New International Version
NKJ	New King James Version
NovT	*Novum Testamentum*
NovTSup	*Novum Testamentum*, Supplements
NRSV	New Revised Standard Version
NTD	Das Neue Testament Deutsch
NTS	*New Testament Studies*
RB	*Revue biblique*
RevExp	*Review and Expositor*
RSV	Revised Standard Version
SBL	Society of Biblical Literature
SBLDS	SBL Dissertation Series
SBT	Studies in Biblical Theology
SEÅ	*Svensk exegetisk årsbot*
SJT	*Scottish Journal of Theology*
SNTSMS	Society for New Testament Studies Monograph Series
SNTW	Studies of the New Testament and its World
ST	*Studia theological*
TDNT	Gerhard Kittel and Gerhard Friedrich (eds.), *Theological Dictionary of the New Testament* (trans. Geoffrey Bromily: 10 vols.; Grand Rapids: Eerdmans, 1964–1976)
TynBul	*Tyndale Bulletin*
TZ	*Theologische Zeitschrift*
USQR	*Union Seminary Quarterly Review*
WBC	Word Biblical Commentary
WMANT	Wissenschaftliche Monographien zum Alten und Neuen Testament
WUNT	Wissenschaftliche Untersuchungen zum Neuen Testament
ZNW	*Zeitschrift für die neutestamentliche Wissenschaft*
ZTK	*Zeitschrift für Theologie und Kirche*

Chapter 1

THEOLOGY AND ETHICS IN PAUL

1. *Purpose of this Study*

This exegetical study challenges the adequacy of three interrelated foci of twentieth-century Protestant Pauline interpretation. Interpreters regularly: (1) distinguish Paul's theology from his ethics; (2) emphasize his oral preaching as the sole or primary vehicle for gospel proclamation and divine revelation; and (3) deny that Paul engages in reasoned, ethical reflection. These traditional perspectives stand in need of comprehensive revision. A new proposal will be offered for understanding how Paul does theology and ethics as a former Pharisee and first-century pastoral theologian[1] – a Christian community-builder with an apocalyptic (i.e. revelatory) perspective.[2]

It will be argued that Paul integrates Christian thinking and living, combining what interpreters frequently (incorrectly) separate as theology and ethics.[3] This becomes evident in Paul's complex process of theological, moral reasoning for which we have coined the phrase 'theo-ethical reasoning'. This characterization captures both the divine and human elements of Paul's behavioural reasoning that is grounded in his interpretation of the divine–human partnership revealed in Jesus Christ. Pursuant to theo-ethical reasoning, Paul associates Christ-conforming conduct with the power of God that becomes manifest in community experiences of new life. This reasoning often lies beneath the surface of the undisputed Pauline texts.[4] Consequently, the present study will explore the underlying logic of Paul's arguments in order to highlight the consistent pattern of reasoning by which he analyses and responds to community behavioural issues.[5]

---

1. The phrase 'pastoral theologian' is used to distinguish this study from those who characterize Paul by using the language of doctrinal theology. For recent interpretations that explore Paul as a pastoral theologian, see Malherbe 1987; 2000a; Dabourne 1999; van Spanje 1999; Gorman 2001.

2. See Chapter 1, section 3.b for interpretative support for using 'apocalyptic' in the context of revelation.

3. A recent comment by Dunn illustrates this problem: 'Paul's ethics have often been rather problematic *for theologians*' (1998c: 628, emphasis added).

4. This study follows the general consensus that the undisputed Pauline texts at least include the canonical letters known as Romans, 1 and 2 Corinthians, Galatians, Philippians, 1 Thessalonians and Philemon. Comparisons will be made with Colossians, Ephesians and 2 Thessalonians, however, since Pauline perspectives have clearly influenced these letters regardless of authorship.

5. For this approach to 'New Testament ethics', see Keck 1996a: 3–16, discussed in Chapter 1, section 4.

It is suggested that theo-ethical reasoning is grounded in Paul's revelatory experience of the risen Christ.[6] These include the appearance of the crucified but risen Christ *to* Paul,[7] the revelation of God's Son *in* Paul,[8] and his visions and revelations of the Lord.[9] Reflecting on this revelatory experience, Paul apparently concluded that God divinely confirmed Christ's human act of self-giving love for others on the cross by raising him from the dead.[10] For Paul this event thus confirmed a new and universal behavioural pattern for all humanity that will hereinafter be referred to as 'Christ's cruciform pattern' or 'cruciformity'.[11] After his experience of this divine life-giving power, Paul understood and taught that conduct conforming to this pattern represents the divinely approved pathway to the experience of new and eternal life from God.

Moreover, Paul also apparently concluded that experiences of God's life-giving power continue to take place in connection with other believers' actions that conform to Christ's cruciform pattern.[12] The present study will argue that the heart of theo-ethical reasoning lies in this discernible link between specific Christ-conforming actions and experiences of new life grounded in the manifest power of God.[13]

We will attempt to show how Paul incorporated this reasoning into his own apostolic ministry and into the lives of the members of his churches. Paul em-

6. For the importance of Paul's revelatory experience to his gospel, see Kim 1984; Segal 1990; 1998; 1999; Morray Jones 1992, Rowland 1982; 1983; 1988a; 1995a; 1995b; Tabor 1986; Ashton 2000; Gorman 2001: 25; Barclay 2002: 140.

7. See 1 Cor. 9.1; 15.8; cf. Gal. 1.12.

8. See Gal. 1.16.

9. See 2 Cor. 12.1, 7. The importance of revelation for Paul is reviewed below in Chapter 1, section 3.b.

10. See 2 Cor. 13.4; Phil. 2.5–11; cf. Gal. 1.1, 4; 2.20.

11. Gorman has recently described this Christ pattern of self-giving love for others as 'cruciformity' (2001: 19–49) and characterized Paul's practical moral reasoning as 'spirituality' (2001: 331 n. 47). In Chapter 1, section 2.e Gorman's work is assessed. Engberg-Pedersen similarly concludes that Paul develops a 'form of human living' grounded in the death and resurrection of Christ (2000: 47), an event that reveals a new 'social norm' of 'love' (1987: 566–67). Engberg-Pedersen's work is reviewed in Chapter 1, section 2.d. Other recent interpreters note Paul's emphasis on the example of the Christ pattern of conduct defined as self-giving for others. According to Hays (1996a: 27–32), this pattern is the central ethical motif in Paul and those who enter into a life that recapitulates Christ's pattern are 'saved by his life' (Rom. 5.10). See also Malherbe 2000b: 115; Bryant 2001: 194; Tomlin 1999: 98; Pickett 1997: 214; Carroll and Green 1995: 131; Cousar 1990a: 186; and Cosgrove 1988: viii. Meeks (1982a: 272) and Tannehill (1967: 6, 75) emphasize 'dying and rising with Christ' as the pattern of living that Paul's community members must follow. See also Keck 1980: 45–49; Hays 1987: 276. Gorman essentially adopts this as the essence of cruciformity.

According to Barclay, Paul moulds the story of his own life into a 'christomorphic historiography' that takes the shape of the crucified and risen Jesus (2002: 151). Paul's life is moulded by the 'master pattern' of the crucifixion and new creation (2002: 155). See also Horrell (2002: 166), who concludes that '[i]t is the paradigm of self-giving seen in Christ's death, and the hope embodied in his resurrection, that gives Paul the new and defining pattern with which to (re)shape his own personal story'; see also Horrell 1999: 323–25; 1997a: 83–114.

12. See, e.g., 1 Cor. 1.5–8; 2.1–5; Gal. 3.1–5.

13. See 1 Cor. 12.4–7 (see Chapter 3, section 3.b).

braced Christ's cruciform pattern as his own exclusive behavioural norm.[14] Through Paul's actions that conform to Christ's cruciform pattern, the crucified but risen Christ continues to become manifest to others.[15] Thus, Paul's embodied proclamation of the crucified and risen Christ takes place by means of both words and deeds.[16]

Moreover, it will be shown that Paul teaches the members of his churches to think, act, and reason in a similar manner by reflecting together to discern the links between Christ-conforming conduct and experiences of new life from God.[17] This study argues that theo-ethical reasoning establishes the conceptual framework for the dialogical, community practice of spiritual discernment in Paul's churches.[18] Believers practise spiritual discernment by *looking for life* in the manifestations of the Spirit that illuminate experiences of this new life.[19] By 'comparing spiritual things with spiritual things',[20] believers distinguish their experiences of this new life from other experiences merely associated with the spirit of the world.[21] These experiences are demonstrations of Spirit and power associated with Christ-conforming conduct that ground believers' faith in the power of God.[22] This association becomes the means by which believers are 'led by the Spirit' in order to 'walk by the Spirit'.[23]

It will also be contended that, according to Paul, believers actively participate in the divine–human partnership in Jesus Christ by conforming their behaviour to Christ's cruciform pattern and practising spiritual discernment in the community.[24] As partners with God and Christ, they participate in God's cosmic redemptive process that was inaugurated in the death and resurrection of Jesus Christ. This process continues as God exercises that same life-giving power to build up Christian communities through the conduct of believers who are led by the Spirit to conform their actions to Christ's cruciform pattern.[25] In this process believers

14. See 1 Cor. 11.1; Gal. 2.17; Phil. 3.10.

15. See, e.g., 2 Cor. 4.6; 12.6–7; Gal. 2.20; 3.1; 4.14; cf. 2 Cor. 13.3–4; Phil. 4.8–9; Barclay 2002: 145–46.

16. See, e.g., Rom. 15.18–19; 1 Cor. 2.1–5; 2 Cor. 4.1–12; 1 Thess. 2.1–14.

17. For the way Paul illustrates this reasoning, see 1 Cor. 1.5–9 (see Chapter 2, section 2.b), 1 Cor. 2.1–5 (see Chapter 2, section 3.c), and Gal. 3.1–5 (see Chapter 4, section 3.a); cf. 2 Cor. 13.5.

18. For various aspects of this practice, see Rom. 8.1–25; 1 Cor. 2.6–16; 12.4–13; 14.1–40; Gal. 5.5–8, 18–25; Phil. 2.1–13; cf. Eph. 3.7–12; 4.17–24; 5.15–21; Col. 3.1–17.

19. See, e.g., 1 Cor. 2.4–5, 12; 12.4–7; Gal. 5.22–23.

20. See 1 Cor. 2.13 (see Chapter 2, section 3.d).

21. For this spirit, see 1 Cor. 2.12.

22. See 1 Cor. 2.1–5 (see Chapter 2, section 3.c).

23. For Paul's references to being led by the Spirit, see Rom. 8.14; Gal. 5.18. For the importance of walking by the Spirit, see Gal. 5.16, 18, 25 (see Chapter 4, section 5); cf. 1 Thess. 4.8.

24. For this partnership, see 1 Cor. 1.9, discussed in Chapter 2, section 2.b.

25. Thus, this study challenges the conclusions of some Pauline interpreters who argue that for Paul the conduct of a believer is controlled by the invasion of an external power that determines how a person will act. It will be argued herein that Paul understands a different sequence. There is a variety of community experiences wrought by external powers (divine or worldly) in connection with particular human actions. God effectuates experiences of new earthly life in connection with conduct that conforms to Christ's cruciform pattern of self-giving love for others (see, e.g., 1 Cor. 12.5–6),

also may come to know Christ and the power of his resurrection as they share in his suffering and conform their actions to his cruciform death.[26]

Chapter 1 is divided into four remaining sections. Section 2 identifies the 'problem of ethics in Paul' and reviews various solutions offered in the history of research. Developments in Pauline interpretation that point toward Paul's religion for a new solution to the 'problem' are reviewed in section 3. Section 4 introduces the alternative solution proposed by this study. The chapter closes in section 5 with a short description of how data was selected for inclusion.

Through exegesis of 1 Cor. 1.1–4.21, Chapter 2 identifies Paul's theo-ethical reasoning and shows how it becomes the conceptual framework for the community practice of spiritual discernment in the church. Chapter 3 (1 Cor. 5.1–16.24) explores how Paul practises spiritual discernment by engaging in theo-ethical reasoning to analyse and address specific behavioural issues. Chapter 4 examines Galatians, similarly showing how Paul combines theology and ethics in theo-ethical reasoning by practising spiritual discernment. The concluding Chapter 5 summarizes the findings and relates them to the field of Pauline interpretation. It also identifies certain parallels between the contemporary theory of moral philosophy known as discourse (communicative) ethics and the role theo-ethical reasoning plays in the structure of community life in Paul's churches.

2. *The 'Problem of Ethics in Paul'*

This section addresses the common distinction between theology and ethics in the twentieth-century history of Protestant Pauline interpretation. It also identifies how some scholars ground their interpretation in a particular understanding of Luther's doctrine of *simul iustus et peccator* and thereby create the 'problem of ethics in Paul'.

a. *Traditional Statements of the 'Problem': Rudolf Bultmann and Victor Furnish*
In 1924 Rudolf Bultmann published 'The Problem of Ethics in Paul' (1924: 123–40).[27] This influential article addressed the perceived contradiction associated with Paul's statements of theological indicative and ethical imperative.[28] As

---

while worldly powers effectuate other experiences in connection with conduct that conforms to the behavioural standards of the world (see, e.g., Gal. 5.19–21).

   26. See Phil. 3.10; cf. 1 Cor. 2.1–5; 2 Cor. 4.10–12; 13.1–5; Gal. 3.1–5.

   27. ET Rosner 1995: 195–216; all citations are to Bultmann 1924.

   28. Bultmann was expressly responding (1924: 123) to Paul Wernle, who had earlier written about the overlooked problem of how those who believed in Christ could continue to commit sins (1897: 1). Interpretative accounts of Paul's theology are often arranged for heuristic purposes according to doctrinal categories drawn from systematic theology. They are usually based on his use of verbs in the indicative mood that are supposed to reflect what God has already fully accomplished in the death and resurrection of Jesus Christ. Within this traditional framework, Paul expresses ethics through verbs in the imperative mood that are focused on prescribing or proscribing particular human behaviour and mental attitudes derived from Paul's doctrinal theology. See, e.g., Dunn 1998c: 631.

with some earlier studies of Paul, Bultmann's analysis presupposes the distinction between ethics and theology in Paul's letters and thought.[29] His conclusions established the parameters for most subsequent discussions of the 'problem',[30] including his own later work on the subject.[31]

Bultmann sought to explain how a person could be at once justified but still require moral exhortation. He identified God's gift of righteousness or justification – in other words, sinlessness – as having the character of divine event arising from God's grace. Bultmann argued that this gift does not involve moral transformation and is not perceptible as human experience or recognizable by behaviour (1924: 136). He concludes that the nature of this new life is purely eschatological. It can only be believed as a gift from God (1924: 136) with the imperative itself constituting part of that gift (1924: 140). He thereby effectively spiritualizes a person's relation to bodily life in the world.[32]

Bultmann thus finds Paul paradoxically exhorting believers who are already justified to 'become what you are'.[33] This distinctive and enduring characterization of Paul's paraenesis is grounded in Bultmann's particular understanding of Luther's doctrine that each Christian is *simul iustus et peccator* – simultaneously justified and a sinner. Bultmann presents an exclusively eschatological framework for understanding the so-called 'already-not yet' tension that many interpreters locate in Paul's letters.[34]

Moreover, Bultmann concludes that 'the salvation-occurrence is nowhere present *except* in the proclaiming, accosting, demanding, and promising word of *preaching*'.[35] Christ and his incarnation become present and active in this oral proclamation (1951: 305). These findings seem to betray Bultmann's commitment to twentieth-century kerygmatic theology where sermon-centred Christian preaching constitutes the modern locus of divine revelation through which God

29. This distinction began at least as early as 1845 in F.C. Baur and continued through the nineteenth and twentieth centuries with interpreters such as Holtzmann (1911), Wernle (1897), Wrede (1904; ET 1907), Enslin (1925) and A. Schweitzer (1931). In his early study of Paul's religion rather than his theology, Pfleiderer (1877) does not emphasize this distinction. Space does not permit an extensive review of these authors and their work.

30. Responses usually assume the same central structure of theological indicative and ethical imperative. See Windisch 1924: 265–81; Furnish 1968: 9, 262–79; Dunn 1998c: 627–29, including n. 11; Dennison 1979: 55–78; Strecker 1987: 60–72; Willis 1996: 306–19; cf. Schrage 1988: 167, 169; Sampley 1991a: 3; Marxsen 1993: 180; Rosner 1995: 18. Engberg-Pedersen has recently offered a comprehensive, alternative approach to resolve the 'problem' that will be discussed below in Chapter 1, section 2.d.

31. See especially 1951: 330–40; 1964a: 15–42.

32. For this criticism, see Käsemann 1971b: 13–14, 19–21; Beker 1980: 276.

33. This phrase appeared later in Bultmann's writings (see, e.g., 1951: 332).

34. See 1924: 139; cf. Luther 1958: 19–29. For other discussions of this 'already-not yet' tension, see Beker 1980: 272–302; Dunn 1998c: 461–72; see generally Lincoln 1981. Marxsen denies that this tension can be resolved logically (1993: 180). His statement of the question highlights that part of the 'problem' lies in a particular interpretation of this Lutheran doctrine: 'If…God has already passed his favorable judgment on humanity (indicative) – which Paul obviously presupposes after Damascus – what significance can be given (theologically) to the imperatives?' (1993: 181).

35. 1951: 302 (original emphasis reduced).

confronts humanity.[36] Bultmann's exegesis thereby appears to impose on Paul a modern way of doing theology that distorts his historical description.[37]

Bultmann fails to acknowledge that for Paul human conduct becomes a vehicle for Christian proclamation and divine revelation.[38] He seemingly ignores Paul's conviction that God transforms earthly human life in ways that become manifest in the empirical lives of believers.[39] The present study shows how this conviction grounds Paul's theo-ethical reasoning and the community practice of spiritual discernment. In this practice, believers seek to associate manifest experiences of new life from God with specific Christ-conforming conduct.

Bultmann's bifurcation of ethics and theology and his overemphasis on Paul's preaching shaped his eschatological solution to the 'problem of ethics in Paul'. He established the parameters for most subsequent discussions of the 'problem'. The distinctions remain important ones, at least in Protestant scholarship, since Paul's theological statements delivered in preaching are still often given priority over his ethics for understanding the apostle's thought and writings.[40]

The legacy of Bultmann can be identified in the important work by Victor Furnish. He concludes that 'the relation of indicative and imperative, the relation of "theological" proclamation and "moral" exhortation, is *the* crucial problem in interpreting the Pauline ethic' (1968: 9, original emphasis).[41] Indeed, Furnish finds that the 'dynamic of indicative and imperative' lies at the centre of Paul's thought (1968: 211). Like Bultmann, Furnish also defines the relationship between Paul's theology and ethics according to various modern doctrinal categories of systematic theology.[42] He concludes that the 'fundamental components' of Paul's 'ethic' are derived from his theological, eschatological and christological convictions that form the root motifs of his preaching (1968: 212–13).[43]

Moreover, Furnish concludes that in Paul's *preaching* the meaning and reality of the eschatological action of God break into the present (1968: 215). Despite

36. For this latter conclusion, see Morgan 1995b: 123.

37. For a similar conclusion, see Kittredge 1998: 15.

38. See, e.g., Rom. 15.18–21; 1 Cor. 2.1–5; 4.16; 11.1; 2 Cor. 12.1, 7; 13.3; Gal. 1.16, 23; 3.1–5; 4.14, 19; Phil. 4.8–9; 1 Thess. 1.6. Indeed, Gorman points out that Paul's body was living proof of his personal story and his scars become the 'present epiphany of the crucifixion of Jesus' (2001: 31, quoting Martyn 1997b: 569); see also Güttgemanns 1966: 185.

39. For a similar critique, see Furnish 1968: 264. For Paul's direct references to the divine transformation of human life, see Rom. 8.29; 12.2; 2 Cor. 3.18; Gal. 4.19; Phil. 2.6–7; 3.21.

40. Indeed, according to Bultmann, in the typical primitive Christian doctrinal and hortatory writings the ethical paraenesis takes second place (1964a: 17). Tuckett posits a similar argument, asserting that 'freedom in relation to ethics and behaviour has to be distinguished sharply from freedom in relation to doctrinal and soteriological matters for Paul: ethical freedom is not allowed to prejudice in any way belief in the full saving work of Christ' and its implications (1991: 324).

Some interpreters still insist that there are even 'theological' and 'ethical' *sections* in Paul's letters. Schrage, for example, stresses this 'well-known fact' (1988: 167). For a critique of this position in connection with Galatians, see Engberg-Pedersen 2000: 136. Dahl assails the unhelpful modern separation between Paul's theology – often described as a dogmatic system – and Paul's approach to mission (1977d: 70).

41. Cf. Beker 1980: 275–78.

42. See Furnish 1968; 1993a; 1999.

43. For a similar position, see Hays 1996a: 19; Fee 1987: 7.

his assertions that Paul's theology and ethics are integral to one another, Furnish nonetheless offers an interpretation that in fact separates ethics from the theology that is proclaimed orally in Paul's doctrinal preaching.[44] According to Furnish, Paul preaches the content of his gospel message involving theological concepts and then tries to correlate this message with human behaviour by *ad hoc* teaching of his own ideas about good and bad conduct based on this message.[45]

Denying that Paul had any ethical theory, Furnish further concludes that Paul does not engage in critical examination or deliberate on the ways in which his ethical concerns are related to his basic theological convictions.[46] He denies that Paul ever establishes any rational standard or propounds any theory of how one knows right from wrong or good from evil in particular instances (1968: 232–33, 236–37).[47] This is true, says Furnish, even though Paul insisted on the urgency of discerning God's will and must have presupposed that it was a practical possibility (1968: 233).

Two things are important in this regard. First, says Furnish, 'the presupposition of Paul's appeal to seek out God's will with one's own critical faculties (δοκιμάζειν, Rom. 12.2) is that those faculties (the νοῦς) have been totally renewed and redeemed in Christ (Rom. 12.1–2)' (1968: 230).[48] He challenges Bultmann's phrase 'become what you are' because it only suggests the '*possibility* of new life' rather than the 'actually and totally new existence' that already has been given the believer through justification on the basis of faith (1968: 225, original emphasis).

It would thus appear that Furnish relies on a particular (incorrect) understanding of Luther's *simul iustus et peccator* in reaching his conclusion. According to Luther, sin is forgiven in baptism and not imputed when 'we believe in Christ' *and* when 'we battle unceasingly against sin' (1958: 28). On the other hand, 'where these two reasons are not present', Luther continues, 'sin is imputed, is not forgiven, and condemns us eternally' (1958: 28). Thus, according to Luther's reading of Paul, the battle against sin must continue after baptism. It involves a *lifelong* battle against sin's power for the new life of Christ to be efficacious for

---

44. Despite his express critique of C.H. Dodd's distinction between 'kerygma' and 'didache' in early Christian proclamation (see Dodd 1944), Furnish's conclusions nonetheless bear a close resemblance to those of Dodd. Even the title of Furnish's study – *Theology and Ethics in Paul* – highlights his perpetuation of this distinction.

45. 1968: 210; cf. Furnish 1993b: 61; Barclay 1988: 27–28.

46. 1968: 211–12; cf. W.D. Davies 1972a: 310; Deissmann 1957: 207, 215. Drawing on the definition of ethics suggested by Wayne Meeks (1993a: 3–6) and Gerd Theissen (1999: 337 n. 1), discussed below in Chapter 1, section 3.a, this study challenges these conclusions. We contend that by engaging in theo-ethical reasoning Paul and other believers practise reasoned reflection to relate their experiences of new life with particular Christ-conforming actions.

47. The present study seeks to show how Paul structures community life around a rational and coherent approach to discerning appropriate behaviour (summarized succinctly in Rom. 12.1–2, discussed briefly in Chapter 5, section 3). This takes place through a reasoning process that includes reflection on conduct and experience in light of the universal cruciform pattern of Christ's self-giving love for others manifest in his death on the cross.

48. See also Cullmann 1964: 228; Dunn 1975: 223–24.

salvation. Furnish thus overstates the *finality* of the baptismal victory.[49] The present study argues that Paul and his churches practise spiritual discernment by engaging in theo-ethical reasoning. This represents the means by which believers unceasingly battle against sin throughout their lives, obtain forgiveness of sins, and avoid the imputation of sin for eternal condemnation.[50]

Second, while Furnish acknowledges that the Holy Spirit serves an important function as 'revealer' for Paul, he denies any connection between these revelations of the Holy Spirit and the discernment of God's will for a Christian's practical decisions and deeds (1968: 231–33). He concludes that Paul's concept of being led by the Spirit does not include reference to any particular patterns of behaviour or moral actions (1968: 232). In effect Furnish weakens the connection between the Spirit and ethics in Paul's religion.

Furnish thus *widens* the conceptual gap between theology and ethics in Paul's letters and thought. Through exegesis of passages that include 1 Cor. 2.1–3.3, Gal. 3.1–5 and 5.18–25, the present study challenges this widening separation. It will be argued that for Paul there is a direct connection between God's will for human conduct and the manifestations of the Spirit. According to Paul's theo-ethical reasoning, the Spirit represents the divine agent whose manifestations illuminate the links between experiences of new life and Christ-conforming conduct. Spiritually discerning these connections provides believers with insight into actions that are pleasing to God and conform to God's will.

b. *Apocalyptic Contours of the 'Problem': J. Louis Martyn*
In recent years there has been growing dissatisfaction with Bultmann's de-mythologized interpretation that strips away Paul's apocalyptic perspective.[51] J. Louis Martyn seeks to remedy this deficiency. He points emphatically towards God's ongoing war of liberation that is crucial for understanding Paul's 'apocalyptic theology' (1997b: 105).[52] According to Martyn, the cosmos becomes a battlefield where the human condition requires liberation from the malignant powers that enslave it. This takes place, he says, not through divine forgiveness but through the divine, invasive act of sending Christ into the world to suffer death for all of humanity (1997b: 273).[53]

On Martyn's reading, however, apocalyptic becomes solely epistemological and does not include an ethical dimension. This unnecessarily separates the 'act

49. Paul appears to suggest an ongoing process of transformation rather than the already-completed one that Furnish describes. See, e.g., Rom. 12.2; 2 Cor. 4.16; Gal. 2.17; Phil. 3.12; cf. Col. 3.10.

50. See now Rom. 8.1, discussed in Chapter 5, section 3, where Paul asserts that there is now no condemnation in Christ. We contend that this assertion applies to those who engage in theo-ethical reasoning and the ongoing practice of spiritual discernment in the churches.

51. Käsemann persuasively argued that the apocalyptic aspects of Paul's thought must be taken seriously in historical reconstruction (see 1969c; 1969d).

52. Although Martyn does not ground his apocalyptic interpretation in the literary genre of 'apocalypse' (1997b: 21–23), he characterizes as 'quite suggestive' (1997b: 21–22 n. 28) the contention of R. Hall (1996: 434–53) that Paul's argument in Galatians does in fact display certain identifiable characteristics associated with arguments from other apocalypses.

53. See Gal. 4.3–5; cf. Rom. 8.1–4.

of thinking' from the 'act of living' in Paul's religion.[54] It perpetuates the distinction between theology and ethics and overlooks certain Second Temple motifs of spatial, temporal and ethical dualism utilized by Paul.[55] With Furnish, Martyn also denies that Paul engages reflectively in doing ethics according to any particular ethical theory (1997b: 502 n. 89).

Furthermore, with Bultmann and Furnish, Martyn unduly emphasizes Paul's oral preaching as the exclusive place where God is revealed at work in the world (1997b: 116; 1991: 161). Martyn equates the 'event' character of the gospel – 'God's apocalyptic act in Christ' (1997b: 116)[56] – with Paul's preaching of the event of Christ's crucifixion. Drawing on terminology from speech-acts theory, Martyn concludes that: 'Paul refers to God's locutionary advent in which the human will is *liberated* into faithful obedience to God when it is *"commandeered"* by the power of God's gracious word' (2002: 88, original emphasis).

Martyn also finds that for Paul there is no autonomy for human beings – only enslavement to sin or the obedience of God that is incited by God's liberating word (2002: 88). He thus joins with Käsemann, insisting that for Paul a person is wholly determined by invasive, external powers.[57] This aspect of Martyn's interpretation creates an unnecessary antithesis between human decision and divine action.[58] It produces an un-Pauline understanding of the divine–human relationship.[59]

The present study challenges Martyn's characterization of this relationship between human conduct and the invasive external powers. The solution to this aspect of the 'problem of ethics in Paul' may lie in understanding that for Paul these powers – whether God or worldly forces – do *not* take possession and control of an individual, thereby causing specific behavioural actions to occur. Rather, from exegesis it will be argued that these external powers work certain discernible effects *through or in connection with* specific human actions.[60] Human action

54. According to Schlatter, this separation was not characteristic of the early church (1997: 19). Brown identifies this as an unnecessary limitation that is present in Martyn's work (1995: 149).

55. For a broader discussion of these apocalyptic motifs in Second Temple Judaism, see Gammie 1974; Adams 2000: 106; Meeks 1982b: 689. They will be examined in Chapter 1, section 3.b.

56. Cf. 1997b: 37 ('God's apocalyptic deed').

57. See, e.g., Käsemann 1971b: 24, 28. For a critique of Käsemann's 'ill-defined' position in this regard, see Barclay 1988: 201–202. Martyn is vulnerable to the same challenge. In responding to Martyn's critique of *Paul and the Stoics*, Engberg-Pedersen similarly challenges Martyn's either/or dichotomy between 'human autonomy' and the work of the 'external powers' (2002: 107, 109–10). Engberg-Pedersen correctly points out that Paul's paraenesis, like any kind of exhortation, presumes that its addressees understand what is being said and may also take action in response. He concludes that this has nothing to do with human autonomy over against God and does not go against Paul's idea that believers are being divinely led by the Spirit (see 2000: 107–108).

58. This tension can be seen clearly at 1997a: 219–20 n. 23.

59. See 1997b: 325 (n. 124), 530, 534. The nature of the divine–human relationship during Paul's time, especially as it relates to the role of angels in Jewish literature and the New Testament, is explored more fully in Sullivan 2004.

60. See 1 Cor. 12.4–7; Gal. 5.19–25; contra Martyn, who contends that in Paul the 'actions… are…effected by the two warring powers' (1997b: 532).

thereby becomes the vehicle through which an external power works specific effects in the world.[61]

Martyn unduly limits the important Pauline 'already/not yet' framework to baptism. He finds that the baptismal 'victory was decisive but it is paradoxically incomplete' (1997b: 501). Consequently, he expressly adopts Bultmann's catch-phrase 'become what you are' (1997b: 535, including n. 184). He concludes that believers must constantly 're-enact' their decisive baptismal victory in the life of the community by repeating the event of crucifixion every day (1997b: 501). Like Bultmann, Martyn by implication grounds his interpretation in a particular understanding of Luther's *simul iustus et peccator*. This requires the eschatological solution to the 'problem of ethics in Paul' that spiritualizes bodily life in the world and distorts any historical reconstruction of Paul's perspective.

Nonetheless, Martyn draws on Luther's conclusion that there is no divine forgiveness in the absence of some form of ongoing practice to battle sin.[62] He also relies on Käsemann's related insight that Christian life is 'a perpetual return to baptism…so long as we keep on the pilgrim way and allow ourselves to be recalled daily to the allegiance of Christ'.[63] These important observations actually suggest that for Paul the baptismal victory is *not* in fact decisive for the believer but must be consistently lived out thereafter.[64] The real issue for believers thus becomes one of how to participate unceasingly in the battle against sin in order to be protected from eternal condemnation. The present study tentatively suggests that for Paul this battle against sin is carried out as believers practise spiritual discernment, engaging in theo-ethical reasoning to reflect on conduct and experience and thereby discern the will of God through testing as part of a community discipline.

Thus, it will be argued that Martyn *does not go far enough* when exploring the ramifications of Paul's apocalyptic (i.e. revelatory) perspective. For Paul, conduct conforming to Christ's cruciform pattern becomes the means by which humans participate with God in the ongoing cosmic warfare. Those who engage in theo-ethical reasoning by practising spiritual discernment are looking for life and its links to Christ-conforming conduct. From Paul's apocalyptic (i.e. revelatory) perspective, the Spirit's manifestations of the experiences of new life provide believers with essential guidance for discerning divinely approved conduct. This in turn allows believers to envision imaginatively those future actions through which they may anticipate other experiences of new life in God's new age and spatial realm that Paul characterizes as life in Christ.

c. *Rethinking the 'Problem'*

Several Pauline interpreters have recently challenged the traditional bifurcation of theology and ethics while trying to resolve the 'problem of ethics in Paul'.

---

61. See, e.g., 1 Cor. 12.4–6; Gal. 5.19–21.
62. See Luther 1958: 28.
63. Käsemann 1969e: 175; see also Barclay 1988: 214.
64. Indeed, the present study will show that the logic underlying Gal. 5.2–4 reflects that the baptismal victory is not necessarily decisive if a later change in practice takes place. See Chapter 4, section 4.

Noting that theology and ethics were not so sharply distinguished in antiquity, Troels Engberg-Pedersen suggests that such a distinction raises more problems than it resolves.[65] So, too, James D.G. Dunn makes a related point:

> For it remains a continuing question as to whether theology is the best label to describe Jewish faith and life; the centre of gravity in traditional Judaism seems to be so much more on praxis, on *Torah,* instruction or direction, on *Halakhah,* how to walk, than on belief. Consequently, a focus on what Paul believed, his *faith,* has probably prejudiced the analysis of how Paul's theology related to his Jewish heritage by starting from an implicit dichotomy between Paul and his parent religion. Consequently, it may be that some will prefer to speak of our larger enterprise as a study of the *religion* of Paul (1998c: 9, original emphasis).[66]

Thus, those who understand Paul's 'faith' as 'belief' within a doctrinal structure drive a wedge between theology and ethics that were integrated aspects of thinking and living for Paul and among early Christians and Jews.[67]

Neil Elliott voices a similar complaint. 'We are accustomed to reading Paul as the architect of a distinctly Christian doctrine of salvation, in effect attributing to Paul a "preferential option" for theology and doctrine over ethics and activism, for right belief (orthodoxy) over right action (orthopraxis)' (1994: 72–73). According to Elliott, this effectively renders Paul's imperative statements 'secondary and derivative' in relation to theological doctrine (1994: 74–75).[68]

A few interpreters have also begun to question the traditional emphasis on Paul's gospel understood as an orally preached, sermon-centred event. For instance, Sally Baker Purvis observes:

> Paul's project did not find completion in the proclamation itself, however foundational and central to his mission proclamation was. Rather, there seems to have been something about the content of the gospel that demanded its enactment in the lives of the persons who heard it (1993: 70).

Through exegesis the present study explores this important but often-overlooked insight. It will be argued that the content of Paul's gospel includes a behavioural standard.[69] We contend that, for Paul, Christ's cruciform behavioural pattern

---

65. Engberg-Pedersen 2000: 6; 1995: 478; see also Deissmann 1957: 207; Horrell 2000: 342; cf. L.T. Johnson 1993: 520–36. Engberg-Pedersen has recently offered a comprehensive proposal that expressly seeks to resolve the 'problem' of theology and ethics in Paul (Engberg-Pedersen 2000; see also Engberg-Pedersen 2002; 1995). His proposal will be considered in Chapter 1, section 2.d.

66. Cf. Deissmann 1957: 5–6 ('Paul at his best belongs not to Theology but Religion'). Although Dunn concludes that he avoids this problem, he nevertheless still privileges the 'belief' or 'talk about God' over the praxis that 'follows directly from such talk' (1998c: 9).

67. See Schlatter 1997: 19: 'These people (the New Testament writers) did not attempt to separate their thinking (*Denkakt*) from the way they lived (*Lebensakt*)'; cf. Hooker 1985: 3.

68. See also Dabourne 1999: 221.

69. Of course, some interpreters do note the correspondence between Paul and the first-century philosophers, who understood that their message and conduct in everyday life must cohere and illustrate one another. See, e.g., Malherbe 1970; 1983b; 1986a; 1986b; 1987; 1990; 1992; 1994; 2000a; Stowers 2001; Glad 1995; cf. Stowers 1984: 80–81. Indeed, in connection with 1 Thessalonians, Malherbe concludes: '[T]hus, Paul again does not think of his preaching as separate from his own life, but the latter is now viewed from the perspective of its providing an example for others to follow in their moral lives' (2000b: 157).

constitutes the new, universal standard for conduct of Jews and Gentiles in God's new age. Conduct conforming to this standard becomes the means of human access to experiences of the power of God that builds communities by giving new earthly life and grounding the hope of future resurrection life after death.[70] This discernible link between Christ-conforming conduct and the life-giving power of God lies at the heart of Paul's gospel and his theo-ethical reasoning. Thus, as believers practise spiritual discernment by engaging in theo-ethical reasoning, they may recognize these important connections that ground Christian faith in the power of God.[71]

Other scholars have recently agreed that 'Pauline theology' is better understood as an activity called *theologizing* rather than as a set of theological propositions or presuppositions about how Paul understands God. This position was recently advocated by Jouette Bassler (1993: 10–11) and has been endorsed by other Pauline commentators.[72] The model urges interpreters to eschew the attempt to uncover 'the centre of Paul's theology' in propositional or doctrinal terms and promotes addressing the 'far more complicated question of how Paul theologized' (Bassler 1993: 17).[73] The present study explores this complex issue, proposing that Paul theologized by practising spiritual discernment as he engaged in theo-ethical reasoning to associate Christ-conforming conduct with experiences of new life from God.

Before presenting this new proposal, however, the recent work of two other scholars must be considered. It appears that only one person, Troels Engberg-Pedersen, has expressly attempted to respond to Bassler's challenge to show how Paul theologized. Another, Michael J. Gorman, addresses the issue by implication in his presentation of Paul's narrative spirituality characterized as 'Cruciformity'. Their work will now be reviewed in the next two sections.

d. *Theologizing Resolves the 'Problem': Troels Engberg-Pedersen*
In *Paul and the Stoics*, Troels Engberg-Pedersen attempts to explain comprehensively how Paul's theologizing activity resolves the 'problem of ethics in Paul'.[74]

---

70. See, e.g., Rom. 5.1–21; 1 Cor. 2.1–5; Gal. 3.1–5.

71. See 1 Cor. 2.1–16.

72. See, e.g., Kraftchick 1993b: 23; Engberg-Pedersen 2000: 15, 47, 79; Hays 1996a: 56 n. 7. The characterization of the activity of doing theology as theologizing is not a new development. For example, Morgan finds Bultmann theologizing through his historical New Testament interpretation, as he does 'New Testament theology' and presents his own individual understanding of theology and Christianity (1973: 12).

73. See also Kraftchick 1993b: 23. Commenting on Beker's analysis of the 'contingency' of Paul's contextual way of doing theology (see Beker 1980; 1991), Dabourne suggests that '[w]hile it is true that Paul was doing theology, and to such good effect that the church has been indebted to him ever since, some such phrase as "pastoring theologically" would better characterize the processes that Beker describes' (1999: 92).

74. Engberg-Pedersen's earlier work on Paul draws on his extensive background in the field of ancient philosophical ethics. See, e.g., 1987; 1991; 1993; 1994b; 1995. For a specific critique of Engberg-Pedersen's conclusion that Paul's approach is distinctly Stoic, see Downing 2001: 278–80. For a challenge to his assessment of Stoic theology and ethics, see Martyn 2002: 73–77; cf. Gorman

He argues that when Paul theologizes (i.e. does theology and ethics) he attempts to develop and describe the content and structure of a general scheme for a Christian 'form of human living' (2000: 47). He concludes that the proper 'theological relationship' between God and Christians and the proper 'ethical relationship' between humans 'belong together and must not be torn apart' (2000: 177). Engberg-Pedersen concludes that Paul's missionary work took the specific form of creating congregations 'engaged in a shared form of life' grounded in Christ's death and resurrection (2000: 37). According to Engberg-Pedersen, this event revealed a new 'social norm' of self-giving love for others (1987: 566–67).[75]

Like Bultmann, Engberg-Pedersen finds Paul focusing on the individual's change of perception regarding personal identity. This involves conversion to a new value system (2000: 34, 47) grounded in the single, objective 'good' found in Christ.[76] This external, objective standard becomes the new one by which any valuation, desire or act is measured (2000: 65). The human mind is thus conformed to the way things actually are in the world (2000: 59, 65–66).[77] He concludes that Paul's ethical system for community life includes practical, reasoned deliberation that precedes human action. He points out that in this system the many particular ends of human acts (the *telos* of any action) may be held together in a single comprehension of an individual's life (2000: 47–50).[78]

Engberg-Pedersen finds that Paul's hortatory practice thus flows directly from his own understanding of the Christ event (2000: 117–18). This generates a new understanding of the divine–human relationship grounded in 'Christ faith' with total directedness towards God (2000: 220–21).[79] Paul's paraenetic goal, argues Engberg-Pedersen, is to bring his audiences to 'full normative knowledge' and self-understanding – a wholly cognitive 'state of mind' (2000: 128). There is always a need for paraenetic reminders, he argues, since there are always degrees of understanding (2000: 238–39).[80] This new understanding began with the baptismal commitment and must be deepened 'until what was basically there to begin with (in baptism) has come to be *all* that there is, a *total* living for God

---

2001: 266 n. 69. Due to their marginal relevance to the present study, these latter two issues will not be addressed.

75. This appears to be the same pattern of conduct that Gorman calls cruciformity (2001: 4–5). Pickett reaches a similar conclusion in connection with Paul's letters to the Corinthians: their 'social harmony' is 'dependent on a unanimous commitment to values which befit a community that has been called into existence through the "word of the cross"' (1997: 68–69).

76. Similarly approaching Paul through the lens of ancient philosophy, Stowers concludes that Paul expresses the 'unitary good' by identifying Jesus Christ as a 'model of human excellence' (2001: 96).

77. Cf. Theissen 1999: 2–3.

78. With these assertions about Paul's ethical theory, Engberg-Pedersen implicitly disagrees with Furnish (1968: 209–10) and Martyn (1997b: 502 n. 89), who conclude that Paul lacks any ethical theory. The exegesis in the present study confirms Engberg-Pedersen's conclusion.

79. Our exegesis will confirm the conclusion that for Paul the Christ event presents a new understanding of the divine–human relationship, although our interpretation of that relationship differs from that of Engberg-Pedersen.

80. The present study argues that for Paul it is not just the paraenesis but also the believers' collective reflection on conduct and experience that contributes to new self-understanding.

through Christ Jesus' (2000: 231, original emphasis). Engberg-Pedersen thus emphasizes Paul's focus on transformation after baptism, without resort to the language of eschatological paradox like Bultmann, Furnish and Martyn. The present study affirms his emphasis.

In response to Martyn and Käsemann, who argue that for Paul a person is wholly determined by outside forces, Engberg-Pedersen observes that 'there is no contrast in Paul...between saying, on the one hand, that people do something "themselves"...that they "understand" or "realize" something...and then, on the other side, saying that they are being guided by some power external to themselves' (2002: 106). He argues that the power talk in Paul does not foreclose the fact that Paul can also be speaking about individual human cognition and individual action out of the human will (2002: 107–10).

Engberg-Pedersen emphasizes the primary importance of paraenesis in Paul's letters and he finds no conflict in the 'already-not yet' nature of human transformation according to this formal structure. He concludes that there is in fact no 'problem of Paul's paraenesis'[81] associated with the indicative/imperative scheme (2000: 224, 232–33, 238–39). The indicative states what is possible when the believer identifies with the Christ event and the imperative provides the reminders that are necessary because believers may not yet have a full and complete understanding of the meaning of the Christ event in their lives.[82] While Engberg-Pedersen expressly affirms Bultmann's descriptive phrase for the indicative/imperative ('become what you are'), he also suggests a 'better alternative': '*remain* what you are – and show it in practice' (2000: 367 n. 12, original emphasis).[83] According to Engberg-Pedersen, Christian practice is the ultimate goal of Paul's theologizing activity. Thus, he concludes, there is no valid distinction between theology and ethics in Paul (2000: 295).

Methodologically, Engberg-Pedersen concludes that the 'coherence of Paul's ideas' cannot be found when they are approached from the 'traditional', 'theological' perspective (2000: 1). He argues that this theological approach usually separates faith from ethical behaviour because the interpreter wrongly distinguishes beforehand between theology and ethics.[84] Moreover, he criticizes those interpreters who combine historical profile with a contemporary theological interest that accepts uncritically Paul's inaccessible and ancient worldview (2000: 16).[85] Therefore, he tries to provide a reading of Paul's anthropology and ethics

81. For this characterization of 'the problem of ethics in Paul', see 2000: 167.

82. The present study argues that Paul is not just interested in the specific conduct that is suggested by Paul's paraenesis, but also the community experiences of new life. Believers must also understand that in the Christ event (properly interpreted) there is a connection between Christ-conforming conduct and experiences of new life through the power of God.

83. This re-characterization of Bultmann's phrase comes very close to that of Käsemann: 'Abide by the Lord who has been given to you and by his lordship' (1969e: 176), whose approach Engberg-Pedersen otherwise criticizes (2000: 19).

84. 2000: 176; see also Engberg-Pedersen 1995: 477–79, 502–503.

85. In his response to Martyn's extended review of *Paul and the Stoics* (see Martyn 2002), Engberg-Pedersen vigorously criticizes Martyn for taking this approach (2002: 110–14).

that offer a 'real option' for modern readers by excising these two categories from their integral connection with Paul's theology (2000: 1, 25).

Despite his challenge to modern theological interpretations of Paul, however, Engberg-Pedersen also presents more than just a descriptive, historical account (his expressed goal). He consistently modernizes Paul's language and perspective (see, e.g., 2000: 86, 87). This sacrifices historical reconstruction for contemporary theological accessibility.[86] Moreover, because of his methodological decision to exclude Paul's inaccessible theology from historical reconstruction, Engberg-Pedersen refuses to include an adequate account of the role that Paul attributes to God, Christ, and the Spirit in his structure for community life and in the logic of his moral reasoning.[87]

The present study seeks to build on Engberg-Pedersen's contentions, while also challenging his seemingly exclusive focus on human self-understanding. We explore Paul's conviction that God builds communities in connection with conduct that conforms to Christ's cruciform pattern. This pattern is what Engberg-Pedersen identifies as the 'shared form of life', the new social norm of self-giving love for others revealed in Christ's death on the cross. This will be accomplished in the present study by acknowledging Paul's theological rationale and moral reasoning, as illuminated by his apocalyptic (i.e. revelatory) perspective, an approach Engberg-Pedersen refuses to incorporate. It will be shown that, by engaging in theo-ethical reasoning, believers are led to greater self-understanding because they are better able to associate Christ-conforming conduct with the identifiable experiences of new life that ground their faith in the power of God.[88] By highlighting these important aspects of theo-ethical reasoning, this study provides a more adequate historical reconstruction of the way that Paul theologizes in his religion.

e. *Combining Theology and Ethics in 'Cruciformity': Michael J. Gorman*
In *Cruciformity: Paul's Narrative Spirituality of the Cross*, Michael J. Gorman illuminates under the name of 'cruciformity' what Engberg-Pedersen calls the Christian 'form of human living', that new social norm of self-giving love for others manifest in Christ's death on the cross.[89] Gorman applies the term to characterize 'a concept commonly believed to be central to Paul's theology and ethics: conformity to the crucified Christ' (2001: 4). According to Gorman this identification with Christ symbolized in baptism is not a one-time event but an experience of ongoing participation in the death of Christ that becomes a life-

---

86. Indeed, Engberg-Pedersen hesitantly admits that he does, in fact, provide a 'theological' reading that is 'more or less a radical extension' of Bultmann's claim about the relationship between theology and anthropology in Paul (2000: 30).

87. For a similar critique, see Martyn 2002: 67.

88. See 1 Cor. 2.1–5; Gal. 3.1–5.

89. See Engberg-Pedersen 1987: 566–67. Engberg-Pedersen's *Paul and the Stoics* was probably published too late for Gorman to engage the work in detail. In the two places where he does acknowledge *Paul and the Stoics*, however, Gorman essentially affirms specific aspects of Engberg-Pedersen's interpretation (see Gorman 2001: 129 n. 18; 266 n. 69).

style (2001: 32–33). The Christ pattern manifest in cruciformity, concludes Gorman, is one of sacrificial, self-giving love for others (2001: 173).[90] Neither belief nor love (which he equates with ethics) are independent realities for Paul. Instead, cruciformity is a 'seamless garment' (2001: 177). It is a narrative spiritu-ality where Paul combines theology and ethics.

Gorman takes this approach because 'most accounts of Paul the theologian and of Paul's theology pay insufficient attention to his religious experience – his spirituality – and to his fondness for narrating that experience' (2001: 3).[91] According to Gorman, this 'significant blind spot in New Testament scholarship' produces an interpretation that presents Paul's letters as a way to 'teach theology' rather than their intended purpose of moulding behaviour by affirming or altering patterns of living and patterns of experience (2001: 3–4).[92] He concludes that the purpose of Paul's letters is 'pastoral or spiritual before it is theological', a goal that today might be called 'spiritual formation' (2001: 4). Gorman further argues that interpreters must 'consider Paul first and foremost as a pastoral or spiritual writer, rather than as a theologian or ethicist' (2001: 4).[93] With Furnish and Martyn, however, Gorman expressly denies that Paul engages in critical reflec-tion on his own religious experience (2001: 3–4).[94]

Paul's basic conviction, says Gorman, is that to the extent that people share in the death of Jesus, so they will also share in his resurrection life (2001: 319). The present life of cruciformity initiates a person into a process of transformation that culminates in the final goal of conformity to the already-glorified Christ (2001: 323). Thus, Gorman finds that the certainty of the future is already beginning. The final transformation into glory has begun as the Day of the Lord and the glory of the Lord have been inaugurated in the experience of cruciformity (2001: 347). The identity, values and practices of those who belong to God's new cove-nant come from the future that is already present (2001: 354).

---

90. This is essentially the same conclusion as that of Engberg-Pedersen (1987: 566–67).

91. See also L.T. Johnson 1998: 4; Chapter 1, section 3.e below.

92. See also Elliott 1994: 72–73. Over a century ago, William Wrede made a similar observation that imposing doctrinal theological categories in connection with the New Testament 'makes doctrine out of what is itself not doctrine' in texts that were in fact focused on giving 'practical advice, direc-tion for life, instruction for the moment.' Wrede 1973: 75; see also Deissmann 1957: 182 and Chapter 1, section 4, below.

93. In support of this position, Gorman points to Pickett's related conclusion: '(S)cholarship on the death of Jesus in Paul has largely been preoccupied with questions of…what Paul *thought* about its significance' (1997: 13, original emphasis). Gorman affirms Pickett's attempt 'to move beyond the ideas represented by the symbol of the crucified messiah to a consideration of the social norms and values which it supports' (Pickett 1997: 31). This move to emphasize the social norm symbolized by the cross is also one of the strengths of the work of Engberg-Pedersen. These positions are incorpo-rated in the present study.

94. The present study argues otherwise. We contend that Paul's complex theo-ethical reasoning interprets the cross as God's revelation of the new and universal social norm of self-giving love for others. Conduct conforming to this new standard leads to experiences of new life. This reasoning process provides the conceptual framework for the community practice of spiritual discernment. This discipline involves reflection on community experience and conduct, seeking to discern the links between Christ-conforming actions and experiences of new life from God. Thus, these categories are not mutually exclusive as Gorman implies.

Although the present study builds on these important conclusions, it will also be argued that these values and practices do not come from the future, understood *temporally*. Instead, they are revealed from God's new spatial realm/ temporal age in Christ that already exists and somehow overlaps the 'present evil age'[95] and 'this world'.[96]

For Paul, cruciformity cannot be attributed to human effort, says Gorman, since a person is wholly 'determined' by invasive, external powers, including the divine power 'that somehow...produces Christ-like qualities' (2001: 49, 299, 400).[97] Thus, concludes Gorman, consciously imitating Christ is an 'impossibility' for the believer (2001: 400). As with Martyn, Tannehill, Käsemann and Hays,[98] Gorman never resolves the 'problem of ethics in Paul'. He fails to explain satisfactorily the need for exhortation/paraenesis if this external, invading power always takes complete control of believers' actions from the outside. Conversely, he also fails to explain why the external power does *not always* take such control.

The present study argues that the 'problem of ethics in Paul' is resolved by understanding the role of theo-ethical reasoning in Paul's religion. As believers practise spiritual discernment by engaging in theo-ethical reasoning, they are led by the Spirit to identify the connections between experiences of new life and actions that conform to Christ's cruciform pattern. Thus, according to Paul, the power of God works in connection with specific human conduct, but does not wholly determine it from the outside.

Although Gorman emphasizes Paul's experience of 're-presenting' in living form the word of the cross,[99] he surprisingly points to the central role of Paul's *preaching* of the cross as the event that 'unleashes the power of the Spirit' (2001: 59) in the communication of the gospel (2001: 31). He concludes that in Paul's preached gospel message, God's 'word has "performed" salvation' (2001: 275). Gorman's focus on Paul's narrative spirituality – one that 'tells a story, a dynamic life with God that corresponds in some way to the divine "story"' (2001: 4)[100] – necessarily leads him to overemphasize Paul's oral preaching.

This creates an unnecessary tension among Gorman's primary conclusions. On the one hand, he asserts that the gospel is communicated by God's salvific, preached word. On the other hand, he argues that Paul promotes Christ's cruciform pattern of conduct lived out in a believer's body as constitutive of new life in Christ. Indeed, Gorman affirms that '[f]or Paul the most faithful interpretation

95. See Gal. 1.4; cf. Rom. 12.2; 1 Cor. 1.20; 2.6, 8; 3.18; 2 Cor. 4.4; see also Eph. 1.21.
96. See 1 Cor. 3.19; 5.10; 7.31; cf. Eph. 2.2.
97. Gorman's argument remains subject to the same critique levelled by Barclay (1988: 201–202) against Käsemann's similarly ill-defined position.
98. Hays similarly argues in connection with Gal. 2.20 that 'Paul is provocatively denying his own role as the acting "subject" of his own life and claiming that he has been supplanted in this capacity by Christ' (2002: 154, 168).
99. Indeed, Gorman also refers to Paul and his communities as 'living exegesis of the same story' (2001: 400).
100. Gorman expressly draws on the work of Hays (1991; 1983/2002), Fowl (1990) and Witherington (1994a), who stress the importance of narrative for Paul.

of the Messiah's story is not a letter or an argument but a living body, one whose life unfolds step-by-step in ways analogous to Messiah Jesus' (2001: 367; see also 2001: 293). Thus, Gorman effectively separates theology from ethics. He fails to identify the critical relationship between Paul's preaching of Christ's cruciform pattern and his embodied behavioural interpretation of that pattern in the context of his own life.[101]

The present study affirms and incorporates Gorman's conclusion that 'cruciformity' represents for Paul the new behavioural paradigm for life in the world. We seek to illuminate how Paul promotes the cruciform pattern as constitutive of the human means of access to experiences of the power of God that gives new life in Christ. Paul thereby links specific conduct that conforms to Christ's cruciform pattern with concrete experiences of new life given by God in the community.[102] This connection between conduct and experience lies at the heart of theo-ethical reasoning. It becomes the basis for Paul's (and other believers') embodied proclamation of Christ crucified and the focus of the community practice of spiritual discernment.

The study challenges Gorman's attempt to cast the pastoral and spiritual approach to Pauline interpretation as an exclusive alternative to understanding Paul as one who does theology and ethics. We attempt to show that Paul combines theology and ethics in theo-ethical reasoning. The community that practises spiritual discernment by engaging in theo-ethical reasoning remains submissive to the guidance of the Spirit. Through this discipline, community members participate individually in the process of divine transformation into the image of Christ – a process that God set in motion in the death and resurrection of Christ. Concurrently, with the aid of this disciplined practice, God shapes the community into a body of Christ, where it takes its place as a collective reflection of the goal of God's cosmic redemption in Christ. For this reason, we contend that theo-ethical reasoning lies at the heart of Paul's religion.

3. *Paul's Religion: A Solution to the 'Problem'?*

A number of other developments in Pauline studies point to specific aspects of Paul's religion for possible solutions to the 'problem of ethics in Paul'.

a. *Defining Paul's Religion and Ethics*
Gerd Theissen recently defined religion as 'a cultural sign language which promises a gain in life by corresponding to an ultimate reality' (1999: 2).[103] This

---

101. According to Barclay, Paul's own story and the stories of other believers have significance so long as the crucifixion of Jesus is a present reality in their lives, present not only in the single act of baptism but also in the continuing experiences and sufferings of their lives (2002: 155). Thus, says Barclay, believers both live from the story of Jesus and live in it as their lives become paradigms of 'the presence and continuance of the Christ story and the Christ grace that keeps punctuating the folds of time to reenact the new creation' (2002: 155–56).

102. See, e.g., 1 Cor. 2.1–5; 2 Cor. 4.1–12; Gal. 3.1–5; 4.1–20; Phil. 1.27–30; 4.8–9; 1 Thess. 2.1–14.

103. Theissen acknowledges (1999: 324 n. 2) the influence of Clifford Geertz (1973: 90) on this definition.

'objective sign system' provides a specific interpretation of the world based on signs that correlate human cognitive, emotional and pragmatic relationships to the reality they signify (1999: 2).[104] According to Theissen a religious sign system combines three forms of expression – myth, rites and ethics – that establish the special feature of any particular religious sign system (1999: 2–3).

Theissen defines 'myth' as the narrative form that fundamentally determines the world and life by characterizing the actions of gods. In the biblical tradition, he says, these actions take place in history in connection with the true God's 'one social partner' – the people of Israel as representative of all humanity (1999: 2–3). For Theissen, ethics are characterized as 'theological reflection on moral norms and values' (1999: 337 n. 1).[105] The 'ethic' of a particular group involves 'the behaviour which is in fact practiced and required in a group' because it corresponds to the group myth and interprets it (1999: 63, 78).[106] Further, Theissen finds that the group 'ethic' of the early church is a 'constitutive part' of the significance of the Christian religious myth (1999: 63). Each reinforces the other as the narrative sign language of the myth finds its parallel in the pragmatic sign language of the 'ethic' (1999: 79). Thus, Theissen essentially argues that, in early Christian religion, theology and ethics are integral to one another.

In his important studies of early Christian morality, Wayne Meeks similarly defines ethics as a second-order, reflective activity: morality rendered self-conscious (1993a: 3–6). For Meeks, ethics is about the logic of moral discourse and action. It is the 'science of morality', where 'morality' names a dimension of life that is a pervasive and, often, only a partly conscious set of value-laden dispositions, inclinations, attitudes and habits that are subsequently internalized by doing ethics. By engaging in ethical reflection to provide a more rational explanation for actions, the person becomes a more dependable moral agent (1993a: 3–6; see also 1988: 17–30).

David Horrell has recently begun to examine Paul's ethics through the lens of discourse (communicative) ethics associated with the contemporary moral philosophy of Jürgen Habermas and Seyla Benhabib.[107] This modern approach assumes that moral questions cannot be answered by simply appealing to an unquestionable authoritative tradition. They must be solved by discourse or argumentation among the participants who are actually involved, since legitimate solutions cannot be imposed by the powerful nor can they reflect only the interests of a certain group. The community must discern and interpret the applicability of specific injunctions. Any moral norm must be something that everyone can agree is in the interests of all concerned. Discourse (communicative) ethics makes no

104. See also Ashton, who finds that religion 'covers a variety of practices and beliefs, all relating somehow or other to unseen powers, some feared, some honoured' (2000: 22–23).

105. See also W.D. Davies, who defines ethics as philosophic reflection on human conduct (1972a: 310).

106. Similarly, in connection with the phrase 'walk worthily of the Lord' in Colossians, Meeks concludes that doing ethics is a hermeneutical process that involves the behavioural interpretation of a particular metaphor-laden religious view of the world (1993b: 47).

107. Horrell 1999: 321–25. See Habermas 1984–88; 1990; Benhabib 1986; 1989; 1990; 1992. Horrell's approach has been introduced into Old Testament studies by Rogerson (1995: 17–26).

substantive contribution to the formulation of moral norms but outlines conditions necessary for the community discernment of such norms to take place. The focus is on the structure of human communication necessary for moral discourse to occur.[108]

According to Horrell, discourse ethics thereby provides the 'underpinning for a "way of life" in which dialogue and mutual understanding can flourish'.[109] Horrell proposes a shift in the study of Pauline ethics *from* a focus on Paul's substantive ethical pronouncements *to* the ways in which he seeks to structure community relationships and communicative structures so that this discernment can take place (1999: 321). At the very least, argues Horrell, Paul can be read and appropriated in ways other than as a supporter of particular ethical stances on specific modern ethical issues (1999: 325). Thus, Horrell's ultimate interest lies in grounding contemporary applications of scripture in historical reconstruction. He concludes that, perhaps, Paul's most valuable and enduring contribution to moral discourse is his vision of community construction in which a moral way of life is created to foster dialogue because each and every member is treated with equal respect and care (1999: 325).

This study applies Theissen's definition of religion, draws on the related definitions of ethics offered by Theissen and Meeks, and takes up Horrell's suggestion to examine the way that Paul structures community life so that effective moral discourse may take place therein. We highlight certain aspects of Paul's religion that may be directly reconstructed or inferred from the logic of his arguments. It is contended that Paul's theo-ethical reasoning provides the framework for the community practice of spiritual discernment in his churches. By means of this practice, church members collectively discern the will of God and render their morality self-conscious by linking particular experiences of God's life-giving power with specific actions that conform to Christ's cruciform pattern. By engaging in theo-ethical reasoning, Paul and his churches attempt to correlate certain human cognitive, emotional and pragmatic relationships to the ultimate reality that they signify: new and eternal (resurrection) life with God in Christ.[110] In this way, they reason together to discern spiritually what actions represent the common advantage and the interests of all members of the community (see Horrell 1999: 325).

b. *The Apocalyptic Contours of Paul's Religion*
The term 'apocalyptic' is widely used in biblical studies, although there is no commonly accepted definition of the term (Adams 2000: 106). For this reason, some interpreters call for a moratorium on the use of the word 'apocalyptic' in connection with Pauline studies.[111] Nevertheless, this study employs the term for several important reasons. For Paul, the terminology of 'apocalyptic' – primarily

108. For this summary, see Horrell 1999: 321.
109. 1999: 321, citing Benhabib 1992: 23–67.
110. Cf. Horrell, who concludes that 'Pauline ethics is firmly grounded in a character-forming narrative that has its essential basis in the Christian community and its corporate life' (2002: 170).
111. See Matlock 1996; Stanton 2000.

understood as *revelation* – plays a central role in his religion.[112] For this reason alone, the use of the term 'apocalyptic' is potentially appropriate if rightly understood. Throughout his letters Paul consistently applies language associated with the event of divine revelation that is part of the broader semantic field associated with human knowledge and its assorted sub-domains.[113] It will be argued that Paul, like many of the early Christians, understood his religious experiences as revelations that became sources of knowledge for direction in religious matters.[114]

This study attempts to show how Paul frequently uses the broad semantic field of revelatory language to articulate the connection between Christ-conforming conduct and experiences of God's life-giving and community-building power. First, Paul describes how the crucified and risen Christ appeared *to* him, that God's Son was revealed *in* him, and that he has had visions and revelations of the Lord.[115] Thereafter, Paul's 'ongoing life in Christ was punctuated with additional "mystical" or "apocalyptic" experiences – "visions and revelations of the Lord" he calls them in 2 Corinthians 12:1' (Gorman 2001: 20). These must be understood as the unveiling (i.e. revelation) of Christ's resurrection life that otherwise lies hidden with God in heaven.[116]

The present study will try to show that, through various revelatory events, Paul *experienced* the same power of God that raised Jesus from the dead. Moreover, we shall argue that through other experiences he also came to know that God exercises this same power in the lives of believers, giving new earthly life to those who inhabit the community that is divinely built in connection with conduct that conforms to Christ's cruciform pattern of self-giving love for others.[117]

---

112. For Paul's use of the noun ἀποκάλυψις, see Rom. 2.5; 8.19; 16.25; 1 Cor. 1.7; 14.6, 26; 2 Cor. 12.1, 7; Gal. 1.12; 2.2; cf. Eph. 1.17; 3.3; 2 Thess. 1.7. For his use of the related verb ἀποκαλύπτω, see Rom. 1.17, 18; 8.18; 1 Cor. 2.10; 3.13; 14.30; Gal. 1.16; 3.23; Phil. 3.15; cf. Eph. 3.5; 2 Thess. 2.3, 6, 8. For Paul's use of 'revelation' as an 'event', see Martyn 1997b: 115; 1997a: 219; Snodgrass 1994: 301. For a general discussion of the importance of 'revelation' for Paul, see Bockmuehl 1990: 133–77; Via 1997: 49–94.

113. For a discussion of the terminology drawn from the broader semantic field of 'knowledge' and its sub-domains that include 'revelation', see Louw-Nida 1994 (Vol. I, §28); cf. Burton 1921: 433–35. Included within this 'sub-domain' are such important Pauline terms as φανερός; φανερόω; φανέρωσις; ἀποδείχις; δείκνυμι; ἀπέδειχεν; ἔνδειχις; ἐπιγνώσκω; οἶδα; ἐπίγνωσις; ἀγνοέω; δηλόω; βέβαιος; βεβαίωσις; and βεβαιόω. For a discussion of Paul's broad use of these terms in 1 Corinthians and their correlation with human perception, see Brown 1995: 24–25 n. 22. For Paul's use of over 30 different terms for 'revelation' in Romans alone, see Snodgrass 1994.

114. See Hurtado 2000: 183, 187–89, 196–99, 204; see also Chapter 1, section 3.d below.

115. See 1 Cor. 9.1; 15.8; 2 Cor. 12.1, 7; Gal 1.12, 16. These passages lead some interpreters to make the claim that Paul was a Jewish apocalyptic visionary and/or mystic and that these experiences, particularly the one described in 2 Cor. 12.1–7, ground Paul's apostolic claims. See, e.g., Kim 1984; Segal 1990; 1998; 1999; Morray-Jones 1992; Rowland 1982; 1983; 1988a; 1995a; 1995b; Tabor 1986; Ashton 2000; and Gorman 2001: 25. For a less positive view of this claim, see Barrett 1973: 33–34; cf. Bornkamm 1971: 21–22.

116. See Gorman 2001: 20; cf. Col. 3.1–4.

117. See, e.g., 2 Cor. 4.10–12. Gorman contends that Paul's transformed bodily life constitutes a present resurrection to new life (2001: 34 n. 34; 131 n. 23), thereby attributing to Paul 'a kind of two-stage resurrection: first, resurrection to new life in Christ, and second, resurrection to eternal life in Christ' (2001: 322).

This takes place when God manifestly exercises the same life-giving power that raised Jesus from the dead to give new earthly life among believers who conform their actions to Christ's cruciform pattern.[118]

These proposed Pauline convictions ground this study's contention that 'apocalyptic' (correctly understood as *revelation*) is an aspect of theo-ethical reasoning. Therefore, this study's use of 'apocalyptic' is true to Paul's use because it focuses on the importance of present revelation, rather than simply referring to Paul's eschatology – that is, what he thought would happen in the future at the consummation of the ages.

Indeed, several Pauline interpreters contend that Paul's theology was integrally related to his apocalyptic perspective.[119] Some apply the term 'apocalyptic', however, to refer to an eschatological presumption, defined as Paul's expectation of the *future* but imminent *parousia* of Christ to establish a transcendent kingdom.[120] The present study challenges this understanding, to the extent that it limits Paul's use of the term 'apocalyptic' to his eschatological expectation regarding only the future.[121] We offer a different context for understanding Paul's use of apocalyptic terminology and motifs grounded in the recent work of several scholars.

First, Christopher Rowland provides an alternative approach to Christian origins that emphasizes its apocalyptic interest in 'revelation'. He suggests that the term apocalyptic should be defined in the context of Second Temple Judaism, where it was focused on the acquisition of 'higher wisdom through revelation' (1988a: 207).[122] Rowland further observes that much (though not all) of the apocalyptic literature of this period generally focuses on 'the improvement of the religious and moral life which such knowledge may bring' (1983: 79 n. 5).[123]

Consequently, Rowland contends that the traditional stress on future eschatology in Christian interpretation should *not* be seen as the key element for

118. Indeed, this is precisely what Paul says in Rom. 6.4. Believers were metaphorically buried with Christ through their baptism into his death, so that, just as Christ was raised from the dead, they, too, might walk in newness of life.

119. See Käsemann 1969c: 82–107; Käsemann 1969d: 108–37; Beker 1980: 19; Martyn 1997a; 1997b. Adams concludes that the 'dominant theological perspective of 1 Corinthians is an apocalyptic one' (2000: 106) and presents a balanced discussion of the present and future dimensions of this apocalyptic perspective. Nevertheless, it will be argued in Chapter 2 (1 Corinthians 1–4) that even Adams overemphasizes the future aspects of Paul's perspective.

120. See, e.g., Käsemann 1969d: 109 n. 1; Beker 1980: 19. For a thorough discussion and analysis of this connection between apocalyptic and 'eschatology' in Käsemann's Pauline interpretation, see Way 1991: 125–31.

121. For statements that seem to limit this eschatological expectation to the future, see, e.g., Beker 1980: 58; Käsemann 1969c: 82–107; 1969d: 108–37.

122. Cf. Hengel 1974: 210–15. Keck similarly argues that 'apocalyptic' includes an 'epistemological' category that involves the revelation of 'otherworldly knowledge, privileged information' (1984: 234–35, including n. 17).

123. Aune similarly suggests that one purpose of the apocalyptic genre is to encourage cognitive and behavioural modifications based on the message communicated from the transcendent world (1986: 90); see also Bockmuehl, who identifies the ethical intention of the *pesher* revelation at Qumran (1990: 48).

understanding the apocalyptic perspective of late Second Temple Judaism and early Christianity (1988a: 213). He emphasizes a Jewish 'this-worldly eschatology' that remained an important component of Christian belief until the end of the second century (1995b: 285).[124] Thus, suggests Rowland, 'the divine presence of the eschaton is vividly present in the lives of the Christian communities' (1995a: 48).[125] Moreover, he concludes that, while Paul certainly encouraged his readers to look forward to the future revelation of Christ, this 'awesome glory' is in some sense being fulfilled in the presence of the apostle himself (1995a: 48).[126]

The present study proceeds by incorporating Rowland's definition of 'apocalyptic' because it reflects the importance of divine 'revelation' for the individual and for the community in Pauline Christianity.[127] Accenting the present, earthly nature of Paul's eschatological perspective, the definition replaces those that make God's future, final eschatological victory the primary emphasis of 'apocalyptic'.

Through exegesis this study attempts to extend Rowland's interpretation. We argue that Paul allowed for the possibility that certain aspects of the 'awesome glory' of the revelation of Christ were becoming manifest not only in Paul, but also in other believers whose conduct conforms to Christ's cruciform pattern. It will be contended that, according to Paul's theo-ethical reasoning, each revealed experience of new life was somehow connected to the reflection of the 'awesome glory' of the revelation of Christ taking place in association with believers'

124. For similar views about the historical importance of revelation, see Bockmuehl 1990: 2, 26; Goulder 1994: 56. The present study differs materially from that of Bockmuehl, however, in that his work concentrates on the Christian 'outworking and re-appropriation of *principles* that were held to be divinely revealed' (2000: 14 n. 30, emphasis added). It is argued here that for Paul it is not 'principles' being revealed, but the manifest power of God that gives new life in connection with Christ-conforming conduct.

125. Wrede (1907: 114–15) makes a similar observation: 'Paul('s)...mode of thinking is purely historical. All his thoughts about salvation are thoughts about a series of events, in which God and man take part, whose scene is on earth and also in heaven – it proceeds, properly speaking, in both places at the same time.' Bockmuehl also observes that certain apocalyptic visionaries received an 'anticipatory "glimpse" ' that could not be equated with the eschatological (i.e. end-time) revelation of the mysteries but that did constitute 'a selective disclosure of their content' (1990: 39).

126. Tabor argues that the vision of heavenly glory 'would have closely correlated with what...is at the core of his [Paul's] message, namely, his expectation of the glorification of the many Sons of God' (1986: 45). Gorman applies these observations to the entire Christian community: 'Those who belong to the new covenant are therefore a people who, in a fundamental sense, do not belong to the age in which they reside...[t]heir identity, values, and practices come from the future, which is already present' (2001: 354). Barclay seems to argue against this conclusion: 'Apocalyptic turns his [Paul's] gaze continually to the future and it no longer matters to Paul if his churches are vindicated in the historical and political realm' (1996a: 393).

Our study contends that Paul's primary focus is the *present reality* of the experience of God's kingdom that from time to time becomes manifest through the practice of spiritual discernment. Just as with the world, God's kingdom has both present and future temporal dimensions.

127. As with Tabor 1986 and Morray-Jones 1993, Rowland's own Pauline interpretation begins with the importance of 2 Cor. 12.1–11. While the event described in 1 Cor. 12.1–5 was more important for Paul than allowed by Barrett (1973: 33–34) or W.D. Davies (1962: 197–98), we suggest that the relative importance of this heavenly ascent journey must be distinguished from the primary significance of other revelations that take place in connection with human conduct and Paul's community-building activities (see, e.g., 2 Cor. 12.6–7a; Phil. 4.8–9).

Christ-conforming actions.[128] As a result, Paul encouraged his communities to practise spiritual discernment by engaging in theo-ethical reasoning. Using Rowland's language, the purpose was to try to identify moments of this 'awesome glory' being revealed in the experiences of new life linked to Christ-conforming actions.

Second, J. Louis Martyn has also effectively characterized certain aspects of Pauline apocalyptic thought (see, e.g., Martyn 1997b: 99–105; 148–51; 393–408).[129] Martyn equates the 'divine event' that Paul calls 'gospel' with the revelation of God's power that creates a 'new history' unfolding in a series of 'gospel events' (1997b: 130; 1991: 164, 174).[130] Similarly, addressing the reason that Paul recounts his own personal stories in his letters, John Barclay concludes that all of these stories concern grace – understood as the action of God in history. They derive their pattern from one central point: 'the apocalypse of Jesus Christ' (2002: 154). Thus, all three interpreters focus on Paul's apocalyptic thought, understood in the context of some type of present revelation of Jesus Christ and the manifestations of God's power bringing new life into the world.

The present study builds on these positions. It attempts to show that for Paul each divine event that he calls 'gospel' constitutes a moment of divine revelation of Christ's 'awesome glory' – where a revelation of Jesus Christ takes place when God's life-giving power is linked to conduct that conforms to Christ's cruciform pattern. This revelation provides believers with higher wisdom for improving the religious and moral life that such knowledge may bring. The revelation confirms the divine approval of specific Christ-conforming actions. This constitutes an essential aspect of Paul's theo-ethical reasoning.

Further, it will be argued that these revelations must be collectively evaluated and that additional revelations may even take place during this dialogical evaluative process (see 1 Cor. 14.29–32). Our study characterizes this dialogical process as the practice of spiritual discernment. Paul and his churches engage in theo-ethical reasoning as they try to discern specific Christ-conforming actions that may be linked to the manifestations of new life from God.

This study also utilizes the term 'apocalyptic' because Paul applies certain dualistic motifs that are grounded in revelation and have been identified with late Second Temple Jewish apocalyptic thought.[131] He uses one motif that contrasts two different spatial realms.[132] These realms are distinguishable based upon the

128. According to Hurtado, powerful religious experiences in early Christianity were perceived as revelations and helped to generate the religious motivation of the Christian movement (2000: 183).

129. Although the present study builds on Martyn's findings in this context, section 2.b above challenged Martyn's understanding of the 'problem' in the relationship between theology and ethics in Paul.

130. Elsewhere, Martyn acknowledges his dependence on Käsemann (1969e: 168–82) for the formulation of the gospel as the 'event' that defines God's power (Martyn 1997a: 219 n. 23). Similarly, Schütz concludes that the 'gospel' is a power of reversal in the world that was inaugurated in the death and resurrection of Jesus and that Paul's interpretation of the gospel represents those events as power and thereby extends them in the world (1975: 281).

131. See Meeks 1982b: 689; Adams 2000: 106.

132. For Paul's use of this cosmic, spatial duality contrasting heaven and earth, see Lincoln 1981;

discernible impact of God's exercise of power upon the human inhabitants of one realm or the exercise of power by the forces of the world in the other.[133] Paul also applies two distinct levels of temporal dualism.[134] For instance, he refers to 'the present evil age' (Gal. 1.4) that is now being brought to an end (see 1 Cor. 10.11). He distinguishes between the wisdom of God revealed in Christ and the wisdom of this age and its rulers.[135] He encourages believers not to be conformed to the standards of this age.[136] For the inhabitants of the dualistic spatial realms, there is a present time and a future time when the unfolding destruction or salvation will be brought to completion.[137] Paul also employs a motif involving ethical dualism in connection with his use of the spatial and temporal dualisms.[138] For Paul this ethical dualism usually refers to a social duality,[139] such as the distinction between those being saved or perishing (1 Cor. 1.18–21), believers and unbelievers (14.22–25), or the saints and the unrighteous (6.1–2).

Three recent interpreters have utilized certain aspects of these motifs in connection with what they refer to as Paul's apocalyptic ethics.[140] Nancy Duff concludes that the living Lord draws people into his 'lordship' or the orbit of power that represents a 'new space' created by his death and resurrection. In this space human behaviour in the imitation of Christ becomes a fragmentary foretaste and living parable of the fulfilment already on its way (1989: 281, 284). Similarly, Alexandra Brown briefly addresses Paul's 'ethic of apocalyptic perception' (1995: 154; cf. Brown 1998: 271–85). She argues that Paul calls for the 'integration of epistemology and ethics' as part of his 'apocalyptic theology' (1995: 159–60). Bruce Longenecker finds that relationships between Christians constitute the sphere where the eschatological power of God becomes evident when people manifest Christ-like relationships and social character (1999: 104). He argues that much of Paul's case in Galatians depends on the connections he establishes between a person's pattern of life and the work of suprahuman, spiritual powers

---

Adams 2000: 109; Meeks 1982b: 689; Cousar 1998: 43. For the importance of spatial dualism in Jewish apocalyptic and wisdom writings, see Gammie 1974: 356–85; Rowland 1988a: 211. E.P. Sanders's assessment of the importance for Paul of 'getting in' and 'staying in' (1983: 6–10) is suggestive of the importance of this dualistic spatial imagery.

133. R. Hall points out how the writers of some Jewish apocalyptic material – including Paul – argue that divine revelation shows them how God acts to distinguish between the inhabitants of God's righteous realm and those who dwell in the realm of the wicked (1996: 436, 441, 444, 447–48; cf. Tabor 1986: 14).

134. Meeks 1982b: 689; Keck 1984: 234; Cousar 1998: 43. For the importance of temporal dualism in Jewish apocalyptic and wisdom writings, see Gammie 1974: 357.

135. See 1 Cor. 1.24, 30; 2.6; 3.18; 2 Cor. 4.4; cf. Eph. 1.21; 2.2, 7; Col. 1.26.

136. Rom. 12.2, discussed below in Chapter 5, section 3.

137. See 1 Cor. 1.18–20; 15.23–28; Keck 1993: 27–38. Lincoln shows how Paul integrates the temporal and spatial dimensions of his eschatological perspective, including its christological content and orientation (1981: 178).

138. For the importance of ethical dualism in Jewish apocalyptic and wisdom literature, see Gammie 1974: 356–85.

139. Adams 2000: 107; cf. Martyn 1967: 269–87; Meeks 1982b: 689; R. Hall 1996: 444; D. Martin 1995: 176.

140. See Duff 1989: 279–96; Brown 1995; B. Longenecker 1999: 92–108.

with which one is ultimately aligned in the respective worlds where these powers operate (1999: 100).

The present study also builds on these contentions. It will be shown that Paul's theo-ethical reasoning incorporates these related, dualistic motifs and emphasizes human relationships as a central aspect of God's new kingdom in Christ. Paul's reasoning thereby integrates human behaviour and perception with the discernible power of God that creates a new time and space. He thus distinguishes between experiences of the new life given in connection with Christ-conforming conduct and life in the world, experienced through conduct that conforms to worldly standards. Moreover, drawing on Theissen's definition of religion, it will be contended that Paul applies these motifs as part of the 'cultural sign language' of his religion. He uses them to correlate human cognitive and pragmatic relationships in his specific interpretation of the world (see Theissen 1999: 2). These motifs help Paul illuminate new life 'in Christ'.[141] There, through the power of God revealed when Jesus was raised from the dead, Christianity's promised gain of new earthly life and resurrection life after death correspond to the ultimate reality of eternal life in and with God (see Theissen 1999: 2).

c. *Paul's Understanding of His Religion*

Addressing the issue of whether the 'gospel' of the New Testament canon has a 'centre', Krister Stendahl suggests that '[t]he crucial problem is whether we interpret "Christianity" primarily as a message (gospel, kerygma, witness), or primarily as a community, a people, the church' that depends in all respects on God's acts and deeds in Jesus Christ (1984: 59–60).[142] The present study emphasizes the role of community formation in Pauline Christianity.[143] It will be argued that the centre of Paul's gospel lies in his understanding that God calls new communities into existence and builds them up in connection with conduct that conforms to Christ's cruciform pattern. Because this life-giving exercise of God's power is discernible as community experience, those who practise spiritual discernment by engaging in theo-ethical reasoning may associate this new life with specific

141. Deissmann called the phrase 'in Christ' the 'characteristic expression' of Paul's Christianity (1957: 140). The phrase reflects a believer's relationship with Christ that can be experienced here on earth – but one that is qualitatively less than the 'face to face' (1 Cor. 13.12) relationship that will be experienced in the future (Deissmann 1957: 217–19). Schweitzer saw the phrase as the key to Paul's theology, expressing a kind of Christ mysticism for the believer that results from having died and risen with Christ (1931: 10, 19). In his published doctoral thesis, Käsemann concluded that the centre of Paul's proclamation is the life 'in Christ' (1933: 183). Gorman emphasizes the spatial aspects of Paul's phrase 'in Christ' and characterizes it in the language of Käsemann as a 'sphere of influence' where believers experience the influence of Christ's power (2001: 35–39). For other discussions and studies of the phrase 'in Christ', see Best 1955: 1–29; Neugebauer 1957–58: 124–38; Neugebauer 1961; E.P. Sanders 1977: 458–61.

142. Cf. Barclay 1996b: 204; Banks 1994: 189; Stowers 1990: 266; Purvis 1996: 419.

143. In the context of Philippians, Engberg-Pedersen concludes that the object of Paul's behavioural exhortation is to bring into existence, as far as possible, a preliminary form of the future heavenly *politeuma* (1994: 290). Similarly, Horrell concludes that 'Pauline thought cannot be conveyed as a series of propositions to be believed, but only as a story that is "lived", retold, and embodied in the practices of the community that celebrates that story' (2002: 170).

actions that conform to Christ's cruciform pattern. They are able to discern spiritually the ways that individuals are being transformed into the image of Christ, as God continues to shape the community into the body of Christ through Christ-conforming behaviour.

In this context the present study also builds on the work of Wayne Meeks.[144] He has regularly shown how the Pauline texts functioned to create and strengthen communities as moral reference groups with a distinctive way of life.[145] Noting Paul's view that a robust ethical life requires moral confidence *based on social phenomena*, Meeks persuasively argues that it is through a social process of forming and re-forming moral intuitions that Paul creates moral confidence among members of his churches (1988: 17). According to Meeks, Paul was forming moral communities by admonishing, instructing, cajoling, reminding, rebuking, reforming and arguing new converts into ways of acting that were worthy of the God who called them (1988: 17).

The present study affirms Meeks's contentions by exploring the nuances of Paul's theo-ethical reasoning and showing how it provides the framework for the dialogical practice of community spiritual discernment. Community reflection on the links between conduct and experience point the members of Paul's churches toward the social phenomena that confirm the community's robust ethical life. As they identify the manifestations of new life from God, the community gains confidence that conduct conforming to Christ's cruciform pattern constitutes the divinely approved pathway that leads to eternal life in Christ, understood as both present experiences of new earthly life and resurrection life after death.

d. *Paul as an Interpreter of Community Experience*
Individual and community experience play important shaping roles in the more fluid way that Paul theologizes.[146] Paul was like many of the early Christians who understood their religious experiences – including but not limited to the appearances of the risen Christ – as revelations that proved to be sources of cognitive content and provided direction in religious matters (Hurtado 2000: 183, 187–89, 196–99, 204). For the most part, however, modern scholarship does not deal with the religious experience and power that were of first importance to the New Tes-

144. See Meeks 1982a; 1982b; 1983; 1986a; 1986b; 1986c; 1987; 1988; 1990; 1991; 1993a; 1993b; 1996. This study also emphasizes, however, the 'apocalyptic' or 'revelatory' foundation for the way that Paul theologized, a focus that for the most part Meeks does not pursue. Martyn (1997b: 533 n. 182) and Bockmuehl (2000: 14 n. 30) also make this latter observation about Meeks's work.

145. See, e.g., Meeks 1988; 1990; 1993a. This understanding also grounds the recent work of Mouton, who focuses on reading a New Testament document ethically (2002: 189–91, including nn. 48, 49).

146. See Bassler 1993: 11; also, Chapter 1, section 2.c, above. Indeed, Ashton affirms the important role of religious experience for understanding Paul's theology (2000: 23, 26, 27, 78). This approach is not new, having been an important part of the *Religionsgeschichtliche* school of biblical interpretation that focused on reconstructing Paul's religion. See, e.g., Wrede 1907; Deissmann 1957; Reitzenstein 1978. Even the conservative scholar Adolf Schlatter emphasized nearly a century ago that 'a person can only become clear about the course of his own life by seeing the past as it exercises its power upon us' (ET Morgan 1973: 119).

tament writers.[147] Indeed, in modern scholarship there appears to be a 'bias in favor of theology against religion' and a 'lack of an epistemology specifically calibrated to the religious dimensions of human existence'.[148]

Seeking to respond to this perceived deficiency, Neil Elliott suggests an alternative model that embraces the role of reflection on experience and practice in Paul's religion:

> In all of Paul's letters…we see the apostle engaged in the constant interplay of praxis and reflection. The appropriate object for the study of Paul's theology, then, is not a set of theological propositions, an 'essence' or 'core' of ideas, but the direction in which he sought to move others in the course of his apostolic activity. The proper approach to Paul's letters begins with an understanding of his thought that resembles Gustavo Gutiérrez's definition of theology. In Paul's letters we see the apostle engaged in 'critical reflection on praxis in the light of the word of God' (1994: 83, citing Gutiérrez 1973: 300).

Elliott thus stresses the importance of Paul's applied theology in practical situations rather than viewing Paul's theology as a system of doctrinal beliefs.[149]

The present study will highlight this aspect of Paul's religion often overlooked in Pauline interpretation. With Rowland, we argue Paul 'made much of the dramatic, charismatic and experiential basis of his arguments', since 'access to privileged knowledge of the divine purposes was in certain cases linked to decisive actions' (Rowland 1995a: 47). The exegesis thus illuminates how critical, reasoned reflection on the links between human conduct and experience constitutes a central component of theo-ethical reasoning.

e. *The Historical and Rhetorical Context of Paul's Gospel Proclamation*
In the late Second Temple period, as evidenced by 4QMMT and other texts, *halakhic* interpretations and debates were a vehicle for theological discourse.[150] These debates and disputations were voiced in the context of a more specific 'discourse of revelatory authority'.[151] This discourse presupposed a divine interest and intervention in human affairs.[152] Further, during this time certain Jewish

147. L.T. Johnson 1998: 4; Hurtado 2000: 184. Johnson's work on the Pauline corpus regularly seeks to account for these important aspects of Paul's religious experience (see 1998; 1996; 1993).
148. L.T. Johnson 1998: 4; see also Hurtado 2000: 184.
149. See also Hurtado 2000: 185.
150. Hendel 1998: 20; see also Dunn 1997b: 147–53. In addition one need only consider: (1) the gospel stories that consistently characterize Jesus debating practical Torah concerns with other Jewish leaders; and (2) the later Mishnah, a codification of oral Torah involving *halakhic* debates that date back to the first century CE.
151. For use of this phrase, see Polaski 1999: 43. She places Paul's use of the language of power and his claim to revelatory authority within a broad discourse that includes Jewish wisdom literature of the period, the writings of Josephus, Jewish apocalyptic texts, Qumran scrolls, and Graeco-Roman philosophical material. Likewise, R. Hall argues that Paul models his logical argument in Galatians on a revelatory argumentative *topos* from Jewish apocalypses that involve authority based on divine revelation (1996: 436).
152. Polaski 1999: 22; see also Martyn 1997b: 220 n. 23. The present study argues that this divine interest and intervention in human affairs is a key component of Paul's theo-ethical reasoning. It is an important factor often overlooked in modern analyses of Pauline ethics, especially those of Bultmann

apocalyptic writers made claims to knowledge about the interpretation of the heavenly mysteries and the mysteries of human existence.[153] These were obtained either from revelations gained through otherworldly journeys or through a type of 'historical non-otherworldly' revelation.[154] This apocalyptic literature must be understood within the context of the 'phenomenology of ancient revelatory experience and practice' (Matlock 1996: 272). It is a complicated issue involving the question of the authenticity of revelatory experiences narrated in apocalypses (Aune 1986: 82–83).[155]

The resulting discourse involves two things: (1) persuasion that the particular writer has divine authority by virtue of the revelation received; and (2) the identification of specific criteria by which that divine authority might be recognized and assessed by the recipients of the argument or claim (see Polaski 1999: 20). Indeed, the criteria that are accorded validity by the listeners and readers will determine whether the arguments for revelatory authority by a given claimant prove persuasive among the recipients (see Hall 1996; Polaski 1999: 20).

Paul proclaims his gospel within this broad first-century discourse. In theo-ethical reasoning Paul embraces this discourse's presupposition that God is interested in human affairs and intervenes in the world. Paul focuses on identifying the will of God that is specifically connected to attitudes and conduct that conform to a particular ethical, social norm among those who accept Jesus as Messiah.[156] Thus, Paul proclaims his gospel by means of his own conduct, preaching, and letter-writing through which the 'awesome glory' of the revelation of Jesus Christ might be identified in association with the experiences of new life occurring through the power of God.[157]

The present study further argues that, like other contributors to this discourse, Paul also provides his communities with a criterion for determining his revelatory authority. It will be shown that Paul establishes community edification as the criterion for identifying where and how the power of God is working in connection with conduct that conforms to Christ's cruciform pattern. This criterion becomes essential for the ongoing life of the community after Paul leaves his churches, since it is well known that other people followed Paul into these churches and challenged his gospel, teaching, and authority. In response Paul does not argue doctrinal theological principles. He exhorts his communities to continue conform-

---

and Engberg-Pedersen, who do not incorporate Paul's theology/cosmology because they conclude it is inaccessible to modern readers.

153. Rowland identifies at least two distinct contributions to the origins of apocalyptic involving both prophecy and the Wisdom tradition (1988b: 203). See now E.E. Johnson 1989, who identifies how Paul brings together wisdom and apocalyptic motifs in the context of Romans chs 9–11.

154. J. Collins 1979: 13–14; see also R. Hall 1996. Collins concludes that only about one-third of apocalyptic literature involves the 'historical non-otherworldly' type of revelation.

155. Aune characterizes this issue as 'an insoluble problem'; cf. Polaski 1999: 19–22.

156. See Horrell 2000: 323–24. For differing views about the breadth of this discourse in which Paul is a participant, see Engberg-Pedersen 2000: 3; Deissmann 1957: 226; Barclay 1996b: 209; Elliott 2000: 21–22; Polaski 1999: 43.

157. For use of the phrase 'awesome glory', see Rowland 1995a: 48, discussed above in Chapter 1, section 3.b.

ing their actions to Christ's cruciform pattern, remaining convinced that this is the
means chosen by God to provide humans with access to experiences of God's life-
giving power that builds up the community. Thus, Paul regularly reflects on the
example of his own conduct to remind his converts about the connection between
Christ-conforming actions and the new life they have experienced together.
Moreover, by teaching his churches to practise spiritual discernment by engaging
in theo-ethical reasoning, Paul encourages them to determine for themselves the
links between Christ-conforming conduct and the discernible power of God
experienced in their new life together.

Paul's letters thus fall within this broad first-century discourse of argumentative persuasion. As the very existence of the letters establish, Paul lacked the
power to compel a specific community to accept his arguments for what to believe
or how to act.[158] Indeed, the letters do not claim to be authoritative in their own
right. Such a claim would render redundant the necessity for the very arguments
set out in the letters (Wire 1990: 10). For Paul, the intrinsic authority of his proclamation and his letters belonged only to God (Wire 1990: 10).[159] Paul was less
focused on the best argument winning the day than he was on creating communi-
cations by word and deed through which divine power could operate to persuade
the recipients.[160] Paul's audience thus had to experience the truth of his arguments
by conforming their actions to Christ's cruciform pattern and reflecting on the
connection between such behaviour and their experiences of new life in the community. By making these associations, they might be divinely persuaded of the
legitimacy of Paul's gospel that conduct conforming to Christ's cruciform pattern
constitutes the means by which believers gain access to experiences of God's
life-giving power as God builds up the community into the body of Christ.[161]

Paul's style challenges his readers to weigh what he has said against the other
views accessible to them, reflecting the 'competitive market' that Paul had entered
as an apostle of Jesus Christ.[162] As instruments of persuasion, his letters are fruitfully explored by rhetorical criticism.[163] This focus on the role of persuasion in
Paul's letters is historically appropriate, given the first-century understanding of
rhetorical techniques and terminology, including the important Pauline word
πίστις.[164] This study suggests that, for Paul, 'faith' is a matter of divine per-

158. See Gorman 2001: 296; Polaski 1999: 20; Engberg-Pedersen 2000: 107; Stowers 1986: 108–
109.
159. This is also the overall thrust of Schütz 1975.
160. Cf. Wire 1990: 11; Elliott 2000: 25; Martyn 1991: 161.
161. In connection with Gal. 5.8, discussed below in Chapter 4, section 4.c, we refer to this process
as one of 'divine persuasion'.
162. See Wire 1990: 11; Meeks 1988. This logic is inherent in the overall analysis of Paul's paraenesis by Engberg-Pedersen (see 2000; 2002).
163. For the importance of rhetorical criticism for Pauline studies, see the pioneering work of
Betz (1979) and, more recently, Elliott 1990; 1994; Mitchell 1991; Pogoloff 1992.
164. Kinneavy (1987) argues that the Graeco-Roman roots of the term 'faith' lie in the ancient rhetorical process of persuasion. For the application of Kinneavy's insights in the context of Pauline
interpretation in Galatians, see S.K. Williams 1997. R. Collins acknowledges that in classical Greek,
πίστις denoted the quality of an object that inspired confidence or otherwise evoked a positive
response (1984: 212).

suasion that takes place as believers participate in a disciplined process. It will be argued that believers grow in faith as they practise spiritual discernment by engaging in theo-ethical reasoning to reflect on the associations between conduct and experience. Faith increases as believers become more persuaded that God continues to exercise the same power that raised Jesus from the dead by giving them new earthly life in connection with cruciform conduct. Regularly identifying these connections gives believers confidence that God is redeeming the world in and through Christ and believers participate in that process through their own Christ-conforming actions.[165]

The close readings of the texts in this study acknowledge Paul's letters as instruments of persuasion. The exegetical studies of 1 Corinthians (chs 2 and 3) and Galatians (Chapter 4) proceed as the experience of one who is hearing (or reading) particular letters from beginning to end.

4. A Solution to the 'Problem' Grounded in Paul's Religion:
Theologizing in the Practice of Spiritual Discernment
by Engaging in Theo-Ethical Reasoning

Over a century ago William Wrede advocated the study of early Christian religion and argued against imposing doctrinal theological categories in connection with the New Testament texts. To do so, said Wrede, 'makes doctrine out of what is itself not doctrine' in texts that were focused on giving 'practical advice, direction for life, instruction for the moment' (Wrede 1973 [ET]: 75).[166] According to Wrede, the 'New Testament is not concerned merely with theology, but is in fact far more concerned with religion' (Wrede 1973 [ET]: 116).[167] Consequently, as part of his programmatic essay defining the task and method of 'New Testament theology',[168] Wrede argued that the descriptive task of reconstructing early Chris-

---

165. Paul's use of the language of 'faith' and 'believing' will be considered below in the context of 1 Corinthians (see Chapter 2, section 3.f) and Galatians (see Chapter 4, section 5).

166. Cf. Deissmann 1957: 182.

167. In Paul's case, said Wrede, the 'religion of the apostle is theological through and through' (1907: 76).

168. For a general discussion of the history and future of 'New Testament theology' and for comparisons of the various approaches to this undertaking, see Morgan 1973; 1995a; Morgan and Barton 1988; Räisänen 2000; Boers 1979; Ebeling 1963.

Furnish has observed that there is an 'inseparable' connection between the concerns of 'Pauline theology' and the 'more fundamental questions about the meaning and aims of…"New Testament theology"' (1990a: 19). Both 'Pauline theology' and 'New Testament theology' may be understood as ways of doing theology by providing theological interpretation of the biblical text that communicates the theological message in a way that makes it credible today. See Morgan (1995b: 104, 106, 107), who speaks only to 'New Testament theology' but by implication also 'Pauline theology' as a sub-category of the broader discipline; *pace* Wrede (1897; ET Morgan 1973), who argues to limit the understanding of 'New Testament theology' to purely descriptive, historical reconstruction. For a challenge to this latter aspect of Wrede's argument, see Morgan 1973: 61; 1995a: 115.

From the historical perspective, there is a risk in writing 'Pauline theology' or 'New Testament theology'. The interpreter may conflate the task of providing a descriptive, historical reconstruction with that of modern theological appropriation. This takes place when aspects of Paul's theological

tian religion involved identifying what was believed, taught, thought, hoped, striven for, and required in the religion (1973 [ET]: 84, 116). He thus implies an integral connection between theology and ethics in Paul's religion.[169]

Leander Keck recently extended Wrede's critique of the methodology of 'New Testament theology' by applying it to the modern attempt to write 'New Testament ethics' and by implication its sub-category 'Pauline ethics' (1996a: 3–4). Keck argues that 'New Testament ethics' does not consist in using the biblical texts as a quarry from which various stones are cut and applied as needed (1996a: 4).[170] Instead, he says, the interpreter must bring to the surface the rationale or moral reasoning that 'undergirds enjoined morality', in particular biblical exhortations, even if this rationale is not apparent on the surface of the text (1996a: 8). Keck contends that this is the 'real "stuff"' of New Testament ethics (1996a: 7). It necessitates the reconstruction of early Christian history and encourages the search for the consistent outlook and ways of thinking that give particular texts a character sufficiently clear to differentiate them (1996a: 10).[171]

This study enters the debate about 'the problem of ethics in Paul'. Responding to Bassler's challenge (Bassler 1993: 17), the study addresses the complicated question of how Paul theologized in the practice of spiritual discernment by engaging in theo-ethical reasoning. Following Wrede, it presents a descriptive, historical account of certain key aspects of Paul's religion that highlights how he understood the complex divine–human relationship. Taking up Keck's proposal, this study regularly looks beneath the surface of the texts to bring to light the logic and rationale of theo-ethical reasoning that establish the consistent pattern of thinking that characterizes the way Paul theologized.

We highlight certain aspects of Paul's religion that may be directly reconstructed or inferred from the logic of his arguments. Of course, any proposed historical reconstruction always remains subject to debate and is beyond irrefutable proof – especially one that seeks to identify aspects of Paul's religion based on rationale inferred from the logic of his arguments. Nevertheless, we offer this proposed historical reconstruction of Paul's religion, aware that it challenges several well-accepted principles of Pauline understanding. We suggest that it presents

---

perspective are disregarded in the historical reconstruction. For instance, both Bultmann and Engberg-Pedersen argue that Paul's basic worldview – his apocalyptic and cosmological outlook that Engberg-Pedersen describes as ' "theology" *cum* "cosmology" ' (2000: 19) – cannot be appropriated by modern readers as it stands. Consequently, these two interpreters disregard Paul's perspective despite their claim to be doing historical reconstruction. This potentially distorts the historical presentation of Paul for purposes of making the ancient writer accessible today. The present study seeks to place greater emphasis on historical reconstruction.

169. For an early discussion of the inseparability of religion and ethics in Paul, see Hermann von Soden 1892: 111. Like Cullmann (1964: 228) and Dunn (1975: 223–24) who followed, however, von Soden interprets Paul as saying that the individual is moved to ethical action from 'within', not from something 'outside' the person (1892: 125). The present exegetical study challenges this narrow interpretation that overlooks the external, guiding role of the Spirit that illuminates the importance of community experience.

170. For similar conclusions, see Horrell 1999: 325; Dennison 1979: 55 n. 1.

171. Cf. Horrell 1999: 321–25; Dennison 1979: 55 n. 1.

a valuable set of reflections and a plausible historical reconstruction based on a close exegetical reading of the texts.

It has become commonplace to assert that Paul was not a 'systematic theologian',[172] a truism since the discipline of systematic theology did not arise until mediaeval scholasticism. But it has been far less common to analyse Paul alternatively as a pastoral theologian.[173] The present study explores the pastoral contexts and methods of reasoning by which Paul associates the experiences of new life with Christ-conforming conduct. We highlight the way that Paul theologizes as a pastoral theologian focused on discerning how God builds communities in connection with Christ-conforming conduct.[174]

Focusing on certain aspects of Paul's religion, this study provides a new framework for understanding the close connection between what are traditionally distinguished as Paul's ethics and theology. It is argued that the 'problem of ethics in Paul' does not lie in the eschatological paradox or contradictory nature of Paul's indicative and imperative statements or structure. Instead, the 'problem' lies in the failure of interpreters to recognize how Paul integrates thinking and acting as a first-century pastoral Christian community-builder and former Pharisee with an apocalyptic perspective. This integration becomes apparent in Paul's theo-ethical reasoning that provides the framework for the important practice of spiritual discernment. By engaging in this reasoned practice, believers associate experiences of God's life-giving power with particular actions that conform to Christ's cruciform pattern.

Thus, the solution to the 'problem of ethics in Paul' is recognizing that there is no 'problem'. As part of his apocalyptic (i.e. revelatory) religious perspective, Paul combines ethics with theology as integrated aspects of Christian living and thinking.[175] This fusion becomes clear in his coherent and complex process of theo-ethical reasoning.[176] It will be shown how this reasoning incorporates Paul's understanding of the divine–human relationship in which Christians bear a missionary responsibility for working with God in the divine plan for cosmic reconstruction.[177] Through believers' actions that conform to Christ's cruciform pattern,

---

172. See, e.g., B. Longenecker 1996: 94–97; Barclay 1996c: 287; cf. Thurén 2000: 11; Doty 1973; Furnish 1968: 208–12; Jaquette 1995: 208.

173. See Malherbe 1987; 2000b; Dabourne 1999; van Spanje 1999: 62–71; Gorman 2001: 4.

174. According to Barclay, the way Paul sometimes tells stories or parts of stories is not incidental to his theologizing, but is in some sense constitutive of it (2002: 133). This study affirms that these stories (in Paul's life and the lives of others) are constitutive of the way Paul theologizes because they show how he reasons – identifying where God is manifestly working to give new life in connection with Christ-conforming conduct.

175. According to Engberg-Pedersen, for Paul theology and ethics are not two different things, but two sides of the same coin bound together by the divine–human relationship (2000: 137); cf. Cousar 1996: 145–46; Barclay 1996c: 287; Gorman 2001: 177.

176. Sampley describes Paul's 'complex moral reckoning' as a process by which the moral agent 'must constantly keep track of the progress of one's own faith toward maturity and where, at the same time, one is to do the calculus of a contemplated action's impact upon others...[and] to live the proper life before God...to monitor a delicate balance regarding self and others at every point in one's life' (1990: 238).

177. See Beker 1980: 277–78.

God continues to reclaim the world for God's sovereignty, giving new earthly life by exercising the same power that raised Jesus from the dead.[178] In Paul's religion each individual and the gathered community engage in theo-ethical reasoning by practising spiritual discernment. In this collective, dialogical process of *looking for life*, community members practise reasoned reflection to associate Christ-conforming conduct with the manifestations of new life. This reveals to them where and how God is reclaiming the cosmos by building Christian communities, changing human perceptions, and guiding Christian practice. In this way it may be concluded that theo-ethical reasoning lies at the centre of Paul's religion.

5. *Selection of Data*

The next three chapters assess the coherence and consistency of the thesis through an exegetical study of two of Paul's *Hauptbriefe* – 1 Corinthians and Galatians. The letters will be examined in sequence from beginning to end in order to identify the rhetorical strategy of the unfolding argument. Each letter's primary role as an instrument of persuasion rather than a resource for extracting theological principles demands such a reading (see Wrede 1973 [ET]: 75). While this approach sometimes makes it more difficult for the reader to 'see the forest for the trees', it highlights the pervasive influence of theo-ethical reasoning throughout each letter and thereby establishes the legitimacy of the thesis.

The letter known canonically as 1 Corinthians was chosen because it is generally recognized as the letter where Paul most consistently and directly deals with contingent matters involving concrete behaviour among believing Christians (Furnish 1999: 142). Thus, the interpreter would most expect Paul to engage in theo-ethical reasoning in 1 Corinthians, where he addresses so many issues associated with community conduct and experience. Therefore, this letter proves an important starting point for testing our thesis.

Galatians was selected for analysis because, along with Romans, it is often conidered one of Paul's 'more theological' letters (Furnish 1999: 123). It points towards the coherency of Paul's theology, doctrinally stated, so the letter has played an important role in the history of Protestant doctrinal theology. As a more theological letter, Galatians presents a challenging test case for the hypothesis that Paul brings together theology and ethics as part of his theo-ethical reasoning by which he integrates Christian living and thinking. Only in recent years has the importance of the letter's ethics been shown to be directly relevant and rhetorically connected to the letter's statements of theology.[179] Galatians was selected over Romans because Paul founded the churches in Galatia but had no personal experience with the Roman Christians upon which to reflect at the time he wrote them. Thus, Galatians presents a better source for testing the hypothesis that Paul

---

178. See Furnish, who concludes that for Paul the eschatological power of God – i.e. God's transcendent power – has a present dimension as the meaning and reality of the ultimate triumph of God's power become manifest in the present (1968: 215).

179. See Barclay 1988; Engberg-Pedersen 2000.

attempts to associate community experience with specific conduct as part of the
way that he persuades others about the truth of his gospel.

If this study shows that in these two very different letters Paul consistently
theologizes by means of theo-ethical reasoning, then the viability of the proposed
solution to the 'problem of ethics in Paul' will be established. This paradigm that
shows Paul's consistent way of integrating Christian thinking and living may
then be explored fruitfully in Paul's other letters, although space limitations pre-
clude such a detailed analysis in this study. The study's conclusions appear in
Chapter 5.

Chapter 2

IDENTIFYING THEO-ETHICAL REASONING
(1 CORINTHIANS 1.1–4.21)

1. *Introduction*

Through exegesis of 1 Cor. 1.1–4.21, this chapter seeks to identify and illuminate Paul's theo-ethical reasoning and its role in the community practice of spiritual discernment. It attempts to show that Paul's gospel proclamation does not take place exclusively (or even primarily) by oral preaching. Rather, Paul engages in reasoned reflection to emphasize the integration of conduct, speech and experience that *should* be taking place when the whole church gathers for worship and moral dialogue. Thus, this section of the letter addresses the structure of community life necessary for effective moral discourse to take place in the community (Horrell 1999: 322).

The chapter brings to the surface the rationale or moral reasoning that grounds particular Pauline arguments and exhortations, even when this rationale is not readily apparent.[1] This shows how Paul attempts to transform community perceptions by aligning them with his apocalyptic (i.e. revelatory) perspective (see Brown 1995: 21). He employs extensive 'perceptual terminology' (Brown 1995: 24 n. 22) to point out the links between community experiences of God's life-giving power and conduct that conforms to Christ's cruciform pattern. These discernible connections between conduct and experience demonstrate the proof of Paul's gospel.[2] They ground believers' faith in the power of God (see 1 Cor. 2.1–5). Theo-ethical reasoning and the community practice of spiritual discernment thereby become the means by which Paul theologizes, as he combines theology and ethics in 1 Corinthians chs 1–4.

Diverse interpretative theories attempt to identify the historical cause of the problems that Paul was writing this letter to correct.[3] Our study proceeds on the

1. See Keck 1996a: 7–8, discussed in Chapter 1, section 4.
2. In her important work on 1 Corinthians, Mitchell discusses the use and function of personal example in ancient deliberative rhetoric. She concludes that Paul's use of proofs by example (both personal and from scripture) throughout the letter support her thesis that the letter is a piece of deliberative rhetoric (1991: 39–68). This study argues that Paul's use of proofs by example constitutes part of his broader appeal to identifying the connections between community experience and conduct that lie at the heart of theo-ethical reasoning and the community practice of spiritual discernment.
3. For the theory that 'Gnosticism' was to blame for the Corinthian problems, see Jewett 1971: 23–40; Schmithals 1971; Wilckens 1971. Horsley (1976; 1977; 1980; 1998), Pearson (1973) and Goulder (1991) stress the influence of Hellenistic Judaism, particularly the influence of Philo and the

basis that there were two related problems in the Corinthian church. First, at least some members of the church, being highly integrated into the surrounding culture,[4] were continuing to adhere to social and cultural norms and values reflecting Hellenistic patterns of thought (Adams 2000: 96–97). They were failing to 'appropriate the apocalyptic dimensions of Paul's gospel' (Adams 2000: 96).[5] Through social and ideological compromise with the culture, at least some of the Corinthians were failing to maintain the distinctiveness of their calling.[6] This chapter will argue that in response to this problem Paul reminds the Corinthians that Christ's cruciform pattern of self-giving love for others, supremely manifest in his death on the cross, has become the new behavioural standard for both Jews and Greeks in God's new age (see Engberg-Pedersen 1987: 566–67). Repeatedly during the course of the letter, Paul offers his own pattern of life as an embodied, interpretative paradigm of this new standard for his communities. His goal is that they, too, will imaginatively conform themselves to the exalted, crucified Jesus Christ (see Gorman 2001: 297; cf. Lindemann 1996: 86). Paul insists that conduct conforming to this cruciform pattern becomes the means by which God gives new life and growth to the church in God's new age (see Gorman 2001: 223).

Second, the present chapter and Chapter 3 attempt to show that there was also a breakdown in the community's practice of spiritual discernment. Some influential members of the church were failing to participate in this important community practice, or, at least, were refusing to consider the views of every member of the community in their reflective, dialogical process of decision-making about behavioural matters.[7] The study proceeds on the basis that Paul was writing this letter of exhortation and advice[8] from his apocalyptic (i.e. revelatory) perspective to correct these deficiencies in the moral discourse of the community.

2. *Identifying Theo-Ethical Reasoning (1.1–9)*

a. *The Salutation (1.1–3)*
In the letter's salutation (1.1–3) and thanksgiving (1.4–9), Paul telescopes several keynote themes (see D. Martin 1995: 55). First, the salutation emphasizes God's one 'deliberative assembly' (ἐκκλησία)[9] in Corinth. In non-biblical Greek

---

Wisdom tradition. Thiselton (1977–78) and Tuckett (1996) point to 'overrealized eschatology' among church members. For a critique of the various positions, see Adams 2000: 94–97.

    4.   See Barclay 1992: 57–59; Lindemann 1996: 86.

    5.   Cf. Lampe 1994: 40–41; Furnish 1999: 7, 19. Adams correctly concludes that the 'dominant theological perspective of 1 Corinthians is an apocalyptic one' (2000: 106).

    6.   Adams 2000: 149; see also Barclay 1992: 59, 70.

    7.   M. Mitchell suggests that the goal of the letter is decision-making about behavioural matters (1991: 257 n. 396).

    8.   Furnish 1999: 15, 17–18; cf. Stowers 1986: 91–152. The epistolary unity of 1 Corinthians is assumed. For arguments supporting this conclusion, see Furnish 1999: 12; Fee 1987: 16; Hurd 1965: 47; Conzelmann 1975: 4; R. Collins 1999: 14; Mitchell 1991: 17, 298; Brown 1995: 21; D. Martin 1995: 261–62 n. 54. This conclusion does not preclude interpolations. See, e.g., 1 Cor. 14.34–35.

    9.   For this translation, see Meeks 1993a: 45; Banks 1994: 27; R. Collins 1999: 51; Barrett 1968: 261.

ἐκκλησία denoted, among other things, the voting assembly of the citizen body of a Greek polis that assembled for deliberative or executive purposes to make civic decisions affecting community welfare (see Acts 19.21–41).[10] This suggests that Paul probably understood the ἐκκλησία as the political assembly of the people in Christ in pointed juxtaposition to the official city assembly.[11] Like the city assembly, however, the ἐκκλησία meets to provide a public forum for all sorts of acclamation, discussion, and decision-making apart from the Roman courts (Gorman 2001: 357).

Moreover, the Septuagint applies the term ἐκκλησία to translate the קְהַל יְהוָה that assembled to consider behavioural matters and make collective decisions.[12] Paul appears to agree with general Jewish and Christian usage, characterizing as the ἐκκλησία those who assemble in the divine presence for community decision-making in the context of behavioural concerns (see Thiselton 2000: 75). Thus, the term ἐκκλησία implies the community's task of 'moral self-formation' (Meeks 1993a: 45). The ἐκκλησία is not for Paul 'an optional supplement to a private spirituality of dying and rising with Christ' (Gorman 2001: 367). It represents 'what God is up to in the world: re-creating a people whose corporate life tells the world what the death and resurrection of the Messiah is all about' (Gorman 2001: 367; cf. Stendahl 1984: 59–60). Indeed, the church 'lives the story, embodies the story, tells the story' as 'the living exegesis of God's master story of faith, love, power, and hope' (Gorman 2001: 367). But Paul knew well that the church must have a disciplined evaluative process for reflecting on the ways it was telling this story by embodying the new cruciform pattern. As this study progresses, it highlights the important role of transformative dialogue in the deliberative assembly – where the community should be reviewing and evaluating the propriety of particular conduct.[13]

In 1.2 Paul connects the Corinthians with 'all the ones calling upon the name of the Lord Jesus Christ in every place'.[14] This phrase probably had its roots in the early Christian ritual of baptism into 'the name of Jesus Christ'.[15] In the ancient world a person's name served not only a distinguishing function but also as a manifestation of the nature of the person who bore that name.[16] The name was virtually an expression of the person (R. Collins 1999: 76).

10. As noted by Meeks 1993a: 45; Banks 1994: 27; R. Collins 1999: 51; Barrett 1968: 261. See, e.g., Thucydides, *Histories* 1.187, 139; 6.8; 8.69; Philo, *Spec. Leg.* 2.44.

11. Gorman 2001: 357; Horsley 1997a: 209.

12. See, e.g., Deut. 4.10; 9.10; 18.16; Josh. 9.2; 1 Chron. 13.2, 4; Ezra 10.8, 12; Neh. 8.2; 13.1; Mic. 2.5; Sir. 21.17; 23.24; 38.33; 1 Macc. 2.56; 4.59; 5.16.

13. See, e.g., 1 Cor. 14.1–40, examined in Chapter 3, section 3.d below.

14. For other invocations of the 'name' of the Lord in this letter, see 1.10, 13, 15; 5.4; 6.11; 16.22.

15. Hurtado 1999b: 200; Kramer 1966: 77; Dunn 1970: 117–22. See 1.13, 15; 6.11; cf. Acts 2.38; 8.16; 19.5; 10.48. According to Morray-Jones, there is a particularly Pauline connection between Christian baptism in the name of Jesus Christ and the Jewish tradition of transformational mysticism, whereby the baptizand is conformed to the divine image through the mediation of Christ (1992: 27–31).

16. Käsemann 1980: 14; R. Collins 1999: 76.

Thus, for Paul, baptism into the name of Jesus Christ suggests a commitment to become a living expression or manifestation of the person of Jesus Christ.[17] Indeed, those who were baptized into the name of Jesus Christ clothed themselves with Christ (Gal. 3.27). This does not mean simply a once-for-all time event. It must be consistently repeated – a conclusion indicated by Paul's use in Rom. 13.14 of the same verb ἐνδύω from Gal. 3.27.[18] In baptism believers commit to conform their lives to the name/character of the person of Christ, who becomes manifest through specific acts (see 1 Cor. 11.1).[19] Moreover, to call upon the name of the Lord 'means not to invoke some shadowy, unknown deity, but to commit oneself in trust to the one whose nature and character have been disclosed as worthy of this trust' (Thiselton 2000: 79). Paul expands on this in 1.5–9.

Furthermore, the present participle in 1.2 (ἐπικαλουμένοις) appears to refer to a uniform Christian practice of calling on the risen Lord. To call on the name of the Lord 'signals an act of appeal and request which is simultaneously an act of commitment and trust on the part of the worshiper' (Thiselton 2000: 78–79).[20] The logic of this appeal and request, combined with Paul's use of the present participle, reflect his conviction that the risen Lord plays a *continuing* role in the deliberative assembly. They must seek and expect his guidance in the community task of moral self-formation (see 1.8; 4.1–5; 11.28–32). In their community life, the Corinthians should be collectively calling on the name of the Lord, the 'living guarantor of the salvation promised to those who trust in him' (Hurtado 1999b: 200).

In 1.2 Paul also characterizes the Corinthians as sanctified/set apart for God in Christ Jesus. The perfect participle ἡγιασμένοις denotes an earlier event with continuing effects.[21] In Paul's biblical tradition, the verb ἁγιάζω and the related adjective ἅγιος were frequently used to denote Israel.[22] They were a nation set apart for special relationship with YHWH and to conduct themselves in a way so

---

17. Interpreting the author's use of the phrase 'walk worthily of the Lord' in Col. 1.10 (cf. Phil. 1.27), Meeks argues that 'ethics' is a hermeneutical undertaking, implying that a Christian's conduct constitutes that person's behavioural interpretation of the conduct of the Lord (1993b: 47); cf. *Did.* 11.8.

18. Citing Dionysius of Halicarnassus 11.5, Dunn finds Paul alluding to the stage in these verses: an actor plays the role of a character by 'putting on' that character and assuming that character for the length of the play as the actor 'lives the part' (1998c: 198 n. 58); cf. Rom. 15.1–5. According to Dunn, this is 'equivalent to assuming the persona of Christ' (1998c: 405). Similarly, Käsemann concludes that for Paul the Christian life is 'a perpetual return to baptism...so long as we keep on the pilgrim way and allow ourselves to be recalled daily to the allegiance of Christ' (1969e: 175; see also Barclay 1988: 214).

19. Indeed, in Exod. 3.13–14 (where Moses asks God's name), the divine response is that Moses 'will see what constitutes my [the divine] name by the sovereign and redeeming acts which I shall perform, and which will thereby disclose my identity in terms of character' (Thiselton 2000: 79).

20. See also 1 Cor. 16.22, discussed below in Chapter 3, section 5.b.

21. Paul uses the perfect tense συνεσταύρωμαι in 1 Cor. 1.23, 2.2 and Gal. 2.19 in a similar way.

22. See, e.g., Lev. 11.44; 20.26; Exod. 19.5–6; *1 En.* 62.7–8; *Pss. Sol.* 8.22; 17.26, 43; 1QM 3.5; 1QH 7.10; CD 4.6.

as to be ἅγιος, just as YHWH is ἅγιος (see, e.g., Lev. 19.2).[23] Paul follows this tradition by consistently applying the verb ἁγιάζω throughout his letters to describe the divine action that sanctifies or sets apart God's people.[24] Similarly, he uses the noun ἁγιασμός to denote sanctification, the state of being set apart for God in Christ.[25] As those set apart by God and for God 'in Christ Jesus',[26] believers must bear the character of God as revealed in the name/character of Jesus Christ (see Fee 1987: 32). Thus, Paul's concept of holiness regularly entails observable behaviour (Fee 1987: 32). Holiness requires conduct built on the foundation of the character and nature of the person of Jesus Christ (see 1 Cor. 3.10–11).

The logic underlying Paul's salutation in 1.2 reflects an essential aspect of theo-ethical reasoning. Those who are baptized into the name of Jesus Christ commit to conform themselves to the nature and character of God revealed in Jesus Christ.[27] They commit to conform their behaviour to Christ's cruciform pattern of self-giving love for others as they are initiated into the sphere of new life, where God's power works in and through the person of Christ.[28]

Thus, in 1.2, 'the theological and ethical make contact' (Thiselton 2000: 77). Similarly, the salutation closes in 1.3 by confirming the cooperative work of both God and the Lord Jesus Christ, who are the two sources of grace and peace in the world.[29] Already, in these opening verses, Paul's theo-ethical reasoning has begun to reflect the way he integrates theology and ethics. It sets the tone for the entire letter.

b. *The Thanksgiving (1.4–9)*

For Paul, the formal thanksgiving expresses pastoral concerns and often serves a paraenetic purpose, frequently becoming 'a kind of overture embodying themes which would be developed more fully later in the main body of the work' (Thiselton 2000: 86).[30] That is the case in 1 Cor. 1.4–9, where additional, major components of theo-ethical reasoning may be detected. From a rhetorical perspective,

23. Fee 1987: 32–33; R. Collins 1999: 52; Furnish 1999: 32.
24. See Rom. 15.16; 1 Cor. 6.11; 7.14; 1 Thess. 5.23.
25. See, e.g., Rom. 6.19, 22; 1 Cor. 1.30; 1 Thess. 4.3, 4, 7.
26. The prepositional phrase 'in (ἐν) Christ Jesus' in 1 Cor. 1.2 invokes both the locative and instrumental aspects of the preposition. For Paul's use of the phrase 'in Christ' with both locative and instrumental force, see Furnish 1999: 32–33; Beker 1980: 272; cf. Wedderburn 1985: 95–96 n. 37; Horrell 2000: 325 n. 18; Sampley 1991: 39; contra Fee 1987: 32 n. 20; Conzelmann 1975: 21; Neugebauer 1958; 1961: 103.
27. According to Gorman, Paul understands that 'baptism is a parabolic enactment of faith...as a sharing in, not merely an affirmation of, the narrative of Jesus' (2001: 123). Paul's primary concern in baptism 'is faith understood as participation in the story of Jesus' (2001: 124).
28. According to Thiselton, '[w]hat counts as holy is perceived as *what counts as Christ-like*' (2000: 76, original emphasis). Therefore, 'just as Christ assumes the form of the "image" of God in public (εἰκών, 1 Cor. 15.49), so a holy people *manifest* their consecration to God through the status and character which they derive from Christ' (2000: 76, original emphasis).
29. See Thiselton 2000: 84; Hurtado 1999b: 195; see also Rom. 1.7; 16.20; 1 Cor. 16.23; 2 Cor. 1.4; Gal. 1.3; 6.18; Phil. 1.2; 4.23; 1 Thess. 5.28.
30. Schubert (1939) showed the influence of Greek epistolary thanksgiving forms in Paul's letters.

these verses make hearers attentive, receptive and well-disposed, while orienting them to the arguments that follow (Mitchell 1991: 195). In 1.4–9 Paul reflects on community experience at Corinth. He marks the connection between Christ-conforming human conduct and the χαρίσματα, the manifestations of God's power that reflect new life in the community.[31] Moreover, each divine gift (χάρισμα) – the revelation of which is later attributed to the work of the Spirit sent from God (see 2.10, 12; 12.4, 7) – represents God's power coming to material expression through divinely confirmed, Christ-conforming human words and deeds.[32] The Corinthians experienced specific χαρίσματα that manifested God's exercise of power that Paul calls 'grace'.[33] Continuing to use the spatial imagery introduced in 1.2, Paul underscores God as 'giver'[34] of this new life 'in Christ Jesus' (1.4).

Similarly, says Paul in 1.5a, 'in him' (Christ Jesus) the Corinthians were divinely enriched (ἐπλουτίσθητε)[35] with all kinds of speaking[36] and knowledge.[37] The adjectival forms of πᾶς in 1.5 should be understood qualitatively rather than quantitatively, since Paul is neither implying that all speech or knowledge in Corinth is divinely given nor that the Corinthians have been fully gifted in these areas (see 13.8–12). Indeed, Paul later calls into question the 'communicative effectiveness' (Thiselton 2000: 92) of some of their speaking (14.1–19). He even argues that the possession of knowledge by some is leading them to act in ways that are destroying the community (8.1–13).

Several interpreters point to the conspicuous absence of any reference in 1.5 to the Corinthians' works of love.[38] The reason for this absence lies in the deficient practice of love by some Corinthians, a shortcoming that defines the course of

---

31. In his important study on ministry and community, Käsemann highlights that for Paul the divine gift of God's gracious power (χάρισμα) and Christ-patterned διακονία (1 Cor. 12.5) are 'interchangeable' (1964c: 65). He also notes that the χαρίσματα are 'interchangeable' with the calling of God according to Rom. 11.29 and 1 Cor. 7.7, 17–24 (1964c: 65). In fact, concludes Käsemann, the many χαρίσματα only exist because of the existence of the *one* overarching χάρισμα to which all others are related: eternal life in Christ Jesus according to Rom. 6.23 (1964c: 64). All the other subordinate χαρίσματα represent human participation in the eternal life of Christ that 'quickens and announces its presence within earthly reality' in human, Christ-patterned διακονία (1964c: 65). The present study explores further these links between Christ-patterned service and the exercise of the power of God that gives new and eternal life.

32. See Dunn 1998c: 553–54; see also 1 Cor. 12.4–7.

33. Barclay concludes that 'grace' is 'the action of God in history' (2002: 154). For understanding 'grace' as God's power, see Käsemann 1964c: 65; Nolland 1986: 26–31; Polaski 1999: 107. These conclusions suggest by implication that grace is experienced as a discernible event in the community.

34. Wagner 1998: 286 n. 33; see also 1.30; 2.12; 3.5, 8, 10, 14; 4.5, 7.

35. Paul is the only New Testament writer to use πλουτίζω. It denotes divine enrichment (see 2 Cor. 6.10; 9.11). He similarly employs πλουτέω and πλοῦτος to designate the richness of God and/or the divine enrichment that takes place in connection with Jesus Christ. See Rom. 2.14; 9.23; 10.12; 11.12, 33; 1 Cor. 4.8; 2 Cor. 8.9; 9.11; Phil. 4.19; cf. Eph. 1.7, 18; 2.7; 3.8, 16; Col. 1.27; 2.2.

36. Thiselton contends that 'speaking' more properly conveys the semantic range of λόγος than does its translation as 'word' (2000: 91–92); cf. Fee 1987: 38; *pace* R. Collins 1999: 62.

37. For the importance of 'knowledge' in the letter, see 8.1–13; 12.8–12; Fee 1987: 38; Conzelmann 1975: 27; Thiselton 2000: 91.

38. See, e.g., Barrett 1968: 36; Mitchell 1991: 195; Weiss 1910: 6; cf. Betz 1986: 33.

action that Paul urges throughout the letter.[39] This conclusion also explains the absence of ἔργον in the list of gifts in 1.5 and its presence in 15.58, at the close of Paul's argument. A 'work' emphasizes the *potential* divine fruitfulness of a person's 'labour in the Lord'.[40]

According to 1.6, divine enrichment occurred when (καθὼς) the witness of Christ (τὸ μαρτύριον τοῦ Χριστοῦ) was confirmed (ἐβεβαιώθη) among them.[41] The important phrase τὸ μαρτύριον τοῦ Χριστοῦ is a cipher for Paul's integrated proclamation of the gospel of Christ.[42] This is something that takes place by word *and* deed.[43] A number of interpreters, however, translate τὸ μαρτύριον as the 'testimony' about Christ,[44] thereby highlighting their assumption that Paul's gospel proclamation primarily takes place verbally.

There is no doubt that μαρτύριον includes oral testimony.[45] Paul's only other use of the word (2 Cor. 1.12) and other New Testament applications,[46] however, suggest something more than just oral testimony. These uses reflect that μαρτύριον signifies *communicative conduct* that establishes a 'proof' concerning the subject of the communication.[47] Indeed, in 2 Cor. 1.12 Paul writes that the way he has behaved (ἀνεστράφημεν) in the world toward the Corinthians constitutes the witness/proof of his own conscience. This assertion points out the way that Paul's conduct provides manifest proof of his own self-awareness.[48] Consequently, it is suggested that Paul's use of μαρτύριον in 1 Cor. 1.6 includes behaviour as well as speech. Paul preaches the story of the crucified and risen

39. See Mitchell 1991: 195; see also 2.9; 8.1–3; 13.1–4, 13; 14.1; 16.14; cf. 12.31.

40. See Mitchell 1991: 217, including n. 164. It will be argued that the manifest 'work' wrought in connection with human conduct is the product of the power of God or the powers of the world. Thus, *pace* Betz (1986: 33), the Corinthians' *praxis* is not to be equated with their ἔργον, although there is a direct connection between the two. See, e.g., 3.1–4; 12.4–7; cf. Gal. 5.19–25.

41. The genitive τοῦ Χριστοῦ may be objective or subjective. Thiselton observes that it is difficult to decide this issue on grammatical and textual grounds (2000: 94). For the objective genitive, see Fee 1987: 40 n. 25; R. Collins 1999: 63; Barrett 1968: 37. Barrett also notes the possibility that the genitive is subjective. It will be argued below that Paul uses the phrase with both meanings. For the translation of τὸ μαρτύριον as 'witness', see Thiselton 2000: 94; Furnish 1999: 33; cf. Héring 1962: 3. As will be shown below, effectively there is no real distinction between translating the phrase as 'witness' or 'testimony'.

42. R. Collins 1999: 63. It should be noted, however, that Collins translates the phrase as 'the testimony to Christ'.

43. See Rom. 15.18–19; 1 Cor. 2.4; Phil. 4.9; cf. 2 Cor. 12.6–7.

44. See, e.g., Fee 1987: 40, including n. 25; R. Collins 1999: 63; Barrett 1968: 38; Hays 1997b: 18; Schütz 1975: 91–92; cf. Thiselton 2000: 94.

45. See LSJ, 1082; Mk 13.9 (Mt. 24.14; Lk. 21.13); Acts 4.33; Heb. 3.5.

46. See Mk 1.44 (Mt. 8.4; Lk. 5.14); Mk 6.11 (Lk. 9.15); Mt. 10.18; Acts 7.44; 1 Tim. 2.6; 2 Tim. 1.8; Jas 5.3; Rev. 15.5.

47. For characterizing μαρτύριον as 'proof', see LSJ, 1082, and the New Testament applications in the preceding note.

48. See Käsemann, who concludes in connection with 1 Cor. 6.13 that the human body 'signifies man in his worldliness and therefore in his ability to communicate…in the bodily obedience… carried out as the service of God in the world of everyday', as 'the lordship of Christ finds visible expression and only when this visible expression takes personal shape in us does the whole thing become credible as Gospel message' (1969d: 135).

Christ, while Paul's own communicative conduct becomes the substance and proof of the story that God *continues* to give new life through conduct that conforms to Christ's cruciform pattern.[49]

This constitutes another aspect of theo-ethical reasoning. Paul preaches the revelation of God's power working in the death and resurrection of Christ. He proves that God still exercises this same life-giving power in the lives of believers by showing them the association between Paul's own Christ-conforming actions and the demonstration of Spirit and power that gives them new life and grounds their faith in the power of God (see 2.1–5).

Thus, Paul's μαρτύριον does not just refer to his oral preaching.[50] Instead, as one who seeks to imitate Christ (1 Cor. 11.1; see also 1 Thess. 1.6), Paul offers his witness of Christ that includes his own embodied interpretation of the name/character of Jesus Christ, the one who gave himself for others. Paul lives out the witness of Christ through his own apostolic lifestyle.[51] As one commissioned by God to proclaim God's Son to the Gentiles (Gal. 1.15–16), Paul's witness of Christ necessarily takes place by word *and* deed. It concerns what can be seen, heard, learned, and received 'in' and 'from' Paul (see 2 Cor. 12.6–7; Phil. 4.9).[52] Christ himself comes alive in and through Paul as his own speech and actions conform to Christ's cruciform pattern.[53]

This is what Paul means by the phrase 'witness of Christ'. Effectively, this may also be rendered as Paul's 'testimony about Christ' in 1 Cor. 1.6, *so long as* it is understood that Paul's oral 'testimony' refers not only to preaching the story of Jesus Christ but also to the links Paul identifies between his own embodied, Christ-conforming conduct and the Corinthians' experiences of enriched new life. At other points, Paul variously characterizes this embodied witness of Christ as (1) the proclamation of the cross (1 Cor. 1.18; see also Gal. 6.14; Phil. 3.17–18); (2) Christ crucified (1 Cor. 1.23; 2.2); and (3) weakness (see 4.9; cf. 2 Cor. 12.7–10; Gal. 4.13).

In connection with Paul's 'witness of Christ' in 1 Cor. 1.6, the juridical undertone of βεβαιόω has been consistently noted.[54] This introduces judgment as another central theme in the letter. The community's enrichment with gifts rooted in God's power (χαρίσματα) provides *discernible* proof that the risen Lord has confirmed Paul's embodied proclamation of Christ.[55] These χαρίσματα are 'positive signs' (Conzelmann 1975: 28) that God's power has been at work among

---

49. See also 1 Cor. 2.1–5; 2 Cor. 4.10–12; 13.1–4; Gal. 3.1–5.

50. See Acts 22.14–15; 26.16; *pace* Schütz 1975: 91–92; Furnish 1989b: 73; Fee 1987: 40; Barrett 1968: 37–38; R. Collins 1999: 62–63.

51. See 1 Cor. 1.17–18; 2.1–5; 4.17; Gal. 3.1; 4.14; Phil. 3.17–18; 1 Thess. 1.5–7; 2.1–12.

52. Sampley observes that Paul's teaching is coordinated with his actions so that what his followers see and hear provides a solid example (1991: 88). Similarly, Käsemann points out in the context of Rom. 15.18 that 'word and work' correspond to the Greek distinction between speech and action (1980: 394). Thus, Paul spreads the gospel through both means of communication.

53. See 2 Cor. 4.10–12; 13.4; Gal. 2.19–20; cf. Gal. 4.14.

54. Mitchell 1991: 106; Horsley 1998: 42; R. Collins 1999: 63; Fee 1987: 40.

55. Paul later explains that only the risen Christ closely examines human conduct and either confirms it or judges it. See 1.8; 4.4–5; 7.25; 11.29–32.

members of the community in connection with Paul's embodied proclamation of Christ.[56] Under the circumstances, Paul's actions and speech became the embodied presence of Jesus Christ (see also 2 Cor. 13.3; Gal. 4.14). Jesus Christ becomes the object of Paul's speech and actions as well as the judge of Paul's faithfulness in this undertaking (see 1 Cor. 4.2, 4; 7.25; cf. 1 Thess. 2.4–10). Consequently, this suggests that the genitive τοῦ Χριστοῦ in 1.6 is both objective and subjective.

Moreover, the Corinthians' divine enrichment took place when Paul's witness of Christ – namely, his proof that the story of Christ continues – was confirmed among them (ἐν ὑμῖν).[57] These moments of divine enrichment became manifest to the members of the community as a matter of personal experience in their relationships with one another (see 2.12; 12.7).[58] Paul frequently applies the phrase ἐν ὑμῖν to emphasize social interaction.[59] For Paul, interpersonal relationships constitute the important apocalyptic (i.e. revelatory) battlegrounds where the cosmic warfare takes place between God and the powers of the world. The manifestations of this conflict may become apparent to those who are discerning (see 3.3).[60] With this particular use of ἐν ὑμῖν in 1 Cor. 1.6, Paul subtly begins to admonish certain members of the community who are rejoicing in this enrichment that they believe is taking place for their own individual edification. This critique continues throughout the letter (see also 8.1–3; 10.23–11.1; 13.1–13; 14.4).[61]

The subsequent result clause in 1.7 modifies the preceding verse and establishes the potential that God would continue to enrich the Corinthians with additional χαρίσματα.[62] Paul thus identifies another conviction that permeates the letter: God continues to work powerfully for the benefit of the community through specific Christ-patterned acts of service to others (3.5; see also 10.24, 33; 12.4–11). Paul also foreshadows the major theme taken up in 2.6–16 and 12.4–31. Through the practice of spiritual discernment, community members seek to identify the manifestations/revelations of the Spirit (χαρίσματα) that confirm Christ-conforming conduct through which God is working for the common good/advantage of the entire church.[63]

56. See 1.5–6; 12.4–7. This same pattern is also present in Gal. 3.1–5, discussed in Chapter 4, section 3.a.

57. For the translation of ἐν ὑμῖν as 'among' the Corinthians, see Thiselton 2000: 94; Conzelmann 1975: 27.

58. Thiselton inexplicably contends that while this divine confirmation takes place among the Corinthians, it is *not* something experienced individually by members of the community (2000: 94).

59. For Paul's use of the phrase in relational contexts, see, e.g., 1 Cor. 1.10–11; 2.2; 3.3, 16; 5.1; 6.19; 11.13, 18–19; 14.25; cf. 2 Cor. 1.19; 10.1, 15; 12.12; 13.3, 5; Gal. 3.5; 4.19; Phil. 1.6; 2.5, 13; 1 Thess. 2.13; 5.12; see also Col. 1.6, 27; 3.16; 2 Thess. 1.12; 3.7, 11.

60. In connection with Gal. 3.1–5, B. Longenecker observes that the Galatians' early experience of the Spirit was 'evidence that God had been at work among them (ἐν ὑμῖν), even bringing about miracles in their midst' (1999: 95). Cf. Gal. 5.22–23.

61. See Wire 1990: 139.

62. See Fee, who acknowledges that ὥστε with the infinitive ordinarily signals a potentiality in classical Greek rather than an actual result, although he rejects this usual application in 1.7 (1987: 41 n. 28).

63. *Pace* Thiselton 2000: 95. Thiselton also challenges the approach being suggested here because

According to 1.7 these χαρίσματα will continue to become manifest to community members who are expectantly awaiting (ἀπεκδεχομένους) the revelation of the Lord Jesus Christ.[64] Indeed, Paul promises in 1.8 that the risen Christ will continue to confirm (βεβαιώσει) the embodied proclamation of Jesus Christ by other members of the community. This divine confirmation of specific behaviour will continue until the end/completion (ἕως τέλους).[65]

Nowhere else in Paul's letters does he associate the word ἀποκάλυψις with the *parousia* of Jesus at the end of time (Conzelmann 1975: 28). Indeed, 'Paul repeatedly employs revelation terminology in reference to a variety of contemporary disclosures' (Bockmuehl 1990: 144). These were 'important and recurrent in the experience of Paul and his churches' (Bockmuehl 1990: 145).[66] Thus, 'in the message and apostolic ministry of the gospel the present dimension of revelation remains essential for Paul' (Bockmuehl 1990: 145).[67]

These observations strongly suggest that in 1.7–8 Paul's use of this pivotal word ἀποκάλυψις is not limited to the context of the final, end-time revelation of Jesus Christ.[68] In addition to the end-time revelation of Jesus Christ (which this surely includes), Paul seems to use ἀποκάλυψις to refer to the revelations of Jesus Christ that continue to take place when additional manifestations of new life from God (χαρίσματα) confirm the embodied proclamation of Christ in a variety of new contexts (see also 1 Cor. 12.4–7).[69] Each χάρισμα con-

---

its appeal to 'experience' begs the question of what constitutes 'authentic experience' (2000: 95). This modern concern should not be imposed on Paul, since he clearly appeals to community experiences of the power of God that ground their faith (2.4–5; Gal. 3.1–5).

64. For Paul's other uses of the important verb ἀπεκδεχομαι, see Rom. 8.19, 23, 25; Gal. 5.5; Phil. 3.20; cf. Heb. 9.28. For the same reasons discussed above in connection with the genitive τοῦ Χριστοῦ in 1.6, it is unnecessary to debate whether the genitive τοῦ κυρίου Ἰησοῦ Χριστοῦ is objective/epexegetical (denoting the content of the revelation) or subjective (indicating Christ as the agent of the revelation). According to Paul, the Lord Jesus Christ not only serves as God's agent for evaluating the faithfulness of each individual who serves Christ (see 4.1–5), but also as the object or foundation of that faithful service (see 3.10; 11.1; 12.5; cf. 4.6–17). Thus, the genitive is both objective/epexegetical and subjective.

65. For the possibility that τέλους means either 'the end' or the 'completion', see Fee 1987: 43, including n. 40.

66. Bockmuehl also concludes that (1) such occasional revelations are only of temporary value; and (wrongly) that (2) these revelations were not foundational or constitutive for Paul because they did 'not carry the full and immediate authority of the divine word'.

67. Despite these important observations, Bockmuehl further concludes (wrongly) that '[t]he significance of contemporary revelations in the larger pattern of God's saving design is in the final analysis theologically secondary and transient' (1990: 145).

68. Contra Fee 1987: 42–43; R. Collins 1999: 64–65. Thiselton implies the same conclusion (2000: 100).

69. Even though ἀποκάλυψις is singular in 1.7, the implication of 1.6 and 1.8 is that there will be *further* revelations of Christ each time χαρίσματα are discerned by the community as the divine confirmation of specific Christ-conforming actions. Thus, it is appropriate to use the plural 'revelations' in connection with 1.8. Paul confirms this understanding with similar assertions in 2 Cor. 12.1 and 12.7, where he refers to revelations (plural) of the Lord that have already taken place. See now Barclay, who concludes that even though the crucifixion of Christ was a past event in history, it still 'punctures other times and other stories not just as a past event recalled, but as a present event…that

stitutes a present and concrete participation in Christ's eternal life of the end-time.[70]

Thus, both past and present revelations of these χαρίσματα constitute incomplete and 'partial incursions of the new age into this age'.[71] They do not constitute the full and complete revelation of the resurrected Jesus Christ that will occur at the end/completion. They do, however, reflect experiences of the risen Christ's transformed, embodied life that God gives in connection with divinely confirmed conduct that conforms to Christ's cruciform pattern (see 2.1–5).[72] These revelations prove to be foundational for Paul and other believers.[73] They become proof of the way and means by which God continues to exercise the same life-giving power that raised Jesus from the dead. Consequently, these revelations also ground the community practice of spiritual discernment, which is focused on identifying these experiences of new life and associating them with Christ-conforming actions. We contend that this ethic grounded in the confluence of divine revelation and human behaviour is the essence of what some interpreters describe more generally as Paul's apocalyptic ethics.[74]

Similarly, the present study contends that the participle ἀπεκδεχομένους in 1.7 does not refer solely to believers' expectant waiting for the end-time coming of Christ, despite the fact that the verb ἀπεκδέχομαι is frequently called an 'eschatological term'[75] thought to refer to 'the End'.[76] This exclusively end-time interpretation of ἀπεκδέχομαι virtually ignores Paul's understanding that the risen Lord is presently active in the community, a conclusion mandated by Paul's reasoning in 1.8, 5.4, 11.32, 14.30 and 16.22 (see also 2 Cor. 12.1).[77] Thus, the participle ἀπεκδεχομένους refers to future events that include, but are not limited to, the continuing revelations of aspects of Christ's new life that take place from time to time in the community.

---

happens anew…in the "revelation of Jesus Christ"' (2002: 146). Barclay concludes, however, that this past event becomes 'existentially present' in the revelation that takes place in the 'preaching of the gospel' (2002: 146), seemingly limiting his important observation.

70. See Käsemann 1964c: 65, who further concludes that 'to have a charism means to participate for that very reason in life, in grace, in the Spirit, because a charisma is the specific part which the individual has in the lordship and glory of Christ'.

71. For this phrase, see Bockmuehl 1990: 147.

72. This is what Gorman attributes to Paul as 'a kind of two-stage resurrection: first, resurrection to new life in Christ, and second, resurrection to eternal life in Christ' (2001: 322). See now Rom. 6.4.

73. Contra Bockmuehl 1990: 144–45.

74. See Duff 1989: 279–96; Brown 1995; B. Longenecker 1999: 92–108.

75. For this typical doctrinal characterization, see Betz 1979: 262 n. 83; cf. Witherington 1998: 369.

76. Fee 1987: 42 n. 36. Dunn wrongly concludes that the verb 'underlines the "already/not yet" character of Christian existence for Paul', with the (incorrect) implication that the tension of the 'confident but yet unfulfilled expectation' cannot be 'resolved or reduced by seeking to make the hope more certain' through present action (1993a: 270).

77. For further discussion of ἀπεκδέχομαι in the context of Gal. 5.5–6, see Chapter 4, section 4.b below.

While these revelations are 'only precursors'[78] in relation to the Corinthians' future consummation in glory, they are nevertheless highly significant in Paul's theo-ethical reasoning and the practice of spiritual discernment. First, they point to the way that God is building up the community with new life through Christ-conforming conduct. Second, they may be spiritually discerned by the community expectantly awaiting further revelations of the risen Christ. Third, by means of this community practice of looking for life, members of the church reason together to identify these moments of new life and thereby create an environment for other revelations to occur (see 1 Cor. 14.29–32).

Paul's use of the verb βεβαιόω in 1.6 and 1.8 provides additional support for our proposed reading of 1.7, one that better captures Paul's 'already/not yet' understanding of Christian existence. The verb alludes to the building metaphor that becomes one of the central foci of the letter.[79] The building metaphor explains the tense variation of the verb βεβαιόω from aorist passive in 1.6 to future in 1.8 (see Mitchell 1991: 107 n. 256). The community is the 'building' of God now (3.9; cf. 3.16), while it also continues to be built up by means of new χαρίσματα that benefit the whole community (see 12.4–11, 31).[80] These gifts of new life shape it for its climactic judgment and transformation at the end/completion. Indeed, Paul's reference in 1.7 to the potential for continued divine enrichment implies that, despite their manifold χαρίσματα of speech and knowledge now, the Corinthians are not yet complete (see also 3.18; 8.2–3, 13; 13.8–12; cf. 4.8).

Paul confirms this proposed interpretation in 1.8, where he assures them that the risen Christ will continue to guide them in this process of divine growth and community construction. He draws once again on judicial imagery, identifying another element of theo-ethical reasoning that shapes the practice of spiritual discernment. He affirms that it is the Lord Jesus Christ who (ὅς)[81] also will confirm (καὶ βεβαιώσει) the Corinthians. By this he means that the risen Christ will continue confirming the Christ-like conduct of community members until the end/completion (ἕως τέλους), thereby helping them remain without accusation (ἀνεγκλήτους)[82] in the Day of the Lord Jesus.[83] By inserting καὶ and ὑμᾶς in

---

78. For this phrase, see Bockmuehl 1990: 146; cf. Brown 1995: 69 n. 9.
79. Mitchell 1991: 105, 107, 195 n. 54; see 1 Cor. 3.9, 10, 12, 14; 8.1, 10; 10.23; 14.3, 4, 5, 12, 17, 26.
80. Cf. Mitchell 1991: 107 n. 256.
81. For understanding Christ as the antecedent of the pronoun ὅς, see Barrett 1968: 39; *pace* Thiselton 2000: 101; Fee 1987: 44.
82. For this translation, see LSJ, 129; R. Collins 1999: 65; cf. Thiselton 2000: 100; D. Martin 1995: 55.
83. Kramer has persuasively shown, especially in the context of 1 Corinthians, that Paul regularly employs the title 'Lord' when he is speaking of the risen Lord Jesus Christ (see 6.14), who is both the source of discernment of the ongoing Christian lifestyle and the final arbiter and authority for determining the adequacy of the deeds of the Christian's daily life (1966: 169–73, 181; see also Dunn 1998c: 397 n. 38; cf. Schrage 1988: 173). See 4.4; 7.25; 8.6; 9.1–2; 10.22, 26; 11.32; 15.58. For this reason, the present study finds unduly limited Hurtado's argument that 'calling upon the name of the Lord' connoted the one-dimensional 'broader praxis' of merely 'treating the exalted Jesus as recipient of the devotion of the Christian community' (1999b: 198).

1.8, Paul expressly affirms that the risen Lord who confirmed Paul's embodied proclamation of Christ (1.6) will also confirm the Christ-conforming behaviour and speech of the Corinthians.[84] When read in light of the later exhortation to imitation (11.1), Paul appears to reason in 1.5–8 that discernible manifestations of God's power (χαρίσματα) enrich the community through conduct that faithfully imitates Christ (cf. 7.25; 2 Cor. 1.21). Paul's primarily temporal use of ἕως (Fee 1987: 43 n. 40) as a preposition with the genitive τέλους denotes that the risen Lord will continue to confirm their imitation of Christ until the time of the end/completion (see 1 Cor. 4.4–5; 13.10; 15.24–25). Conversely, if community members stumble in the day-to-day conduct of their relationships, no such divine confirmation will take place (see Thiselton 2000: 95 n. 52). In that case they will experience division and strife rather than life and peace (see 3.3; 14.33).[85]

Triumphant interpretations of 1.8 overemphasize the 'already' nature of Christian existence. For instance, some interpreters wrongly argue that in 1.8 'Paul assures the readers that at the last day they will be free from any charge' (Thiselton 2000: 101) or that '[i]n 1.8 he expresses the conviction that the eschatological Lord of the community will maintain it in a blameless condition until the time of judgment' (R. Collins 1999: 65).

Instead, for Paul there can be progress in faith (Phil. 1.25) and the restoration of what is lacking in people's faith (1 Thess. 3.10). This more dynamic, fluid perspective underlies the logic of his assertions in 1 Cor. 1.5–8. The discerning church must seek to associate specific Christ-conforming conduct with the experience of a χάρισμα. When this happens, members grow more persuaded that their faith is grounded in the demonstrated power of God associated with the embodied proclamation of Christ crucified.[86]

Indeed, as Paul points out later in 11.32, the Lord is now presently judging and disciplining certain practices of community members in advance of the end/completion. Paul reasons that this adverse divine judgment of certain conduct is taking place so that the Corinthians might not be condemned with the world when the time of completion finally arrives. This reasoning further suggests that at least some of the Corinthians do *not* presently stand without accusation in God's kingdom. Instead, standing in present judgment, they lack the assurance that they will not be condemned later with the rest of the world.

Paul thus places an important limitation on the state of the Corinthians' present enrichment. Rhetorically, in 1.8 he anticipates his ironic attack in 4.8–13 against some members of the community who over-estimate the completeness of their present enrichment. Moreover, by emphasizing the provisional but expected revelations that continue to take place when a χάρισμα confirms Christ-conforming conduct, Paul lays the groundwork for attacking the certainty of knowledge that is

---

84. From the context of 1.5–8 it is clear that the object of the verb βεβαιόω in 1.8 is the same as it was in 1.6: τὸ μαρτύριον τοῦ χριστοῦ.

85. See Mitchell 1991: 173, including n. 661, who concludes that ἀκαταστασία in 14.33 is the opposite of βεβαίωσις in 1.6, 8 and the adjectives Paul uses in 15.58.

86. See 1 Cor. 2.1–5, discussed in Chapter 2, section 3.c.

now serving for some as a warrant for conduct that is destroying the faith of other community members (see 8.2, 10–12).[87]

The thanksgiving closes in 1.9 with Paul's affirmation that God called the Corinthians into a partnership (εἰς κοινωνίαν)[88] involving Jesus Christ. Paul places the adjective πιστός in the emphatic position, however, to stress the faithfulness of God in this partnership.[89] Thus, Paul once again reminds the Corinthians of God's active and powerful involvement in their lives. God called them into relationship, setting them apart from the rest of Corinth when they committed to conform their actions to Christ's cruciform pattern. God enriched them with experiences of new life that confirmed Christ-conforming actions, as they are being divinely shaped and built into a community that collectively reflects the body of Christ (see 3.6, 7; 12.18, 24). The affirmation that God is faithful points out that it is God rather than any human who gives this new life and that it is experienced only in the context of the believers' partnership with Jesus Christ.

Indeed, Paul's use of κοινωνία throughout the letter highlights this joint participation between God, the risen Lord Jesus Christ, and the Christian believer.[90] It also accentuates that this must be an exclusive partnership if the gospel is to be effectively proclaimed. Further, the logic of Paul's later arguments in 3.9, 7.16, 9.22, 10.16–17 and 10.33 suggests that some people, including but not limited to Paul himself, serve in this exclusive partnership by bringing others to the new life that Paul also refers to as salvation.

The partnership theme effectively sets the stage rhetorically for Paul's transition to 1.10, where he first articulates the letter's important theme of divisiveness in the context of community conduct and gifts. Paul attributes this problem of divisiveness to competition in the church. Therefore, in 1.9 he introduces the divine–human partnership and the cooperation it implies, a theme Paul will develop as the faithful God promises the Corinthians a way out of their problems (see 10.13).[91]

87. According to Brown, Paul is calling the Corinthians' attention to the provisional nature of God's present revelation and setting the scene for 'the toppling of what they think they can know in the present' as he prepares them for a change in perspective (1995: 69).

88. For this translation, see D. Martin 1995: 56. Thiselton rightly notes that the contemporary use of 'fellowship' in church circles may convey an impression quite foreign to Paul's distinctive emphasis (2000: 104). According to Thiselton, the word means communal participation in that sonship derived from the sonship of Christ in which all participants are shareholders (2000: 104).

89. For Paul's consistent affirmation of God's faithfulness, see Rom. 3.3; 1 Cor. 10.13; 2 Cor. 1.18; 1 Thess. 5.24. It appears that Paul shares a similar pattern of moral reasoning with that of the psalmist in the *Psalms of Solomon*. After asserting that God is faithful (14.1), the writer highlights the life – the 'paradise' – that God provides to those who live in the righteousness of the law's commandments (14.2–3). Both Paul and the psalmist thus ground 'life' in the 'faithfulness of God' and directly connect it with human conduct.

90. See 9.23; 10.16, 18, 20; 12.4–7. The noun and related verb may also be found in Rom. 12.13; 15.26, 27; 2 Cor. 1.7; 6.14; 8.4, 23; 9.13; 13.13; Gal. 2.9; 6.6; Phil. 1.5; 2.1; 3.10; 4.15; Phlm. 6, 17. Similarly, Käsemann observes that translations of κοινωνία as 'fellowship' are 'much too weak', although he further emphasizes that the individual undergoes the experience of forcible seizure by the overwhelming power of superior forces (1964d: 124). This latter point, we contend, underestimates the force of Paul's *participatory* partnership language involving believers.

91. Cf. Horsley 1998: 42.

c. *Summary (1.1–9)*
In 1.1–9 Paul identifies some of the letter's central themes. The logic underlying his assertions discloses critical aspects of theo-ethical reasoning. He places the spotlight on the universal baptismal commitment to ground Christian behaviour in the nature and character of the person of Jesus Christ.[92] He alludes to the central role of the deliberative assembly (ἐκκλησία) for moral formation that is centred on each believer's commitment to conform to the nature and character of Jesus Christ.

Paul also makes the important connection between conduct and experience. He links community experiences of the enriching power of God that gives new life (χαρίσματα) with the divinely confirmed, embodied proclamation of Christ. According to his reasoning, these discernible χαρίσματα divinely confirm the occasional revelations of Jesus Christ that take place in connection with conduct that conforms to Christ's cruciform pattern. Paul reminds the church that they must continue to expect these revelations of Christ, who will also confirm their Christ-conforming actions until the end/completion (contra Conzelmann 1975: 28). This is the way that the risen Lord continues to provide the community with behavioural guidance (see also 3.13; 11.19, 28, 32), as they experience collectively how the faithful God gives them new life in connection with believers' Christ-conforming actions.

3. *Practising Spiritual Discernment by Engaging in Theo-Ethical Reasoning (1.10–4.21)*

a. *Recognizing the Problems, Proposing the Solution (1.10–17)*
In 1.10–17 Paul identifies specific problems manifest from his reflection on the community's experience. Their divisions, suggested by their contentious discord (ἔριδες),[93] were recognizable even by Chloe's people (1.10–11). They are the discernible consequences of conduct that conforms to the standards of the world (see 3.3). According to 1.12 (see also 3.21; 4.6b) there is internal competition among church members, who are professing allegiance to particular human leaders and aligning themselves with these leaders to enhance their own individual status (see Adams 2000: 89). The questions in 1.13 further suggest that some church members even may have been attributing their gifts to these human leaders rather than to God or the risen Lord (see Lampe 1990: 118; cf. 1.29, 31; 12.4–7). Paul's relatively rare use of the phrase ὁ χριστός in the questions (see also 12.12) perhaps alludes to the church in Corinth as the body of Christ (see Schrage 1991: 152). This implies that the integrity of the church's social/political

92. Ashton points to Rom. 6.5 as support for the conclusion that the unity of believers in one body is grounded in their spiritual death to their previous existence and their commitment to a new life in the community, as they are knit together by the 'equivalent of Christ's death' (2000: 134, including n. 28).
93. See Mitchell, who calls ἔριδες a 'potent term' for political or domestic discord that she translates as 'contentions' (1991: 81); see also Thiselton 2000: 121.

body, also characterized as the 'deliberative assembly' in 1.2, is just as important
to God as their individual human bodies.[94]

Paul exhorts the Corinthians to action in 1.10, establishing the general paraenetic and advisory purposes of the letter.[95] Echoing 1.2, he invokes the nature and
character of Jesus Christ (i.e. his 'name') as the means by which (διά) he thinks
God will unify them in speech, thought and opinion.[96] Moreover, he identifies his
purposes (ἵνα) for encouraging them and invoking the name of the Lord: (1) so
that all of them might say the same thing; (2) so that there might not be divisions
among them; and (3) so that they might be restored (κατηρτισμένοι) in/by the
same mind (ἐν τῷ αὐτῷ νοΐ) and in/by the same opinion (ἐν τῇ αὐτῇ γνώμῃ).[97]

In 1.10 Paul thus establishes certain themes that he will address throughout the
remainder of the letter.[98] First, by asserting that the Corinthians must all say the
same thing, Paul means that they must make one common confession: only Jesus
is Lord of their lives.[99] Paul thus begins to de-emphasize the role of human leaders (see also 3.7). The Corinthians experience new life by means of the power of
God working through (διά) the one Lord Jesus Christ[100] and through (διά) the
Lord's servants who proclaim only Christ crucified.[101]

Second, Paul refers to their discernible divisions that provide proof that their
conduct conforms to worldly, human standards (see 3.3). He thus alludes in 1.10
to a breakdown in the Corinthians' practice of spiritual discernment. By reflecting together on their common experiences of conflict, strife and division, they
should be discerning this problem for themselves (cf. 11.29–32) during the intimate dialogue that should be taking place among those who share the same
faith.[102] Paul addresses different aspects of this problem in 2.1–16 and 14.1–40.

Third, in 1.10c Paul also challenges another breakdown in their practice of
spiritual discernment. Because they are not adequately engaging in theo-ethical
reasoning, the Corinthians are failing to integrate their thinking and acting. They
are neither thinking with 'the same mind' nor arriving at 'the same opinion'
about what constitutes appropriate conduct. Consequently, they must be restored
(κατηρτισμένοι) by returning to the Christ-like perspectives and practices that
Paul taught and demonstrated for them during an earlier visit (see 4.17). He
implies that by reasoning with the same mind of Christ (see 2.16; cf. Phil. 2.4–5)

---

94. D. Martin persuasively argues that in this letter Paul uses 'body' language on three levels (the
individual, social/political, and universal) pursuant to a cosmological hierarchy where each body represents a microcosm of the larger body (1995: 120–36).

95. See Stowers 1986: 108–109; Mitchell 1991: 25, 33; Engberg-Pedersen 2000: 322 n. 7.

96. For the unifying role of Christ's 'common name', see Mitchell 1991: 68 n. 14.

97. This translation highlights the dual nature of this restoration to distinguish Conzelmann (1975:
32) and Bultmann (1964b: 717–18), who argue there is no difference in meaning between νοΐ and
γνώμη in 1.10.

98. While Mitchell may overstate the role of 1.10 by calling it the thesis statement of the letter
(1991: 66), the programmatic nature of the verse must not be overlooked.

99. See 12.3; cf. 12.5.

100. See 8.6; 15.21, 57; cf. 1.9; 2.10; 12.5–6, 8; 15.2.

101. See 1.21; 2.2; 3.5; cf. 1.29–31; 12.4–6.

102. See Thiselton 2000: 121, citing Tertullian, *On Prescription Against Heretics* 26.

they may arrive at the same opinion about what constitutes Christ-conforming conduct. These practices possibly constitute some of Paul's 'ways in Christ' that he teaches in all his churches (1 Cor. 4.17).[103] Thus, he sent Timothy to *remind* the Corinthians about what he had taught them.

Paul is saying that the entire community must reason together according to the mind of Christ as they seek to discern actions that embody the nature and character of Jesus Christ in service to others. To reason with the same mind means to try to discern actions that conform to Christ's cruciform pattern of putting the interests of others ahead of one's own interests (see 10.24, 33; Phil. 2.4–5). Indeed, '[f]or Paul the mind marks the orientation of the whole person, not just the intellect, towards the Spirit' and it is never separated from its bodily context (Brown 1995: 166). Consequently, mindful life is also bodily life (Brown 1995: 166).

Moreover, in 1 Cor. 1.10 Paul is suggesting that they must seek to have 'the same opinion', collectively agreeing about what specific conduct reflects divine approval (see 1.6, 8). Indeed, Paul consistently uses γνώμη in behavioural contexts, referring to a considered opinion about what conduct will meet with the Lord's approval.[104] Paul thus appears to be encouraging the Corinthians to integrate their thinking and acting.[105] It is suggested that, for Paul, the revelation of Jesus Christ does not take place without such integration at both the individual and community levels. He implies that they must be restored by returning to the spiritual discernment practices and theo-ethical reasoning that he taught them on his first visit to Corinth.

In the transitional 1.17, Paul contrasts the worldly community experience reviewed in 1.10–16 with the manifest power of God that becomes the focus in 1.18–2.5. He introduces the letter's first major argument (1.17–2.5) by redirecting the Corinthians away from human leaders and human power to the power of God associated with the cross of Christ (cf. Horsley 1997b: 242). In this letter Paul uses the cross as a symbol that functions to deconstruct secular norms and values for human conduct (Pickett 1997: 214).[106] It symbolizes Christ's self-giving love, that pattern of other-regarding behaviour that Paul exemplifies and encourages the Corinthians to imitate (see 11.1). Paul implies that some of the Corinthians do not yet perceive the connection between the power of God that raised Jesus from the dead and the behavioural standard associated with the divine wisdom manifest in the cross of Christ.

According to 1.17, Christ did not send Paul to baptize but to proclaim the good news of God's power at work in the death and resurrection of Christ. Paul typically uses the verb εὐαγγελίζομαι to characterize human participation in

103. This possibility is discussed further in Chapter 2, section 3.h below.

104. See 7.25, 40; cf. 2 Cor. 8.10; Phlm. 14.

105. Contra Brown, who concludes that Paul's 'first line of attack against division is epistemological', since Paul's first move is *not* to outline a course of human action (1995: 156).

106. According to Pickett, Paul carries this out by calling the community's attention to the social significance of the cross, reflecting on the symbolic structure of the gospel in connection with specific behavioural issues (1997: 34).

each revelatory event that Paul calls εὐαγγέλιον.[107] In fact, for Paul the gospel is the 'divine event' (Martyn 1997b: 115) inaugurated in the death and resurrection of Jesus Christ. It occurs each time God's power that gives new life – namely, salvation – is revealed (see Rom. 1.16–17).[108] These revelations take place in connection with the embodied proclamation of Christ crucified (see 1 Cor. 1.5–9; 2.1–5; Gal. 3.1–5).

Thus, for Paul, the power of God remains discernibly operative in the world, creating a 'new history' that unfolds in a series of 'gospel events'.[109] By imitating Christ through his own conduct (1 Cor. 11.1), Paul becomes an active participant in the revelation of Jesus Christ (cf. 1 Cor. 1.6–7; Gal. 1.16; 2.20; 4.14).[110] This study suggests that the complex communicative event that Paul calls gospel takes place with each manifestation of God's power that gives new life in connection with specific Christ-conforming behaviour.[111] According to 1 Cor. 1.17, Paul was sent to communicate the gospel. He accomplishes this by proclaiming God's apocalyptic (i.e. revelatory) act in the death and resurrection of Jesus Christ – an event that continues to take place in Christian communities. Thus, Paul proclaims the gospel each time he associates community experiences of new life from God with actions that conform to Christ's cruciform pattern of self-giving love for others (see 1 Cor. 1.5–9; 2.1–5; 2 Cor. 4.7–12; cf. 1 Cor. 12.4–7).

Indeed, in Corinth Paul did not originally make this correlation in wisdom of speech,[112] 'lest the cross of Christ might be emptied of its power' (1.17). With the phrase οὐκ ἐν σοφίᾳ λόγου, Paul does not *per se* condemn wisdom or its pursuit. Instead, he focuses on the worldly attitudes and behavioural standards that are shaping the Corinthians' understanding and pursuit of wisdom (Stowers 1990: 258). He appears to be attacking their adherence to cultural norms, challenging the high value that some of them place on rhetorical eloquence alone (see Adams 2000: 90).

In 1.10–17 Paul highlights the Corinthians' failure to integrate thinking and acting by engaging in theo-ethical reasoning and conforming their actions to the cruciform pattern of the cross. According to Paul, the Corinthians must be restored in/by the same mind. What he means is that they must reason together

---

107. Schütz emphasizes that the verb reflects the human activity relating to the visibly perceptible gospel (1975: 36).

108. Brown similarly concludes that the gospel 'takes place' (1998: 271–85). Schütz characterizes the gospel as the 'field of God's activity as it touches man's life' (1975: 53, 281). For Käsemann, the gospel is the event that defines God's power (1969e: 168–82). For discussions about the role that the word εὐαγγέλιον played in the emperor cult, see Martyn 1997b: 127–20; S.K. Williams 1997: 39.

109. Martyn 1997b: 130; see also Schütz 1975: 52.

110. See Hansen, who concludes from Galatians that Paul is a participant in the apocalypse of Jesus Christ and presents himself as 'a paradigm of the apocalypse' (1994: 194–209). Cf. Rom. 15.18–19; 2 Cor. 12.1–7; Phil. 4.9; see now Acts 22.15.

111. Schütz points out that the power that becomes manifest lies beyond the individual who is merely an instrument through which this power becomes perceptibly visible (1975: 282).

112. See D. Martin 1995: 47; S. Pogoloff 1992: 108–27; Litfin 1994: 187; Thiselton 2000: 142–47; R. Collins 1999: 85. Like most studies of this issue, however, these interpreters distinguish worldly wisdom and eloquence from divine wisdom, but fail to address the behavioural component that was an essential aspect of Paul's proclamation.

according to the single mind of Christ (cf. 2.13–16; Phil. 2.4–5). They must also be restored in/by the same opinion. By this, Paul means that they must reason together with the mind of Christ as they seek to reach agreement on what constitutes divinely confirmed conduct. They must do this, however, not by looking to the standards of behaviour recognized by the world. They must discern actions that conform to the standard of the cross, Paul's cipher for Christ's cruciform pattern of self-giving love for others (see 2.1–16; 14.1–40).

The logic that underlies Paul's argument in 1 Cor. 1.10–17 suggests something central to his understanding of the gospel. The communicative event that Paul calls gospel is the revelation of Jesus Christ, who still lives by the power of God. This requires the proclamation of God's apocalyptic (i.e. revelatory) act in Jesus Christ by means of oral preaching and the embodied proclamation of Christ's cross in people's lives. This integration of speech and action allows believers to associate community experiences of new life wrought through the power of God with specific Christ-conforming actions (see 1.5–8; 2.1–5; 4.19–20; 8.1–3; 2 Cor. 4.7–12).[113]

b. *Proclaiming Christ as the Power and Wisdom of God (1.18–25)*
With the phrase ὁ λόγος ὁ τοῦ σταυροῦ (1.18), Paul introduces his 'principal weapon' (Brown 1995: vii) for attacking community divisions rooted in the overvaluation of culturally-defined wisdom.[114] The vast semantic scope of ὁ λόγος demands that its translation be contextually determined in most cases. Paul's associations of μωρία with ὁ λόγος ὁ τοῦ σταυροῦ in 1.18 and τῆς μωρίας with τοῦ κηρύγματος in 1.21 suggest that 'proclamation' most adequately conveys the aspect of ὁ λόγος in view in 1.18 (Thiselton 2000: 153). Although 'word of the cross' (Brown 1995: xvii n. 2) and 'message of the cross'[115] are appropriate translations, both risk a concentration on cognitive or informational content that is too narrow (Thiselton 2000: 153). They overlook the important role of embodied gospel proclamation for Paul. Indeed, emphasizing the gospel as oral message points away from its capacity to transform (see Thiselton 2000: 153), as people recognize the links between Christ-conforming actions and experiences of new life through God's power.

In 1.18 Paul divides all humanity into two groups: those who are being destroyed and those who are being saved.[116] The two present passive participles indicate alternative processes that have already begun but are not yet complete (cf. 15.24–28).[117] The language creates a social duality that characterizes the

113. Thus, Martyn's characterization of the gospel as an 'aural event' (1991: 163) is too limited. Similarly, those interpreters who understand Paul's communication of the gospel as merely oral preaching without further explanation overlook the integral connection for Paul between conduct and preaching. See, e.g., Brown 1995; Litfin 1994; Schütz 1975; Fee 1987; Dunn 1998c; Furnish 1999.
114. For this latter conclusion, see Adams 2000: 108.
115. Martyn 1988: 5; Barrett 1968: 18; R. Collins 1999: 101; Fee 1987: 67–68. Cf. Gorman 2001: 277.
116. Hays 1999: 402; cf. Tabor 1986: 14; see also 1 Cor. 15.47–49.
117. Indeed, according to Héring, '[i]t is highly characteristic of Paul's soteriology that he does not

inhabitants of two distinct spatial realms.[118] Paul thus argues by implication that his embodied proclamation of the cross represents the power of God to those who inhabit the spatial realm where salvation is underway. Conversely, his cruciform lifestyle is foolishness (μωρία) to those who inhabit the spatial realm where destruction is already taking place among those who continue to act according to the world's behavioural standards (cf. 3.3; 4.9–13; 11.30–32).

Paul introduces the important expression 'power of God' in 1.18. This is a phrase he uses throughout his letters to focus on a central concern: identifying what God has done, is doing, and will do in the world (see Martyn 1997a: 220 n. 23). As a pastoral theologian, Paul regularly seeks to identify 'God newly exerting his own very strange kind of power in the world of human beings'.[119] In connection with 1.4–9 it was argued that the χαρίσματα constitute concrete manifestations of God's life-giving power that enriches community life through Paul's embodied proclamation of Christ. In 1.18 Paul makes the same assertion using the motifs of spatial, temporal and ethical dualism. He associates his embodied proclamation of Christ's cross with the power of God that is giving new life, saving those who inhabit God's new spatial realm in Christ.

Paul also implies a temporal dualism in 1.18.[120] For the inhabitants of each of these two alternative spatial realms, there is a present time and a future time. Each involves an ongoing process of destruction or salvation that will be brought to completion in the future (see 1.7; 15.24–28; cf. 11.32). He later characterizes one of these two temporal alternatives as 'this age' (1.20; see also 2.6, 8; 3.18; cf. Gal. 1.4). Moreover, he yokes the temporal dualism with the spatial and ethical dualisms. He uses 'this age' co-extensively with the spatial realm where destruction is already underway.[121] This realm and age of destruction constitute that part of the world where the inhabitants are being guided by the world's wisdom rather than the wisdom and power of God manifest in Jesus Christ.

As noted above, Paul establishes an ethical dualism in 1 Cor. 1.18.[122] Continuing a strategy introduced in 1.4–9, he once again associates the power of God with his own embodied proclamation of Christ's cross that brought new life to believers in Corinth. The cross becomes a cipher for 'the paradigm of self-giving for the sake of others', a standard for behaviour that defines 'the pathway to life

---

speak of "the saved" (which would be "*sesosmenoi*") but of those who are being saved ("*sozomenoi*")', since salvation is not yet gained in its totality (1962: 8). See also Hays 1999: 404; Furnish 1999: 46.

118. Meeks 1982b: 689. See also 1 Cor. 4.20–21; 6.9–10; 15.50.

119. The quote is from Martyn 1997a: 218 n. 19, though he does not refer to Paul as a pastoral theologian.

120. See Adams 2000: 107. Gammie identifies 'temporal dualism' – an opposition between this age and the age to come – as one of six common characterizations of the dualism that regularly appears in Jewish apocalyptic and wisdom literature (1974: 357).

121. In 10.11 Paul integrates the spatial, temporal and social dualities, referring to believers as the people upon whom the conclusion of the ages has descended.

122. Adams identifies a social and ethical duality associated with the 'saved' and the 'perishing' (2000: 107). D. Martin also observes that '…in 1 Corinthians 1–4, Paul's argument depends on the radical separation of Christ's body from the cosmos, in an apocalyptic, ethical dualism' (1995: 176). For the importance of ethical dualism in Jewish apocalyptic and wisdom literature, see Gammie 1974.

and well-being' from God (Thiselton 2000: 158).[123] Indeed, the cross symbolizes what this study calls Christ's cruciform pattern. This is the new social norm of self-giving love for others that became manifest in Christ's death on the cross for the sake of humanity according to the will of God (see also Gal. 1.4; 2.20).[124] Further, Paul's own embodied proclamation of Christ's cross now 'determines the pattern of Christian discipleship as living for others, at whatever personal cost' (Thiselton 2000: 157).

According to the logic of Paul's reasoning, the cross and resurrection of Jesus Christ constitute God's revelation of the divine alternative to the world's normative system of wisdom and power. Indeed, Christ becomes the wisdom and power of God (1 Cor. 1.24; cf. Rom. 1.3–4; 1 Cor. 1.30; Phil. 2.6–11).[125] The cross signifies the new behavioural norm for conduct through which believers experience new life (i.e. salvation), as God continues to exercise that life-giving power among those who inhabit God's new spatial realm/temporal age in Christ.

Paul confirms the moral context of this new social norm by ironically characterizing it as μωρία to those who are perishing (1 Cor. 1.18). In Stoic philosophy the term μωρία reflected moral stupidity (Engberg-Pedersen 2000: 38). This usage would not be lost on those philosophically-grounded members of Paul's audience. Further, having suggested that the moral component was central to his proclamation, the form of its delivery must necessarily include the way it is lived out in the context of Paul's own life.[126] Thus, Paul reasons that the ones being saved by the power of God are those who inhabit God's new spatial realm/temporal age by conforming their behaviour to this new social norm of self-giving love for others manifest in the cross. Those who are perishing in 'this age' are those who are still conforming their conduct to the wisdom of the world – the old behavioural standards that predate Christ's cross and resurrection.[127]

By implication Paul also connects conduct that conforms to Christ's cruciform pattern of self-giving love for others with 'knowing God' (1.19–25; see also 8.1–3). According to 1.20–21, the world did not know God through (διὰ) the world's wisdom. In these verses Paul uses ὁ κόσμος to refer to the dominant society with its structures, institutions, power-relations, norms, values and goals that Paul sets in antithesis to God's new order (Adams 2000: 80, 113). According to the logic of Paul's argument, a person cannot know God by acting in conformity with the behavioural standards of the world (see also 15.34). Instead, says Paul, God was

123. Similarly, says Pickett, 'Paul employs the symbol of the cross to underwrite certain patterns of interpersonal conduct' (1997: 35).

124. See Engberg-Pedersen 1987: 566–67; cf. Schrage 1988: 173; Lampe 1990: 119–20.

125. Thus, Paul is not attacking wisdom *per se*, but only the wisdom of the world. See Fitzgerald 1988: 117–50; Stowers 1990: 253–86.

126. Malherbe (1987; 1989; 1992) and Engberg-Pedersen (1987; 1993; 1994b; 2000) place Paul in the ancient ethical tradition by showing how he employs the widely practised methods of his day, particularly those of the Greek moral philosophers. For a detailed exploration of the use of personal example in antiquity, see Fiore 1986.

127. Bilde concludes that, for Paul, Christ presented a model or τύπος of the road from death to life which can now be adopted or used by believers with the same result as Christ – transformation of the earthly body into a spiritual body (1993: 24). See also Chapter 3, section 4.e below.

well pleased (εὐδόκησεν) to save the ones believing by means of (διὰ) Paul's embodied proclamation of the cross (1.21; see also 3.5). Paul uses εὐδόκησεν elsewhere to signify approval of particular conduct[128] and twice to characterize the divine approval of human action.[129] When we read 1.21 in light of 1.6–7, it suggests that Paul is referring to the divine confirmation of Paul's witness of Christ – his embodied proclamation of the cross and preaching that associates his conduct with the Corinthians' experiences of new life through the power of God (see also 2.1–5; 2 Cor. 4.10–12).

In fact, since Jews demand signs[130] and Greeks seek wisdom (1 Cor. 1.22), Paul gives them what they seek through his embodied proclamation of Christ crucified (1.23).[131] Ironically and paradoxically, as the 'wisdom of God' and the 'power of God' (see 1.24, 30), the crucified and resurrected Christ meets these expectations of both Jews and Greeks.[132] Paul's repeated references to Jews and Greeks (1.22, 24) emphasizes his focus on all humanity, with its basic cultural division as seen from the (Palestinian) Jewish point of view (Horsley 1998: 50–51).

The logic of Paul's argument suggests that Christ's cruciform pattern represents the universal and unifying ethical standard for the conduct of all people in God's new age.[133] Paul reasons that specific actions conforming to Christ's cruciform pattern now constitute the means by which both Jews and Greeks may know God. This takes place as they experience the power of God that raised Jesus from the dead and now gives new life to those who inhabit God's new age/temporal realm. Paul focuses on the fact that 'a system of reinforcement independent of the old world has appeared with Christ' (Theissen 1987: 371).

The perfect participle ἐσταυρωμένον in 1.23 (see also 2.2; Gal. 2.19) indicates that the event of Christ's crucifixion has continuing effect for those who believe that the embodied proclamation of the cross leads to experiences of new life from God (see also Gal. 3.1–5). The logic of Paul's argument, including his use of ἐσταυρωμένον and his assertion in 1 Cor. 1.8 that Christ will continue to confirm the Corinthians' own cruciform actions, suggests that believers continue to participate in Christ's crucifixion through their own behaviour. They must die daily to the behavioural standards of the world and conform their actions to Christ's cruciform pattern (see 15.31; cf. 11.26).[134] Read in conjunction with

128. See 2 Cor. 5.8; 12.10; 1 Thess. 2.8; 3.1; cf. 2 Thess. 2.12.

129. See 1 Cor. 10.5; Gal. 1.15; cf. Col. 1.19.

130. Paul's use of σημεῖα reflects his Jewish background and refers to a demand for a visible sign of God's powerful approval (Fee 1987: 74–75; 682–83). In this case it would be powerful proof that God is acting through Paul's embodied proclamation of Christ's cross. See 1.4–9; Lampe 1990: 120 n. 8.

131. The δέ is conjunctive rather than adversative (*pace* Fee 1987: 75) or contrastive (*pace* R. Collins 1999: 107).

132. See Lampe 1990: 121–22; Thiselton 2000: 170; Martyn 1997a: 220–221.

133. See also Rom. 6.4–8; 8.16–29; Gal. 2.16; 3.28; cf. Dunn 1998c: 403. For discussion of this conclusion in the context of Galatians, see Chapter 4, section 2.d below.

134. According to Ellis, believers are 'called to actualize the "crucifixion with Christ"' by imitating Paul as they 'seek not their own benefit but that of others' (1974b: 74). This is what Paul illustrates through his own apostolic lifestyle according to 1 Cor. 4.9–13 and 2 Cor. 4.7–12.

1.6–8, Paul appears to be contending that the community will continue to experience concretely the power of God for new life (χαρίσματα) in connection with their own actions that conform to this cruciform pattern.

In summary, the logic underlying 1.18–25 suggests that, as the wisdom and power of God, the person of Jesus Christ is the place where the divine and human meet. These verses reflect Paul's conviction that Christ's self-giving love for others becomes manifest in his death on the cross.[135] This establishes the new social norm for human behaviour (i.e. Christ-conforming love).[136] Christ's divinely confirmed, cruciform pattern now serves as the unifying behavioural norm for all humanity. Moreover, Jews and Greeks alike may now know God by experiencing God's life-giving power (the same power that raised Jesus from the dead) in connection with conduct that conforms to Christ's cruciform pattern. Believers now participate in this divine–human partnership (see 1.9) when they conform their behaviour to Christ's cruciform pattern and experience God's saving power that brings new life.

c. *Reflecting on Experience: Connecting Christ-Conforming Conduct with Demonstrations of God's Power (1.26–2.5)*
Having implied that believers may know God by means of the embodied proclamation of Christ crucified (1.21), Paul now exhorts the Corinthians to reflect (Βλέπετε) on their own experiences (1.26) to prove his argument.[137] The very existence of the community provides empirical proof that the weakness and foolishness of God manifest in Christ's cross remains stronger than anything human.[138] The community is Paul's evidence that 'God has created a new world on the model of self-giving love' that was first manifest in Christ's death on the cross.[139]

Paul reminds the Corinthians that not many among them were wise, powerful, or of noble birth according to human standards (κατὰ σάρκα).[140] God chose the foolish, weak, shameful, low born, despised, and those who amount to nothing in the eyes of the world to overturn the values, standards and expectations of the world.[141] Community experience at Corinth confirms that in Christ's cross God

135. See Engberg-Pedersen 1987: 566–67; cf. Schrage 1988: 173; Horrell 1997a: 109.
136. See Schrage 1988: 212; cf. Schürmann 1974: 282–300.
137. For similar translations of the imperative Βλέπετε, see Conzelmann 1975: 49; R. Collins 1999: 107. Paul consistently uses this plural imperative form to encourage his churches to reflect collectively on the connections between experience and conduct. See 1 Cor. 8.9; 10.18; 16.10; 2 Cor. 10.7; Gal. 5.15; Phil. 3.2; cf. Eph. 5.15; Col. 2.8.
138. Horrell 1996: 132; D. Martin 1995: 61; Brown 1995: 102.
139. Brown 1995: 147; see also 2 Cor. 3.1–3.
140. For this translation of κατὰ σάρκα, see R. Collins 1999: 109; Barrett 1968: 57. For Paul's similar use of σάρξ in Galatians, see Barclay 1988: 206–209.
141. This indicates that a majority of the community members must have come from the lower classes. See Horrell 1996: 132; D. Martin 1995: 61; Theissen 1982: 70–73. Conversely, it also means that some members of the community were from the upper classes (D. Martin 1995: 61) or at least enjoyed higher social status than a majority of other community members. Meeks argues persuasively that Theissen's model does not take sufficient account of the complexities involved in the

re-defined what should be understood as weakness in the world. Against all expectations of the wisdom of the present world order, these representatives of lower worldly status have become God's instruments. Through them God is creating a new social structure that attests to God's power to transform earthly human life and change the world's perception of reality.[142]

According to Paul this upheaval of the world's expectations took place so that no one would boast about worldly things but would boast exclusively in the Lord (1.29–31). He reasons throughout 1.18–31 that God created and continues to build the community as an alternative to the surrounding culture. This divine construction takes place through conduct that conforms to the new social norm manifest in Christ's death on the cross. Since conduct conforming to this standard now constitutes the means by which all Jews and Greeks may know God, any boasting about status must be grounded solely in the Lord Jesus Christ, whose cruciform pattern is the foundation for all new life.[143]

In 2.1–5 Paul's use of 'perception-related terminology intensifies' (Brown 1995: 97). He employs the language of 'paradigm and demonstration' (Brown 1995: 102) to reflect on the Corinthians' experience and connect it with his own ministry among them. Twice in 2.1 he refers back to the time he first came among them, emphasizing the role of his own conduct in proclaiming God's mystery for the end times.[144] He did not come to Corinth proclaiming God's mystery in lofty speech or wisdom (2.1), a reference to one possible mode of attempting to communicate the gospel (Brown 1995: 113).

Instead, he determined not to know (εἰδέναι) anything among them except the crucified Christ (2.2; cf. Gal. 3.1). In this context '"to know" means something like "to experience and to announce in word and deed"' (Gorman 2001: 1). Paul apparently proclaimed Christ crucified through his own concrete, Christ-conforming actions and preached the connection between such behaviour and their experience of the power of God that enriched community life (see also 1 Cor. 1.4–9; cf. Rom. 15.18–19; Gal. 3.1–5). It is suggested that this connection between Paul's Christ-conforming conduct and their experience of new life represents Paul's embodied interpretation of the wisdom of God that was previously hidden in a mystery but has now been revealed through the Spirit (1 Cor. 2.10).[145]

---

various levels of social stratification and, therefore, an across-the-board equation of higher social status with wealth alone is an unjustified leap (1983: 69–70). The same critique would probably apply to D. Martin's analysis.

142. See Pickett 1997: 78; D. Martin 1995: 59–60; Horrell 1996: 132; Adams 2000: 116.

143. For this latter assertion, see 1 Cor. 3.10–11.

144. D. Martin asserts that in 2.1–16 Paul 'turns the spotlight from the Corinthians to himself and his ministry' (1995: 61). This is only partially correct. Martin underestimates the connection Paul makes between his own ministry – his embodied proclamation of Christ crucified – and the Corinthians' experience of new life (see also 1.4–9). For the choice regarding the textual variant τὸ μυστήριον, see Metzger 1994: 480; Brown 1995: 97; Thiselton 2000: 207–11; Kim 1984: 75; Bornkamm 1967: 819 n. 141; *pace* Fee 1987: 88 n. 1; Conzelmann 1975: 53.

145. Brown correctly observes that Paul's statement in 2.7 refers to the '*content* of the kerygma' (1995: 113, original emphasis). Through action and speech Paul communicates the content of the kerygma, God's wisdom formerly hidden in a mystery but now revealed in Christ's cross and resurrection.

Neither the mode nor content of Paul's embodied proclamation conformed to the verbal wisdom and rhetoric highly valued by some Corinthians.

Instead, the participles καταγγέλλων (2.1) and ἐσταυρωμένον (2.2) suggest that Paul communicated the gospel by means of both the embodied proclamation of Christ crucified and oral preaching about the message of the cross. As in 11.26 the present participle καταγγέλλων does not signify something taking place verbally, but something that becomes manifest through concrete actions (Brown 1995: 102).[146] Indeed:

> The unusual use of the term (καταγγέλλων) in 1 Cor. 11.26 may help to illustrate its use here (2.1). In that text, the proclamation is not verbal, but rather issues forth from the concrete *action* of persons in the setting of the Supper. It is what they *show*, not what they *say* that *proclaims the Lord's death*. Notice that what is shown is the *death of Jesus* – for Paul, an *apocalyptic* and *paradigmatic* act. As the death of Jesus on the cross is for Paul the revelation of God's struggle with and victory over hostile forces (1 Cor 15:24), so is bearing and demonstrating that death the apocalyptic sign of the victory whose fruit is reconciliation (Brown 1995: 102, original emphasis).

These insights also illuminate Paul's use of the perfect passive participle ἐσταυρωμένον in 1.23 and 2.2. The participle reflects Paul's continuing behavioural participation in the metaphorical re-enactment of Christ's crucifixion (see also Gal. 2.19; 3.1; cf. 5.25; 6.14).[147] This is the event that continues to be embodied metaphorically in the lives of believers when they die to the standards of the world and conform their actions to Christ's cruciform pattern of self-giving love for others (cf. 1 Cor. 15.31; Gal. 2.19; 6.4). According to Paul's theo-ethical reasoning, the community experiences the life-giving power of God in connection with these Christ-conforming actions.

Thus, for Paul, the self-giving death of Jesus for others on the cross becomes the behavioural norm for conduct that leads believers into the experiences of new life in God's new age/spatial realm in Christ. In this way believers become active participants in the revelation of God's hidden mystery. God's victory over the powers of Sin and Death (see 1 Cor. 15.50–57) in Christ's death and resurrection also becomes manifest in the χαρίσματα that reflect new life from God given in connection with Christ-conforming actions (see 1.4–9).

Moreover, in 2.1 Paul utilizes the language of an apocalyptic visionary, one who has come among them proclaiming the mystery of God. The term μυστήριον suggests the visionary disclosure of apocalyptic (i.e. revelatory) information.[148] It describes the unfolding drama of God's re-creation of the world through Jesus Christ (see also 8.6). In 2.1–2 Paul inextricably links the revelation of God's mystery with his own Christ-conforming conduct *and* the knowledge gleaned by

---

146. Similarly, Thiselton asserts that καταγγέλλων means 'proclaiming in the full sense of the word' in a way that is 'broader than what we think of today as *preaching*' and that 2.1 may add force to the argument that Paul's self-presentation 'and display of the speaker' were at issue (2000: 209, original emphasis). Nevertheless, he concludes that καταγγέλλων merely signifies the spoken word (2000: 209). For a similarly limited conclusion, see Litfin 1994: 204–209.

147. In connection with Paul's embodied proclamation of the cross in Gal. 3.1, see B. Davis 1999: 205–209; Hofius 1991: 384 n. 37; *pace* Martyn 1997b: 283.

148. See Newman 1992: 238; Kim 1984: 74–99.

others from his embodied participation in the crucifixion of Christ (cf. 8.1–3). Indeed, in 2.2 'Paul makes a pointed autobiographical statement about the connection of the cross to *knowledge*' (Brown 1995: 24, original emphasis).

This 'knowing' of 2.2 'proves itself, not in words, but in Paul's demonstration of weakness, fear, and trembling' (Brown 1995: 102). Assessing his own embodied proclamation of Christ crucified in the language of the world's standards, Paul ironically describes it as 'weakness' (2.3).[149] This becomes the vehicle through which God's life-giving power becomes manifest in the world.[150] Later, in 4.9–10, Paul leaves no room for doubt that living in weakness involves death to the behavioural standards and values of the world (see also 2 Cor. 12.5–12; 13.4). He characterizes himself as shameful, weak, and despised in a world that promotes self-advantage as the basis for action. Paul's use of 'weakness' in 1 Cor. 2.3 and elsewhere signifies a sharing with Christ in his humiliation, suffering and death characterized in the language of the world. Paul willingly endures these things so that he might also share in bringing new life to others (see 2 Cor. 4.7–12; 13.1–4).[151] For Paul, '[a]uthentic "apostolicity" entails an identification with Christ in his self-giving and a reaching out beyond one's own personal resources (2 Cor 1.9), in further experience of resurrection power' (Thiselton 2000: 215).

In 1 Cor. 2.4, Paul reminds the Corinthians of the divine effects that were demonstrated in connection with his Christ-conforming manner of life (see also 12.4–6). His speech (ὁ λόγος)[152] *and* his proclamation (τὸ κήρυγμά) were not in persuasive words of wisdom.[153] Instead, using metaphors reaching far beyond oral speech (Brown 1995: 102), Paul points the Corinthians to the demonstration (ἀποδείξει) of Spirit and power[154] that took place in connection with his embodied proclamation of the cross.

Paul's use of ἀποδείξει in 2.4 is a New Testament *hapax legomenon*. It was a technical term in Greek rhetoric that described a type of evidence or proof for an argument (Fee 1987: 95 n. 28). It was a term often connected with rational, argumentative discourse (Lim 1987: 147). Paul uses this noun to establish that the *discernible* power of God provided the Corinthians with *visible* proof of Paul's

---

149. See also 2 Cor. 11.30; 12.5, 9, 10; 13.4; Gal. 4.13.

150. Cf. Thiselton, who concludes that 'Paul's "authority" lay not in smooth, competent, impressive powers of articulation, but in a faithful and sensitive proclaiming rendered operative not by the applause of the audience, but by the action of God' (2000: 214).

151. Cf. Thiselton 2000: 215; Schweitzer 1931: 101–59. Hafemann overemphasizes the aspect of Paul's suffering, calling it the 'revelatory vehicle' through which the knowledge of God is made manifest in the cross (2000: 174–75).

152. Thiselton correctly concludes that in 2.4 Paul clearly intends for ὁ λόγος to refer to his speaking activity (2000: 217).

153. For the textual issues associated with this latter phrase in 2.1, see Metzger 1994: 481; Fee 1987: 82 n. 2.

154. For this translation of πνεύματος καὶ δυνάμεως, see Barrett 1968: 65; Furnish 1999: 94. Fee (1987: 95), Horsley (1998: 54) and Ashton (2000: 163) conclude that 'Spirit' and 'power' are essentially interchangeable, a virtual hendiadys, with the two words representing the same reality. It will be suggested below in connection with 1 Cor. 2.12 that the Spirit is the divine agent that illuminates God's power for those practising spiritual discernment (cf. 12.4–7).

gospel. This is a gospel focused on proclaiming God's apocalyptic (i.e. revelatory) act in Christ as existentially re-presented each time believers experience
new life in association with conduct that conforms to Christ's cruciform pattern
(see also 1.4–9).

Indeed, '[t]he question for Paul is not *whether* the life-creating, resurrection
power of God is real and can be experienced in the present, but *how* that power is
encountered now' (Gorman 2001: 280, original emphasis). By recalling again the
events that took place when he first came among the Corinthians, Paul uses their
community experiences as proof of the connection between God's life-giving
power as manifest in the χαρίσματα and specific conduct that conforms to
Christ's cruciform pattern.[155] He further emphasizes that this experience was a
demonstration of the Spirit. He thereby introduces to the letter the role of the
Spirit, whose importance for community life and the practice of spiritual discernment will be addressed in the following verses (2.6–16).

We contend that this discernible connection between the experience of new life
from God and conduct conforming to Christ's cruciform pattern lies at the heart of
Paul's theo-ethical reasoning and grounds the practice of spiritual discernment.
Indeed, according to 2.5, this demonstration of Spirit and power took place so that
(ἵνα) the Corinthians' faith might be grounded in the power of God rather than
human wisdom. Making his fourth reference to the 'power of God' since he introduced the phrase in 1.18, Paul contrasts this experience of divine power with the
standards and values that define human wisdom (see also 4.18–19). He rejects
these standards and values as the predominant criteria for making distinctions and
judging arguments.

Instead, this demonstration of Spirit and power constitutes proof of Paul's
arguments that: (1) Christ's cruciform pattern is the new, divinely approved
behavioural standard for both Jews and Greeks; and that (2) it constitutes the
pathway that leads to experiences of God's life-giving power. For Paul, the community appropriately engaged in theo-ethical reasoning in the practice of spiritual
discernment understands that Christian faith is grounded not in persuasive words
of human wisdom but in these demonstrations of the Spirit that illuminate believers' experiences of God's manifest power that brings new life. Thus, Paul turns
in 2.6–16 to remind the Corinthians about the revelatory role of the Spirit sent

---

155. According to Gorman, 'Paul never divorces these experiences of God's power from the experience of the cross as the center of divine power', since the 'life-giving power of God is most fully
experienced by Paul in the cross of Christ and in the life of cruciform power that shares in that cross'
(2001: 280). In his recent study of Paul's religion, Ashton argues that it was not Paul's message of
salvation and resurrection that caught the attention of his Gentile audiences but their experience of the
demonstration or 'display of spiritual power' that was the 'attention-grabber' (2000: 163–65). While
the present study generally affirms Ashton's finding, it disagrees with his further conclusion that this
'display of spiritual power' was *limited* to the 'performance of miracles' involving exorcisms and
cures as the most visible feature of Paul's 'preaching' (2000: 164–65). A 'miracle of healing' is but
one of the many manifestations of the Spirit that Paul lists in 1 Cor. 12.8–10 (see also Rom. 12.3–11).
Moreover, it is not one of the two that he mentions in 1 Cor. 1.6–8 as the manifest χαρίσματα that
first confirmed Paul's embodied proclamation of Christ crucified and helped give birth to the church
in Corinth.

from God in the practice of spiritual discernment, an essential *community* discipline associated with this faith-building process.

d. *Divine Revelation in the Practice of Spiritual Discernment (2.6–16)*
Paul has now reminded the Corinthians about their first faith-grounding demonstration of Spirit and power associated with Paul's embodied proclamation of Christ crucified (2.1–5). He turns to explain the revelatory role of the Spirit in this process. He characterizes it as the Spirit sent from God to illuminate experiences of new life given by God (see 2.12). Paul draws again on certain motifs that explain how the revelation of the hidden mystery of God's plan is being carried out in the arena of history.[156]

Paul also recalls for them the practice of spiritual discernment, a process of 'comparing spiritual things with spiritual things' (2.13) that *should* be taking place in the community. Paul's use of the first person plural pronoun throughout the section points to the collective and dialogical nature of this community practice. This suggests that the *locus operandi* of the Spirit is the dialogue taking place in the deliberative assembly (see Thiselton 2000: 229), a conclusion that Paul expressly confirms in 3.16 and 6.19. It is a practice Paul probably taught them in his initial visit to Corinth (see 4.15–17) and a discipline implied in the events recounted in 1.4–9.[157] This section of the letter thus lays a critical foundation for later discussions about the distinctions that must be made between certain broad 'spiritual things' (πνευματικὰ) and those narrower spiritual experiences that reflect new life from God (χαρίσματα) associated with specific Christ-conforming actions (see 1 Corinthians chs 12–14).[158]

The section begins with Paul returning to the use of temporal dualism, claiming that he speaks a wisdom that is not of 'this age' or associated with the rulers of 'this age' who are being destroyed (2.6; cf. 1.18). The present participle καταργουμένων indicates that God is still engaged in the ongoing conflict to defeat the powers of 'this age' (see also 15.23–28).[159] Further, asserts Paul, this wisdom is spoken only in a mystery (2.7) among the 'mature' (2.6).

We suggest that the mature are the believers who reject the behavioural standards and values associated with the wisdom of 'this age' and its rulers. The mature are convinced that God's wisdom and power were revealed in Jesus Christ and that this established a new behavioural standard of self-giving love for others.[160] The mature understand and accept the fact that conduct conforming to

---

156. See Kovacs 1989: 218–19, 223; Brown 1995: 24.

157. Theissen seems to conclude incorrectly that Paul is introducing previously unknown content in 2.6–16. He asserts that the material 'fits poorly into the intellectual world of Pauline theology' (1987: 50). This study seeks to show otherwise by means of Paul's theo-ethical reasoning, an integration of theology and ethics.

158. Kovacs correctly points out that this section also sets up Paul's handling of the resurrection and *parousia* in 1 Cor. 15 (1989: 218).

159. Kovacs 1989: 224; Beker 1980: 159–60.

160. Theissen concludes that only the mature 'emancipate themselves consciously from the compulsive standards of this world' (1987: 385). According to Betz, the Corinthians' practical conduct does not reflect 'maturity', a concept and claim that require the synthesis of eloquence, knowledge

Christ's cruciform pattern must be spiritually discerned, as believers seek to identify the connections between the demonstrations of God's life-giving power and specific Christ-conforming actions (see 2.1–5). Thus, the mature are the ones who have reoriented their outlook to the new age by embracing Christ's cruciform pattern as their behavioural standard and practise spiritual discernment to look for life in their experiences of God's power associated with such Christ-conforming actions.

Indeed, for Paul being mature means perceiving that wisdom comes from God as a gift in Christ, enabling the self to live responsibly and wisely for others and for the good of the whole community (Thiselton 2000: 231). It 'entails integration of character and a long-term stance toward responsibility and hope' (Thiselton 2000: 263). Only the mature 'penetrate what happens to them and in them' (Theissen 1987: 352) because they reflect on the connection between their experience of new life and conduct that conforms to Christ's cruciform pattern.

Although God's plan remained hidden until now, this divine wisdom was previously established by God before the ages 'for our glory' says Paul in 2.7.[161] Paul's δόξα language invokes the horizon of the Jewish scriptures, which use the term to speak of God's past and future worldly visitations (Newman 1992: 245). It denotes the radiance of God and the manifestation of God's power.[162] Paul's use of δόξα in 2.7 not only refers to that which awaits believers in the age to come but also to the glory that is 'to some extent anticipated in the present age' (Barrett 1968: 71).[163]

Indeed, for Paul the concept of human glorification has more than just a future reference.[164] Paul makes this clear in 2 Corinthians. The 'eternal weight of glory' (2 Cor. 4.17) for which believers are being prepared is the 'culmination of the *present* transformation from "one degree of glory (*doxan*) to another"…which results when believers "behold the glory of the Lord" in Christ (2 Cor. 3.18)' (Brown 1995: 112, original emphasis). Thus, '[d]ivine glory is already breaking into the world in the Christ-event' and is 'reflected in the *diakonia* (service) of God by believers who are "daily given up to death for Jesus' sake, so that the life of Jesus may be manifested in their mortal flesh" (4:11)'.[165] Furthermore, according to 2 Corinthians 3–4, the *experience* of glory transforms human beings. This is a transformation that involves a change of perception by which the believer 'becomes the vessel in which the transcendent power of God is manifested (4.7)' (Brown 1995: 113).

From this it may be concluded that in 1 Cor. 2.7 Paul has in mind both the 'eschatological glory (with its present and future connotations) and the trans-

---

and practice (1986: 33). Fee (1987: 102–103) and Dunn (1998a: 321) triumphantly assert (wrongly) that the 'mature' include all who have the Spirit – namely, the whole church.

161. Despite his important study on the background of Paul's use of δόξα language, Newman incorrectly translates the phrase εἰς δόχαν ἡμῶν as 'for his [God's] glory' (1992: 159–60, including nn. 14–15).

162. Brown 1995: 112, citing Ps. 110.3; Isa. 6; Mic. 5.11; *I En.* 63.2.

163. See also 2 Cor. 3.18; cf. 1 Cor. 15.43.

164. Brown 1995: 112, citing the same point made by Bultmann (1985: 82).

165. Brown 1995: 112–13; cf. Käsemann 1964c: 65.

formed perception that results when one beholds the glory of God in the face of Christ *crucified*' (Brown 1995: 113, original emphasis). According to Paul's understanding of glory, believers now share in the 'radiance' of God's self-giving insofar as they share the character of Christ, participating in 'the having-died-with and being-raised-with Christ'.[166] This is the process of embodied human transformation into the image of Christ, from one glory to another (see 2 Cor. 3.18). It concludes with transformation into resurrection life after death, the social and cosmic reality of the risen Christ's full and complete glory. Paul thus appears to understand Christian life as an unfolding process of human transformation into the full image of Christ (see 1 Cor. 15.44–49). This is a bodily process directed by the risen Christ (see 1.8; 4.1–5; cf. Phil. 3.20–21), who has become a life-giving Spirit (1 Cor. 15.45; cf. 2 Cor. 3.17–18).

Against this background, Paul argues in 1 Cor. 2.8 that had the 'rulers of this age' known God's wisdom they would not have crucified 'the Lord of glory'.[167] This unusual characterization of Christ should also be read against the horizon of early Jewish apocalypses, where angelic figures frequently defined God's glory and served as God's chief agents to execute God's mysterious will and plan in the world.[168] Paul seems to ascribe these formerly angelic functions to the crucified but risen Lord. His key uses of the word δόξα in 2.6–8 indicate that God's previously hidden plan for human glorification has now become manifest in Jesus Christ, the crucified one who has also been raised and now reigns as the Lord of *human glory*.[169] Paul thus refers to the experience of new life – the product of God's power mediated to humans through Christ-conforming conduct. These constitute 'the things' prepared for those who love God, previously hidden but now revealed through the Spirit who knows the depths of God (2.9–10).

According to 2.12, the mature believers ('we') received this Spirit sent from God rather than receiving the 'spirit of the world'. This took place so that (ἵνα) the mature might be able to perceive (εἰδῶμεν) these gifts of new life given them by God (χαρισθέντα). On the one hand, '[t]he divine Spirit comes from "beyond" to impart a disclosure of God's own "wisdom"' (Thiselton 2000: 262). On the other hand, the Spirit facilitates a change of human consciousness among the mature. This involves a deepening or growing perception about the new life that God gave them through Christ and his cruciform act of self-giving love for others on the cross.[170] Thus, for Paul, the Spirit sent from God becomes the instrument

---

166. Thiselton 2000: 245; cf. Tannehill 1967.

167. For the debate about whether the 'rulers of this age' refers to human leaders, spiritual powers, or both, see Kovacs 1989: 217–36; D. Martin 1995: 62–63; Bockmuehl 1990: 163; Theissen 1987: 373–86; Thiselton 2000: 233–39.

168. Newman 1992: 237, 244; Thiselton 2000: 247; cf. Brown 1995: 116–17, including n. 28. Apparently, the exact form of this title can be found only in *1 En.* (40.3 and 63.2) and nowhere else in the New Testament (cf. Eph. 1.17; Jas 2.1).

169. Tabor even argues that the idea of heavenly glorification lies at the 'core of Paul's message' and that his uses of δόξα and δοξάζω summarize his overall view of God's plan of salvation (1986: 19). For Paul's references that suggest that the risen Lord presently reigns, see, e.g., Rom. 8.29–30; 1 Cor. 1.8; 4.1–5; 11.29–32; 15.25–28.

170. Cf. Koenig 1978: 169; Brown 1995: 147 n. 103.

of divine revelation and human understanding among the mature.[171] Those who
are less mature continue to receive the spirit of the world. Paul later calls them
infants in Christ (3.1).

In 2.12 Paul uses χαρισθέντα, a synonym for χαρίσματα.[172] This links 2.12
with 1.5–8, where the discernible χαρίσματα that enriched the community
divinely confirmed Paul's embodied proclamation of Christ crucified. Thus, to
the extent that God's wisdom and power in Christ may be known in the present
time, it must be spiritually discerned as it is divinely revealed among the mature.
Conversely, argues Paul in 2.14, the person who lives and reflects solely according to the standards of the world (the ψυχικὸς ἄνθρωπος) does not receive the
'things of the Spirit of God' because they are foolishness (μωρία).[173]

Paul uses the present tense δέχεται in 2.14, meaning that the ψυχικὸς ἄνθρωπος is not receiving the Spirit and is not yet believing (cf. 1.18). This person is
not yet accepting that Christ's cruciform death and resurrection revealed God's
wisdom, including how to walk in God's new age and experience God's life-
giving power in that new realm. The ψυχικὸς ἄνθρωπος fails or refuses to practise spiritual discernment by engaging in theo-ethical reasoning. Thus, this
person does not acknowledge or recognize the connection between these experiences of new life and Christ-conforming conduct. As a result, says Paul in 2.14b,
the ψυχικὸς ἄνθρωπος is not able to know this new life given by God. Later, in
8.1–3, Paul further explains this process involved with acquiring such knowledge, a process that demands that a person's actions conform to Christ's new
behavioural standard of self-giving love for others.[174]

Paul also sets out the *dialogical* nature of the practice of spiritual discernment
in 2.12–16. He thereby lays the foundation for his detailed ordering of this dialogue in 14.1–40. Paul and the mature members of the community speak about
these gifts of new life from God, but not in words taught from human wisdom
(2.13). Instead, they describe them as teachings of the Spirit (2.13).[175] Paul thus
characterizes the reception of revelation from the Spirit as a type of learning
through experience. In these verses, however, he clearly distinguishes two *different* educative processes. On the one hand, the person who receives the spirit of
the world is socialized into the world by conforming to its behavioural standards.
On the other hand, the mature believer who receives the Spirit from God discerns

171. Kovacs shows that in *1 En.* 91.1 the Spirit is the agent of divine revelation of God's plan for
the last days, a plan that concerns human and divine action (see *1 En.* 91.12–17; 93.1–10). Similarly,
she shows that *4 Ezra* 14.19–20 combines the ideas of the reception of the Spirit with the understanding of God's plan (1989: 227–28). This latter text also involves a statement about how humans are to
conduct themselves in the last days so that they might find life.

172. Dunn 1998c: 553 n. 115; BAGD, 876–79.

173. According to Thiselton, the ψυχικὸς ἄνθρωπος in 2.14 is the 'person who lives on an entirely
human level' (2000: 268).

174. See Chapter 3, 2.e.

175. According to D. Martin, these things are 'taught pneumatically' (1995: 63). Similarly, in
1 Thess. 4.9, Paul links Christ-conforming behaviour with being 'God-taught' (θεοδίδακτοί). See
also *Barn.* 21.4, where the author makes use of this same rare word, encouraging the church members to be 'God-taught' (θεοδίδακτοί) through behaviour.

experiences that open up entirely new possibilities for Christ-conforming human behaviour.[176]

For Paul this teaching of the Spirit takes place in the collective dialogue of those engaged in the active process of *diakrisis*.[177] According to the difficult verse at 2.13, one that raises a number of different possibilities,[178] Paul and the mature members of the community are involved in a collective, dialogical process of 'comparing spiritual things with spiritual things' (πνευματικοῖς πνευματικὰ συγκρίνοντες).[179] The present participle συγκρίνοντες, derived from a verb denoting comparisons,[180] describes a community reasoning process.[181] This process involves reflecting on the possible connections between experience and conduct.

Paul's only other uses of the verb συγκρίνω (twice in 2 Cor. 10.12) denote a similar process of evaluative comparison (Gardner 1994: 73). As part of their discernment about whether they truly belong to Christ, Paul exhorts the Corinthians in 2 Cor. 10.7 to re-examine reflectively the experiential evidence that is manifest before them (τὰ κατὰ πρόσωπον βλέπετε). The exhortation reaches a climax in 2 Cor. 10.12, where he criticizes their practice of comparing and measuring one person against another. By doing so, he implies a contrast between their approach, one that involves judging *people*, with the process of comparing spiritual *experiences* described in 1 Cor. 2.13. We suggest that spiritual discernment specifically involves evaluating the links between experiences and particular conduct. It does not involve the judgment of people, something that is reserved solely for the Lord (see 4.1–5).

Moreover, this dialogical and comparative process potentially requires the community to consider the insights and evaluations of *every* member of the deliberative assembly.[182] Every person must have the chance to be heard as the group seeks to discern these links between conduct and experience (see 14.1–5,

---

176. For these two contrasting processes, see Theissen 1987: 368.

177. The verbs and nouns in 2.13 are all plural, suggesting a community practice. Thus, both Barrett (1968: 75) and Dunn (1975: 235) unnecessarily overemphasize the inward and individualistic apprehension of these gifts. In the related context of 1 Cor. 12.9, however, Dunn correctly concludes that the 'discernments of spirits' suggest a process of *diakrisis* that involves determining the sources of the prophecy – such as an evil spirit or the Holy Spirit – and evaluating or interpreting the prophecy as to its content and what it means for the community (1998a: 314).

178. See Schrage 1991: 262; cf. Thiselton 2000: 264.

179. Dunn correctly suggests that this 'difficult phrase' must include the thought that inspired speech, as well as the gifts divinely bestowed, should always be subject to some sort of evaluation (1998a: 314). Unfortunately, however, his translation of the phrase ('judging spirituals by spirituals') misses the point in two respects. First, it does not adequately capture the comparative nature of the process as suggested by the participle συγκρίνοντες. Second, his translation emphasizes a comparison of people rather than experiences, a distinction that will be explored below.

180. BAGD, 774; LSJ, 1667.

181. See Lietzmann 1949: 12–14; Gardner 1994: 73–74.

182. Indeed, the logic that grounds Paul's exhortation to the 'strong' in chs 8–10 to defer to the needs of the 'weak' presumes that the positions of the 'weak' have been made known to the whole community. For the way that Paul gives voice to every position as he writes 1 Corinthians 8–10, see Meeks 1988.

26–32).[183] Even Paul himself expects to become a participant in this congregational dialogue, as 5.3–5 and Rom. 1.11–12 imply.[184]

In 1 Cor. 2.13 Paul first uses the word πνευματικά ('spiritual things').[185] Apparently, the πνευματικά were the subjects of an earlier letter to Paul (see 12.1; 14.1). The word was probably being used by some of the Corinthians (Käsemann 1964c: 66). Paul later characterizes this group within the church as being eagerly desirous of spirits (14.12). For Paul, the πνευματικά are 'spiritual realities' that can come from any source and lead in any direction (L.T. Johnson 1996: 117). Paul later points this out again in 12.1–2.[186] The πνευματικά do not refer *only* to gifts from God, nor do they constitute the equivalent of the χαρίσματά, and do not even become interchangeable parallels to them.[187]

Instead, in 2.15–16 Paul suggests that the πνευματικά must be distinguished one from another through this comparative process by which the 'spiritual person closely examines all things' (ὁ δὲ πνευματικὸς ἀνακρίνει πάντα). According to Paul's underlying logic, this discernment must take place to distinguish whether spiritual realities are rooted in the Spirit sent from God or the spirit of the world (see 2.12; cf. Eph. 6.12). Thus, Paul appears to be suggesting that believers must compare spiritual experiences in order to distinguish those greater χαρίσματα (see 1 Cor. 12.31) that represent new life given by God for the community's common good (see 12.7). Indeed, Paul later confirms community edification as the evaluative criterion for making this spiritual assessment.[188]

Later, in 1 Corinthians 12–14, Paul describes this comparative, dialogical process of spiritual discernment in more detail (see 12.1–3; 14.1–5, 23–32). According to the first-century social custom known as the symposium, this process should have been taking place in the deliberative assembly during the period of conversation that followed dinner.[189] By emphasizing the collective nature of this discourse in 1 Corinthians 14, Paul responds to certain individuals who were undermining the community practice of spiritual discernment through their 'self-reliant revelatory prowess'.[190]

183. According to Dunn, in 2.12–16 Paul implies that all members of the community become participants in the discernment process focused on recognizing and understanding the 'gifts' from God and making 'Spirit-informed' judgments on matters involving the Spirit, including prophecy (1998d: 282). For discussion of the role of prophecy in Paul's theo-ethical reasoning and the practice of spiritual discernment, see Chapter 3, section 3.d.

184. Cf. Koenig 1978: 174. For discussion of Paul's contribution to this dialogue in connection with the issues raised in 1 Cor. 5.1–13, see Chapter 3, section 2.a.

185. See also 9.11; 12.1; 14.1.

186. For this distinction in 12.1–2, see Käsemann 1964c: 66; Chapter 3, section 3.b.

187. Contra Koenig 1978: 169; Fee 1987: 576–77; R. Collins 1999: 135, 447; Conzelmann 1975: 204; Horsley 1998: 167.

188. See 8.1, discussed in Chapter 3, section 2.e, and 10.23, addressed in Chapter 3, section 2.h.

189. For consideration of the social custom of the symposium in first-century society, see D. Smith 2003; Aune 1978: 70–78. The conclusion that first-century Christian gatherings included a post-supper, symposium-like event has been recognized by D. Smith 2003; Aune 1978: 74–75; Lampe 1990: 37, 40; 1991a: 190–91. For discussion of the role of the symposium-like event in Paul's churches, see D. Smith 2003: 173–217; Chapter 3, section 3.d below.

190. For this latter phrase, see Newman 1992: 236.

Paul also introduces the term ἀνακρίνω in 2.14–15.[191] This verb was used regularly in connection with judicial proceedings, especially to describe the process where magistrates closely examined the conduct of the parties in preparation for trial.[192] The translation used here ('closely examine') reflects this aspect of the judicial assessment of behaviour in advance of final judgment.[193] This is a theme Paul incorporates throughout the letter (see, e.g., 1.7–8; 3.10–18; 4.1–5; 11.17–24). Indeed, the ability to know things given by God 'depends on the ability to carry out the "spiritual judging or investigation"' implied by the verb ἀνακρίνω (Gardner 1994: 74).

We suggest that Paul uses the verb ἀνακρίνω in 2.14 to join this reflective process of closely examining people's *conduct* with the process of comparing spiritual *experiences* described in 2.13. Paul thereby emphasizes the importance of reflecting on conduct and experience and links the two in ways that he illuminates throughout the letter. Further, the present participle συγκρίνοντες (2.13) and the present tense uses of ἀνακρίνω in 2.14–15 highlight Paul's expectation that the spiritual discernment of these connections between conduct and experience should be a discipline consistently practised in the deliberative assembly.

Moreover, says Paul in 2.15, the spiritual person closely examines all *things* (πάντα) – namely, all conduct and experiences – but that *person* will not be closely examined by anyone (see also 4.4; 2 Cor. 10.12). To combat the intense personal competition in the church (see 1 Cor. 1.10–17), Paul makes it clear that the spiritual person does not closely examine another person.[194] Thus, it would appear that Paul's goal for the practice of spiritual discernment is to *distinguish* the gifts of new life by means of God's power (χαρισθέντα/χαρίσματα) associated with Christ-conforming conduct (see 1.4–9) from other 'spiritual things' (πνευματικὰ) experienced in connection with the spirit of the world and behaviour that conforms to the standards of the world.

Paul's assertion in 2.16 that 'we have the mind of Christ' makes yet another important distinction. There are those who are reasoning with a Christ-like perspective (see also Phil. 2.1–5) and there are those who are probably claiming to know the mind of the Lord (see Brown 1995: 140). It would appear that for Paul the 'mind of Christ' is the 'same mind' that should be unifying the Corinthians (see 1 Cor. 1.10). It is the same mindset or attitude with which every member of the community should be reasoning.[195] If everyone was reasoning with this same mindset, the group would be better able to reach the 'same opinion' about what constitutes Christ-conforming action (see 1.10). Thus, the 'mind of Christ' is the

---

191. See also, 2.15; 4.3 (2x), 4; 9.3; 10.25, 27; 14.24.

192. See LSJ, 109; Fee 1987: 117.

193. Cf. Barrett 1968: 77 ('investigate'); Fee 1987: 117 ('discern'); R. Collins 1999: 136–37 ('judge').

194. Cf. Dunn 1975: 235. Pursuant to this same reasoning, Paul later affirms in 4.1–5 that only the Lord Jesus Christ 'closely examines' the individual person for purposes of determining whether that person has been 'faithful' as a 'servant of Christ'. Cf. Gal. 1.10; 1 Thess. 2.14.

195. L.T. Johnson 1996: 113, 127. D. Martin notes that all the Corinthians *potentially* have the 'mind of Christ' (1995: 63).

appropriate perspective for those who practise spiritual discernment, trying to associate Christ-like conduct with community experiences of new life.[196]

Indeed, for Paul, the mind is never separated from its bodily context (Brown 1995: 166). It marks the orientation of the whole person, not just the intellect, towards the ways of the Spirit (cf. Rom. 8.1–25; Gal. 5.5–6, 18–25).[197] Later, in 1 Corinthians 14, Paul emphasizes the importance of the mind for discerning appropriate behaviour through the practice of spiritual discernment.

Paul thus concludes this discussion of the dialogical and comparative practice of spiritual discernment. Just as Christ's cruciform pattern of self-giving love for others has become the new behavioural norm for conduct in God's new age/ spatial realm in Christ (1.18–25), so, too, the 'mind of Christ' serves as God's new, unifying standard for thinking and reasoning (see also Phil. 2.1–13).[198] These two new, divinely revealed standards shape Paul's theo-ethical reasoning and the practice of spiritual discernment that lie at the heart of his religion.

Paul's argument in 1 Cor. 2.6–16 also sheds light on the earlier discussion of 1.4–9. In Chapter 2, section 2.b it was suggested that the revelation of Jesus Christ was not just a future event that would occur at the close of the ages. Paul and believers eagerly expect such revelations to continue to take place each time an experience of new life through God's power (χάρισμα) confirms Christ-conforming actions. In light of 2.6–16, it would appear that the χαρίσματα constitute the present manifestations of the glory of God in Christ, who will be fully revealed only at the end time.[199] Paul expects that those who now participate actively in Christ's crucifixion – dying to the world's standards of behaviour and conforming their actions to Christ's cruciform pattern – will reflect the earthly glory of God revealed in the crucified and risen Christ (see 15.40–49).[200] They become instruments by which other believers experience God's life-giving power manifest in the χαρίσματα that build up the community into the body of Christ.

Consequently, this study tentatively concludes that, for Paul, conduct conforming to the new behavioural standard embodied in Christ's cruciform pattern becomes the means by which the risen Lord continues to mediate God's own

196. Willis concludes that Paul's real concern in the passage is with conduct more than reasoning (1989: 111). While this conclusion understates the role of comparative reasoning in the passage, Willis's emphasis on conduct is generally overlooked by many interpreters.

197. Brown 1995: 166.

198. See Willis, who concludes that the 'mind of Christ' is an ethical outlook formed around the message of the cross which is manifest in the proper attitudes and conduct of believers (1989: 121).

199. Ashton argues that Paul's use of 'glory' or 'glorification' points to God's final purpose that has already commenced, an idea that Paul got from a personal revelation (2000: 140–41). Paul's use of the title 'Lord of glory' in 2.8 might even suggest that in his resurrection vision of the Lord (1 Cor. 9.1; 15.8) Paul identified Christ with the human form of God's glory as described in *1 En.* 40.3 and in the throne-room vision scene of Ezekiel ch. 1. For the possible links between Paul and early Jewish apocalyptic tradition involving *Merkhaba* mysticism and meditation on Ezekiel ch. 1, see Segal 1990: 60–61; 1998; 1999; Rowland 1988; Newman 1992; Morray-Jones 1993; Ashton 2000: 105–42.

200. For a discussion of the different aspects of 'glory' associated with earthly life, see Chapter 3, section 4.e.

glory to the world.[201] Paul seems to understand δόξα as representing some type of material manifestation of an aspect of God's own glory.[202] This involves the rewards given to those favoured by God.[203] Moreover, a believer's primary contact with this divine δόξα must be through perception, especially through some type of seeing (Koenig 1990a: 161). Thus, Paul appears to forge a direct link between the experiences/manifestations of God's life-giving power (χαρίσματα) and conduct that conforms to Christ's cruciform pattern.[204]

The importance of recognizing these connections highlights the critical role of practising spiritual discernment by engaging in theo-ethical reasoning. By reflecting comparatively on their conduct and experience, community members seek to identify the manifestations of new life from God revealed by the Spirit (2.12). With the guidance of that Spirit, they try to associate these experiences with conduct that conforms to Christ's cruciform pattern. Paul thereby anticipates his arguments in 15.35–44, where he distinguishes between the earthly and heavenly manifestations of glory associated with the different forms of earthly and heavenly bodies being shaped by particular behaviour.[205]

e. *Illustrating Spiritual Discernment: Reflecting on Conduct and Experience (3.1–4)*

The revealing verses in 3.1–4[206] illustrate the 'real pulse of the argument in the first four chapters' (Willis 1989: 120).[207] Paul actually models the practice of spiritual discernment, engaging in theo-ethical reasoning to illuminate the Corinthians' situation by linking conduct with community experience.[208] He asserts in 3.3 that they are still fleshly, walking according to human standards (κατὰ ἄνθρωπον περιπατεῖτε) characteristic of the wider world (Adams 2000: 93). He discerns this because (γὰρ) jealousy and discord are manifest in their community relationships (3.3; cf. Gal. 5.19–23).[209] Their experience provides clear evidence that they are not mature (Betz 1986: 38). Paul thereby calls their attention to the link between their community experience of contentious discord and their conduct that conforms to worldly human standards.

Moreover, Paul also implies that their divisions exist because some members of the church lack the spiritual maturity that only develops as believers practise

---

201. Cf. Newman 1992: 245; Tabor 1986: 19.

202. See Koenig 1990a: 160–61, 163; cf. Savage 1996: 103–29.

203. See Kovacs 1989: 220, who cites *1 En.* 62.15; *2 Bar.* 51.12; *4 Ezra* 7.91.

204. Newman overemphasizes Paul's preached message at the expense of his behavioural proclamation (1992: 245). Indeed, Paul exhorts the Corinthians in 10.31 that everything they do should be for the glory of God and in 6.20 to glorify God in their body. In Rom. 8.30 he characterizes those who are justified as the object of God's glorification.

205. See Chapter 3, section 4.e.

206. For this characterization, see Barclay 1988: 206.

207. Cf. Funk 1966: 275–305; Baird 1959: 425–32.

208. According to Brown, 1 Corinthians 3–4 extend the 'experiential implications' of the noetic shift that takes place in the letter's first two chapters (1995: 21).

209. In a later letter to the Ephesians, Ignatius concludes that the community was 'living according to God' since there is no strife among them (Ignatius, *Eph.* 8.1).

spiritual discernment according to the 'mind of Christ'.[210] Characterizing the
Corinthians as fleshly, as infants in Christ, Paul is unable to address them as
'spiritual ones' (1 Cor. 3.1). They are not spiritual because at least some of them
are not practising spiritual discernment to associate their experiences and conduct. Paul uses the verb δύναμαι three times in 3.1–2, creating an emphatic
verbal link back to the ψυχκὸς ἄνθρωπος characterized in 2.14. This implies
that at least some of the Corinthians are not able to know and receive the gifts of
new life from God because they refuse to practise spiritual discernment. Paul's
critique is thus levelled at any person – whether a believer or not – who fails to
walk in conformity with Christ's cruciform pattern and to practise spiritual discernment in order to identify the links between conduct and experience.

f. Clarifying Roles in the Divine–Human Partnership (3.5–23)
Paul applies a variety of images associated with agricultural and construction
imagery in 3.5–23, metaphorical language that illuminates aspects of theo-ethical
reasoning. To reduce the factional divisions, Paul downplays the importance of
individual human leaders. He emphasizes that only God's power is responsible
for giving growth to the community (3.6, 7). In 3.9 he characterizes Apollos and
himself as fellow workers with God (θεοῦ...συνεργοί).[211] They cooperate with
one another and with God (Mitchell 1991: 98). They are servants through whom
the Corinthians came to faith, as the Lord assigned distinct ministries to each of
them (3.5; see also Rom. 12.3).[212]

The preposition διά in 1 Cor. 3.5 highlights that Paul and Apollos were simply the means or channels by which God worked powerfully through their
specific actions (Thiselton 2000: 300). Indeed, in 3.5–13 Paul uses ἕκαστος five
times to emphasize not the person involved in ministry but the particular roles
assigned to each of them by the Lord (cf. Rom. 12.3–10).[213] Thus, Paul's 'task-
oriented perception of leadership...concentrates on the particular task each leader
is accomplishing' (Clarke 1993: 119). 'The issue concerns "their role" and
"function as servants" (v. 5)' (Thiselton 2000: 301, quoting Schrage 1991: 288).
Thus, God's power that builds the community works through specific Christ-
conforming acts of service/ministry (see 1 Cor. 12.4–7). This conviction lies at
the centre of theo-ethical reasoning.

In 3.5 Paul applies the ingressive aorist ἐπιστεύσατε.[214] It denotes the moment
when the Corinthians entered into the continuing state or process of 'believ-

---

210. Brown reaches a similar conclusion: the Spirit facilitates the transforming of the human mind
into the 'mind of Christ' (1995: 147); cf. Bultmann 1951: 327 (they lack 'ethical maturity').
    211. For this translation of συνεργοί, see W.D. Davies 1972a: 322; Betz 1986: 39; Weiss 1977: 77–
78; Robertson and Plummer 1914: 58; *pace* Furnish 1961: 369; Thiselton 2000: 305–306; R. Collins
1999: 146. See now Furnish, who characterizes each similar phrase in 2 Cor. 6.1 and 1 Thess. 3.2 as
a 'striking expression' that Paul works together with God (1984: 341, 352).
    212. For this characterization of ἔδωκεν, see R. Collins 1999: 145; Thiselton 2000: 300.
    213. Clarke 1993: 119; Thiselton 2000: 301.
    214. Schrage 1991: 288; R. Collins 1999: 145; Thiselton 2000: 300; *pace* Fee 1987: 131. For other
uses of the ingressive aorist of πιστεύω, see Rom. 13.11; 1 Cor. 15.2; Gal. 2.16.

ing'.[215] Elsewhere, Paul's use of πιστεύω also suggests a continuing state or condition.[216] The rhetorical background of the word πίστις in late antiquity is important in this regard. In the first-century Graeco-Roman world, the terms πίστις and πιστεύω often carried connotations associated with persuasion.[217] Thus, it is arguable that for Paul and his churches these terms frequently denoted the status of 'being convinced or persuaded' (S.K. Williams 1997: 65–66, generally citing Kinneavy 1987). This suggests that, as a faithful servant of Christ and steward of God's mysteries (see 3.5; 4.1–2; 7.25), Paul was participating in a process of divine persuasion (see Gal. 1.10; 5.8).[218] This process was one by which Paul sought to cooperate with God through his embodied proclamation of Christ crucified. The goal was to persuade others that in the gospel of Christ there is a link between Christ-conforming conduct and the discernible experience of God's life-giving power in the community.

The building metaphor introduced in 3.9 becomes a dominant theme for the remainder of the letter.[219] The community constitutes God's building. This image leaves no room for the destructive divisions that endanger the church. It points to the corporate structure that is central to Paul's theological and pastoral concerns in the letter.[220] Moreover, he emphasizes that it is God who gives growth (3.6, 7; cf. 1.5, 7) to the community characterized as God's 'field' and, by implication, it is God who constructs the θεοῦ οἰκοδομή (3.9).[221]

In 3.10–17 Paul focuses on the human role in this divine process of building or destroying the community.[222] For emphasis he uses the verb ἐποικοδομέω four times in these eight verses. It is a member of the οἰκοδομ- word group that Paul normally uses in moral exhortation, suggesting a paraenetic function here as well (R. Collins 1999: 155). Paul claims the role of a skilled master builder who laid the foundation of Jesus Christ (3.11) that others are now 'building upon' (ἐποικοδομεῖ). He once again affirms that God gave him grace/power (χάρις) in this specific task.[223] In 3.10d he also challenges every Corinthian[224] to reflect

215. Generally, Moule, citing Burton, suggests that the ingressive aorist represents the 'point of entrance' that is used with verbs whose present tense denotes a state or condition (1959: 10). More specifically, Schrage characterizes the ingressive aorist in 3.5 as the inception of the event denoting when the Corinthians first came to faith (1991: 291).

216. See, e.g., Rom. 3.22; 4.24; 9.33; 10.4, 9–10; 15.13; Gal. 2.16; 3.22; 1 Thess. 1.7; 2.10, 13.

217. This is one of the main conclusions of Kinneavy's 1987 study that focuses on the Greek rhetorical origins of Christian faith.

218. This will be examined in the context of Galatians in Chapter 4, section 4.c.

219. Horsley 1998: 64. See, e.g., 8.1; 10.23; 14.3–5, 12, 17, 26.

220. See Schrage 1991: 295; Thiselton 2000: 307; Mitchell 1991: 37.

221. *Pace* Castelli, who interprets 1 Cor. 3.9 as a verse 'rendering the women and men of Corinth as passive objects of apostolic working, the products of apostolic production' (1991b: 213).

222. Horsley points out (1998: 64) that in Paul's culture the 'building' metaphor was a common one for personal growth and spiritual enlightenment, not only in Hellenistic philosophy (see, e.g., Epictetus, *Diss.* 2.15.8) but also in Philo's mystical theology (see, e.g., *Somn.* 2.8; *Gig.* 30; *Mut. Nom.* 211). Thus, Paul is once again re-defining a term from its ordinary understanding, this time emphasizing the communal rather than individual nature of edification (see also 1 Cor. 10.23–11.1).

223. For understanding 'grace' as divine power in Paul, see Käsemann 1964c: 65; Nolland 1986: 26–31; Polaski 1999: 107.

(βλεπέτω) on how (πῶς) they are contributing to the construction process through their own actions (R. Collins 1999: 151). Paul's reasoning suggests that they should be practising spiritual discernment. He implies that there are discernible manifestations for assessing how the building process is progressing in connection with their own actions (cf. 3.1–4; 11.29–32).

Indeed, Paul's question in 3.16 demands that the Corinthians affirm that their community belongs to God (see 3.6, 7, 9) and that the Spirit of God dwells among them (ἐν ὑμῖν).[225] Paul's two-pronged question implies that some community members have forgotten (or are ignoring) that the Spirit dwells among them as the source of their behavioural discernment (see 2.10, 12, 14–15; 3.1). There will be accountability to God for such failure. According to the logic of his argument in 3.10–17, conduct conforming to worldly standards will destroy the community that is God's temple. It should otherwise be set apart (ἅγιός)[226] as the work of God being constructed through conduct that conforms to Christ's cruciform pattern.[227] Divine judgment will befall those whose actions conform to the standards of the world and destroy God's holy temple in Corinth (see 11.29–32).

Paul closes this section by re-emphasizing the importance of Christ-conforming conduct. He exhorts anyone who thinks they are wise in 'this age' to become foolish in order that they might become truly wise (3.18). Paul echoes his earlier uses of the foolishness motif (1.18, 21, 23, 25, 27; 2.14). Once again he contrasts the wisdom of 'this age' and its various behavioural standards (see Adams 2000: 118) with God's wisdom of the new age/spatial realm manifest in Christ Jesus and his new behavioural standard of cruciform self-giving love for others. Paul's logic implies that the Corinthians become truly wise when they know God because they identify their own experiences of God's life-giving power and associate them with actions that conform to Christ's cruciform pattern (cf. 8.1–3).

g. *Household Management Images Clarify Roles (4.1–7)*
In the short section in 4.1–7, Paul continues the argument (οὕτως). He introduces household management imagery to clarify the roles and responsibilities in the divine–human partnership introduced in 1.9. In 4.1 he characterizes himself and Apollos as contributing subordinates (ὑπηρέτας) of Christ and stewards of the mysteries of God entrusted with secret things.[228] He thereby establishes his

---

224. For the conclusion that Paul is referring to every member of the community, see Kuck 1992: 172, 174; R. Collins 1999: 150–51; Yinger 1999: 224; Mitchell 1991: 213; cf. Horsley 1998: 65; Fee 1987: 139–45. The fact that both 3.9 and 3.16, the verses that enclose the subject passage, are clearly addressed to the entire community makes it highly improbable that Paul has narrowed the audience for his remarks in 3.10–15, notwithstanding that his references in 3.10–15 become more singular rather than collective.

225. Cf. Rom. 8.9, 11.

226. Paul is reprising his 'holiness' theme from 1.2 according to R. Collins (1999: 153).

227. Cf. Jaquette 1995: 223. One of Gärtner's four points of contact between Paul's symbolism and that found in the Qumran community involves the close association between the Spirit's presence and the demand for purity, a clear reference to the connection between the Spirit and behaviour (1965: 57–58).

228. For this translation, see LSJ, 1872; cf. Fee 1987: 159; *pace* Rengstorf 1972: 542; see Acts 26.16.

role in the hierarchy of relationships set out in 3.21–23 (cf. 12.4–6; 15.20–28). He also echoes 2.6–16, where he described his own role of interpreting God's wisdom in a mystery through the practice of spiritual discernment.[229] Correspondingly, the performance of these duties will be divinely assessed. The steward must be found faithful (πιστός) in the discharge of the duties (4.2). This is a standard apparently derived from Paul's conviction that God is faithful (1.9; cf. 10.13; 1 Thess. 5.24).

In the important verses at 1 Cor. 4.3–4,[230] Paul clarifies that for the present time it is only the risen Lord, the one Master and Lord of the household, who appropriately judges the faithfulness of the conduct of his subordinates (see also 1.6, 8).[231] Paul again uses the verb ἀνακρίνω introduced in 2.14, drawing on the judicial imagery of the magistrate who closely examines the conduct of the parties in preparation for trial. According to the logic underlying Paul's argument in 4.1–7 (see also 1.6–8), 'the Lord is the authority to whom the believer is responsible and from whom the believer derives his or her lifestyle and ethics' (Thiselton 2000: 926). The Lord closely examines Paul's actions to assess them and (possibly) confirm that they faithfully conform to Christ's cruciform pattern (see 1.6; cf. 1.10; 4.17; 7.25). In 4.3–4 Paul thus describes the role of the Lord who judges conduct in advance of the end time, with the present participle ἀνακρίνων indicating an ongoing process of regular evaluation (cf. 9.26–27; 1 Thess. 2.4).

Paul views as insignificant the close scrutiny that some Corinthians are giving him on a personal level (1 Cor. 4.3; cf. 2.15). He also rejects any evaluation 'by a human day' (ὑπὸ ἀνθρωπίνης ἡμέρας), apparently referring to any tribunal that judges him according to human standards (cf. 6.1–8). Despite his hyperbole that he does not even closely examine himself (4.3), he asserts in 4.4 that he 'knows nothing against himself'. Paul thus implies that he has reflected on his own conduct and experience and that this provides him with a confident self-awareness of the faithfulness of his own actions.[232] Nevertheless, Paul's main point is that spiritual discernment remains fallible and inadequate, whether that discernment is positive or negative (cf. 13.8–12).[233]

Consequently, even as a discerning apostle, Paul affirms that he has not thereby been justified (δεδικαίωμαι) by his clear conscience. Even if the practice of

---

229. According to Koenig, Paul is charged with the duty of disclosing the future eschatological mysteries – the visions of God's final purpose – so as to empower others for ministry during the period between the resurrection and the *parousia* (1978: 172).

230. Thiselton finds that 4.3b–4 have 'pivotal importance' for Paul's 'theology' (2000: 339).

231. D. Martin 1995: 65; 1990: 15, 17, 80; Thiselton 2000: 337.

232. The verb σύνοιδα in 4.4 is related to the noun συνείδησις (see 8.12; 10.25–29), often translated as 'conscience'. In New Testament usage συνείδησις carries a sense of 'consciousness' or 'self-awareness' in relational contexts. See, e.g., Horrell 1997a: 89 n. 18; Maurer 1971: 914–15; D. Martin 1995: 180–82; cf. 1 Cor. 11.28; 2 Cor. 13.5; Gal. 6.4; 1 Thess. 5.21. Sampley correctly points out the importance of self-evaluation for Paul and links it to the interrelationship between self-giving love for others and the growth of faith (1991a: 50). But he overstates the case when he attributes the view to Paul that the final judgment is not a fearful prospect because of the believer's capacity for self-assessment (1991a: 69). Paul makes it clear in 4.4 that his own self-assessment does not completely resolve the issue. See now Keck 1996b: 4 n. 7.

233. Cf. Thiselton 2000: 340; Schrage 1991: 322.

Looking for Life

spiritual discernment cannot provide certainty with regard to final judgment and divine justification, however, this does not mean that the practice is unimportant for Paul (see 7.25).[234] Although the final adjudication of every person belongs only to the risen Lord (4.4–5), his present judgment may be spiritually discerned so that believers may reform their actions accordingly (see 11.29–32; cf. 1.6, 8).

Paul emphatically concludes this part of the argument with an imperative in 4.5. He exhorts the Corinthians not to judge anything before the proper time – that is, when the Lord comes among them. At that moment, says Paul, the Lord will bring to light the hidden things of darkness and will manifest the counsels of hearts. There will be recognition given to each person from God rather than other humans.[235]

Commentators generally conclude that 4.5 contains only a reference to the Day of the Lord, understood as the day of final judgment when Christ returns to turn over the kingdom to God (see 15.23–24).[236] Nevertheless, there are reasons for concluding that this is not just an exhortation to the Corinthians to refrain from making any judgments until Christ's final return at the end of time.[237] First, elsewhere in this letter Paul consistently calls on the community to distinguish, closely examine, and judge among themselves about the adequacy of particular conduct.[238] Emphasizing the evaluation of *conduct* and *experience* rather than people, Paul has argued that the spiritual person closely examines all things even though that person is not closely examined by anyone (2.15). Second, Paul's real concern is not to limit the Corinthians' ability to make judgments about conduct, but about the timeliness and context of those judgments. In the practice of spiritual discernment, the whole gathered community makes such behavioural judgments.[239] They do so, however, only when they discern the Lord's guiding presence among them.

Paul expands the focus of his argument in 4.6, bringing the Corinthians within its purview through his use of the word μετεσχημάτισα. He appears to confirm that he has been using the rhetorical device of covert allusion evident in the argument from as early as 3.5.[240] The word μετεσχημάτισα suggests that Paul has

---

234. *Pace* D. Martin 1995: 181; Fee 1987: 162–63.

235. Mitchell points out that in 4.5 Paul is reminding the Corinthians (who are boasting in themselves) that it is better to be praised by others, especially God (1991: 91).

236. See, e.g., Horsley 1998: 68; Thiselton 2000: 343–44; R. Collins 1999: 174; Mitchell 1991: 91; Héring 1962: 27–28; Fee 1987: 163–64; cf. Lietzmann 1949: 19.

237. This is a point acknowledged but otherwise ignored by Fee 1987: 163.

238. See, e.g., 1.8; 2.13–16; 5.1–3, 12–13; 6.1–8; 10.25–29; 11.29–32; 14.24–25, 29–30. Noting these verses, some commentators try to cure a perceived inconsistency by arguing that Paul is speaking only about the Corinthians' incompetence to judge the apostle himself. See, e. g., Fee 1987: 163; R. Collins 1999: 170. This attempted reconciliation misses Paul's point.

239. Paul emphasizes the importance of the whole gathered community coming together in the same place (see, e.g., 11.20; 14.23) with all the members participating (see, e.g., 14.26). His concern suggests that some in the community may be judging him and others without the evaluative counsel of the whole group.

240. See Fiore 1985: 85–102; Adams 2000: 121; Stowers 1990: 256–57; R. Collins 1999: 176; cf. Schrage 1991: 334; Thiselton 2000: 351.

'changed the form' of the argument by focusing the discussion on himself and Apollos as a covert allusion for its application to all the members of the congregation. In the ancient Graeco-Roman world the use of covert allusion to soften criticism was closely associated with irony (see 4.13–18), νουθεσία (see 4.15), and the use of positive contrastive models (see 4.15–17).[241] In contrast to the conceit and strife manifest among the Corinthians, Paul and Apollos cooperated in their ministries as fellow workers with God (3.9). Paul thus implies that cooperation rather than competition grounds community growth through the power of God.

Moreover, the two purpose clauses in 4.6 combat factionalism by emphasizing the cooperation demanded by the community practice of spiritual discernment. The first clause suggests that Paul has utilized covert allusion so that the Corinthians might learn by the cooperative example of Paul and Apollos how not to conduct themselves 'beyond what is written'.[242] Paul probably alludes to the six specific scriptural citations he has already used earlier in the letter.[243] Each of the cited passages identifies how God destroys human standards of perception and reasoning and replaces them with God's own divinely revealed norm. In 2.16 Paul characterized this new standard for reasoning as the mind of Christ (cf. 1.10; Phil. 2.2–5). Paul thus uses scripture to try to reshape the minds and perceptions of his readers, challenging them to recognize that in Christ God has established new norms for thinking and acting. He wants them to understand how God may now be known in the world through demonstrations of Spirit and power in connection with the embodied proclamation of Christ crucified (see 1 Cor. 2.1–5; 12.4–7).

The second purpose clause in 4.6 is dependent upon the first (Hooker 1990a: 107). In their service as διάκονοι (3.5; cf. 12.5), as fellow workers with God (3.9; cf. 12.4–6), and as servants of Christ and stewards of God's mysteries (4.1), Paul and Apollos cooperated rather than competed with one another. Thus, neither became 'puffed up' against the other. Throughout the remainder of the letter, Paul pursues this attack on competition among members of the community who have become 'puffed up' against one another.[244] Thus, in 4.6 Paul recommends himself and Apollos as models of constructive cooperation. He later affirms that the Corinthians should imitate this model that is grounded in the example of Christ himself (see 4.16; 11.1; cf. Gal. 4.12, 14; 1 Thess. 1.6).

In 1 Cor. 4.7 Paul ties together various strands of his argument with several questions. He introduces another distinctive verb (διακρίνω) with the same

---

241. Fitzgerald 1988: 120–22; Stowers 1990: 257.

242. The enigmatic phrase ἵνα ἐν ἡμῖν μάθητε τὸ Μὴ ὑπὲρ ἃ γέγραπται in 4.6 has evoked considerable debate. In addition to the commentaries see, e.g., Hooker 1963–64: 295–301; Wagner 1998: 279–87; D. Hall 1994: 143–49; Tuckett 2000: 403–24; Welborn 1987: 320–46; Hanges 1998: 275–98; Hays 1999: 391–412.

243. Hays 1999: 402–403; cf. Wagner 1998: 279–87; Hooker 1963–64: 295–301; *pace* Schrage 1991: 334–35; Barrett 1968: 106–107. For these citations see 1 Cor. 1.19 (modified Isa. 29.14); 1.31 (Jer. 9.23 and/or 1 Kgs 2.10); 2.9 (although no exact scriptural correlation has been found, possibly citing portions of Isa. 64.3 and 65.16); 2.16 (modified Isa. 40.13); 3.19 (Job 5.13); and 3.20 (Ps. 93.11).

244. For Paul's other uses of φυσιόω in the letter, see 4.18, 19; 5.2; 8.1; 13.4.

– κρινω root as ἀνακρίνω (2.14, 15; 4.3, 4) and κρίνω (2.2; 4.5). He employs διακρίνω consistently to signify the legitimate exercise of human judgment as the product of community spiritual discernment. The verb implies that it is the Lord who will distinguish their Christ-conforming actions from conduct that conforms merely to worldly standards (cf. 1.8; 3.1–4). Moreover, the intensive use of the aorist form of λαμβάνω three times in 4.7 dramatically highlights the Corinthians' misplaced trust in themselves and their human leaders as the sources of their own enrichment. They must understand that it is God who works through Christ-conforming conduct (cf. 3.5) to enrich them with the χαρίσματα/ χαρισθέντα (see 1.5–9; 2.10, 12; 12.4–7).[245]

Paul has now set the stage for 4.8–13, where he reminds the Corinthians about the nature of his own apostolic lifestyle and preaching that served as the means by which he 'fathered' them through the gospel (4.15; cf. Gal. 4.19). He appears to recall once again that divine event that took place when there was a demonstration of Spirit and power associated with Paul's embodied proclamation of Christ crucified (see 1 Cor. 2.1–5). It is the event that divinely confirmed Paul's gospel and grounds their faith in the power of God (1 Cor. 1.5–8; 2.4–5; cf. Gal. 3.1–5).

h. *Discerning the Kingdom of God that is Power Not Speech (4.8–21)*

Paul concludes this first long section of the letter by associating his own embodied proclamation of the gospel of Christ crucified with the Corinthians' birth 'through the gospel' – in other words, their first experience of new life in Christ Jesus (4.15; cf. 1.21; 2.1–5). In 4.8–21 he describes some of his own conduct with greater specificity. He then calls on the Corinthians to imitate him by conforming their actions to the pattern they saw lived out among them through him (see 4.8–16; cf. Phil. 4.9). Paul once again utilizes the motifs of ethical and spatial dualism to characterize their experiences of new life in God's kingdom as the discernible power of God that operates in connection with Christ-conforming conduct.

In 1 Cor. 4.8–13 Paul characterizes his own apostolic lifestyle in language drawn from a 'this-worldly' perspective (Adams 2000: 124). He is (literally, 'we are') weak (ἀσθενεῖς) and dishonoured (ἄτιμοι),[246] a fool for Christ's sake according to the standards of the world.[247] Paul ironically contrasts his own cruciform lifestyle with that of some of the Corinthians who think they are 'discerning in Christ' (φρόνιμοι ἐν Χριστῷ), 'strong' and 'honoured' as seen through the eyes of the world.[248] Paul understands his apostolic lifestyle as God's cosmic

245. According to Dunn: 'the charism is a function of the member…of the body…the contribution which the individual member makes to the whole' (1998c: 554). This actually seems to be the position of the Corinthians that Paul criticizes in 4.7.

246. With these adjectives in 4.10, Paul anticipates his use of their related nouns in 15.43 to highlight the characteristics of how resurrection from the dead is sown in an earthly body but raised into a heavenly body. See Chapter 3, section 4.e.

247. See also 1.25, 27; 2.3; cf. 8.1–13; Gal. 4.13; 2 Cor. 12.9–10.

248. Brown argues that in 4.8–13 Paul lists the characteristics of the 'wise in Christ' that are very different from the Corinthian ideal (1995: 163).

spectacle to the world, angels, and all humanity (4.9). His life is a theatrical performance of the cross that leads directly to the Corinthians' experience of God's life-giving power, a performance of the gospel of Christ crucified that is a living commentary on the gospel (see Gorman 2001: 367). Paul holds up for imitation his own attempt to conform his actions to Christ's cruciform pattern (see 11.1).[249]

Paul's two uses of ἤδη in 4.8, describing the Corinthians' 'enrichment' (cf. 1.5) and 'satiation', suggest that he thought some of the Corinthians understood their present life in Christ as completely fulfilled.[250] Moreover, his sarcastic assertion that they reigned (ἐβασιλεύσατε) in the world (4.8) implies that some of them were not submitting to the present reign of the risen Lord (see 15.25), who still rules over community life (1.8; 11.32). Employing techniques from the rhetorical form known as the letter of admonition (see 4.14), Paul tries to convey the proper sense of how they should conduct themselves according to Christ's cruciform pattern.[251] Thus, imitation means conforming to a general pattern of behaviour rather than heeding specific precepts or a core of ethical teachings.[252]

Paul thus identifies his primary purpose in writing: seeking to persuade some Corinthians to modify their conduct. While the church members might have innumerable moral guides (μυρίους παιδαγωγοὺς)[253] in Christ, contends Paul, they do not have many 'fathers in Christ' (4.14). Elsewhere, even if he does not use the image of the παιδαγωγός, Paul recognizes the importance of those whose conduct serves as examples for others (see Phil. 3.17). In 1 Cor. 4.14–16 he appears to draw on his Pharisaic tradition. The one who teaches Torah to the child of another parent becomes like a father to that child.[254] Rather than teaching Torah as the pattern for life, however, Paul proclaims Christ's cruciform pattern (cf. 1 Cor. 1.18; 2.2).[255] He encourages them to become his imitators (4.16).[256]

---

249. According to Keck, this passage shows how the ethic of Christian existence appears strange and discontinuous from the ethic of this world (1988: 86).

250. For a discussion of whether this enthusiastic existence was based on their 'realized eschatology' compare Hays (1999: 396–97, including n. 17) with Tuckett (1996: 247–75) and Thiselton (1977–78: 510–26).

251. Cf. R. Collins 1999: 192.

252. Lietzmann 1949: 21–22; contra Belleville 1996: 123; Michaelis 1967: 668–69.

253. For a discussion of the role of the παιδαγωγός as a moral guide in the first century, see N.H. Young 1987: 150–76; R. Collins 1999: 193.

254. R. Collins 1999: 193 (drawing on *b. Sanh.* 19b). The feminist critique of Castelli misses the point of Paul's analogy in these verses (1991a: 100–101). She limits her analysis to the nature of the paternal role in Graeco-Roman society rather than considering Paul's Pharisaic training as the background. She overlooks how Paul uses traditional patriarchal language to recommend conduct that promotes an *anti*-patriarchal status reversal among those who presently enjoy higher status in the Graeco-Roman society. See D. Martin 1990: 142.

255. R. Collins concludes that Paul replaces Torah with the gospel as the means of the generation of life in the child being taught (1999: 193).

256. The characterization that Paul renders of his apostolic lifestyle in 4.8–13 is not capable of direct mimesis within the Corinthian community. Thus, Castelli incorrectly insists that Paul's call to unity and imitation involves the repetition of a 'sameness' that encourages everyone to look like Paul himself (1991b). For similar critiques of Castelli, see Horrell 1999: 323; Thiselton 2000: 371–73.

Like Paul and Christ before him (cf. 12.22–24), the Corinthians must voluntarily accept a low-status evaluation according to the standards of the world by conforming their actions to Christ's cruciform pattern (cf. Gal. 2.19).

Having exhorted them to imitation, Paul says that for this reason he is sending Timothy, a man who is also faithful (πιστός) in the Lord. This characterization does not just refer to Timothy's acceptance of Christ as his Lord (*pace* R. Collins 1999: 200). It describes Timothy as another 'living exemplification of the gospel lifestyle' (Thiselton 2000: 374).[257] Paul sends Timothy 'to instantiate in their presence the flesh-and-blood living out of the gospel of the cross' (Thiselton 2000: 374). Timothy will bring to their minds (ἀναμνήσει) other actions that conform to Christ's cruciform pattern that was first modelled for them by Paul. Timothy will not bring these things to their minds 'by intellectual teaching, but by his own very stance and conduct' (Thiselton 2000: 374). He will illustrate for them again Paul's way of life.[258] This is the way he lives by word and action in every church (1 Cor. 4.17).

The phrase τὰς ὁδούς μου τὰς ἐν Χριστῷ in 4.17 cannot be adequately translated as 'my ways in Christ', since the noun ὁδοί denotes the equivalent to the rabbinic *halakhah* involving ways of walking in the world.[259] The word 'conveys a dimension of *moral standards* which the Greek alone, without its Hebrew-Christian biblical background, would fail to convey' (Thiselton 2000: 374, original emphasis).[260]

Moreover, as another aspect of Paul's ὁδοί ἐν Χριστῷ, this study further suggests that Timothy will address the community practice of spiritual discernment and its grounding in theo-ethical reasoning. Paul has probably already taught them this practice (see 4.17) and modelled it in this letter (see 1.4–9; 2.1–5; cf. 4.8–13). Timothy, too, will focus the Corinthians on this important practice by which they discern demonstrations of Spirit and power that divinely confirm actions that conform to Christ's cruciform pattern. Timothy will remind them of the link between conduct and experience that has been the central focus of the first four chapters of the letter and is the foundation for all that follows.

Paul sends Timothy because in Paul's absence some people have become 'puffed up' (4.18; cf. 4.6). They talk human wisdom rather than living out the wisdom of God manifest in the cruciform pattern of Christ's death (cf. 4.19).[261] Paul threatens to come and 'know by observation' (γνώσομαι),[262] namely to experience, the power rather than the speech of those who are arrogant (4.19–20). Paul's threat accomplishes two things. First, it once again re-emphasizes that the

257. Cf. 7.25; Gal. 2.7; 1 Thess. 2.4.

258. For this characterization of the phrase τὰς ὁδούς, see R. Collins 1999: 200.

259. Thiselton 2000: 374; see also Schrage 1961: 32–33; D.M. Stanley 1959: 859–77; Spencer 1989: 51–61; B. Sanders 1981: 353–63.

260. Cf. Barrett, who concludes that 'Paul's ways in Christ Jesus are moral standards, expressed to some extent in recognized patterns of behaviour which can be taught' (1968: 117).

261. Spencer emphasizes Paul's criticism of mere talk rather than action (1989: 60).

262. For this translation of γνώσομαι, see LSJ, 350. R. Collins (1999: 201) notes that Paul uses the verb 'to know' in its Semitic sense of 'to experience' (cf. 2.2).

focus of spiritual discernment is the demonstration of power manifest in their community experience. Second, it clearly implies that whatever power is being exercised in connection with this talk will be manifestly discernible to Paul (see 1.11–12; 3.3).

The verses in 4.19–20 clearly reflect on the 'awkward tension' between Paul's 'unconcealed use of power as a threat' and the ideal communicative dialogue that Paul has been describing, where all participants are equals in the argumentative discourse through which moral norms are agreed (Horrell 1999: 322). It may be that Paul concludes that if he is going to persuade those who are full, rich, and reigning like kings (4.8), he must exercise blunt power (Horrell 1999: 322). This forceful exercise of verbal power extends into Paul's prophetic assessment of the situation that immediately follows in 5.1–13, possibly even subverting the ideal communicative dialogue by over-emphasizing Paul's own position in the matter.

Drawing on the motif of spatial dualism, Paul also affirms that the kingdom of God is not a matter of speech but of power (4.20).[263] What Paul means by this is that the kingdom of God is the place where God exercises the power that gives new life in connection with Christ-conforming conduct. Indeed, for Paul the kingdom of God represents the locus of 'the power of dynamic action' (G. Johnston 1984: 149) manifest in the world as a present, yet uncompleted, reality.[264]

Paul thus follows the logic he used in the critical argument in 2.1–5. The Corinthians' faith in the power of God is grounded in the demonstration of Spirit and power that took place in association with Paul's embodied proclamation of Christ crucified (cf. Gal. 3.1–5). Paul thus associates the kingdom of God with the discernible manifestations of new life in the community through God's life-giving power (R. Collins 1999: 202). When Paul gets to Corinth, he will seek to know by observation 'what manifests the reality of God-in-Christ and his sovereign deeds' (Thiselton 2000: 377).

In other words, Paul asserts that he will practise spiritual discernment by engaging in theo-ethical reasoning when he arrives in Corinth. He will be looking for life in the χαρίσματα/χαρισθέντα that divinely confirm conduct that faithfully conforms to Christ's cruciform pattern (see 1 Cor. 1.5–8; 2.1–5; 4.1–5). He will distinguish these spiritual experiences manifesting new life from God from the effects wrought by worldly powers associated with the talk about worldly wisdom of those who are 'puffed up'. He will distinguish the embodied proclamation of Christ crucified from speech and conduct that merely conform to the wisdom and standards of the world. Paul thus sets the stage for the letter's transition to 5.1, where he begins to engage in theo-ethical reasoning, modelling the practice of spiritual discernment in the context of specific behavioural issues.

---

263. For Paul's use of the phrase 'kingdom of God', see also Rom. 14.17; 1 Cor. 6.9, 10; 15.24, 50; Gal. 5.21; cf. Eph. 5.5; Col. 1.13; 4.11; 2 Thess. 1.5. Fee correctly concludes that despite its rare occurrence in Paul, his casual use of the phrase in 1 Cor. 4.20 indicates that it was a regular part of his understanding of the gospel (1987: 192); see also Sampley, who concludes the phrase is a commonplace in Paul's moral instruction (1990: 231 n. 19).

264. Fee 1987: 192; see also 1 Cor. 13.8–12.

4. *Summary*

Chapter 2 has attempted to show how Paul consistently engages in theo-ethical reasoning in 1 Corinthians 1–4. It highlights the way Paul the pastoral theologian brings together theology and ethics by interpreting through conduct and speech what God has done and is doing in the world through Jesus Christ. It has been shown that for Paul the revelation of the wisdom and power of God in Jesus Christ establishes three foundational aspects of theo-ethical reasoning. First, in the death of Christ, God made manifest the behavioural standard for the new age: the cruciform pattern of self-giving love for others. Second, in raising Christ from the dead, God demonstrated to the world the power that gives new life after death and divinely confirmed Christ's cruciform pattern as the world's unifying behavioural standard. Third, those who believe in Christ as the wisdom and power of God may also experience new earthly life and the hope of eternal resurrection life after death in God's new age/spatial realm (i.e. God's kingdom in Christ). This takes place through the power of God in connection with conduct that conforms to Christ's cruciform pattern. Chapter 2 has also suggested that Paul's preaching is the means by which he connects his embodied proclamation of Christ crucified with community experiences of new life from God.

Chapter 2 also attempts to show from 1 Corinthians 1–4 that believers must practise spiritual discernment by engaging in theo-ethical reasoning. Throughout the letter, Paul models this practice by pointing the Corinthians to various links between conduct and experience. He reminds them that their faith in the power of God was first grounded in the demonstration of Spirit and power that they experienced in connection with his own embodied proclamation of Christ crucified. Paul also explains the role of the Spirit for understanding the divine gifts of new life associated with Christ-conforming conduct. The community must compare spiritual experiences to be able to distinguish between experiences of the life-giving power of God associated with specific Christ-conforming actions and experiences of worldly power wrought through conduct conforming to worldly standards.

Moreover, it has been shown that Paul applies the motifs of temporal, spatial and ethical dualism to make these contrasts. On the one hand is the new life of salvation in the kingdom of God, experienced in connection with conduct that faithfully conforms to Christ's cruciform pattern. On the other hand is life in 'this age' and 'this world', lived according to the behavioural standards and wisdom of the world that is already undergoing destruction.

Paul has set the stage rhetorically for the remainder of the letter that will now be examined in Chapter 3. The present study will attempt to show how Paul contextually analyses behavioural issues according to theo-ethical reasoning, modelling the practice of spiritual discernment. Paul consistently challenges the Corinthians' failure to act in ways that conform to Christ's cruciform pattern and their failure to practise spiritual discernment in the deliberative assembly. These failures block or impede the revelation of Jesus Christ from taking place. They inhibit the process by which God exercises power to transform each person into the image of Christ and builds the entire community into the social, spiritual body of Christ.

Chapter 3

ENGAGING IN THEO-ETHICAL REASONING: ASSOCIATING EXPERIENCE WITH CONDUCT (1 CORINTHIANS 5.1–16.24)

1. Introduction

This chapter's exegesis of 1 Corinthians 5–16 will show how Paul consistently practises spiritual discernment by engaging in theo-ethical reasoning. He analyses and responds to a variety of behavioural issues inside and outside the church. Paul evaluates whether various community experiences suggest divine confirmation of Christ-conforming conduct or divine judgment on actions that conform to the standards of the world. Further, he emphasizes community edification as the goal of Christ-conforming conduct. We argue that in the practice of spiritual discernment this becomes the criterion for identifying community experiences of God's life-giving power associated with Christ-conforming behaviour.

Paul assesses the conduct of church members as participants in the broader culture in 1 Cor. 5.1–11.1. This is reviewed in Chapter 3, section 2. In 11.2–14.40 he takes up concerns about particular actions inside the deliberative assembly (ἐκκλησία). These are examined in Chapter 3, section 3, which also highlights the dialogical nature of the practice of spiritual discernment described in 2.1–16. The letter reaches its zenith in 1 Corinthians 15, where Paul links conduct conforming to Christ's cruciform pattern with the unfolding transformation of the physical body into the spiritual body through the power of God, a process that culminates in resurrection life after death (Chapter 3, section 4). Paul concludes the letter in 1 Corinthians 16 just as he began it. He exhorts church members to conform to Christ's cruciform pattern and to call on the name of the Lord in their practice of spiritual discernment (Chapter 3, section 5). As he did in 1.4–9, Paul reminds the Corinthians that this is a discipline through which the risen Lord will continue to guide them through the Spirit and keep them blameless in the presence of God and the risen Lord. Chapter 3 closes with a short summary in section 6.

2. Engaging in Theo-Ethical Reasoning: Evaluating Actions Taken Outside the Church (5.1–11.1)

a. Evaluating a Clear-Cut Issue from Paul's Perspective (5.1–13)

Paul begins his reflective assessment of the links between specific experiences and practices in 5.1–13. He acknowledges the important reality that Christians

84   *Looking for Life*

must continue to live in relationships with the sinful inhabitants of 'this world', since otherwise believers would have to go out of the world (5.10). For the present time, they must leave to God the judgment of those outside the church, while exercising their responsibility to judge the conduct of those inside the community (5.12–13).

More specifically, Paul challenges an extreme example of πορνεία that was even unacceptable according to first-century social standards and values (5.1).[1] Nevertheless, Paul's *primary* concern is not the offender's act of sin, but that other community members have become puffed up (5.2).[2] This conclusion, grounded in community experience, is supported by: (1) Paul's emphatic placement of the plural ὑμεῖς in 5.2; (2) his re-emphasis of the point in 5.6; and (3) the fact that after 5.1 he never again mentions the specific offence.[3] Paul underscores the church's own error in judgment based on his evaluation of the experience of the whole community.[4] This breakdown in community discernment allows the offensive conduct to continue as a destructive force within the community.

Indeed, the compound subjects of the verb συναχθέντων in 5.4 seem to point toward the community practice of spiritual discernment that should be taking place in the deliberative assembly.[5] Paul is present in that process by his spirit communicated primarily through his letter[6] and, possibly, through Timothy's presence with them (see 4.17).[7] In this way Paul offers his own prophetic word on the matter as part of the dialogical community practice that should be evaluating this controversial action being taken 'in the name of the Lord Jesus'.[8] Indeed, this latter phrase further confirms what this study consistently argues: believers' should seek to have their actions conform to Christ's cruciform pattern. They must conform themselves to his self-giving nature or character that constitutes his 'name'.[9] Thus, any action taken or word spoken by a believer should be done 'in the name of the Lord Jesus'.

While some commentators characterize Paul's judgment in this situation as a binding exercise of apostolic authority,[10] he seems rather to be 'at great pains to proceed with the Corinthian assembly' (Horsley 1998: 80).[11] In fact Paul actually qualifies his judgment in 5.3 through his use of the key phrase 'as one who is

1. See Fee 1987: 200 n. 24; Horsley 1998: 79.
2. Roetzel 1972: 123; *pace* Fee 1987: 202 n. 28; cf. 4.19; 8.1.
3. For this latter observation, see Minear 1983: 343; cf. Rosner 1992b: 471.
4. See Conzelmann 1975: 96; Gorman 2001: 229; Fee 1987: 197; Horsley 1998: 79; Roetzel 1972: 118; M. Mitchell 1991: 112–16; Meeks 1983: 130; *pace* Barrett 1968: 127.
5. Murphy-O'Connor correctly translates the phrase: 'when you and my spirit are gathered together with the power of the Lord Jesus' (1977a: 241); cf. Käsemann 1969b: 70; Horsley 1998: 80; see also 14.23–26, 29–32.
6. See Barrett 1968: 124; Fee 1987: 205.
7. See B. Dodd 1999: 76.
8. For this translation of 5.3b–5.4a, see Horsley 1998: 79; A.Y. Collins 1980: 253; Murphy-O'Connor 1977a: 240–41; cf. Sampley 1991b: 68; Meeks 1993b: 37–58.
9. See 1.2; cf. 1.10, 13; 15. This is discussed in Chapter 3, 2.a above.
10. See, e.g., Käsemann 1969b: 70–71; Conzelmann 1975: 97; Fee 1987: 206; Mitchell 1991: 229; Horsley 1998: 80.
11. See also Murphy-O'Connor 1977a: 244.

present' (ὡς παρών) in the deliberative assembly. This phrase would be super-fluous *if* Paul's apostolic authority *solely* empowered him to render a final judg-ment in the matter.[12]

Thus, we suggest that he gives his own *participatory* rather than conclusive prophetic assessment of the worldliness of the offending conduct. As with any prophetic utterance, Paul's judgment must be evaluated along with others in the deliberative assembly (see 14.30, 32).[13] Paul thereby models the prophecy that should be taking place.[14] He encourages the Corinthians to conclude for them-selves that the offender must be expelled (5.5, 7, 13) so that the Spirit sent from God might be saved in the day of the Lord (5.5).[15]

Paul thus models a reasoning process that he thinks will enable the community to discern what action should be taken, to understand why, and to assume respon-sibility for correcting the situation (Pascuzzi 1997: 120–21). When the commu-nity practices spiritual discernment by engaging in theo-ethical reasoning, all positions on the matter must be considered (cf. 9.3; 14.29–32). Paul thus illus-trates a particular discourse that should build moral confidence in the community, as all participants become better moral agents through their involvement in the community dialogue (see Meeks 1988: 17, 19–21, 28).

b. *Disputes Resolved According to One Behavioural Standard (6.1–11)*
In the context of a dispute between community members in 6.1–11, Paul once again distinguishes the standards for conduct outside the church from the norm associated with the character and nature of Jesus Christ (i.e. his 'name'). As in 5.1–13, Paul criticizes not only the particular conduct of the church members, but also the failure of the community to exercise properly its community judgment responsibility.[16] His real concern is the very existence of the lawsuit itself (6.7). This situation suggests not only a behavioural failure of church members to con-form to Christ's cruciform pattern (see Gorman 2001: 230), but also another breakdown in the community practice of spiritual discernment.

Paul is incredulous that the Corinthians are acting as if they are unworthy to make the smallest present decision involving the affairs of daily life (6.2–3). The two insiders have turned over their dispute to be judged by those outside the church who are unrighteous (ἄδικοι) or have no faith (ἄπιστοι). According to

12. Paul also rejects such authority in 2 Cor. 1.24.
13. Stowers correctly notes the persuasive, rather than authoritative, approach taken by Paul in his admonition (1990: 262). For how the prophetic debate might unfold in the deliberative assembly and turn out contrary to the thrust of Paul's position, see Wolter 2003.
14. Cf. B. Dodd 1999: 75.
15. *Pace* Roetzel, who concludes that it is the man's spirit that will be saved (1972: 123). In Gal. 3.5, 1 Thess. 4.1–8 and 5.19, Paul closely links God's supply of the Spirit with human conduct that is pleasing to God.
16. For the conclusion that it was the 'strong' at Corinth (measured by social and class signifi-cance) who were making use of the courts to settle their differences, see B. Winter 1991: 559–72; Chow 1992: 123–41; cf. Theissen 1982: 97. D. Martin concludes that it was the higher-status Corin-thian Christians taking the lower-status members to court (1995: 77). The present study does not require resolution of this issue.

Paul the matter should be resolved by those in the church who have been set apart (ἅγιοι) in Christ Jesus (6.1; cf. 1.2, 10, 13, 15). In this way the conduct of every member will be evaluated equally[17] pursuant to a single behavioural norm. Paul's distinction thus appears to reflect his concern that the outsiders will adjudicate the matter according to the world's behavioural standards (cf. 1.18–25).[18]

Paul's use of ἄπιστος is unique to the Corinthian correspondence, highlighting further its extensive use in this particular letter.[19] There are clear connections between the ἄπιστοι referenced in 6.1–8, Paul's use of πίστις in 2.4–5, and the context of the verb πιστεύω in 1.21 and 3.5.[20] They suggest that the ἄπιστοι are those who have not yet known God (cf. 15.34). They have not yet experienced the demonstration of Spirit and power that grounds faith in the power of God and is connected with the embodied proclamation of Christ crucified (see 2.1–5).

With regard to the community, Paul inquires sarcastically in 6.5 whether there is no one among them who is wise enough and empowered to distinguish (διακρῖναι) the conduct of its members (cf. 4.10).[21] He thus challenges the community failure to measure these specific actions against the standard of Christ's cruciform pattern as part of their reasoned practice of spiritual discernment.[22]

Having rebuked the community for its collective failure, Paul models how to reflect on the conduct of the individuals and measure it against the new standard of cruciformity. He finds that the one seeking recompense was unable to be injured or defrauded without seeking recourse in the courts (6.7). He was deprived of an opportunity to proclaim the cross in the context of his own situation.[23] Similarly, Paul chastises the perpetrator of the injury and fraud in 6.8. He uses the same verbs from 6.7 in the active voice to imply that such conduct, especially towards a community member, does not conform to Christ's cruciform pattern.

In 6.9–11 Paul turns to another important aspect of the problem, challenging their 'eschatological certainty' that they will inherit the kingdom of God.[24] He cautions them not to be led astray by those who promote, condone or engage in conduct that conforms merely to worldly standards (6.9; cf. 15.33; Gal. 6.7). The use of the logical future indicative κληρονομήσουσιν in 1 Cor. 6.10 (see

---

17. Cf. D. Martin 1995: 78; see also A. Clarke 1993: 59–72; Chow 1992: 123–41.

18. Barclay concludes that the 'unbeliever' represents the 'world' which makes them inappropriate judges of the affairs of believers (1992: 59 n. 15). Fee argues that the pagan judges are the ones whose values and judgments the church has rejected by its adoption of different standards (1987: 236). Roetzel, on the other hand, thinks that Paul does not object to the lower ethical standards of the heathen courts, but only to the church's moral and theological failure (1972: 126). This is an unduly limited conclusion.

19. See 7.12–15; 10.27; 14.22–24; cf. 2 Cor. 4.4; 6.14, 15.

20. Cf. 14.22; 15.2, 11.

21. Cf. Barrett, who finds that in connection with 11.29 the verb διακρίνω means to 'mark one out as different from others' (1968: 274).

22. Thiselton correctly concludes that '[t]he give-and-take of subjecting self-interest and personal desire to a consensus among capable people of integrity…is part and parcel of respecting the corporate self-discipline and discernment of the Other-than-self, or other than a closely like-minded group' (2000: 435). Cf. Fee 1987: 237.

23. Gorman 2001: 230; cf. Fee 1987: 241; Thiselton 2000: 437.

24. Roetzel 1972: 129; cf. 3.18; 8.2; 10.12.

Thiselton 2000: 439) reflects Paul's conviction that those who practise evil actions cannot inherit the kingdom of God, either now or in the future.

The logic of Paul's theo-ethical reasoning that lies beneath the surface of these arguments may now be identified. Believers who anticipate experiencing new life in God's kingdom must conform their actions to Christ's cruciform pattern and practise spiritual discernment. They must reason together to evaluate their experiences and discern how they are linked to specific actions. This is a necessity if they are to hold one another accountable for conforming to Christ's cruciform pattern.[25] Their failure to distinguish offensive action and to hold one another accountable to this cruciform standard leads to further experiences of community conflict.

c. *Integrating Theology and Ethics in the Body (6.12–20)*
Paul linked life in God's kingdom with individual behaviour and community discernment practices in 6.1–11. He then takes up both in the context of the body (σῶμα), a term used eight times in 6.12–20. Paul argues against some members of the community who appear to be acting as if bodily relationships are no longer meaningful to their new life in Christ (Doughty 1975: 67). This section demonstrates once again that for Paul there is an 'inseparability of Christian identity and Christian lifestyle, or of theology and ethics' (Thiselton 2000: 458).

In 6.12 Paul addresses what appears to be a Corinthian behavioural slogan (πάντα μοι ἔξεστιν).[26] Rather than denying its applicability, he qualifies it by adding that, while lawful, all actions may not prove advantageous (συμφέρει). He thereby introduces the theme of 'advantage' by appealing to the self-interest of the individual as a major criterion of decision-making about specific conduct.[27] Paul immediately begins to re-define the 'advantage', however, directing the Corinthians away from their highly individualistic approach for discerning what conduct is advantageous.[28] Building on 5.1–6.11, he highlights that individual bodily actions may prove meaningful by virtue of their *destructive* effects on other community members and the larger social body (see also 8.1–13; 10.1–13; 11.17–34).

Emphasizing that the body is 'for the Lord and the Lord for the body' (6.13), Paul implies two things. First, serving the Lord with one's individual body means conforming one's actions to Christ's cruciform pattern. Second, the Lord serves

25. By way of encouragement in 6.11, Paul reminds them that, despite their past behavioural failures, they were nonetheless washed, sanctified and justified in the name of the Lord Jesus Christ and by the Spirit of God. They know where and how to turn for restoration to life in the kingdom.

26. For the conclusion that this is a Corinthian slogan, see Mitchell 1991: 35–36; Horrell 1996: 122; Conzelmann 1975: 108. P. Marshall, citing Dio Chrysostum (*Diss.* 62.3; 3.10), points out that this phrase not only characterizes rulers obsessed with their power and rights but also is a familiar assertion from people of rank and status about their independence from those who would impinge on their freedom (1987: 278); see also D. Martin 1995: 72.

27. Mitchell 1991: 33, 35. Mitchell further notes that Paul uses a variety of words to exploit this theme (1991: 33 n. 57). See, e.g., 7.35; 9.18, 20; 10.23, 24, 33; 12.7; 13.3, 5; 14.6; 15.32, 58.

28. As part of this strategy, Paul later employs οἰκοδομέω and οἰκοδομή to characterize the new criterion for discerning what represents the community 'advantage'. See 8.1; 14.3–5, 12, 17, 26.

the body by leading the church's collective behavioural discernment practice (see 1.8; 4.4–5). Indeed, the one who is joined to the Lord is one Spirit (6.17; cf. 12.13; 15.45; 2 Cor. 3.18).[29] By this Paul means that the same Lord (1 Cor. 12.5) who has become the life-giving Spirit (see 15.45; cf. 2 Cor. 3.18) sent from God (1 Cor. 2.12) continues to lead believers who practise spiritual discernment. By means of the Spirit, the risen Lord helps believers identify experiences of new life associated with Christ-conforming conduct.[30]

Indeed, says Paul in 6.15, believers' bodies (σώματα) are the limbs and organs of Christ (Thiselton 2000: 465). But when one of these limbs and organs is joined (κολλώμενος) to a prostitute through the practice of sexual immorality, that person becomes one body and one flesh with the prostitute (6.16). More importantly, such conduct also lifts out (ἄρας) from the realm of Christ other limbs and organs, a thought Paul cannot bear to endure (6.15). On the other hand, by using the same present participle κολλώμενος in 6.17, Paul seems to suggest that being joined to the Lord continues to take place when believers' actions conform to Christ's cruciform pattern.

According to the logic of the entire argument, having already raised the Lord, God will also raise 'us' (i.e. the corporate body) by means of that same power (6.14). In other words, God will raise the 'single in-Christ corporeity, for whom "bodily" existence matters'.[31] Thus, if one expects to be raised in the end at the time of the completion (see 1.8), one must be a member of this body of Christ rather than a worldly body. Believers do this by following the same Spirit sent from God, who leads them as they seek to conform their actions to Christ's cruciform pattern.

In these verses Paul's argument 'depends on the radical separation of Christ's body from the cosmos, in an apocalyptic, ethical dualism' in which Christ is opposed to 'this world' (D. Martin 1995: 176). Instead of placing the human will or soul on one side and food and the body on the other, Paul sets πορνεία (as representative of the estranged cosmos) in opposition to God, Jesus Christ, and believers in their earthly existence (D. Martin 1995: 176). For Paul, the human act of sexual immorality contradicts the Lord's reign over the individual body that takes place through Christ-conforming conduct. Such action lifts a person out of the body of Christ and returns that person to the world (cf. Gal. 1.4; 5.4). The person is taken back into the domain of the 'not-Christ' (Thiselton 2000: 473), with terrible consequences for the individual and the community.[32]

Paul closes this complex argument in 1 Cor. 6.19–20. He suggests that the individual human body has no freedom or independent ontological status of its own,

---

29. D. Martin asserts that for Paul 'the individual body has no independent ontological status… [t]he prostitute's being is defined by her status as a representative of the cosmos; the Christian man's being is defined by his participation in the body of Christ' (1995: 176).

30. See 1.4–9; 2.1–5, 12–16; 3.16–17; 4.1–5; 12.4–13; cf. 1.5–8; 15.34, 58; Phil. 3.10.

31. Thiselton 2000: 464. According to Thiselton, Paul's logic of bodily resurrection is expounded in detail in 15.12–58 and involves two principles of bodily resurrection: there is both a continuity of identity and a transformation of mode of being (2000: 463–64).

32. Cf. 1 Cor. 10.1–12; 11.30; J.A.T. Robinson 1952: 80 n. 1.

but is a microcosm of a larger social body (D. Martin 1995: 178). As individuals bought with a price (6.20), believers become like slaves under Roman law. They are now servants of the one Lord Jesus Christ (cf. 4.1; 12.5). They must conform their actions to his cruciform pattern of self-giving love for others if they expect to continue experiencing new life from God in the community (see 12.4–7). They do not have an independent existence, but are participants in the larger, corporate body of Christ of which they are merely members.[33]

Echoing 3.16–17, where the community rather than the individual body is clearly in view, Paul reminds them in 6.19 that their body (singular) is a temple of the one Holy Spirit that is 'among them'. The phrase ἐν ὑμῖν suggests that Paul is referring to the single *spiritual* body that is the corporate body of Christ where the Spirit dwells (see 15.44).[34] We contend that Paul is referring to the church, made up of many individual bodies of its members (6.15) who are each joined to the Lord and to one another by their Christ-conforming actions. The logic of Paul's argument is that the deliberative assembly (ἐκκλησία) is the spiritual body where the one Spirit dwells among them (see also 3.16). In that body the members share the behavioural guidance of the risen Lord who is now the one life-giving Spirit that leads them in their community practice of spiritual discernment (cf. 15.45; 1.8; 2 Cor. 3.18). This Spirit leads those who practise spiritual discernment to recognize the manifestations of God's life-giving power working in connection with divinely confirmed conduct that conforms to Christ's cruciform pattern.[35]

Consequently, in 1 Cor. 6.20, Paul closes with an exhortation to glorify (δοξ-άσατε) God in their body. Paul's use of the plural σώματα in 6.15 to refer to the many individual bodies who make up the one larger body accentuates his use of the singular σώματι in 6.20. This probably reflects Paul's conviction that, both individually and collectively[36] through their interpersonal conduct, the Corinthians manifest to the world their understanding of the character and nature of God revealed in Jesus Christ.

In this short but important section, Paul stresses that bodily conduct is meaningful for the individual and the community. He insists that the Corinthians consider the impact of their individual actions on others as he redefines what constitutes the 'advantage' for purposes of discerning appropriate conduct. He alludes again to the important community practice of spiritual discernment, whereby the community should be identifying the detrimental effects on the corporate spiritual body of worldly behaviour by individual members of that body. Rather, as the social body where the Spirit dwells, they must glorify God collectively. They do so by practising spiritual discernment together, evaluating how they will continue being joined to the Lord through individual actions that

33. D. Martin 1995: 178; see 12.12–26.
34. As discussed above in Chapter 2, section 2.b, Paul consistently uses the phrase ἐν ὑμῖν throughout the letter to refer to interpersonal relationships in the community.
35. See 1.4–9; 2.1–5, 12; 12.4–7, 11, 13.
36. According to Mitchell, σώμα in 6.20 can refer to both the individual body and the communal body of Christ (1991: 120 n. 338). Cf. Wire 1990: 77; Glancy 1998: 495 n. 62.

conform to Christ's cruciform pattern. Thus, as they engage in theo-ethical reasoning, Paul and his churches combine what are known in contemporary terminology as theology and ethics.

d. *Discerning Faithful Conduct is Situational (7.1–40)*

In 1 Corinthians 7 Paul presents a notable example of how he applies theo-ethical
reasoning to concrete situations. He gives his opinions on matters of conduct
involving marital relations about which the Corinthians made inquiry.[37] Far from
advocating that rational deliberation be subordinated to blind faith, divine com-
mands, or even to his own authoritative leadership, Paul models a dialogical
process of free, cooperative, and openly participatory moral deliberation.[38]

First, in 7.1–2, Paul causally links the practice of abstinence with the sexual
indiscretions taking place.[39] He thereby associates specific conduct with community experience and recommends that the practice be curtailed.

Second, in 7.17–24, where Paul grounds his paraenesis to the married (7.1–16)
and to the unmarried (7.25–40),[40] the language of 'calling' dominates (eight times
in eight verses). Along with Paul's earlier uses of the various forms of 'call' in
1.1, 2, 9, 24, and 26–30, this suggests that the Corinthians had not grasped what
he meant by the concept of 'call', an important theme of the letter (Bassler 1993:
15). Thus, Paul exhorts the Corinthians each to walk (περι πατείτω) 'as God has
called' them (7.17). He refers to God's act of calling each person by exercising
life-giving power in connection with that person's specific Christ-conforming
service.[41] Paul's doubling of ἕκαστος in 7.17 and its recurrence as the subject of
the framework sentences in this section (vv. 17, 20, 24) emphasize both the individual character of the 'call' and the diverse nature of the social settings in which
it takes place (Fee 1987: 310 n. 17).

Third, addressing unmarried community members, he offers his own opinion
(γνώμην) in 7.25 and 7.40 concerning conduct that he *anticipates* will please
God in the particular circumstances (cf. 1.10).[42] As in 5.1–13 Paul does not
attempt to control the outcome by means of a coercive authoritarian decree. He
engages in dialogical persuasion, offering warrants for his opinions and affirming
that he has been mercifully found to be faithful by the Lord (7.25).[43] Indeed, he

---

37. For this latter conclusion grounded in Paul's use of the introductory phrase περὶ δὲ ὧν
ἐγράψατε, see Horrell 1996: 90; Dunn 1995: 54; cf. Mitchell 1989: 229–56. See also 7.25; 8.1; 12.1;
16.1, 12.

38. For this general conclusion not tied to 1 Corinthians 7, see Stowers 1990: 266; Meeks 1988:
17; Lategan 1990: 318, 326–27.

39. See Fee 1987: 267–71, 277–79.

40. R. Collins 1999: 274.

41. See 12.5–6; Thiselton 2000: 548–49; cf. Rom. 8.29–30; Gal. 1.15.

42. In connection with 1 Cor. 14.1–40 (Chapter 3, section 3.d), it will be argued that prophecy for
Paul included a concern for the future as focused on the consequences of present action. Thus,
prophecy involves the way that believers imaginatively envisage future actions that may conform to
Christ's cruciform pattern, with the expectation that the Spirit will illuminate experiences of new life
in connection with such conduct.

43. See also 4.1, 5, 17; cf. Rom. 15.18–19; 1 Cor. 9.1–2; 2 Cor. 3.2; 12.6–7; Gal. 2.7–8; Phil. 4.9;
1 Thess. 2.4.

thinks he has the Spirit of God (7.40). Paul thus attributes his confident opinion about the future consequences of particular behaviour to the guidance of the Spirit, alluding to the practice of spiritual discernment. He thereby expresses confidence but not certainty about his opinion.[44] This segues into the following verses in 8.1–13, where he challenges some Corinthians who are acting on the basis of a certainty about their own knowledge of God and thereby destroying community life.

Finally, in 7.29–35, Paul intensifies his insistence that the community adopt a more apocalyptic perspective on their life in the world (see Adams 2000: 131). The enigmatic sentences in 7.29 and 7.31b emphasize that the once distant, future new age has been brought temporally forward and spatially nearer by the death, resurrection and present reign of the risen Lord.[45] The future is now in plain view (Fee 1987: 339). God has compressed the time (ὁ καιρὸς συνεσταλμένος ἐςοτίν) and brought forward the future into the present. According to Paul, the Spirit guides those who engage in theo-ethical reasoning, enabling them to recognize these temporary and partial experiences of the new life of the future (cf. 2.10, 12; 13.8–12) associated with Christ-conforming conduct.[46] In these *present* experiences of new life, believers identify where and how God is working to bring about both historical and cosmic transformation.[47]

The five ὡς μὴ clauses in 7.29b–31 illustrate the apocalyptic context. Paul encourages every member of the community to be more conscious about acting in ways that do not conform to human, worldly standards, that is, to the σχῆμα of this world.[48] This does not mean, however, that Paul calls for the renunciation of worldly relationships.[49] Instead, he criticizes the Corinthians' high degree of commitment to the standards of the present world and their participation in the surrounding culture *on those terms* (see Adams 2000: 136). By implication Paul summons them to reflect on their experience and conduct in order to discern which actions prove faithful because they manifest the divine fruitfulness that confirms that they are pleasing to the Lord as they conform to his cruciform pattern. In this way believers conform their actions to the revelation of God in the death and resurrection of Jesus Christ. This is the essence of Paul's 'apocalyptic ethics' rightly understood.

---

44. *Pace* Furnish, who argues that in 7.25 and 7.40 Paul invokes only his 'apostolic authority' as identified in 1.1 (1999: 23); cf. Gorman 2001: 297. See now Schütz 1975.

45. Cf. Fee 1987: 339; J.T. Sanders 1986: 63, 66.

46. According to Brown, Paul's 'apocalyptic ethics' are about: (1) 'both perception and action, both assurance of the power of God's reign now and active hope for its culmination in the future'; and (2) about being 'drawn into freedom's orb by the revelation of the new creation and then, despite every conventional claim to the contrary to live the freedom one sees' (1995: 168–69).

47. See Schrage 1995: 176. Transformation is not inconsistent with believing that the present form of the world as it exists will end at some future time. See, e.g., Conzelmann 1975: 134; Adams 2000: 135; Fee 1987: 342 n. 23.

48. See Doughty 1975: 70; Adams 2000: 131.

49. Doughty 1975: 71; *pace* Dunn, who concludes that 'earthly ties should now be disregarded' (1998c: 311).

e. *Acquiring Knowledge: A Process That Requires Practising Love and Reflecting on Experience (8.1–13)*
In 8.1–11.1 Paul considers a number of complicating variables that make eating food sacrificed to idols an issue 'open to a broad range of valid interpretations by individual believers' (D. Newton 1998: 305). Rather than trying to arrive at a clear, simple rule, Paul seeks to let all legitimate voices be heard. He encourages even the most vociferous speaker to become a *listener* participating in a communal dialogue through which all appropriate Christian action must be discerned (see Meeks 1988: 19–20).

Framing this entire discussion are two important passages that illuminate theo-ethical reasoning (8.1–13; 10.23–11.1). Both emphasize Christ's cruciform pattern of self-giving love for others as the new behavioural standard for experiencing life in God's new age/spatial realm in Christ. In 8.1–13 Paul attempts to moderate the Corinthians' enthusiasm for knowledge. He cautions them that the acquisition of knowledge is a process that unfolds over time as the community consistently reflects on the connections between experience and conduct. Continuing a theme addressed in 6.12–20, Paul redefines the 'advantage' in 10.23–11.1. He asserts that community rather than individual edification represents the new criterion for discerning advantageous conduct (see Gorman 2001: 227–28). The logic underlying these two framing passages suggests that over time knowledge of God arises from the connections made between acts of cruciform love and community experiences of new life characterized as edification.[50]

The section opens with Paul quoting a Corinthian phrase in 8.1,[51] acknowledging that all people possess knowledge. Some Corinthians, however, were apparently using their knowledge that there is only one true God (8.4) to justify their freedom to eat food sacrificed to idols at cultic events. As in 5.1–6.11, these actions were being taken without concern for their impact on other community members. The problem arises, says Paul, because not all people in the church possess this particular γνῶσις (8.7). By following the example of the ones who claim to have a certainty of knowledge about eating the food sacrificed to idols (8.10), other believers (who are less certain about this theological principle) are defiling and destroying themselves (8.7, 11).

In response Paul begins to redefine knowledge of God as a process inextricably bound to the active practice of love (8.2–3).[52] He cautions them in 8.1 that

---

50. The long passage at 8.1–11.1 has been the subject of close scrutiny in recent monographs and articles. Gardner (1994) investigates the section as part of his discussion about the function of the gift of the Spirit called γνῶσις. Horrell (1996) addresses the idol food issues in the larger context of challenging Theissen's characterization of Paul's social ethics as 'love patriarchalism'. Horrell further focuses on Paul's preference for 'christological praxis' (i.e. cruciform conduct) over 'theological principles' in 1 Corinthians 8–10 (1997a: 83–114). D. Newton (1998) reviews the Graeco-Roman background for a variety of cultic practices and feasts celebrating gods in Corinth and its impact on the Corinthian controversy. Cheung (1999) assesses the Jewish background of idolatry in the context of Paul's approach in 1 Corinthians 8–10 and the church's interpretation of Paul on the same issue in the 200 years after he wrote to Corinth.

51. Thiselton 2000: 620; cf. R. Collins 1999: 309.

52. Cf. Thiselton 2000: 624; Héring 1962: 67; D. Newton 1998: 276.

knowledge puffs up while love builds up (οἰκοδομεῖ).[53] The perfect infinitive ἐγνωκέναι (8.2) corrects the claim by some to possess knowledge of God as the product of a *completed* process (see also 13.12).[54] The ingressive aorist ἔγνω (8.2) indicates that the ones claiming to possess knowledge of God have only begun to know and understand what they are claiming.[55] The aorist infinitive γνῶναι that follows καθὼς δεῖ completes the contrast. It is necessary to differentiate between the triumphant claim to possess definitive knowledge of God and the Christian process of coming to know God as one is known by God.[56]

Thus, as against those who prefer a life guided by the certainty of such knowledge rather than by practising love (see Gorman 2001: 232), Paul challenges the manner by which their knowledge was acquired (Stowers 1990: 284). A person must actually practise love to participate in the process of coming to know God. Such knowledge only occurs as one is known by God through Christ-conforming acts of love (see 8.3; cf. 13.12; 15.34; Gal. 4.6–9).[57]

This study suggests that for Paul this process of acquiring knowledge of God takes place in the community practice of spiritual discernment, a position identified during our discussion of 1 Cor. 2.1–16. There, Paul reviewed the practice of spiritual discernment, reminding the Corinthians that no one has known (ἔγνωκεν) the 'things of God' except the Spirit of God (2.11). According to Paul's logic, the 'things of God' are the experiences of new life revealed by the Spirit (2.12) – those demonstrations of Spirit and power occurring in connection with the embodied proclamation of Christ crucified (see 2.1–5). Conversely, the ψυχικός person is unable to receive and know (γνῶναι) these 'things of God' because this person refuses to practise spiritual discernment (2.14). Only those who think, reason and act with the mind of Christ have the potential to know the mind of the Lord (2.16).[58] Thus, knowledge acquired in the absence of practising love and spiritual discernment is immature knowledge (see 13.8–12). This serves as an inadequate basis for autonomous action.[59]

53. Paul continues his attack on those who are 'puffed up' that began earlier in the letter (see 4.6, 18, 19; 5.2; cf. 13.4; Col. 2.18).

54. Cf. Héring 1962: 67; Thiselton 2000: 624.

55. Cf. Thiselton 2000: 624; Héring 1962: 67 ('you are not even at the beginning of knowledge').

56. Cf. Thiselton 2000: 624. In support of this textual version of 8.3, see R. Collins 1999: 312; Schrage 1995: 233–34, including n. 131; *pace* Fee 1987: 364 n. 26; Horrell 1997a: 86 n. 14; Horsley 1998: 118; Thiselton 2000: 625.

57. Cf. Horrell, who suggests that true knowledge is actually connected with those who love; it is a love informed and shaped by the pattern and example of Christ (1997a: 87). Similarly, D. Newton finds that ' "[l]ove" and "knowledge" go hand-in-hand and are inextricably intertwined'; thus, love rather than knowledge is the sole basis for true Christian ethics and behaviour according to 8.1–3 (1998: 277).

58. Phil. 2.2–8 clearly indicates that having the same perspective/mindset as Christ involves integrated thinking and acting.

59. Holladay concludes that love is the sole prerequisite for participating in the divine mystery (1990: 94). It must be added, however, that believers come to know God by practising spiritual discernment, as they associate acts of cruciform love with their experiences of new life through the power of God.

Paul also introduces the important verb οἰκοδομέω in 8.1. The concept of community edification is a central component of theo-ethical reasoning and plays an important role in the dialogical practice of spiritual discernment. For Paul community edification is the criterion by which church members evaluate their community experience.[60] According to Paul's reasoning, God builds up the community through acts of cruciform love, defined as acts that seek the advantage of others rather than self-gratification.[61] This community edification becomes the *discernible* goal of the practice of love. Indeed, Paul later exhorts the Corinthians to seek the edification (οἰκοδομὴν) of the deliberative assembly rather than the individual (14.12), taking every action so that the church might be built up (οἰκοδομὴν) by each act (14.26).

The logic underlying the entire argument suggests that believers are known by God when they practise Christ-conforming love. They come to know God by spiritually discerning the demonstrations of Spirit and power associated with these Christ-conforming acts of love. Paul thus advocates acts of cruciform love as the antidote to the problems arising from eating idol meat.[62]

Paul's unusual reference to God and Christ in 8.5–6 also illuminates theo-ethical reasoning.[63] Paul places together God and Christ, creation and redemption, in a way that is uniquely Pauline.[64] He affirms that God is the source of all existence (cf. 3.23), meaning that everything derives its life from the power of God. The preposition διά appears twice in 8.6, thereby attributing to Christ a mediating function.[65] Through Christ, believers are being newly created by God (cf. Col. 1.16). The preceding emphasis on acts of love conveys Paul's conviction that it is through specific actions conforming to Christ's cruciform pattern of self-giving love for others that God is now creating life anew among those who inhabit God's new age/spatial realm in Christ.

Having identified the behavioural norm of cruciform love and the discernment criterion of community edification, Paul essentially exhorts the Corinthians to practise spiritual discernment in connection with the consumption of meat sacrificed to idols. The imperative βλέπετε (1 Cor. 8.9) once again invites church members to reflect on their experience and conduct. They must discern from that experience whether their actions are adversely affecting others in the community. Paul does not want the ἐξουσία that allows them to choose between specific actions (cf. 11.19) to be grounded solely in the certainty of their knowledge about God, since it is also creating a 'stumbling block' for others (8.9).[66] Indeed, his

60. According to L.T. Johnson, 'Paul's understanding of edification provides the church with a formal criterion for discernment' (1996: 112).

61. See 6.12–20; 10.23, 24, 33; 14.4.

62. See Horrell 1997a: 91; Gorman 2001: 232; cf. Thiselton 2000: 638; Horsley 1998: 124.

63. For Dunn these references to God are 'fascinating and at times puzzling' (1998c: 36) because he has not focused on the logic of theo-ethical reasoning.

64. For the possibility that 8.6 is some type of pre-Pauline creedal formula, see Conzelmann 1975: 144 n. 38; cf. Fee 1987: 373–74.

65. R. Collins 1999: 315, 320; Langkammer 1970–71: 197; Horsley 1998: 120.

66. In Rom. 14.1–23 Paul similarly addresses and responds to the issue of how eating particular foods becomes a 'stumbling block' for others.

ironic question in 8.10 suggests to those with such knowledge that their conduct will build up or embolden (οἰκοδομηθήσεται) others to eat the food. As a result the others stumble in their own walks. They miss the experience of new life through the power of God that works in connection with the Christ-conforming actions of others (see 8.13; cf. 1.4–9; 2.1–5).[67] As in 5.1–6.20, Paul stresses the adverse effects of one community member's conduct on the conduct and faith of another.[68]

As Paul models spiritual discernment by engaging in theo-ethical reasoning, he reasons his way toward a solution to the particular behavioural issue in question. Acting on the knowledge that food may be a stumbling block to others means choosing not to exercise one's own ἐξουσία if it causes someone else to stumble. The 'sin against Christ' (8.12) is not eating the idol meat. Rather, it denotes a relational concern – causing a fellow believer to stumble (Horrell 1999: 323).

The logic of the argument points to the necessity for community dialogue. Every person must be heard so that the group becomes aware of one person's stumbling block. This allows the entire community to envision the contours of appropriate cruciform behaviour for the future. Effectively, Paul tells the Corinthians that a moral decision cannot be made by the individual in isolation, but only in the context of community patterns of relationship and interaction (Horrell 1999: 323).

To illustrate the anticipated outcome of such a discernment dialogue, Paul pledges that he will never eat meat again if that is what it takes to prevent others from stumbling (8.13). By citing his own behavioural discernment, he confirms that surrendering ἐξουσία for the sake of others may actually constitute an act of cruciform love. Thus, by offering this personal example, Paul also introduces the theme of 1 Corinthians 9: just as Christ gave up his own ἐξουσία by dying for others (cf. Phil. 2.6–11), so, too, Paul surrenders his own ἐξουσία for the sake of those for whom Christ died.

f. *Specific Examples Illuminate the Divine-Human Partnership (9.1–10.13)*
Paul has just challenged the Corinthians to try to build up the community through acts of love rather than exercising their own ἐξουσία for individual benefit. In 9.1–27 he seeks to prove that he conforms his own actions to this pattern suggested in 8.1–13.[69] He then cites a story from scripture (10.1–13), reflecting on the example of Israel's conduct and experience in the wilderness. It illustrates the practice of idolatry that has been the prominent focus since 8.1 and introduces the theme of discernible divine judgment that Paul addresses in 11.17–34. The section again shows how Paul engages in theo-ethical reasoning by reflecting on conduct and experience to assess behavioural issues.

---

67. See Fee 1987: 384 n. 45.

68. According to Keck, Paul regularly emphasizes the accountability of each believer for the integrity of all believers' faith (1996b: 9); see also D. Martin 1995: 135.

69. For the links with ἐξουσία in 1 Corinthians 9, see 9.4–6, 12, 18. For the integral role of 1 Corinthians 9 in the structure of Paul's argument see Horrell 1997a: 90–91; D. Newton 1998: 314–16; *pace* Conzelmann 1975: 151.

Paul establishes his apostleship and freedom in 9.1, pointing to a vision (ἑώρακα)[70] of the risen Lord Jesus as a warrant for his apostolic defence in 9.3–23 (cf. 15.8).[71] As in 1.26–31 and 2.1–5, he invites the Corinthians to reflect on their own experience for proof of what Paul calls his 'work in the Lord' in 9.1d.[72] The community itself constitutes the divine 'seal' of Paul's apostleship 'in the Lord' (9.2).[73] The legal metaphor characterizes the divine community enrichment that confirms Paul's embodied proclamation of Christ crucified (see 1.4–9; 2.1–5). This community edification provides divine proof of Paul's apostolic status to those members of the community who are 'closely examining' (ἀνακρίνουσίν) him (9.3).[74]

Moreover, the vision referenced in 9.1 grounds his ἐξουσία to accept financial support from the Corinthians. As one of those who sowed (ἐσπείραμεν) 'the spiritual things' (τὰ πνευματικὰ) among the Corinthians,[75] he is even more entitled to reap from them the 'fleshly things' (τὰ σαρκικὰ) that represent the physical necessities that are his share in the harvest (9.11–12). This foundation allows him, however, to set a Christ-like example by surrendering this right to accept support. Paul thereby contrasts his own abdication of ἐξουσία with the use made of it by the Corinthians he criticized in 8.1–13. He does not want to take any action that becomes an obstacle to others (9.12). It might block another person's perception of the gospel, that 'divine event' (Martyn 1997b: 115) that 'takes place' (Brown 1998: 271–85) to ground people's faith in the power of God by means of a demonstration of Spirit and power associated with the embodied proclamation of Christ crucified (see 2.1–5).

Paul then re-emphasizes his own behavioural example in 9.15, consistently surrendering ἐξουσία to model Christ's pattern of self-giving love for others (9.16–18). His earthly 'ministry becomes a living paradigm of the gospel' (Fee 1987: 421). This is what he means in 9.21 when he says that he is in the law of Christ (ἔννομος Χριστοῦ).[76] As one who now understands that Christ's love constrains (συνέχει) believers (2 Cor. 5.14),[77] Paul's sole behavioural norm is Christ's cruciform pattern of self-giving love for others manifest in his death on the cross.[78] This fundamental paradigm grounds the example he sets for others

70. For understanding this verb as visual perception, see Dunn 1975: 104–109; Kim 1984: 55–56; *pace* Michaelis, who concludes it is merely a revelation in *word* (1967: 355–60).
71. Newman 1992: 186; Kelly 1979: 112.
72. Conzelmann 1975: 152. See also 15.58; cf. 2 Cor. 3.1–3; Gal. 3.1–5.
73. See also Rom. 4.17; 2 Cor. 1.22.
74. Gardner 1994: 76. The present, active participle ἀνακρίνουσίν suggests an ongoing assessment. Other early Christian texts, probably written later than Paul, also emphasize the importance of examining the behavioural life of the prophet to determine the authenticity of the prophecy. See *Did.* 11.8, 10, 11; Hermas, *Man.* 11.7–21; cf. Mt. 7.16, 20.
75. For Paul's related use of σπείρω to connect human conduct with the 'sowing' of the resurrection body, see 15.36, 37, 42–44; cf. 4.8–13. This is discussed in Chapter 3, section 4.e.
76. See C.H. Dodd 1969: 134–48; Thiselton 2000: 703–704; cf. Gal. 6.2.
77. Cf. 1 Cor. 8.1; 12.31. The genitive in the phrase ἡ ἀγάπη τοῦ Χριστοῦ in 2 Cor. 5.14 is subjective.
78. See Engberg-Pedersen 1987: 566–67; cf. Hays 1996a: 46 (the christomorphic life); Horrell

(1 Cor. 11.1). Though he is free (9.1, 19), Paul ironically enslaved himself to all people (9.19). This practice makes no sense in the absence of its grounding in the status-renouncing, self-enslaving love of Jesus (Gorman 2001: 233), who was raised to resurrection life by the power of God (see Phil. 2.6–9).

Paul takes this action so that he 'might gain more' (1 Cor. 9.19). He uses the verb κερδαίνω five times in these four verses, indicating that he is making an important word play on a verb that frequently means gaining a profit or advantage. Thus, he continues his strategy of redefining the meaning of profit or advantage.[79] He argues that it is no longer about economic advantage according to the world's standards, but gaining more people as participants in the gospel.[80]

Consequently, in 9.23 Paul argumentatively asserts that every action he takes is for the sake of the gospel, so that he might become a partner with the gospel (ἵνα συγκοινωνὸς αὐτοῦ γένωμαι) in connection with his Christ-conforming manner of life.[81] Through Paul's embodied proclamation of Christ crucified, he expects to become a partner/participant in the divine event that takes place each time there is a demonstration of Spirit and power that grounds human faith in the power of God (2.1–5; cf. 1.9). Paul takes every action in the public domain for the purpose of 'making transparent by his daily life…the character of the gospel which he proclaims as the proclamation of the cross'.[82] According to 9.24–27, he consistently endures the hardships of the apostolic lifestyle.[83] As one who proclaimed Christ's cruciform pattern to others (ἄλλοις κηρύξας), Paul does not want his own conduct to be found ἀδόκιμος, thus failing the test of divine scrutiny outlined in 1.4–9 and 4.1–5.[84]

Paul broadens the ἀδόκιμος theme in 10.1–13.[85] He turns to the example of Israel as a warning of what happens when conduct does not withstand the test of divine scrutiny (cf. Mitchell 1991: 250–51). Drawing parallels to Corinth and using τινες with repetition, he points out that some became idolaters (10.7), some engaged in sexual immorality (10.8), some put the Lord[86] to the test (10.9), and some grumbled (10.10). He draws again on the theme of divine judgment,[87] reflecting on Israel's wilderness experience when many were struck down. Paul associates that experience of divine judgment with their idolatrous conduct. For Paul these wilderness events are examples (τύποι; τυπικῶς) for the benefit and admonishment of Paul and the Corinthians (10.6, 11), the ones upon whom the

---

1997a: 105–106 ('christological praxis'); Schrage 1995: 345 ('the command to love' means conformity to Christ). See also Gal. 2.20.

79. See Mitchell 1991: 33; Stowers 1986: 108–109.

80. See Fee 1987: 426–27 n. 24; Thiselton 2000: 701–702, 705.

81. Hooker 1996: 87; cf. Thiselton 2000: 707–708; Schütz 1975: 51–52.

82. Thiselton 2000: 708. See also 1 Cor. 1.18–25; Gal. 3.1–5.

83. See also 1 Cor. 4.8–13; 2 Cor. 4.7–12.

84. See 1 Cor. 4.4–5; 2 Cor. 13.5.

85. Horrell 1997a: 95; cf. Schrage 1995: 387–88.

86. With the RSV, NIV and manuscripts ℵ, B, C, P, 0150, 33, 104 and some early Church Fathers, this study accepts 'Lord' as the best textual referent rather than 'Christ'; *pace* NRSV, Fee 1987: 450; Metzger 1994: 494.

87. See 3.10–17; 4.5; 5.5–6; 6.12–20.

'completion of the ages' (τὰ τέλη τῶν αἰώνων) has now 'descended' (κατ-ήντηκεν) according to 10.11.

Consequently,[88] Paul exhorts the Corinthians in 10.12 to reflect (βλεπέτω) once again on their experience and conduct so that those who think they are standing might take heed, lest they fall (cf. 10.8; 15.1–2; Gal. 5.4).[89] He alludes to 1 Cor. 9.27, always concerned that believers might be divinely judged ἀδόκιμος for conduct that fails to conform to Christ's cruciform pattern. He also foreshadows his discussion in 11.17–34 of the discernible, divine judgment that has already befallen the Corinthians. Some of their actions during worship do not conform to Christ's cruciform pattern and, by implication, have been found ἀδόκιμος.

Paul closes this warning section, however, with a statement of hope (10.13). God will provide the 'way out' (ἔκβασιν) of the temptation of the temple meals, so that the Corinthians might be taken out from under the present danger. Reasserting that 'God is faithful', Paul echoes aspects of the divine–human partnership with Jesus Christ identified in 1.4–9. This echo implies that their way out of danger lies in spiritually discerning conduct that will conform to Christ's cruciform pattern. By doing so, they may anticipate that the faithful God will enrich them once again with experiences of new life that confirm such Christ-conforming behaviour (see 1.7–8). Thus, they must practise spiritual discernment by reflecting on their own actions and experiences in light of the examples of Paul and Israel. Paul is confident that, if they do so, they will discern the way out from under their danger.[90]

g. *The Divine-Human Partnership in Christ is Exclusive (10.14–22)*

Building on the hope that God will provide the way out of the danger when they reflect on the situation, Paul urges the Corinthians in 10.14 to avoid or depart from the pagan temples and meals (see also 8.6–10). He echoes 4.10, ironically suggesting in 10.15 that he is speaking as to discerning people (ὡς φρονίμοις).[91] He thus alludes again to the importance of reflection on conduct and experience. Following his consistent pattern of theo-ethical reasoning, Paul also exhorts them to judge for themselves what he is saying.[92] As he has done throughout, Paul provides a series of reasoned arguments to support his recommended action.[93] He thereby seeks to influence the dialogue that should be taking place in the deliberative assembly.

Paul's exhortation is grounded in the partnership theme that provides the lynchpin for his reasoning (D. Newton 1998: 335; cf. 1.9). All those participating

---

88. Gardner argues that ὥστε shows the centrality of 10.12 to Paul's argument (1994: 152); cf. D. Newton 1998: 330.

89. According to Gardner, the verb alludes to the Old Testament concept of 'standing' before or in the presence of the God who judges God's people (1994: 152–53). Gardner also concludes that 10.12 is the heart of Paul's argument (1994: 153).

90. Horrell finds that 'the whole passage is a warning against complacency' (1997a: 96).

91. For this translation, see LSJ, 1956. Gardner notes the irony (1994: 168).

92. See 4.5; 5.3, 12; 6.1–3; 11.13.

93. D. Newton 1998: 335; cf. Meeks 1988.

in the unifying Christian cultic meal share both in the partnership (κοινωνία) of the 'body' and the partnership (κοινωνία) of the 'blood' of Christ (10.16). By appealing to what is probably a well-known sacramental tradition in 10.16 (see Käsemann 1964d: 109), Paul insists that participation in the Lord's Supper entails 'not only communal participation in a covenant pledge of "belonging" and faithfulness to that pledge but also communal participation in the actual physical lifestyle' (Thiselton 2000: 763). This participation 'signifies identification with Christ in his death as both the source of redemption and the pattern for life and lifestyle' (Thiselton 2000: 763). Paul thus emphasizes the link between conduct that conforms to Christ's cruciform pattern (the partnership in his 'blood') and the community experience of new life (the partnership in his 'body').

To support this argument Paul makes two related points. First, he invites the Corinthians to reflect on the experiential and behavioural example of historical Israel (βλέπετε τὸν Ἰσραὴλ κατὰ σάρκα), where the ones eating the sacrifices are partners of the altar (10.18). Second, he concludes that those who partake of the food sacrificed to demons become partners (κοινωνοὺς) with the demons (10.20). According to the logic of the argument, it is the practice of eating that makes one a partner either with God or demons.[94]

A concluding question in 10.22 further suggests that some Corinthians may be participating in two different partnerships by virtue of their two different cultic associations. These divided loyalties may provoke the Lord (who is the more powerful partner) to jealousy (10.22). By implication Paul reminds them that the Lord plays an active and continuing role in the community (see 1.8; 4.4–5). His jealous judgment must be reckoned in the deliberative assembly (see 11.29–32).[95]

The fact that Paul does not specify the precise contours of unacceptable, non-Christian cultic participation places the responsibility for discerning the appropriate level squarely on the shoulders of community members.[96] He implies again that the important community practice of spiritual discernment will help them resolve this issue. Participation by all community members in the dialogical reflection will help them determine the appropriate limits of non-Christian cultic participation.

h. *A Single Behavioural Standard and Discernment Criterion (10.23–11.1)*
In 10.23–11.1 Paul summarizes his arguments since 5.1. He affirms cruciformity as the new norm for conduct and divine edification as the new criterion for evaluating community experience.

He begins in 10.23 by refining the Corinthians' individualist slogan introduced in 6.12. Though all conduct might be lawful, not all actions are advantageous (συμφέρει) and build up the community (οἰκοδομεῖ). Individual believers are encouraged to seek no longer their own good but that of others (10.24), just as Paul does not seek his own advantage (σύμφορον) but that of many (10.33). The imperative phrase in 10.24 appears to be grounded in the 'act of faith (or

---

94. Fee 1987: 470; *pace* D. Newton 1998: 338, 340.
95. Cf. Hurtado 1999b: 203.
96. See Horrell 1997a: 100–101; D. Newton 1998: 367–71.

faithfulness) toward God' that became manifest in Christ's self-giving love for others on the cross (Gorman 2001: 162). As Paul showed in 1 Corinthians 9, the actions of his own life embody this divinely approved pattern of cruciform love that does not seek its own advantage but builds up others (see also 8.1; 13.5).[97]

Indeed, the Corinthians are to become imitators (μιμηταί) of Paul, just as he is an imitator of Christ (11.1). 'By claiming to be an imitator of Christ in this regard, Paul implies (a) that Christ acted similarly, (b) that this way of Christ was an expression of love, and (c) that this love is paradigmatic not only for Paul but for all who belong to Christ' (Gorman 2001: 162). Thus, Paul expressly embraces Christ's cruciform pattern as the behavioural norm for experiencing life in God's kingdom.[98] The human Jesus established the behavioural foundation for the community – that building or temple that God is constructing through acts of cruciform love (see 1 Cor. 3.6–16). As the context of 8.1–11.1 suggests, conforming to the example of Christ takes place by setting aside personal rights and privileges for the good of others.[99]

Actions conforming to Christ's cruciform pattern are highly situational, however, and incapable of being stated in predetermined rules. Paul makes this point clear in 9.19–23. The 'right action must be discerned on the basis of a christological paradigm, with a view to the need of the community', since 'ethics cannot be sufficiently guided by law or by institutionalized rules' (Hays 1996a: 43, 46). Instead, 'Spirit-empowered, Spirit-discerned conformity to Christ is required' (Hays 1996a: 46). As Paul has argued and illustrated throughout the letter, Christ-conforming behaviour must be spiritually discerned. It is the product of reasoned, dialogical reflection that identifies the links between conduct and experience. This reflection determines, to the extent possible, what actions appear to manifest divine confirmation because they are linked with experiences of new life (see 1.4–9; 2.10–16).[100]

This also means that believers must have a criterion by which to make this experiential evaluation – the product of comparing spiritual things with spiritual things (2.13). As a result, in 10.23–11.1 Paul redefines the τέλος for every action to be taken: community edification (see Mitchell 1991: 37). He 'overtly and consciously redefines what is τὸ συμφέρον for the Corinthian community' (Mitchell 1991: 36). The parallel structure of 10.23a and 10.23b suggests that the advantageous act is the one that builds up the community (Mitchell 1991: 37, 257). This implies that the community must identify experiences of edification – experiences of new life from God.

The logic of Paul's argument suggests that this new life is the life of salvation from God. Indeed, says Paul, every action he takes seeks the advantage of others, 'so that they might be saved' (10.33). Moreover, in 10.31 he exhorts the Corinthians that whatever they do, including eating or drinking, should be done 'for the glory of God' (cf. Phil. 2.11). He uses 'glory' once again to denote some

97. See Gorman 2001: 161–62.
98. See also Phil. 2.4–8; Gal. 2.19–20.
99. Belleville 1996: 126; Horrell 1997a: 102, 104, 105.
100. See also Rom. 12.1–2; 2 Cor. 13.3–5; Phil. 1.9–10; 4.8–9; 1 Thess. 2.4; 5.21; cf. Eph. 5.9–10.

manifest aspect of the revelation of God's own glory that reflects eternal life.[101] Thus, God's power to save – in other words, the power that gives eternal life – becomes manifest in connection with specific actions that conform to Christ's cruciform pattern because they seek the advantage of others rather than self.

The argument in 10.23–11.1 illuminates the role of theo-ethical reasoning and the community practice of spiritual discernment. Believers' actions must imitate those of Paul just as his behaviour imitates that of Christ. Christ-conforming behaviour is conduct that seeks the common advantage of the community rather than the benefit of the individual. Christ-conforming behaviour is divinely confirmed when God builds up the community through these actions. Consequently, this divine confirmation of Christ-conforming behaviour must be discerned in reflection on the experiences of community edification. Thus, Paul identifies the new criterion of community edification to guide their collective deliberations in the practice of spiritual discernment. It becomes the standard by which they collectively evaluate their community experiences as they try to identify divinely confirmed, Christ-conforming actions.[102]

3. *Engaging in Theo-Ethical Reasoning: Evaluating Actions Inside the Deliberative Assembly (11.2–14.40)*

In the letter's third long section, Paul engages in theo-ethical reasoning to respond to concerns about conduct inside the deliberative assembly (ἐκκλησία). As with 5.1–11.1, he points to community experience as proof that a variety of actions do not conform to Christ's cruciform pattern and do not manifest the exercise of God's life-giving power.

In the difficult and arcane passage at 11.2–16, he addresses the relationship between hair, head coverings, and angels in community worship. For purposes of this study, only two things must be noted. First, after making specific suggestions, Paul exhorts the Corinthians to judge for themselves the resolution of the behavioural issue (11.13). Second, he points out in the context of these deliberations that neither he nor his churches tolerate anyone who seems to be fond of victory (φιλόνεικος).[103] In the community practice of spiritual discernment, certainty of knowledge is unacceptable (see 8.1–13). Participants must always remain open to revelation. They must be willing to change their positions during the course of the dialogue as the Spirit opens them to new insights (see 14.29–32).[104]

---

101. See Koenig 1990a: 160–61, 163; cf. Savage 1996: 103–29. Similarly, Beker concludes that 'glory' has a physical connotation that refers to the quality of the messianic new age that is the new creation – the glorious life of the kingdom of God (1980: 282–83).

102. Mitchell notes the importance of community experience in Paul's argument (1991: 256) without addressing the way that Paul seeks to link community experience with particular actions that conform to Christ's cruciform pattern.

103. For this translation, see the possibilities discussed in Wire (1990: 14) and Thiselton (2000: 846–47).

104. According to the contemporary theory of discourse (communicative) ethics, this dialogue is transformative as its participants are open to changing their previously held beliefs during the course of the conversation. See Benhabib 1986: 313–16.

a. *Even Now the Lord is Disciplining the Community (11.17–34)*
Paul challenges community worship practices in 11.17–34, including events taking place in the symposium-like dialogue that follows the meal.[105] The forensic
shading of the passage is unmistakable and refers to a judicial event now taking
place in the congregation (Roetzel 1972: 137).

The key verb συνέρχομαι, used by Paul only in this letter, holds together the
entire argument from 11.17–14.40 (Fee 1987: 536).[106] As the acknowledged term
in antiquity for the official assembling of the people (Käsemann 1964d: 119), the
verb makes it clear that Paul is focusing on conduct during worship. Both
Aristotle and Paul use this verb to refer to the process by which human beings
joined together to form a society (Mitchell 1991: 154–55). Moreover, for Aristotle
(as with Paul) dialogue plays a central role in community formation among those
who assemble:

> For it is possible that the many, though not individually good men, yet when they
> come together (συνελθόντας) may be better, not individually but collectively…for
> where there are many, each individual, it may be argued, has some portion of virtue
> and wisdom, and when they have come together (συνελθόντας), just as the multitude
> becomes a single man with many feet and many hands and many senses, so also it
> becomes one personality as regards the moral and intellectual faculties.[107]

For Aristotle, community formation takes place when individuals share wisdom
and virtue in dialogue and partnership with one another.[108] The first-century
Middle Platonist Plutarch makes a related point. He complains that the party's
goal of good partnership/fellowship (κοινωνείας τὸ τέλος) is lost and the god
Dionysius is outraged ('Table Talk', *Moralia* 615A) when the conversation in the
after-dinner symposium does not include the participation of everyone.

It is suggested that Paul shares with Aristotle and Plutarch a similar commitment to the importance of partnership and dialogue in the moral formation of the
deliberative assembly. First, he has already emphasized the divine–human partnership (1.9; 10.16). Second, he has argued that the Corinthians must reason with
the same mind (the 'mind of Christ') to reach the same opinion about appropriate
behaviour (1.10; 2.16). Hearing that there are σχίσματα manifest among them
when they come together (11.18; see also 1.10), Paul sets out to correct the way
they are inappropriately assembling (11.17; see also 14.1–40). The disorder-
liness, drunkenness and inequality (11.21) of their proceedings point out how
some members of the group are bringing practices and perspectives from the
surrounding culture into the conduct of church affairs.[109] These attitudes and

105. Lampe 1991a: 188–91; 1994: 40. Aune concludes that the structure of the assembly of the
Corinthian Christians was influenced by cultural symposia patterns: a ceremony that begins with a
dinner and concludes with a session involving wine (1978: 78). What takes place in this after-dinner
symposium is discussed in connection with 1 Corinthians 14 in Chapter 3, section 3.d below.
106. See 11.17, 18, 20, 33, 34; 14.23, 26.
107. Aristotle, *Pol.* 3.6.4, quoted by Mitchell (1991: 155).
108. See *Pol.* 3.5.10. For Paul's partnership language in 1 Corinthians, see 1.9; 9.23; 10.16, 18, 20;
cf. 1.2; 3.9.
109. Adams 2000: 89. According to Lampe, the conduct was 'the result of their unreflected
prolongation of their prebaptismal behaviour' (1994: 40).

practices are reinforcing worldly economic and social status distinctions between community members.[110] Their divisions distort the celebration of the Lord's Supper (11.20) and impede the post-dinner moral dialogue.[111]

Before identifying and challenging the offending conduct, however, Paul builds on the ἀδόκιμος theme regarding the divine confirmation or disapproval of people based on their specific actions (11.19). He intentionally replaces σχίσματα from 11.18 with αἱρέσεις.[112] He thereby introduces a word play that concludes with his use of διαιρέσεις in 12.4–6,[113] where he emphasizes the importance of the *varieties* of experiences, services, and divinely-wrought effects. In 11.19 Paul stresses the constructive aspect of having to make behavioural choices (αἱρέσεις).[114] It is even 'necessary' for there to be such choices, says Paul, so that manifest among them will be the ones whose behaviour has been divinely confirmed through reflective testing (οἱ δόκιμοι φανεροὶ).[115] This underscores Paul's consistent argument throughout the letter that the Corinthians are failing to distinguish between actions that appear to reflect divine confirmation and those that do not. Not all of them are practising spiritual discernment by engaging in theo-ethical reasoning to make these important behavioural and experiential distinctions.[116]

Indeed, some of the Corinthians are disregarding (καταφρονεῖτε) the deliberative assembly (11.22).[117] Paul may be describing not so much a feeling of some community members toward others (the verb is usually translated as 'despise'), but the refusal by some members to participate or listen to others in the symposium-like period of moral dialogue that follows the Lord's Supper. Later, he repeatedly emphasizes that, when the whole deliberative assembly comes together in the same place (14.23), it is important that *all* members of the church participate in this dialogical practice of spiritual discernment (see 14.5, 23–24, 26, 31). The argument implies that some were not participating and this was proving detrimental to the church's attempt to make the kinds of behavioural and experiential distinctions that Paul has been addressing since 5.1. Thus, Paul's overarching concern is to challenge those who continue to act according to worldly standards in the deliberative assembly.[118]

110. See D. Martin 1995: 74–80; Theissen 1982: 69–174; Meeks 1983: 67–68; Mitchell 1991: 264.

111. Paul is thus focusing on the 'ways in which the cliques affect community life when these contentious persons come face to face ἐν ἐκκλησίᾳ' (Mitchell 1991: 152).

112. See Horrell 1996: 151 n. 127; R. Campbell 1991: 65. R. Collins (1999: 421), Mitchell (1991: 153), Fee (1987: 538 n. 34) and Barrett (1968: 261) are certainly correct that these two terms are *normally* essentially synonymous, as Gal. 5.20 suggests.

113. R. Martin suggests this possibility (1984: 12–13), one that Fee calls an 'intriguing suggestion' (1987: 586 n. 13).

114. For this translation, see LSJ, 41; R. Campbell 1991: 65.

115. See Horrell 1996: 150–51; contra R. Campbell 1991: 65–69.

116. R. Collins correctly observes that the rhetoric of 11.17–22 invites the Corinthians to make a judgment about their own behaviour (1999: 417). Paul is not insisting, however, that the community determine 'who is or is not a genuine Christian' (contra R. Campbell 1991: 68), a conclusion that runs afoul of Paul's conviction that the church judges conduct, not people (see 4.1–5).

117. For this translation, see BAGD, 420.

118. Horrell 1996: 105; Lampe 1994: 40; cf. Mitchell 1991: 264.

Paul amplifies his assault on these practices in 11.26–27, focusing on the manner in which they are gathering to eat and drink the Lord's Supper (Horrell 1996: 152). The emphatic placement of the phrase 'the death of the Lord' makes it the focal point of the Corinthians' unworthy declarative conduct in the deliberative assembly. Indeed, 'the connection that Paul makes between the sacramental proclamation of Christ's death and ethics' constitutes the 'central question of the text' (Lampe 1994: 45). Some of the Corinthians are still coming together to consume the meal in ways that maintain worldly distinctions based on social status.[119] This manner of declaring the meaning of the Lord's death that took place for everyone,[120] including the weak (see 8.11), is not meeting with the Lord's approval (see 11.32). Indeed, Christ's death and resurrection dissolved all the world's behavioural standards. It established his cruciform pattern of self-giving love for others as the universal standard for conduct through which God is bringing about a new order.[121]

With his phrase 'until he comes' (11.26), Paul echoes earlier admonitions, thereby suggesting that he is making a paraenetic use of the phrase.[122] For instance, in 1.7–8 he asserted that the community should be eagerly expecting the revelation of Jesus Christ to continue taking place to confirm Christ-conforming conduct. In 4.5 he warned the Corinthians not to judge anything before the time when the Lord comes. The logic of Paul's reasoning points to his conviction that the risen Lord continues to come among them to evaluate their actions.

Indeed, Paul proceeds directly into further paraenesis in 11.27–34. In these eight verses filled with judicial imagery and the central theme of judgment, the authoritative example of the 'parousiac Lord' provides the principal argument in Paul's rhetoric (R. Collins 1999: 436–37). He contends that the Lord has already evaluated some of their behavioural choices, coming among the gathered community to judge and discipline them. The logic of the unfolding argument since 11.17 indicates that the guiding presence of the Lord *should* be apparent if the *whole* community is engaged in theo-ethical reasoning, dialogically practising spiritual discernment by reflecting on the links between experience and conduct.[123]

Paul thus exhorts each person to prove themselves through testing (δοκι-μαζέτω). By this he means that church members must examine whether their own actions are conforming to Christ's cruciform pattern, lest they bring judgment on themselves if they do not (11.29). He expects each person to discern the presence and participation of all members of the community, irrespective of social status, before anyone proceeds to eat the bread and drink the cup (11.28–29).[124] Before proceeding with the meal, they must discern the presence of the

---

119. Horrell (1996: 152), citing Lampe (1991a: 211), notes that the Corinthians' conduct does not reflect the pattern of Christ's action in his death for others. Cf. R. Collins 1999: 429.

120. Cf. Käsemann 1964d: 121.

121. According to Lampe, 'our love for others represents Christ's death to other human beings' (1994: 45).

122. See Bornkamm 1969: 174–75; cf. Lampe 1994: 43.

123. According to S. Barton, the presence or absence of the judgment of the Lord is well able to be discerned (1986: 241).

124. For this characterization of the phrase μὴ διακρίνων τὸ σῶμα in 11.29, see D. Martin 1995:

entire social body (cf. 3.16; 6.19). '[T]he Lord's Supper is essentially a demonstration, a ritual enactment, of the truth that the diverse members of the Christian community have become one body in Christ' (Horrell 1999: 322). Therefore, to count as the Lord's Supper the meal must include all members of the body to demonstrate their oneness (Horrell 1999: 322).

Paul thereby amplifies his concern that the Corinthians have actually divided the one social body of Christ (see 1.13). Indeed, they are failing to embody the cross by not looking out for the interests of every member of the deliberative assembly and exercising the same care for one another (see 12.25–26). They are unworthily announcing the Lord's death to worldly standards (see 11.26–27; cf. 1.18, 23) and thereby subjecting community members to the Lord's judgment and discipline (11.31–32; cf. 4.5; Phil. 3.18–19).

Consequently (διὰ τοῦτο), concludes Paul in 1 Cor. 11.30, many of the Corinthians have become weak, feeble, and are even dying. Paul draws on the popular Jewish notion that sickness and death are forms of punishment for sin.[125] He offers these experiences as discernible proof that the Lord has come among them and unfavourably judged some of their actions.[126] This judgment on particular conduct is taking place, however, so that (ἵνα) the Corinthians might avoid future condemnation with the world (11.32; cf. 1.18) by amending their practices.[127]

Paul thus continues to divide humanity into two groups by means of his use of spatial, temporal and ethical dualities.[128] He also emphasizes the importance of practising spiritual discernment to identify the presence of the risen Lord who distinguishes, guides and judges their conduct in the deliberative assembly (see 1.8; 4.1–5). In 11.33–34, Paul offers his advice for future conduct that he thinks will meet with the Lord's approval. When coming together to eat they are to wait for one another (ἀλλήλους ἐκδέχεσθε), so that the worldly distinction between the have and have-nots may be overcome (see Horrell 1996: 154).

Some commentators concede that 11.27–34 reflects Paul's understanding that there are present aspects to divine judgment on the entire community.[129] Nevertheless, this troubling passage is often treated as if it were not paraenesis or warning. For interpreters trying to rescue Paul from the apparently superstitious logic of such reasoning, the verses represent an inexplicable exception to the general rule that divine judgment language in Paul addresses an event that will take place in the future and final Day of the Lord.[130] The embarrassing 'vigour, crudeness and naïveté' (Hurd 1965: 286) of the language is regularly taken as

---

74; Mitchell 1991: 265; Engberg-Pedersen 1993: 120, 122; Bornkamm 1969: 148. Barrett strips the passage of its pragmatic, social dimension by interpreting 'the body' as the body and blood of the Lord (1968: 275).

125. R. Collins 1999: 436. See Mk 2.9; Jn 9.12; Gal. 4.14.

126. As elsewhere in Paul, the proof through testing of particular conduct is divinely given. See 1.5–8; 3.13; 9.27; 11.19; see also Rom. 12.1–2; 14.18; 2 Cor. 10.18; 13.5–7; Phil. 1.10; 1 Thess. 2.4.

127. According to Horsley, Paul implies that when the world is condemned the assembly itself would be vindicated as the society of the new age (1998: 163).

128. See Adams 2000: 143; Chapter 2, section 3.b.

129. See, e.g., Roetzel 1972: 83–85; Fee 1987: 565; Kreitzer 1987: 100.

130. See, e.g., Fee 1987: 561–62; Kreitzer 1987: 100.

evidence that it belongs to an earlier stage of Paul's preaching that no longer holds true.[131]

The passage nonetheless reflects a critical aspect of Paul's theo-ethical reasoning.[132] The reference to the Lord's 'coming' in 11.26 is not only an implied reference to the future Day of the Lord understood as the time of final judgment. It is also an aspect of the Lord's active reign in the present time (see 1.7–8; 15.25).[133] He comes among the gathered community to assess their conduct as 'the judging presence of the Lord' (Roetzel 1972: 139). To discern this guiding presence, however, the entire church must be present and practising spiritual discernment.

b. *Theo-Ethical Reasoning and the 'Spiritual Things' (12.1–30)*

In 12.1–30 Paul continues to connect the role of the Spirit to behavioural life in God's new age/spatial realm.[134] He responds to the Corinthians' inquiry about the 'spiritual things' (τὰ πνευματικά) and presents a 'theological critique' of their position (Käsemann 1964c: 66).[135] He builds on the implication that 'all pneumatic and ecstatic experiences are ambiguous' (Lampe 1991c: 21).[136] Paul implies that they must distinguish between various spiritual things (see 2.12–13; 12.2; 14.29–32).[137]

Paul distinguishes the category of χάρισμα (associated with the service of Christ and his community) and the 'spiritual things' that result from demonic spirits that are the counterpart of χαρίσματα (Käsemann 1964c: 66). This makes πνευματικά a *broader* term than the more limited χαρίσματα that Paul references in 12.4.[138] Paul's point lies precisely in the fact that, because the spirit of the world competes with the Spirit sent from God (see 2.12; cf. Gal. 5.17), the spirits and spiritual things that people experience in connection with particular actions must be distinguished (see also 1 Jn 3.24–4.2). Thus, the Corinthians must learn to recognize the authentic manifestations of new life through God's power illuminated by the one Holy Spirit dwelling among them (see R. Collins 1999: 449). Apparently, such community testing of the spirits had not been common practice in Corinth, as 14.29–32 also suggests (R. Collins 1999: 445).

131. See, e.g., W.D. Davies 1962: 291.

132. Lampe argues that '[a]s strange as this little speech in 11.29–32 about the judging Lord may seem to us, it is theologically important' (1994: 46).

133. Indeed, Käsemann acknowledges that in the passage the self-manifestation of the Lord 'sets men in the perspective of the Last Day and therefore bears within itself the marks of the divine action which will characterize that Day', thus constituting 'a kind of anticipation of the Last Day within the community' (1964d: 122, 125).

134. According to Beker, Paul 'ethicizes' the Spirit in this section (1980: 291).

135. For the conclusion that περὶ δὲ usually introduces a subject the Corinthians inquired about, see Chapter 3, section 2.d above.

136. Cf. Dunn 1998a: 313.

137. According to Dunn, of all the early Christian writers Paul appears to have grasped most clearly the danger of an inspiration whose source was demonic and whose utterance could not be trusted but must be subjected to careful evaluation (1998a: 314).

138. *Pace* R. Martin 1984: 36; Dunn 1998c: 554–55.

Contrasting two intelligible statements in 12.3 (Holtz 1971–72: 365–76), Paul appears to distinguish those who are led by the spirit of the world from those who are being led by the Holy Spirit sent from God (cf. 2.12). The first statement ('Jesus is a curse') is one that is inspired by the spirit of the world because it characterizes the death of Jesus according to worldly standards. Emphasizing the human Jesus who died as a curse under the law (see Gal. 3.10–13),[139] the statement is grounded in the law's behavioural standards (Deut. 21.23; 27.26) that no longer apply after the advent of Christ and the revelation of 'the faith' (see Gal. 3.22–25).[140]

The second statement, a confession in 1 Cor. 12.3 that 'Jesus is Lord', proclaims Christ's status as the risen, vindicated and exalted Lord. He remains active through the Spirit (cf. 15.45; 2 Cor. 3.18) to communities 'calling upon his name' for behavioural guidance (see 1 Cor. 1.2, 8; 4.1–5; 16.22; see also Rom. 10.6–13). This confession by means of the Holy Spirit (ἐν πνεύματι ἁγίῳ) establishes the Spirit's guiding influence. The Spirit's illumination of experiences of new life associated with Christ-conforming conduct becomes the means by which believers are empowered to confess that 'Jesus is Lord'. Those who are thereby 'led by the Spirit' (see Rom. 8.14; Gal. 5.18) are set apart from the rest of the world because they practise spiritual discernment in order to conform their actions to Christ's cruciform pattern to which they were committed in baptism. This sequence suggests one or more demonstrations of Spirit and power that take place in connection with the embodied proclamation of Christ crucified (see 1 Cor. 2.1–5, 12; cf. 12.13). Thus, the confession that 'Jesus is Lord' indicates a commitment to serve God through an appropriate, Christ-centred lifestyle (Thiselton 2000: 926–27).

In 12.4–11 Paul amplifies this critical connection between Christ-conforming behaviour, the manifest power of God, and experiences of new life illuminated by the Spirit. In the sequence in 12.4–6, he identifies three specific divine agents[141] with distinct roles.[142] Paul thus highlights the essence of theo-ethical reasoning in this crucial sequence held together by the phrase 'the same Spirit' that encloses the section (12.4, 11).[143] This is the same Holy Spirit (12.3) sent from God to help believers perceive God's gifts of new life in connection with Christ-conforming conduct (see 2.1–5, 10, 12, 14). Those who are thereby led by the Spirit from God are set apart from those who are merely zealots for all spirits (cf. 14.12).[144]

First, while there are varieties (διαιρέσεις) of experiences of God's life-giving power (χαρισμάτων),[145] there is only 'the same Spirit' (12.4). By this

139. See van Unnik 1973: 120.
140. See 1 Cor. 16.13, discussed in Chapter 3, section 5.a below, where Paul exhorts the Corinthians to stand firm in 'the faith'.
141. See Horsley 1998: 169; Hurtado 1999b: 212; cf. Fee 1987: 586–87.
142. See Hurtado 1999b: 212.
143. For this latter observation, see R. Collins 1999: 449.
144. Cf. Käsemann, who concludes that 'there is manifested in the heathen counterparts of the charismata a demonic spirit which causes them [the Corinthians] to remain unfruitful and does not issue in service' (1964c: 66).
145. For this characterization of χάρισμα, see Chapter 2, section 2.b.

Paul means that there is only the one Holy Spirit sent from God to help those who
practise spiritual discernment perceive their experiences of new life (see 2.10,
12–16). Paul's choice of χαρίσματα functions as a theological corrective to the
Corinthians' use of the broader term πνευματικά.[146] The word πνευματικά fails
to distinguish between the manifest experiences of new life given by God and
those individual spiritual experiences associated with conduct that does not benefit
others.

Second, there are also varieties of services (διαιρέσεις διακονιῶν) that are
all grounded in the 'same Lord' (12.5; cf. 11.1). This is the one Lord Jesus Christ,
whose cruciform pattern of self-giving love for others became manifest in his
death on the cross. This has become the new social norm for life in God's kingdom (see Engberg-Pedersen 1987: 567–68). Paul thus reasons that believers serve
this same Lord (see 3.5; 4.1; 16.15) through a multitude of actions. Paul characterizes these actions as the 'service' of others that conform to the cruciform
pattern of the 'same Lord' who is Jesus Christ.

Third, there are also varieties of effects (διαιρέσεις ἐνεργημάτων) wrought
by the 'same God' who works (ἐνεργῶν) all things in everyone (12.6; cf. 2.4–5;
8.6).[147] This is the same God who enriches the community with gifts that are
experienced as new life and associated with Christ-conforming actions (see 1.5–
8; 2.1–5; cf. Rom. 12.6). Indeed, Paul regularly applies forms of the verb ἐνεργέω
to characterize God's power working in connection with human conduct.[148]

Moreover, by using διαιρέσεις in each of these three verses, Paul completes
the word play begun in 1 Cor. 11.19. It is necessary for there to be different
choices (αἱρέσεις) for conduct so that those whose actions reflect divine confirmation become manifest. Paul's logic suggests that this divine confirmation
becomes manifest in connection with actions that are grounded in the διακονία
of this same Lord Jesus Christ. Discernment of this divine confirmation takes
place by means of the same Spirit, who points the community toward the connections between acts of cruciform love and the varieties of experiences of new life
being wrought by the same God. Thus, for Paul, 'ethics' becomes a hermeneutical undertaking by the actor who interprets Christ's cruciform pattern of serving
others in the course of daily living.[149]

Paul's repeated use of the phrase 'to one…to another' (12.8–10) highlights
two related concerns: (1) the activity of the Spirit; and (2) the unique roles
played by each member of the community, as their particular Christ-conforming
actions become the means by which they experience the new life God effectuates in the community.[150] Each person is being given (δίδοται) the manifestation

146. Käsemann 1964c: 66; see also R. Collins 1999: 450; Lampe 1991c: 22; *pace* Conzelmann
1975: 207; Dunn 1998c: 554–55.
147. Fee points out that Paul's use of ἐνεργημάτων emphasizes the effects produced and not just
the activity itself (1987: 161 n. 279; *pace* BAGD, 265). Later, in 12.18, 24 and 28, Paul re-emphasizes
that God is the one who has placed each person in the 'body of Christ' as God has best determined.
148. See Gal. 2.8; 3.5; Phil. 2.13; 1 Thess. 2.13; see also Eph. 1.11, 20; 3.20; Col. 1.29; cf. Gal.
5.6; 2 Cor. 4.12; but see Rom. 7.6; Eph. 2.2.
149. Cf. Meeks 1993b: 37–58.
150. Cf. Horsley 1998: 170.

(φανέρωσις) of the Spirit for the common advantage (τὸ συμφέρον). The present passive δίδοται suggests a divine activity that is still occurring (cf. 1.7–8). With his use of φανέρωσις, Paul continues to focus on the visible, demonstrated power of God that is illuminated by the Spirit (see 2.1–5, 12).[151] He insists that these manifestations are being given only for the community's advantage rather than for individual enrichment or satisfaction (Mitchell 1991: 38 n. 83).

Moreover, the logic of 12.4 and 12.7–11 effectively renders χαρίσματα and φανέρωσις τοῦ πνεύματος as synonymous.[152] Thus, it is more accurate to say that the χαρίσματα should be understood as particular spiritual events (Dunn 1998c: 558) or experiences.[153] These χαρίσματα, wrought by God but made manifest by the Spirit to confirm Christ-conforming conduct, reveal experiences that constitute present aspects of believers' embodied participation in eternal life.[154] These gifts of new life always remain beyond human control and solely reflect God's exercise of life-giving power to benefit the community in connection with specific Christ-conforming actions.[155] Christ continues to reign in the world (see 1 Cor. 15.25; cf. 1.8), subjecting everything to the power of God in connection with actions that conform to his cruciform pattern.[156] This becomes the means by which believers participate as partners in the divine mystery – God's unfolding plan for transforming the world.

Paul's two distinct references to the 'one Spirit' in 12.13 serve as the fulcrum for linking the preceding verses to 12.13–30. Building on the argument he introduced in 6.12–20, his logic emphasizes the entire community as one body, the 'body of Christ' according to 12.27. As Paul asserted earlier (3.16; 6.19), this one social body constitutes the locus of the Spirit's activity (Gillespie 1994: 127). All (πάντες) members of the community – whether Jews or Greeks, slaves or free persons – were baptized into this one body by the one Spirit (12.13). This language indicates that all pre-existing social distinctions are integrated into the one body of Christ. They no longer serve as appropriate distinctions for discerning specific actions that conform to Christ's cruciform pattern.[157]

Moreover, all (πάντες) the Corinthians were 'made to drink' (ἐποτίσθημεν)[158] of that one Spirit. The verb may allude to the Graeco-Roman practice of drinking

151. According to Fee, what distinguishes the listing of manifestations in 12.8–10 is 'the concretely visible nature of these items' (1987: 591).
152. For this conclusion, see Conzelmann 1975: 208 n. 10; Dunn 1998c: 554; cf. Fee 1987: 589.
153. Cf. Lampe 1991c: 22; Reiling 1977: 65.
154. Cf. Käsemann 1964c: 65. According to Lampe, the community experiences a piece of the divine heavenly sphere – some of the eschatological reality now as an anticipation of the eschaton – through the active practice of loving service to others (1991c: 25).
155. Similarly, in Gal. 5.23–25, Paul associates the 'fruit of the Spirit' (i.e. experiences of new life from God) with those who walk in line with the Spirit; see also Rom. 12.3–8.
156. Cf. Käsemann, who concludes: 'Grace pushes home its attack to the very heart of the world; it liberates it from the demons' (1964c: 72).
157. See Gal. 3.27–28; cf. 1 Cor. 1.26–31; Wire 1990: 138; *pace* Castelli 1991a: 116, 129–33.
158. For the debate about the proper translation and interpretation of ἐποτίσθημεν in 12.13, compare Fee 1987: 603–605, including n. 28 ('made to drink'), with Dunn 1998c: 450 and Cuming 1981: 283–85 ('watered/irrigated').

from the same cup of wine ('spirit') that marked the transition from the dinner event in the formal parties of the Hellenistic world to the subsequent symposium that was centred on moral dialogue.[159] If so, with another word play Paul may be pointing them toward the practice of spiritual discernment that should be taking place after the meal is completed and the cup of wine is passed. In this community practice it is the one guiding Spirit that unifies the church by illuminating their common experiences of new life associated with Christ-conforming conduct. In other words, by illuminating these experiences of new life, this one Spirit leads believers to walk in a variety of ways that conform to Christ's universal, cruciform pattern. Through these actions God forges believers into one unified social body.

Indeed, the body metaphor that Paul employs throughout 12.12–30 applies a common *topos* in Graeco-Roman rhetoric that compared the human body with the city-state.[160] The *topos* was used frequently to argue that inequality among people is both necessary and salutary.[161] Paul seeks to reverse that understanding. He argues that God has arranged the body (12.18, 28) with a variety of members, all of whom are important. Similarly, 'God has mixed together the body' and given more abundant honour to the ones lacking worldly status (12.24; see also 1.18–31).

With this affirmation of divine placement in the social body, he challenges the world's expectation that nature establishes the order and hierarchy of any political and social body.[162] This is occurring so that there might not be any division (σχίσμα) in the community (12.25; see also 1.10; 11.18). Paul thereby rebukes those in the community who think they are more important than other church members. His 'vision of community seems to contain at its heart a commitment to the value and contribution of each member' (Horrell 1999: 323).[163]

Christ and his cruciform pattern of self-giving love for others lie at the centre of Paul's reasoning in 12.22–30. Referring to the inferior one to whom God has given greater honour (12.24; cf. Phil. 2.6–11), Paul not only refers to certain community members but also alludes to Christ and his cruciform pattern that have become the foundation for all community conduct (see 1 Cor. 3.10–11; 4.16–17; 11.1).

159. See D. Smith 2003: 187, 201–202, 207; R. Collins 1999: 463. For further discussion of the formal parallels between Hellenistic dinner parties and the Christian Eucharist, see D. Smith 2003; Lampe 1991a: 183–213; Lampe 1991b: 1–16. This symposium-like period of moral dialogue in the church is addressed in Chapter 3, section 3.d below.

160. See, e.g., Marcus Aurelius, *Med.* 2.1; 7.13; Epictetus, *Diss.* 2.10.3–4; Seneca, *Ep.* 95.52; *Anger* 2.31.7; Dio Chrysostom, *Disc.* 9.2; 33.34; 34.32; 39.5; 40.21; 41.9; 50.3.

161. D. Martin 1995: 92–96; R. Collins 1999: 459; Meeks 1983: 89; Horsley 1998: 171; Horrell 1996: 178; 1999: 323; see also M. Douglas 1973: 98.

162. See D. Martin 1995: 39; R. Collins 1999: 458; Horrell 1999: 323. Horrell considers and rightly rejects the possibility that in 12.18 Paul appeals to divine ordering as an element of a conservative ideology that legitimates the existing, 'worldly' social hierarchy (1996: 179–80).

163. Horrell also observes that Paul's basic moral concerns seem 'surprisingly similar' to those of Habermas and his contemporary theory of discourse (communicative) ethics that is grounded in 'equal respect' for the individual and 'empathy and concern for the well-being of one's neighbors'. Horrell 1999: 323, quoting Habermas 1990: 200; see also Benhabib 1992: 9.

Thus, church members should exercise the same care for each and every member of the body (12.25) no matter what their social status according to the world's standards. Paul thereby refers to the new, universal behavioural standard of Christ's self-giving love for others. If one member suffers, all the members suffer with that one, just as all members rejoice when one member is divinely glorified (12.26; see 2.7–8). Paul advocates the equality of care, mutual regard, and esteem that should be afforded to every member of the group, irrespective of their worldly social status and power.[164] Later, in 14.5, 24 and 31, he uses various forms of πᾶς to reinforce that each and every member of the church must be afforded equal participation in the practice of spiritual discernment in the post-dinner dialogue of the community.[165] According to the divine plan, there must be mutual respect and openness among community members in the post-dinner conversation. All who are present should be allowed to participate actively in the deliberations.[166] Paul points out how Christ-conforming conduct 'disempowers the powerful and revalues the nobodies, so that the community may be united in the kind of agreement that is founded on equal care and mutual regard' (Horrell 1999: 324). Paul calls the powerful to imitate Christ, because things are not as they should be in the community and that should be apparent to everyone (see Horrell 1999: 324).

Finally, in 12.27–30 Paul concludes the argument begun in 12.4. Each person is a member/organ of this political and social body of Christ 'for his/her own part' (12.27).[167] He identifies particular roles that serve an important *chronological* function in the formation and growth of this body that he also characterizes as the deliberative assembly (12.28).[168] The fact that Paul later suggests in 1 Corinthians 14 that every member of the community should seek to prophesy and should be allowed to do so (14.1, 5, 31) belies the argument that in 12.28 he is establishing a hierarchy of formal offices or positions in the church.[169] Although he does not use the term διακονία as he did in 12.4, the remainder of 12.28 identifies a number of different, essential services that build on the apostolic work through which God gave birth to the church (see 4.15) and continues to give it growth (see 3.6–15).[170]

---

164. See Horrell 1996: 182; 2 Cor. 8.13–15.

165. For the conclusion that the subject of 1 Corinthians 12 and 14 involves the problem of proper conversation or verbal instruction at the Christian assemblies in Corinth following the Eucharistic meal, see D. Smith 2003: 203–209; cf. Frör 1995: 65–66.

166. Aune 1978: 77. According to the contemporary theory of discourse (communicative) ethics, the willingness to reason from another person's point of view demonstrates the readiness to seek understanding with others and reach some reasonable agreement in an open-ended conversation (Benhabib 1992: 9).

167. For this translation of μέλη ἐκ μέρους, see R. Collins 1999: 470; Fee 1987: 618 n. 7.

168. For the conclusion that Paul is not establishing a hierarchy of offices – or of 'gifts' – see Fee 1987: 623 n. 34; *pace* Horsley 1998: 173.

169. See Gillespie, who concludes that the exhortation in 12.31 suggests that prophecy was a 'manifestation of the Spirit' not limited to those called 'prophets' (1994: 127). Cf. Forbes 1995: 246; Aune 1983: 198.

170. According to Horrell (1999: 323), Paul's description in 1 Corinthians 12 of the diversity of

Fundamental aspects of theo-ethical reasoning appear in 12.12–30. God exercises the power to arrange disparate people into a community that manifests the unified social body of Christ. This takes place in connection with conduct that conforms to Christ's cruciform pattern. The one Spirit sent from God illuminates community experiences of this divine power that build up the whole church by means of this life. Believers' faith is thereby grounded in the power of God (see 1 Cor. 2.1–5).

c. *Seeking the Greater* Χαρίσματα *through the Way of Love (12.31–13.13)*
Having emphasized the great variety of services grounded in the one Lord's cruciform pattern of self-giving love for others (12.5, 27–30), Paul turns in 12.31–13.13 to describe this 'way' of love that is 'beyond comparison'.[171] He asserts its link to particular spiritual experiences of new life from God (χαρίσματα). In 12.31a he exhorts the Corinthians to seek zealously (ζηλοῦτε)[172] the 'greater χαρίσματα'.[173] He thereby continues his theological critique of their pursuit of πνευματικά by privileging as 'greater' certain πνευματικά that he calls χαρίσματα.[174]

Paul's earlier arguments against internal competition make it highly improbable that he is encouraging the Corinthians to seek some χαρίσματα that are greater than others.[175] Instead, the χαρίσματα are those varied experiences of new life that enrich the community and are associated with God's life-giving power that works in connection with conduct conforming to Christ's cruciform pattern (see 1.4–9; 12.4–6). The verse at 12.31 also serves as a transition into 13.1–7, where Paul presents his own apostolic behavioural paradigm to illustrate this way of love that is beyond comparison (Holladay 1990: 80–98).

The shift from the second-person plural exhortation in 12.31a to first-person singular in 12.31b signals a change from paraenetic appeal to the use of personal example to illustrate that appeal (Mitchell 1991: 58).[176] The present tense δείκνυμι

---

these services within the functioning body belies Castelli's claim that Paul's exhortation to imitation is a 'call to sameness' and an 'indictment of difference' (1991a: 116).

171. For this translation of καθ' ὑπερβολὴν see BADG, p. 407. The phrase is used attributively with ὁδὸν rather than adverbially with δείκνυμι. Conzelmann 1975: 216; Fee 1987: 625; contra R. Collins 1999: 474–75.

172. According to Fee, the verb ζηλοῦτε is imperative rather than indicative (1987: 623 n. 32); cf. 14.1, 39.

173. The verse at 12.31 has been characterized as a 'puzzle' (Fee 1987: 623), a 'notable crux' (R. Martin 1984: 33) and a 'shift of accent' that does not go smoothly into the following chapters (Conzelmann 1975: 215). Our interpretation of 12.31 resolves perceived difficulties or tensions.

174. Baker (1974: 224–34), R. Martin (1984: 34–35, 65) and E. Ellis (1974a: 129), building on the work of Käsemann, agree that χαρίσματα is Paul's word that serves as a theological corrective to the Corinthians' use of πνευματικά. The two words are not synonymous (*pace* Bultmann 1952: 156; Conzelmann 1975: 207).

175. For this same conclusion, see Iber 1963: 43–52; R. Martin 1984: 34; Bittlinger 1967: 73; *pace* Fee 1987: 624–25.

176. Holladay shows that this shift, also evident in 8.13b as a transition to the personal example Paul employs in 1 Corinthians 9, was typical of Graeco-Roman paraenesis. It reflected the belief of ancient moralists that personal example was far superior to precept as a means of illustrating and reinforcing appeals to a particular mode of life (1990: 83–87).

used with ἔτι suggests that through his own life Paul has consistently tried to illustrate for them this way of love that he is about to describe (cf. 2.1–5; 4.8–13).[177]

With δείκνυμι Paul applies another verb that signified various visual experiences and the unveiling of divine secrets in both non-biblical and biblical Greek (see Schlier 1964b: 25–30). The New Testament itself provides a number of important examples.[178] The force of the verb is 'demonstrative' rather than 'pedagogical' (Holladay 1990: 87). Only once does it serve as a synonym for 'teach' (Mt. 16.21). Even more frequently – and to the point here – the verb involves revelations of God's action in the world that disclose some aspect of the heavenly mystery.[179] In fact δείκνυμι can be used synonymously with φανερόω and ἀποκαλύπτω (Schlier 1964b: 29), two other verbs closely associated with Paul's theo-ethical reasoning and the practice of spiritual discernment.

Moreover, the verb δείκνυμι has a history of being used in paraenetic contexts where a particular ethical lifestyle was being promulgated, especially in contexts where the preacher provided the paradigm.[180] While Paul's use of δείκνυμι in 12.31 is unique to his letters, a similar, compound form of the verb (ἀπέδειξεν) appears in 4.9.[181] Similarly, the latter verb's related noun form (ἀπόδειξις) was used in the critical verses in 1 Cor. 2.1–5, where Paul reminded the Corinthians that a visible demonstration of Spirit and power not only authenticated Paul's embodied proclamation of Christ crucified but also grounded their faith in the power of God.

In 12.31b Paul associates this important revelatory verb δείκνυμι with ὁδός, a word indicating the 'way' that the Corinthians should walk and conduct themselves in the world.[182] He thereby establishes a link between human conduct that conforms to this 'more excellent way' of love and experiences of new life that Paul characterizes as the greater χαρίσματα. A Septuagint equivalent of δείκνυμι (δείκνυω) was regularly used in conjunction with ὁδός to signify God's direct revelation or disclosures made through prophets to guide God's people in the proper way of conduct.[183] Thus, Paul's use of ὁδός in 12.31b is intended to point the Corinthians toward the way that they should walk.[184] According to the logic

---

177. See R. Collins, who concludes that the 'way' Paul puts before the Corinthians is the 'way' of his own life (1999: 474).

178. See Holladay 1990: 87 n. 35; Schlier, 1964b: 25–26; Mt. 4.8; 8.4; Mk 1.44; 14.15; Lk. 4.5; 5.14; 20.24; 22.12.

179. See, e.g., Lk. 24.40; Acts 7.3; 10.28; Jn 2.18; 5.20 (2×); 10.32; 14.8–9; 20.20; Heb. 8.5; Jas 2.18; Rev. 1.1; 4.1; 17.1; 21.9–10; 22.1, 6, 8.

180. Holladay 1990: 87. See, e.g., Epictetus, *Diss.* 3.22–26; *Diss.* 3.22, 45–49.

181. Cf. Acts 2.22; 25.7; 2 Thess. 2.4.

182. Michaelis indicates that in the New Testament the sense of ὁδός as 'walk' or as 'conduct' is 'plain in many passages' (1967c: 85–87); see also Conzelmann 1975: 216. By means of a dubious argument, however, Michaelis denies this application in 1 Cor. 12.31, where he renders ὁδός as merely an 'attitude'.

183. See, e.g., Exod. 13.21; Deut. 1.33; 1 Sam. 12.23–24; Ps. 49.23; Isa. 40.13–14 (cf. 1 Cor. 2.16); Isa. 48.17; Mic. 4.2.

184. According to Fee, to miss the parenetic thrust of this chapter is to miss the point altogether (1987: 627 n. 10).

of Paul's argument, cruciform acts of love lead to experiences of the greater χαρίσματα that manifest the experiences of new life through the power of God that builds up the community (see also 8.1–3). Paul thus forges a critical connection between human conduct and divine revelation, identifying a central component of theo-ethical reasoning and the practice of spiritual discernment.[185]

In 1 Corinthians 13, Paul continues to employ the self-referential first-person singular introduced in 12.31b. He emphasizes that this 'more excellent way' of love involves relational action rather than an attitude or emotion. In 13.1–3 he presents negative, hypothetical examples of conduct set in the context of his own apostolic ministry.[186] Of particular importance is 13.2, where Paul asserts that, even if a person has potentially powerful prophecy and 'has all the faith so as to move mountains', this person must nevertheless offer them in love if there is to be a benefit for others.[187] Shortly, Paul will highlight that the purpose of prophecy is to edify and encourage others rather than self (14.1–32). Thus, what Paul means in 13.2 is that prophecy must be offered to help others to walk in ways that are pleasing to God.

The overwhelming tendency of commentators is to deny Paul's use of πίστις in 13.2 as a reference to 'justifying faith'.[188] There is no linguistic or theological reason, however, for imposing such a limitation on Paul's use of πίστις in this context. Throughout Paul's letters, 'faith' refers to a level of confidence that God continues to act powerfully in connection with conduct that conforms to Christ's cruciform pattern. In 13.2 Paul is simply referring to a believer's confidence (i.e. 'faith') that God's power may even move mountains in connection with the believer's actions. Even in this exaggerated, metaphorical scenario, argues Paul, the contemplated action must nevertheless be one that benefits others rather than self.

In 13.4–7 Paul changes course, writing about love descriptively. He makes love the subject of the sentence to characterize the ways that love acts towards others. He thereby underscores love's behavioural grounding (Roetzel 1972: 160). In these verses Paul appears to use verbs that echo his earlier reflections on the conduct of some Corinthians (see 3.3; 4.6, 18–19; 5.2; 7.36). Similarly, according to 13.5, love does not seek its own way. This phrase recalls one of the most conspicuous shortcomings in the behaviour of some Corinthians (Holladay 1990: 96). Paul also suggests in 13.6 that love does not rejoice (χαίρει) in wrongdoing, but in the truth. The phrase ἐπὶ τῇ ἀδικίᾳ echoes the adjective ἄδικος and verb ἀδικέω used in 6.1–11, thus implying that the community members addressed there are not acting in love.

185. According to Segal, through Paul interpreters discover a whole social and ethical side to first-century mystical writings, normally missed in the modern separation of ethics, apocalypticism, and mysticism (1990: 59–60).
186. See Holladay 1990: 83–84; R. Collins 1999: 472; Horsley 1998: 176; cf. Horrell 1997a: 91–92.
187. Cf. R. Martin 1984: 44.
188. See, e.g., Fee, who limits it to 'special faith for mighty works' (1987: 632); Holladay, who says it means the ability to perform miracles of healing, particularly exorcisms (1990: 90). But Paul clearly distinguishes πίστις from 'miracles of healings' in 12.9.

Conversely, the verb συγχαίρω in 13.6 echoes 12.26, where Paul argued that every community member must have the same care and concern for others by rejoicing together when another member is glorified. These parallels suggest that exercising the same care and concern for one another constitutes the active practice of love grounded in Christ's universal cruciform pattern of self-giving love for others. Finally, Paul asserts in 13.7 that 'love bears all things' (πάντα στέγει), echoing 9.12. There, he recalled for the Corinthians his own apostolic conduct by which he voluntarily gave up rights to compensation. He bears all things (πάντα στέγομεν), lest he might place some obstacle to the gospel in the path of others. By implication, Paul's own action has the look of love.

Paul concludes his description of the 'more excellent way' of love in 13.8–13, where he contrasts the enduring, eternal nature of relational love with the partial, incomplete and temporary quality of earthly human life. He implies the divine source and character of love, contrasting it with the faith and hope associated with mortal Christian life (13.13). When the complete comes (ὅταν δὲ ἔλθη τὸ τέλειον), the prophecy, knowledge and tongues that are part of earthly human life will cease (13.8, 10). Paul thereby minimizes the importance of the individual spiritual experiences valued so highly by some members of the community (Horsley 1998: 178).

In 13.11 Paul returns to the key word νήπιος. He uses it this time not to refer to the Corinthians (see 3.1), but to contrast the 'then' and 'now' of his own life (Holladay 1990: 97). Speaking of the time before Christ appeared to him, Paul says that he was once infant-like because he spoke, thought (ἐφρόνουν)[189] and reasoned (ἐλογιζόμην) as one who was infant-like. He insinuates that at least some of the Corinthians are still speaking, thinking and reflecting according to infant-like standards (see 3.1).

Paul attempts to change their immature perspectives grounded in worldly standards. In 13.12 he describes the heart of his apocalyptic (i.e. revelatory) outlook encased within two-age dualism. He uses ἄρτι and τότε twice to make a temporal *and* qualitative distinction. On the one hand is earthly human life, where humans 'see' and 'know' indirectly and only 'in part'. On the other is fully transformed life at the completion (13.10; see also 15.24). This is the time when believers see (God and Christ) face to face and fully know (ἐπιγνώσομαι) just as they have been fully known (ἐπεγνώσθην). The divine passive ἐπεγνώσθην (13.12b)[190] suggests that the active ἐπιγνώσομαι refers to knowing God fully, an important concern expressed throughout the letter (see 1.21; 8.3; 15.34; see also Gal. 4.8–9). Paul thus continues to challenge those who claim certainty about their *present* knowledge of God without actually practising love (see 1 Cor. 8.1–13).

Indeed, explains Paul in 13.12a, humans now see through a mirror in a riddle (βλέπομεν γὰρ ἄρτι δι᾽ ἐσόπτρου ἐν αἰνίγματι).[191] He continues to use

189. Cf. 4.10; 10.15; 11.22.
190. See R. Collins 1999: 497.
191. For this translation of αἴνιγμα, see LSJ, 39; Fee 1987: 647 n. 42; Barrett 1968: 307; cf. Ashton 2000: 137.

βλέπω, a verb of sight. In ancient Greek literature the mirror symbolized, among other possibilities, the indirectness of vision.[192] Paul employs the metaphor in 13.12a in a similar way (see also 2 Cor. 3.18).[193] In a mirror one sees one's own image (Fee 1987: 648). What Paul means is that when a believer looks into the mirror he or she *should* be seeing (indirectly) the image of Christ reflected in certain actions taken in the context of his or her own life or actions taken in the context of the lives of other believers.[194] Thus, this present, but indirect, vision to which Paul refers takes place 'in a riddle'.

According to the deeper logic of theo-ethical reasoning that lies beneath the surface of the text, Paul's phrase is not pejorative. He is speaking metaphorically about the way the community tries to solve this riddle through the practice of spiritual discernment in the deliberative assembly. By reflecting on conduct and experience, the community seeks to identify indirect visions of the image of Christ. These may become manifest in connection with a believer's conduct when it conforms to Christ's cruciform pattern and is divinely confirmed by its link to experiences of new life in the community. If someone tentatively identifies such a connection, it must then be evaluated by the entire community (1 Cor. 14.29–32). Only then, through seeing this indirect vision of the image of Christ, will believers be transformed into that same image of Christ from one glory to another (cf. 2 Cor. 3.18). We suggest that this is what Paul means in 1 Cor. 1.7–8 when he encourages the Corinthians to expect that the revelation of Jesus Christ will continue to take place among them until the end – the time of the completion.

The Corinthians must learn anew to see and recognize the image of Christ as it is indirectly reflected in the mirror. They must do so in the practice of spiritual discernment by identifying their experiences of new life from God and associating them with divinely confirmed, Christ-conforming behaviour. Paul thus sets the stage rhetorically for 1 Corinthians 14, where he addresses the community's failure to practise spiritual discernment by engaging in theo-ethical reasoning.

d. *Practising Spiritual Discernment: Reflecting on Conduct and Experience Builds Up the Community (14.1–40)*
Paul's criticism of the Corinthians' inadequate practice of spiritual discernment reaches its climax in 14.1–40, where Paul addresses their failure to engage adequately in the moral dialogue that should be taking place in the symposium-like period that follows the Lord's Supper.[195] It is one in which all church members

192. Conzelmann 1975: 227–28, citing Plato, *Tim.* 71b and Philo, *Decal.* 105; Fee 1987: 648.
193. The mirror also symbolized clarity in Plato (*Tim.* 72c) and the Platonic tradition (Conzelmann 1975: 227; Horsley 1998: 178). Paul does not intend that meaning in 13.12. Horsley, thinking that Paul enlists the metaphor in this sense, wrongly concludes that 13.12 actually 'subverts' the mirror image (1998: 178). Instead, Paul exploits one of its meanings to clarify his apocalyptic (i.e. revelatory) perspective on the link between human conduct and experience.
194. See 11.1; 15.49; 2 Cor. 3.18; cf. Gal. 3.27.
195. This type of post-supper, symposium-like event in Christian gatherings has been recognized by Aune (1978: 74–75) and recently explored in more detail by Lampe (1991a: 190–91).

must participate, as they prophesy to one another by seeking to associate past actions with particular experiences (see 14.1–5). What Paul means is this: by making such connections believers are better able to imaginatively envision future Christ-conforming actions that they anticipate might lead to other experiences of God's life-giving power that builds up the community.[196] In this section Paul sets out an ordered process that elevates rational and cognitive prophecy over the ecstatic, stressing the importance of the mind in the theo-ethical reasoning and the practice of spiritual discernment.[197] This dialogue that attempts to evaluate diverse prophecies and the 'spirits' associated with them requires intelligible communication, with the expectation that revelation may take place in the conversation.[198] Thus, Paul responds to those church members who were convinced that the gift of unintelligible, inspired utterance was the principal, divinely authenticating sign of Christian prophecy associated with life in the Spirit (Gillespie 1978: 80–82). It may have even been a practice that some viewed as a symbol of high status within the community (see D. Martin 1995: 88).

The content of 1 Corinthians 14 serves as the basis for all discussion about prophecy from Paul's point of view.[199] The evidence is so limited that interpreters must make inferences from that evidence (Forbes 1995: 237). Thus, this study will continue looking beneath the surface of the text to try to identify how Paul understands prophecy, as seen through the interpretative lens of theo-ethical reasoning. Before looking at the text, however, Paul's broader place in first-century prophecy will be explored briefly.

Paul associated himself in at least some nominal way with the classical Hebrew prophets.[200] They were not primarily predictors of the future but social, moral and religious critics who addressed their own situation and called for reform (Gray 1993: 167). Although prophecy was not a phenomenon that had ended by the first century, its evolution had led to differences of degree and kind from the ancient prophets. First-century prophets believed that God controlled the events of history in a direct and immediate way (Gray 1993: 166). Moreover, they thought that God revealed God's intentions through prophets who sought to warn and lead people by encouraging them to follow the path that the prophet had chosen

---

196. Beker concludes that Paul's churches discern the will of God in particular circumstances not through casuistry but flexible interpretation arrived at through communal discussion and consensus, collective investigation of 'that which counts'; there is no isolated existential decision in ethical situations since the group comes together to investigate, test and approve what is the will of God (1980: 320–21). Similarly, Hauerwas observes that the church's focus on 'gathering' makes it impossible to divorce Christian ethics from ecclesiology (1995: 157).

197. According to D. Martin, Paul's deference to the 'mind' was an aspect of his understanding of the gospel as reversal: Paul was raising the status of the mind to the same level as that of the spirit (1995: 103).

198. See 14.29–33; cf. Rom. 1.11–12. According to Koenig, Paul also understands this interpretative work as a reciprocal affair done in community (1978: 169, 174, including n. 14).

199. Forbes 1995: 237; see also Aune 1983: 19. For Paul's references to prophecy or a prophet other than the historical prophets of Israel, see Rom. 12.6; 1 Cor. 12.10, 28, 29; 13.2, 8; 14.6, 22, 29, 32, 37; 1 Thess. 5.20; cf. Eph. 2.20; 3.5; 4.11. Paul uses the verb προφητεύω only in 1 Corinthians (11.4, 5; 13.9; 14.1, 3–5, 24, 31, 39).

200. See Gal. 1.15, discussed in Chapter 4, section 2.c.

for them (Gray 1993: 166).[201] The prophet was one who enjoyed a special relationship with God and thereby gained access to privileged information and knowledge about the proper conduct of life that was not otherwise available (J. Barton 1986: 96–140).

Prophecy during Paul's time was concerned with the future as focused on the consequences of present action (J. Barton 1986: 200–202).[202] Our study has already identified and established this as an aspect of Paul's theo-ethical reasoning. He reflects on the links between past conduct and experience to envision imaginatively future actions that he anticipates will reflect divine approval (cf. 7.25). More specifically, prophecy for Paul involved the exercise of a teaching ministry that was pastorally oriented to build up the community and to reveal the word and will of God (see 14.1–3).[203] It involved pastoral preaching that by its nature offered guidance and instruction to the community, thereby serving a broad paraenetic function to get people to change their ways (D. Hill 1977: 114–16).[204] For Paul, prophecy also included the practice of critical reflection necessary to make these kinds of connections (Thiselton 2000: 1093). Indeed, for Paul, revelation grounds prophecy (cf. 14.30), which may be understood as the public proclamation of a revelatory event or experience[205] associated with behavioural matters.

With this as background, Paul opens this important section of the letter with twin imperatives in 14.1 that reflect the application of theo-ethical reasoning. He encourages the Corinthians to pursue love and to be zealous for the spiritual things (τὰ πνευματικά), especially so that they might continue to prophesy. Once again he affirms their desire for πνευματικά, while reinforcing the link made in 12.31–13.13 between the practice of love and experiences of God's life-giving power that Paul calls the 'greater χαρίσματα'. According to the logic underlying Paul's assertion, the Corinthians themselves must actively *pursue* acts of Christ-conforming love, since this is a human behavioural matter. They may

201. Gray points out, however, that Josephus appears to limit the biblical prophets' activities to that of prediction and minimizes their didactic and hortatory roles (1993: 268).

202. Barton's characterization of prophecy has drawn express approval from at least one Pauline scholar (Matlock 1996: 298).

203. D. Hill 1977: 127–28. According to L.T. Johnson, prophecy for Paul was 'a form of ordered and controlled speech that reveals God's action in the world and calls the church to response' (1996: 119).

204. For unpersuasive criticism of Hill's conclusions in this context, see Aune 1983: 13. A similar criticism is that of Gillespie, who argues (wrongly) that Hill's characterization of prophecy as 'pastoral preaching' grounded in 1 Cor. 14.3 distorts 'gospel proclamation' and leads to the 'trivialization' of early Christian prophecy (1994: 28). The problem lies in Gillespie's understanding that 'doing theology' involves doctrine rather than a focus on pastoral matters involving the discernible power of God working to build up the community in connection with specific Christ-conforming behaviour. Thus, it may be concluded that Gillespie privileges doctrine over ethics (see Elliott 1994: 72–75, discussed in Chapter 1, section 2.c). Moreover, Gillespie underestimates the central role of revelation in Paul's gospel proclamation.

205. See Turner 1996: 10–12; Grudem 1982: 116, 142. Turner erroneously understands this, however, only in connection with *spontaneous* utterances that take place without the benefit of critical reflection.

only *desire* spiritual experiences, however, since these are wrought by powers external to believers and beyond their control, although they are experienced in connection with specific conduct (see 3.1–3; 12.4–7; see also Gal. 5.19–25).

The purpose clause in 1 Cor. 14.1 shows that Paul understands prophecy as something that derives from making this connection between Christ-conforming conduct (i.e. acts of love) and spiritual experiences of new life from God (χαρίσ-ματα). This implies that the prophet and others must practise spiritual discernment by engaging in theo-ethical reasoning to identify these links. This is a method of reasoning and a practice that Paul thoroughly described in the letter's opening chapters and has illustrated throughout the letter. Indeed, for Paul, prophesying 'depends on the active agency of the Holy Spirit mediated through human minds and lives to build up, to encourage, to judge, to exhort, and to comfort others in the context of interpersonal relations'.[206]

It would thus appear that prophets imaginatively envision specific, future actions that might conform to Christ's cruciform pattern. They anticipate the future consequences of such actions, expecting that such behaviour will be divinely confirmed through experiences of new life that enrich and build up the community (see 1.4–9). It is suggested that this is one of the regular practices by which the community seeks to solve the riddle identified in 13.12. Prophets are those who look into the mirror and try to discern the image of Christ through their own Christ-conforming actions or those of other believers. The more they see the face of Christ in the mirror through these actions, the more they are divinely transformed into the image of Christ (see 2 Cor. 3.18). Prophets also point to experiences of community edification that confirm such Christ-conforming conduct (see 1 Cor. 1.4–9) by which the *body* of Christ is being transformed through the power of God working in connection with such Christ-conforming actions (see 15.44, 46, 49).

According to 14.3, the one prophesying speaks edification (οἰκοδομὴν). Paul probably means that prophecy provides 'encouragement and consolation'[207] when the speaker identifies connections between conduct and experiences (see also 14.1). The church is built up when someone intelligibly communicates the discernible links between specific Christ-conforming conduct and experiences of new life, as community members rejoice together under such circumstances (see 12.26).[208] In this way they gain confidence, growing in faith as they perceive that conduct conforming to Christ's cruciform pattern constitutes the pathway to experiences of God's life-giving power (cf. Phil. 2.5–11). On the other hand, when the prophet asserts that actions do not conform to Christ's cruciform

---

206. Thiselton 2000: 1094; see also 2000: 956–65, 1087–94; cf. D. Hill, who concludes that for Paul prophecy is inspired 'pastoral preaching' – as distinguished from 'evangelistic' preaching (1977: 112).

207. See D. Hill 1979: 122–23. Reiling (1973: 13) and Aune (1983: 19) both raise the concern that the phrase οἰκοδομὴν καὶ παράκλησιν καὶ παραμυθίαν does not express specific characteristics. But it is the encouragement and consolation that are the community benefits derived from hearing about the articulated connections between conduct and experience.

208. See Cullmann 1953: 26.

pattern because they are associated with painful or divisive experiences (see, e.g.,
1 Cor. 1.11–16; 3.1–3; 5.1–6.11; Gal. 5.19–21), there is a need for mutual and
shared suffering (see 1 Cor. 12.26), admonition (see 1 Thess. 5.12–21) and consolation (cf. 1 Cor. 14.3, 35).

For these reasons Paul insists that prophecy must be intelligible if it is to build
up the community by providing encouragement and consolation. In fact no one
'hears' the person who speaks mysteries to God through uninterpreted tongues
(14.2). Literally, of course, listeners undoubtedly hear the audible sounds of uninterpreted tongues. For Paul, however, the verb ἀκούω also encompasses comprehension and response to the content of what has been spoken.[209] This is not
surprising, since in the Septuagint the verb ἀκούω and the related noun ἀκοή are
regularly used to translate various forms rooted in the Hebrew verb שׁמע.[210] We
suggest that there can be no 'hearing' without: (1) intelligible prophecy that identifies past experiences of the greater χαρίσματα; and (2) prophetic association of
these experiences with acts of cruciform love. This allows the prophet and other
listeners to envision imaginatively other actions that may also lead to experiences
of new life through God's life-giving power.

Indeed, in 14.14, Paul characterizes the mind of the one speaking in a tongue
as unfruitful. By this, Paul means that this person is not intelligibly identifying
the important connection between conduct and experience so that others might be
encouraged or consoled. The speech proves unproductive because it provides
only individual rather than community edification (see 14.4). Paul thereby
devalues the unintelligible *glossolalia* that some members of the community
were viewing as the supreme spiritual gift (Bassler 1982b: 415) or, at the very
least, were accepting as the only form of divine confirmation of the speaker's prophetic powers and spiritual status (L.T. Johnson 1996: 116). As with other sections of the letter, Paul's vision of church life shows a clear tendency to elevate
the rational and cognitive over the ecstatic (Alexander 1994: 82).

Paul's uses of οἰκοδομὴν or οἰκοδομέω in 14.3–5 and 12 continue his
prominent use of the building theme (see also 3.9; 8.1; 10.23). The metaphor
characterizes the goal of Christ-conforming conduct: building up the community through the power of God that gives new life in connection with Christ-
conforming behaviour. The prophet's intelligible statements benefit the entire
deliberative assembly (ἐκκλησία) and not just the individual (14.4). The point is
so critical in Paul's theo-ethical reasoning that he rephrases it in 14.5. The one
prophesying is greater than the one speaking in unintelligible tongues, unless
the latter interprets the tongues so that the ἐκκλησία might receive edification.
Being 'zealots of spirits', they must seek the edification (οἰκοδομὴν) of the

---

209. Paul elsewhere uses the verb ἀκούω and the related noun ἀκοή at several key points in his
arguments concerning how believers receive gospel proclamation. See, e.g., Rom. 10.10, 14, 16–18;
11.8; 15.21; 2 Cor. 12.6; Gal. 3.2, 5; 4.21; Phil. 4.9; 1 Thess. 2.13; cf. 1 Cor. 2.9. It will be argued in
Chapter 4 that the 'hearing of faith' in Gal. 3.2 and 3.5 that leads to the receipt of the Spirit includes
both the listeners' understanding and behavioural response to the way Paul proclaimed Christ
crucified. See Chapter 4, section 3.a below.

210. See, e.g., Exod. 15.26; 19.5; Deut. 28.1, 2.

deliberative assembly (ἐκκλησία) so that they might flourish with new life (14.12). What Paul seems to suggest is that through the practice of spiritual discernment, described in 2.12–16, they must *distinguish* spiritual experiences of new life from God that build up the whole church (i.e. the 'greater χαρίσματα') from those unintelligible and/or individual spiritual experiences that do not benefit the entire community but only individuals (see 14.18–19).

The logic consistently underlying Paul's argument suggests that the community is built up when all of its members are able to perceive, understand and affirm how their experiences of new life from God are linked to Christ-conforming conduct (cf. 14.16–17). Paul makes the connection to specific behaviour clear in 14.19. He would rather speak five words with his mind than a myriad of words in tongues so that (ἵνα) he might instruct (κατηχήσω) others (14.19). The verb κατηχέω (see also Gal. 6.6) links intelligible prophecy with behavioural instruction.[211] Speaking with the mind for the benefit of others implies a community dialogue. This involves various prophecies that must be evaluated with the expectation that revelation might take place during the conversation in the deliberative assembly (see 1 Cor. 14.29–32). Thus, it may be said that, for Paul, the goal of prophecy is to declare the will of God for the present, expressed by means of reasoned and intelligible speech (see Käsemann 1980: 340). In fact it may even be concluded that the public affirmation of the connection between specific Christ-conforming actions and experiences of new life from God lies at the heart of Paul's gospel proclamation that grounds believers' faith in the discernible power of God (see 2.1–5).[212]

With an exhortation and hypothetical illustration in 14.20–25, Paul concludes his lengthy contrast between self-edifying, uninterpreted tongues and intelligible prophecy that builds up the church because it benefits others. The illustration shifts the focus from Paul's critique of tongues to the dialogical practice of spiritual discernment that becomes the main subject in 14.26–40. Moreover, the illustration models this practice that should be taking place in the symposium-like period of moral dialogue that follows the Lord's Supper.

Paul challenges the Corinthians in 14.20 to stop being children and become mature in their discernment practices (ταῖς φρεσίν).[213] By citing Isa. 28.11–12,[214] he suggests that uninterpreted tongues do not lead to obedience (εἰσακούσονταί) to the Lord (1 Cor. 14.21). This compound verb rooted in ἀκούω is used frequently to translate שׁמע in the Septuagint.[215] Once again it shows that for Paul

---

211. See Rom. 2.18; cf. Acts 18.25; 21.21. Fee concludes that κατηχέω is not the ordinary word for 'teach' and has to do with 'informing' or 'instructing' another in 'religious matters' (1987: 676); *pace* Conzelmann, who asserts that the verb is used only in connection with 'dogmatic' instruction (1975: 240).

212. The failure to see this connection leads Gillespie to distinguish unnecessarily between Paul's gospel proclamation and pastoral preaching (1994: 24).

213. For this translation of φρεσίν as 'discernment', see Conzelmann 1975: 241; Fee 1987: 678 n. 9.

214. Fee discusses Paul's divergences from known versions of Isa. 28.11–12 (1987: 679–80).

215. In the Septuagint this verb is used over 200 times in connection with obedience to the voice of the Lord and frequently translates the Hebrew verb שׁמע. See, e.g., Deut. 30.8, 10, 17, 20.

'hearing' not only involves listening to the spoken word but also includes an appropriate behavioural response (cf. 14.2; Gal. 3.2, 5). Uninterpreted tongues do not build up the community by helping others identify how to respond to what is heard. Imagined future behaviour must be communicated through intelligible prophecy that predicts, based on previously discerned links between conduct and experience, how such conduct may be connected to another anticipated demonstration of Spirit and power that grounds believers' faith (see 1 Cor. 2.1–5).

Paul's hypothetical example in 14.23–25 illustrates how intelligible prophecy becomes a sign for believers (14.22), as the connections between conduct and experience are identified. He depicts a scenario where the whole deliberative assembly has come together in the same place. Present are people who have no faith (ἄπιστος) or are uninstructed/unpractised (ἰδιώτης).[216] Reading between the lines, we tentatively suggest that, when members of the community prophesy, they closely examine (ἀνακρίνεται) the actions of the outsider (cf. 4.3–4). According to 14.24–25, through this dialogue the conduct of the outsider is brought to light (ἐλέγχεται) and the hidden things of the outsider's heart become manifest (φανερά). This language parallels 4.4–5, where Paul describes how the Lord will come and closely examine (ἀνακρίνων) their behaviour and bring to light (φωτίσει) the purposes of people's hearts.

Paul states the main purpose of his illustration in 14.25. By means of the community dialogue, intelligible prophecy may even become revelatory to the uninstructed one who has no faith and is merely a passive participant in the conversation. The outsider sees, hears and understands things about the outsider's own life. In the process this person may recognize and acknowledge the way that God is actively working among members of the community, even as they reflect on experiences associated with the actions of those outside the community.

In early Christianity 'prescriptive oracles' were a form of prophetic speech involving ethical issues in which the speaker enjoins a particular type of action or behaviour in a specific context (Aune 1983: 321–22). There was frequently a claim made to some form of divine inspiration that provided authority for this type of paraenesis because it was often applied in contexts of conflict where some in the audience might not fully share the speaker's convictions (Aune 1983: 322). Paul's illustration implies that the revelation that may take place in community dialogue provides divine authentication of the prophecy offered.[217] Paul confirms this in the following verses.

In 14.26–40 he provides order for the community practice of spiritual discernment that includes the articulation and evaluation of prophecy. He frames both ends of the passage with an imperative (γινέσθω), thereby emphasizing the importance of their behaviour during this symposium-like period of moral dialogue. During this conversation all speech and actions must be taken for

---

216. For this latter translation, see LSJ, 819.

217. Christian literature of the late first century and early second century consistently reflects the importance of community dialogue involving prophecy and the evaluation of appropriate conduct that serves the common advantage of the community. See *Barn.* 4.9–11; 21.4–6; *Did.* 16.2; Hermas, *Sim.* 9.26.3; Ignatius, *Eph.* 13.1.

building up (οἰκοδομὴν) the community (14.26). Paul thus highlights again the goal of Christian behaviour (whether inside or outside the deliberative assembly) and the new discernment criterion that must be applied to evaluate community experiences associated with such actions. Moreover, he stresses once again that *all* community members must participate in this collective discernment process. When they come together each person (ἕκαστος) may offer something to the worship and dialogue (14.26).[218]

Apparently, the meetings of the whole deliberative assembly had become chaotic with a great number of spontaneous utterances (possibly overlapping) and the offering of unintelligible, uninterpreted tongues (Lampe 1991c: 20).[219] Consequently, Paul sets out a procedure in 14.29–33 to address the problem and thereby establishes the *dialogical* nature of spiritual discernment. The Corinthians must collectively test all prophetic speech for content (14.29, 32).[220] Apparently, such testing had not been the regular practice in this church.[221] With this exhortation Paul may be contributing to a broader debate in the early church focused on how Christian communities authenticate prophecy.[222] His earliest extant correspondence suggests that the community practice of spiritual discernment, including the evaluation of prophecy, already played an important role in his churches.[223]

Moreover, Paul's repetitive and emphatic use of πάντες three times in 14.31 emphasizes another of his concerns expressed throughout the letter. It may be that some were dominating the 'deliberative assembly' (cf. 11.22).[224] They may have been proceeding with the post-Supper, symposium-like period of moral dialogue before everyone had arrived and had an equal opportunity to participate. Alternatively, it may be that some were simply ignoring the prophetic contributions of others who they deemed to be less important members of the assembly

218. In 14.26 Paul is describing what should be happening (Fee 1987: 690) rather than reproaching the Corinthians for too much that is happening (*pace* R. Martin 1984: 78).
219. For the possibility that the size of the community may have been contributing to the problems, see the characterization of Frör 1995: 3.
220. Cf. 12.10; see also Rom. 12.1–2; 1 Thess. 5.19–22.
221. R. Collins 1999: 445. Horsley identifies two separate steps in this discernment process: evaluating the content of prophecies and the testing of 'spirits' (1998: 187).
222. In early Christian history, prophetic speech was regarded as authentic only when the community collectively discerned the authenticity of such prophecy. See *Did.* 11.8, 10, 11; Hermas, *Mand.* 11.7–21; cf. Mt. 7.16, 20. According to *Did.* 11.8a this determination was based not on the content or manner of delivery of the prophetic speech but on community agreement that the voice of the Lord was speaking through the prophet. This conclusion was authenticated by the manifest effects of that prophetic word in the life and behaviour of the prophet. See also Hermas, *Mand.* 11.7a, 16; cf. 11.10, 11; 1 Cor. 2.1–5; 4.8–13, 19–20; 2 Cor. 6.3–10; 13.1–3; Gal. 3.2, 5; 4.12–20; D. Hill 1977: 130; Niederwimmer 1998: 178–79.
223. See 1 Thess. 5.19–22, where Paul links the Spirit and prophecy with holding fast to 'the good' as it is collectively proved through testing (δοκιμάζετε). Indeed, throughout his letters, Paul consistently uses the verb δοκιμάζω and its related noun (δοκιμήν) and adjective (δόκιμος) to refer to the community process of discerning the divine proof that confirms conduct conforming to Christ's cruciform pattern of self-giving love for others. See also Rom. 1.28; 2.18; 5.4; 12.2; 14.18, 22; 16.10; 2 Cor. 2.9; 8.2, 8, 22; 9.13; 10.18; 13.3, 5–7; Gal. 6.4; Phil. 1.10; 2.22; 1 Thess. 2.4; 5.21; cf. Eph. 5.10. Paul's use of ἀδόκιμος also supports this argument. See Rom 1.28; 1 Cor. 9.27; 2 Cor. 13.5–7.
224. See Fee 1987: 695.

Looking for Life

(see 12.22–25). Either way, the deliberative assembly is impoverished and the evaluative process of engaging in theo-ethical reasoning is potentially thwarted as a result.[225] Indeed, all members of the community must be singly able to prophesy in order that (ἵνα) all members might learn and all members might be encouraged (see 14.31).[226]

The imperative in 14.29 to let two or three prophets speak does not limit the number of prophecies to be offered in the assembly.[227] Rather, Paul proposes a more orderly procedure that recognizes the need of each person to hear the prophecies offered in turn. Paul's use of the verb ἀποκαλύπτω in 14.30 points out that revelation may occur in the course of this dialogue.[228] This indicates that revelatory insight is an essential source of prophecy.[229] Thus, it would seem that, for Paul, prophecy involves the divine unveiling of the heavenly mystery. It is disclosed when believers associate experiences of new life from God with conduct that conforms to Christ's cruciform pattern (cf. 2.1, 7, 10–12).

Building on the comparative process of spiritual discernment described in 2.13–16, Paul exhorts the Corinthians in 14.29 to distinguish (διακρινέτωσαν) between prophecies after two or three have spoken. He gives priority to the listeners' assessments of the prophecies, implying that prophecy must be collectively evaluated (Wire 1990: 147, 149). The verb διακρινέτωσαν highlights the practice of distinguishing among several behavioural possibilities, just as Paul has suggested throughout the letter by using this same verb (see 4.7; 6.5; 11.29, 31; cf. 11.19). This collective evaluation must occur in close proximity to the time the prophecies are presented to establish some order for this potentially contentious conversation (cf. 11.16).

Thus, it appears that, for Paul, proclamation and preaching are not the task of one person but a task for several, if not every member, of the congregation. Thus, the worship service comprises dialogue, sometimes even dispute, requiring some order for the sequence (Lampe 1991b: 18, 20). Indeed, in these verses Paul appears to be reminding the Corinthians of something they already supposedly practise (Horsley 1998: 187; cf. 1 Thess. 5.19–21).

In 14.32–33 Paul asserts that the spirits of prophets are ordered by prophets. He thereby builds on his earlier characterization of this dialogue as the process of comparing spiritual things with spiritual things (2.13). This is an important aspect of distinguishing various prophecies (see 14.30). The goal of this comparative process is to identify and acknowledge the greater χαρίσματα (cf.

225. Aune points out (1978: 73) that in Plutarch's ideal symposium practice there must be equality among the guests (*qu. conv.* 613F) and that disorder in the proceedings threatened its effectiveness (*qu. conv.* 615E; 618C), possibilities that cannot be dismissed for the church in Corinth.

226. The only other Christian text to discuss prophecy in any detail, Hermas, *Mand.* 11, also suggests that the gathered church as a whole is a prophetic body and that any member may be called upon by the Spirit to speak as the Lord wills. See Reiling 1977: 74–75.

227. Fee 1987: 693; *pace* R. Collins 1999: 519.

228. According to one perspective within the contemporary theory of discourse (communicative) ethics, these conversations must be viewed as 'moral-transformative processes' (Benhabib 1986: 312–16), thus implying that revelation takes place during the course of the dialogue.

229. See Fee 1987: 695; Cullmann 1953: 20; Reiling 1977: 70.

12.31) that are distinct from the other 'spiritual things' (τὰ πνευματικά) that often edify only the individual or may even destroy the community (see also 14.18–29; cf. 3.3, 16–18; 8.7–13). The spirits of prophets must be ordered or prioritized (14.33) because God is not the God of anarchy or confusion (ἀκατασ-τασίας) but peace.[230] This comparative, dialogical process must be undertaken in an orderly fashion so that the power of God may even be experienced in the course of the discernment dialogue (see 14.22–25).

Paul winds down this section of the letter in 14.37–38, issuing a challenge to all those who think that they are prophets or spiritual people. They must recognize fully (ἐπιγινωσκέτω) that his suggestions for order in the practice of spiritual discernment are a command of the Lord (cf. 7.19). As he has done throughout the letter, he puts his own 'spiritual authority' on the line (Wire 1990: 158). He leaves the final decision about his behavioural suggestions for the community to discern, however, relying on the one and the same Holy Spirit to persuade them that the Lord is speaking through him in the circumstances.[231] He remains confident that the living God will vindicate him.[232]

In the enigmatic 14.38, however, he takes a parting shot at those who are not practising spiritual discernment. Anyone who does not recognize his ordering recommendation as a commandment of the Lord is not being known (ἀγνοεῖται) by God (see 8.1–3; 15.34; cf. 1.21).[233] Paul thereby implies that the disorder and judgment presently being experienced by members of the community lead him to conclude that their present practices are not meeting with the Lord's approval.[234]

Consequently, Paul closes with one further imperative: let all things be done (γινέσθω) decently and according to order (14.40; cf. 14.26; 16.14). But it is not the good order *per se* through which God works to build up the community.[235] Rather, God continues to build up the church by giving it new life, experienced in connection with specific Christ-conforming acts of believers. Believers must identify this connection, however, in order to envision imaginatively other actions that may lead them to anticipate other experiences of new life. This means that the prophecy must be undertaken in a way that makes it intelligible for everyone in the deliberative assembly.

4. *The Divine Mystery of Bodily Transformation (15.1–58)*

This climactic section of the letter also 'provides the key to its meaning' (Barth 1933: 11).[236] Paul presents his interpretation of the events God set in motion with

---

230. The phrase 'as in all the deliberative assemblies of the saints' in 14.33b begins the probable interpolation about women remaining silent in the churches. This interpolation continues in 14.34–35. See R. Collins 1999: 520; contra Fee 1987: 697–98.

231. Cf. Wire 1990: 158; 2 Cor. 13.3.

232. Cf. Käsemann 1969b: 74.

233. Käsemann acknowledges that the passive verb denotes divine action (1969b: 68–69).

234. Cf. Käsemann 1969b: 68–69.

235. According to Scroggs, the imperative in 14.40 does not reflect that 'order' and 'decency' are the primary aims of an 'overly-rigid Paul', but that mutual edification and learning cannot take place in the midst of ecstatic disorder (1996: 24 n. 22).

236. See also Gorman 2001: 323.

Christ's crucifixion and resurrection. Responding to doubts and questions about
the resurrection of the dead, he argues that God established a process of bodily
transformation that is already underway.[237] For proof Paul points to his own experience of the risen Lord and to the Corinthians' experience of the power of God in
connection with Paul's embodied proclamation of Christ crucified.[238]

The chapter begins with a warning about conduct and ends with an exhortation,
thereby making clear the chapter's 'practical intent' (Meeks 1996: 802). Paul sets
out not to teach 'correct beliefs' but to 'reassure and stabilize a community that
has work to do in the world' (Meeks 1996: 802). Believers who were called by
God into partnership with Jesus Christ (1.9) become active participants with God
in this process of bodily transformation by conforming their behaviour to Christ's
cruciform pattern. Paul integrates earlier arguments, concluding that God is now
exercising the power that gives new life and transforming bodies in connection
with conduct that conforms to Christ's cruciform pattern. Thus, theo-ethical reasoning shapes Paul's interpretation and presentation in 1 Corinthians 15.

a. *God's Power is Manifest in Christ's Resurrection Body (15.1–11)*
Paul begins by reminding the Corinthians that they received the gospel – that
divine event that reveals God's power giving new life in the world (15.1–2; cf.
Rom. 1.16–17).[239] Their experience became part of the gospel's revelatory history, a history that continues to unfold through a series of gospel events that occur
each time God's life-giving power becomes manifest in the world.[240] According to
1 Cor. 15.1–2 this divine event first took place by means of Paul's communicative act (τίνι λόγῳ εὐηγγελισάμην).[241] This includes both his preaching and
cruciform lifestyle (see 2.2; cf. Gal. 3.1).[242] Indeed, Paul regularly applies the
verb εὐαγγελίζωμαι (used in 1 Cor. 15.1, 2) to describe all of his actions as an
apostle.[243] He thus begins this climactic chapter just as he began the letter –

---

237. According to Schweitzer, Paul 'asserted that the solidarity of the Elect with Christ was already
working itself out in the period between His Resurrection and Return, and that only thereby would
their union with Him in the Messianic Kingdom be rendered possible' (1931: 109). Gorman characterizes this as 'a kind of two-stage resurrection' in Paul: 'first, resurrection to new life in Christ, and
second, resurrection to eternal life in Christ' (2001: 322).

238. According to Thiselton, Paul's reference to 'knowing God' in 15.34 is the lynchpin of the
entire argument (2000: 1178). Gorman makes the point that 'Paul is convinced that experience and
theology are closely connected to each other' (2001: 323).

239. For the characterization of the gospel as divine event, see Martyn 1997b: 116, 130; 1991: 164,
174; cf. Schütz 1975: 53, 281.

240. See Martyn 1997b: 130, 150. In connection with 2 Cor. 12.1, Segal correctly makes the point
that Paul's use of the plural 'revelations' is important because it 'states surely that Paul's reception of
revelation was progressive' (1999: 261). Moreover, there is progressive revelation to the entire community. See Bockmuehl 1990: 138, 144, 146. In this context 'progressive' means 'ongoing' or 'continuing' revelations. See now 1 Cor. 1.7–8.

241. For the possibility of this translation of λόγος, see Thiselton 2000: 1185.

242. Schütz argues that through his 'preaching' Paul interprets God's power and makes it available to others (1975: 43, 281–82), thereby overlooking the role of Paul's behaviour in his gospel
proclamation.

243. Friedrich, 1964: 719.

reflecting on the Corinthians' experience of God's power associated with Paul's proclamation of Christ crucified by word and deed (see 1.5–8; 2.1–5; cf. Gal. 3.1–5).

For Paul the gospel is also the power of God that creates a place (see 1. Cor. 4.19–20).[244] It is where the Corinthians have taken their stand (ἑστήκατε) and are being saved (15.2; see also Rom. 5.2). The present passive σῴζεσθε in 1 Cor. 15.2 echoes σῳζομένοις in 1.18. Both describe a process *presently underway* by which God's saving power is being experienced as new earthly life. Thus, as in 1.18, Paul links these experiences of God's saving power with Christ-conforming conduct by means of spatial, temporal and ethical dualisms.

New life in God's kingdom is not to be taken for granted, however, and to make the point in 15.2 Paul employs the conditional clause εἰ κατέχετε (R. Collins 1999: 533–34). He implies that some of them lack a coherent grasp of practical discipleship (see Thiselton 2000: 1186). The conditional clause contrasts two groups (cf. 1.18). On the one hand are those who are being saved. They are experiencing new life from God in connection with those who continue to conform to Christ's cruciform pattern. On the other hand are those who are living by the world's behavioural standards and perishing along with that world (cf. 11.32).

The perfect passive verb ἐγήγερται in 15.4 emphasizes a related aspect of Paul's reasoning. Christ's past resurrection continues to have significance for those who believe that his cruciform pattern is the divinely confirmed pathway to experiencing new life from God.[245] Paul dramatically illustrates this in 15.6–11. He reflects again on his own experience, describing when that divine event (i.e. the gospel) first occurred in his own life. Despite the fact that he was not worthy to be called an apostle because he persecuted the church (15.9), he experienced God's grace/power when the resurrected Christ appeared to him (15.8; see also 9.1). Paul uses the important verb form ὤφθη four times in 15.5–8 to describe this visual experience that in his view confirmed the inauguration of God's new age of transformed bodily life.[246]

Indeed, Paul immediately links this visual experience with his own transformed life (15.10). After this visual experience of the risen Christ, he put into action his faith in God's life-giving power. That faith has not been without fruit (see also 15.14; cf. 15.58).[247] Through his active labour accompanied by the power of God that was with him, Paul's life has been fruitful since the time the risen Christ appeared to him (see also Rom. 15.18–19; Gal. 2.7–8; 1 Thess. 2.4). Through Paul's embodied proclamation of Christ crucified by word and deed, the Corinthians believed in the power of God (see 1 Cor. 15.11; cf. 2.1–5; 3.5; Gal. 3.1, 5). By implication Paul once again presents his own life as an example for

---

244. According to Schütz, 'the focus is less on the gospel as what they believed than on the gospel as where they are' (1975: 42).

245. Cf. Furnish 1993b: 76.

246. See Segal 1998: 404; cf. Newman 1992: 192; R. Collins 1999: 531–32. For understanding the verb ὤφθη as visual perception, see Dunn 1975: 104–109; Kim 1984: 55–56; *pace* Michaelis, 1967b: 355–60; R. Collins 1999: 535.

247. For this translation of κενὴ as 'without fruit', see LSJ, 938.

the Corinthians to follow,[248] a point he makes clear in 1 Cor. 15.58 by echoing this language from 15.10 (see Mitchell 1991: 287).

Paul's theo-ethical reasoning thus shapes his introduction in this climactic chapter. Through his preaching and lifestyle grounded in Christ's cruciform pattern, the Corinthians have *already experienced* the gospel, understood as God's life-giving power of salvation experienced in connection with faithful conduct conforming to Christ's cruciform pattern (cf. Rom. 1.16–17). This connection between the embodied proclamation of Christ crucified and the experience of transformed life lays the foundation for the rest of Paul's argument in 1 Corinthians 15.[249]

b. *Faith and Proclamation are Without Fruit if there is No Resurrection from the Dead (15.12–19)*

Having reminded the Corinthians in 15.1–11 that they have already experienced the same power of God that Paul experienced when the risen Christ appeared to him, Paul now responds to some who are claiming that there is no resurrection from the dead (15.12). He reasons that the reality of bodily resurrection is linked directly with the power of God that raised Christ from the dead (15.12–13). He continues to offer as proof the experiences of that power in his own life and in the lives of the Corinthians.

If Christ has not been raised, then his own embodied proclamation (κήρυγμα) is without fruit (15.14). The Corinthians know better, however, since Paul has previously reminded them of the link between his κήρυγμα of Christ crucified and the visible demonstration of Spirit and power that grounded their faith in the power of God (2.1–5; 15.1–2). He recalled for them earlier that he fathered them through the gospel (see 4.15). By this, we suggest that Paul is referring to the way that he 'sowed' the 'spiritual things' among them (9.11). The Corinthians experienced these as new life through the power of God (χαρίσματα) in connection with Paul's embodied proclamation of Christ crucified (see 1.4–9; 2.1–5). The resulting community that God arranged (see 12.18, 24) reflects a social body that does not mirror other social bodies shaped by conduct that conforms to the standards and values of the world (see 1.26–31). Thus, the Corinthians should already know from their own experience that Paul's embodied proclamation was fruitful. This proves that their denial of resurrection is groundless.

In this short section Paul alludes to the knowledge of God's power that the Corinthians should have inferred from their own experiences. Through the practice of spiritual discernment, they should be able to link their experiences of God's enriching power with Paul's embodied proclamation of Christ crucified. They lack maturity, however, and by failing to practise spiritual discernment they do not perceive this discernible connection that grounds people's faith in God's resurrection power.

---

248. See also 4.16; 11.1; cf. 8.13–9.27; 13.1–11.
249. Cf. Thiselton 2000: 1177.

c. *God's Plan for Cosmic Liberation: Believers are Being Made Alive in the Presence of Christ (15.20–28)*
In 1 Cor. 15.20–28 Paul evokes the theme of cosmic revolution (D. Martin 1995: 133). He includes an imaginative characterization of the sequence by which God and Christ are now liberating the cosmos and subjecting every rule, authority, and power of the world to the power of God.[250] For the present time, the risen Christ continues to reign until all his enemies, including death, have been subjected to him through the power of God.[251]

Paul's use of the first and last Adam typologies (15.21–22) highlights his dualistic, apocalyptic thrust centred on the antithesis between death and life (Beker 1980: 100). For Paul, the two figures are agents, one for life and the other for death (Scroggs 1966: 83). Just as death has come into the world through a human being, so, too, through (διά) a human being resurrection from the dead has taken place (15.21). In these verses where Paul's reasoning parallels his rationale in Rom. 5.12–21, he implies that death came into the world through Adam's sinful behaviour (see Rom. 5.12, 17–19), while implying that new and eternal (resurrection) life comes through the one righteous act of the man Jesus Christ (see Rom. 5.16–19). In light of this seemingly parallel reasoning, it is plausible to suggest that in 1 Cor. 15.21–26 Paul is making a connection between Christ-conforming conduct and new and eternal (resurrection) life. This is a relationship he amplifies throughout the remainder of 1 Corinthians 15. Paul's use of this typology also exemplifies his first-century perspective that the individual human body has no reality apart from its participation in a larger body identified with a greater cosmic reality (see D. Martin 1995: 131, 133).

For as in Adam all die, says Paul, so too, in Christ all will be made alive (πάντες ζῳοποιηθήσονται) in the proper order (15.22–23). Having already been raised from the dead, Christ is the first fruit (ἀπαρχή)[252] of those who have died (15.20, 23). Then the ones belonging to Christ in his presence (ἐν τῇ παρουσίᾳ αὐτου)[253] will be made alive (15.23). This is a process that has already begun among those who conform their actions to Christ's cruciform pattern and experience new life from God (χαρίσματα) because they are calling on the guiding presence of the risen Lord in the practice of spiritual discernment.[254] Then (εἶτα) comes the consummation (τὸ τέλος),[255] when Christ turns the kingdom over to God (15.4). That will be the time when every enemy

---

250. According to Thiselton, this is 'Paul's demonstration of a divine purposive order' (2000: 1224). Utilizing the language of doctrinal theology, Käsemann argues that 15.20–28 is a passage that 'lays bare as no other does the dominant motif of Paul's theology of the Resurrection' (1969d: 133).
251. See 15.25–28; cf. 1.8; 4.4–5, 19–20; 11.29–32.
252. For Paul's other uses of ἀπαρχη, see Rom. 8.23; 11.16; 16.5; 1 Cor. 16.15; cf. 2 Thess. 2.13.
253. For the translation of παρουσία as 'presence', see LSJ, 1343.
254. Cf. 1.5–8; 2.1–16; 4.4–5; 5.4; 11.32; 16.22. The verb ζῳοποιηθήσονται in 15.22 is a logical future. Cf. Fee (1987: 751 n. 24), who observes that believers 'rise to "life" because they have already been given "life" in Christ'.
255. For this translation of τέλος see LSJ, 1772.

of God and Christ have been destroyed and God becomes all things in all things (15.4, 25, 26, 28).[256]

Notwithstanding Paul's focus on this unfolding cosmic transformation, the primary purpose of 15.20–28 is 'practical rather than theoretical' (Meeks 1996: 802). Christ's human experience is no anomaly. The resurrection of the dead began through the human Jesus (15.21), a reference to Christ's *earthly* life and self-giving death for others. Indeed, Paul's portrayal of Christ's heavenly reign in 15.20–28 (cf. 4.8) illustrates the *supreme example* of his self-giving love for others. In this cosmic process, Christ sacrifices his own status and advantage for the sake of others as a faithful servant of God (Meeks 1996: 806).[257] Just as he did in his earthly life, the *risen* Christ places his present reign in the service of God (cf. 1 Cor. 12.5–6), who is liberating the cosmos from the powers that prevail through human conduct conforming to the standards of the world. Christ's eternal and enduring pattern of cruciform love (see 13.13) remains the paradigm and example for all those who 'belong to Christ' or are 'in Christ' (see Gorman 2001: 323).

In 15.20–28 Paul engages in theo-ethical reasoning by linking Christ's eternal pattern of self-giving love for others with the process of divine transformation into embodied resurrection life. He seeks to change attitudes and behaviours within the Corinthian community rather than emphasizing theoretical questions about the future unfolding of the divine mystery (Meeks 1996: 806–807). As Paul has argued from the letter's opening verses, the process of being made alive in Christ has already begun for believers living in his guiding presence in the deliberative assembly (see 1.5–8; cf. 11.29–32). Implied in Christ's eternal pattern of self-giving love for others is a rebuke of the worldly competition for status that is infecting the Corinthian community. Paul thereby reinforces his earlier appeal for some of them to give up their hierarchical claims to status and privilege (cf. 3.21–23). He subtly reminds them that Christ's 'more excellent way' is the way of self-giving love for others that seeks the common good rather than individual advantage.

d. *Knowledge of God Requires Conduct that Conforms to Christ's Cruciform Pattern (15.29–34)*
Not surprisingly, Paul follows his characterization of Christ's supreme example of self-giving love for others with a short section that includes a 'very strong hortatory word' (Fee 1987: 775). The difficult and enigmatic reference to those who are 'being baptized on behalf of the dead' (15.29) will not divert the exegesis. Instead, this study focuses on Paul's primary point: knowledge of God requires actions that declare a person's death to the behavioural standards of the world (cf. 11.26) by conforming to Christ's cruciform pattern (see 8.1–3).

---

256. For the interpretation that God is the ultimate subjecting subject in this passage, see Thiselton 2000: 1236; Barrett 1968: 359. For those who think Christ is the subjecting power, see Fee 1987: 756; R. Collins 1999: 554. Our study of Paul's theo-ethical reasoning points to God as the subjecting power (see 1 Cor. 12.6).

257. See also 2 Cor. 8.9; Phil. 2.5–11.

In this section Paul offers another personal example of his own Christ-centred perspective, recalling for the Corinthians that he puts himself at risk every hour (15.30) and 'dies daily' (15.31).[258] 'Death' becomes a metonymy for Paul's intentional rejection of the world's behavioural standards and his acceptance of Christ's cruciform pattern of self-giving love for others as his new norm (see also Gal. 2.19–20; 6.14–15).[259] Indeed, according to human standards (κατὰ ἄνθρωπον)[260] there would be no advantage (ὄφελος)[261] to Paul's self-giving and suffering for the benefit of others if God had not raised Jesus from the dead (1 Cor. 15.32). In the absence of transformed resurrection life, human conduct becomes irrelevant since death would then be the final victor (15.32).

He sharply warns the Corinthians not to be deceived or led astray in 15.33 (cf. Gal. 6.7).[262] He applies a popular epigram (φθείρουσιν ἤθη χρηστὰ ὁμιλίαι κακαί) to discourage them from continuing to engage in practices that are based on human standards (cf. 1 Cor. 5.6; Gal. 5.9). The broad term ὁμιλίαι involves human relations and suggests both 'companionship' and 'conversation'.[263] Paul almost certainly is casting aspersions on the 'bad conversations' taking place in the symposium-like period of moral dialogue that was his focus in 1 Corinthians 14.[264] These bad conversations are supplanting the otherwise efficacious practice of spiritual discernment. They are having a corrupting effect that is perpetuating their problematic behaviour and denial of the resurrection (cf. Horsley 1998: 208).

Indeed, they must 'sin no longer' says Paul in 15.34, with the present imperative ἁμαρτάνετε implying action already in progress (Fee 1987: 774). Paul thus ends his argument for the reality of the resurrection from the dead with an abrupt and pointed *moral* admonition. This indicates the close connection he finds between the worldly behaviour of some Corinthians and their denial of resurrection (cf. Horsley 1998: 208). Conversely, it confirms what this study has argued throughout: for Paul there is a direct and discernible connection between the experience of new and eternal life from God and conduct that conforms to Christ's cruciform pattern.

258. According to Hafemann, 'Paul is called as an apostle to "die every day" (1 Cor. 15.31) as a means by which the significance of the cross and resurrection are made real to those to whom the gospel is preached' (2000: 179). While Hafemann's emphasis on preaching overlooks the role of the cruciform lifestyle in Paul's proclamation, his point is otherwise helpful.

259. According to Hafemann, Paul uses 'death' as a metonymy for his life of suffering as an apostle (2000: 179).

260. Mitchell concludes that 15.32 reflects the theme of subscribing to earthly and secular values of political glory and strength (1991: 82, including n. 97).

261. Mitchell includes ὄφελος from 15.32 in a list of Paul's appeals to 'advantage' throughout the letter (1991: 33 n. 57).

262. The imperative does not come as a surprise (*pace* Fee 1987: 773), since it follows directly from Paul's emphasis on 'dying' to human standards of conduct in the preceding verses and repeats similar warnings in 3.18 and 6.9 (Horsley 1998: 208).

263. Fee 1987: 773; Horsley 1998: 208; LSJ, 1222.

264. Cf. Horsley, who similarly notes that ὁμιλίαι includes 'conversations', concluding that 'Paul is almost certainly casting aspersions on the "bad conversations" of *gnosis* that accompany the Corinthians' "bad relationships" with *Sophia*' (1998: 208).

Moreover, it is not surprising that as a warrant for this strong behavioural exhortation in 15.34 Paul asserts that *some* of them (τινες) have no knowledge (ἀγνωσίαν) of God. Paul thus makes a direct connection between ignorance of God and sin (see Conzelmann 1975: 279) – actions that do not reflect divine approval because they do not conform to Christ's cruciform pattern.[265] For Paul knowledge of God takes place when believers practise spiritual discernment and associate divinely confirmed, cruciform actions with manifestations of God's life-giving power (cf. 1.4–9; 2.1–16; 8.1–3). Knowledge of God (through an experience of the power that raised Jesus from the dead) has been the lynchpin of Paul's argument. Verse 34 thereby becomes the hinge to the remainder of the chapter.[266] Their ignorance of God results from three interrelated causes: (1) some of them are still living by human standards (3.3) rather than seeking to act in ways that conform to Christ's cruciform pattern; (2) their conduct blocks them from experiencing the discernible, life-giving power of God; and (3) the break-down of the post-dinner dialogue prevents them from identifying the connections between conduct and experience being illuminated by the Spirit and the guiding presence of the Lord.

The Corinthians are failing to discern spiritually the Lord's present judgment on their worldly behaviour (see 11.29–32; cf. 4.3–5). Consequently, Paul calls the entire congregation back to the 'sensible, rational examination of what is "good and acceptable and perfect"...before God and neighbor' (Bornkamm 1969: 41). They must engage in theo-ethical reasoning, returning to the practice of spiritual discernment, if they expect to identify what conduct is 'good and acceptable and perfect' (see also Rom. 12.2) and to continue experiencing the power of God that gives new life in connection with such Christ-conforming actions.

e. God Transforms the Body in Connection with Conduct that Conforms to Christ's Cruciform Pattern (15.35–58)
Paul turns in 15.35–58 to address concerns probably voiced by some of the Corinthians about the nature of the resurrection body and how the dead are actually raised.[267] The response seems to draw on the appearance of the risen Christ to Paul, an experience that proved to him the reality of embodied resurrection life. Thus, Paul focuses on the body as the principle of continuity in the transformation of earthly human life into embodied resurrection life.[268]

In this section it will be argued that, for Paul, Christ-conforming acts of self-giving love for others are the means by which God continues to transform individuals into the image of Christ and communities into the body of Christ. This

265. According to R. Collins, that some 'deny the resurrection is contrary to their experience of God' (1999: 558–59). Cf. Thiselton, who concludes that the key to the resurrection transformation is not knowledge of 'truths' but knowing God (1977: 525).
266. See Thiselton 2000: 1256–57. Similarly, Fee concludes that in light of 15.20–28, those who deny the resurrection are those who are 'ignorant of God' (1987: 774).
267. D. Martin 1995: 125; Horsley 1998: 208–209.
268. Cf. Horsley 1998: 208–209.

conduct becomes the means by which earthly bodies manifest glory as part of the bodily transformation that is already underway and will become complete at the consummation (see 15.23–28).

In 15.36–38 Paul returns to agricultural imagery (see also 3.6–9; cf. Gal. 6.7–9), making use of a first-century cultural understanding that the individual's experience of nature was considered the source of wisdom (Horsley 1998: 209). His seed-sowing metaphor underscores that the seed must die to be transformed into a different mode of existence as the crop or fruit (i.e. new life).[269] This death to new life sequence takes place in the context of earthly human life. Believers die daily to the behavioural standards of the world (cf. 15.31) by conforming their actions to Christ's cruciform pattern and experiencing transformation into the spiritual body.[270] This is a process that will become complete only at the consummation. Nevertheless, there remains a continuity of identity between the fruit and the seed throughout the process (Thiselton 2000: 163).

Paul also emphasizes the importance of each seed being sown (σπείρεις). At the individual body level, the metaphor probably signifies specific Christ-conforming actions. Paul's emphatic placement of σύ in 15.36 ('what *you yourself* are sowing') points to this conclusion (cf. Jn 12.24). He anticipates a variety of different Christ-conforming actions (see 11.19; 12.5) through which believers have a variety of experiences of new life that are advantageous to the social body (see 12.4, 7). Through these actions each believer plays an important participatory role in the divine construction of the social body of Christ that is underway (see 3.6–15; 12.24–27).

In Paul's metaphor, what is sown is not made alive (ζῳοποιεῖται) unless it dies (15.36). Indeed, God is giving (δίδωσιν) to each seed its own new body (15.36, 38).[271] The present tense δίδωσιν points to a transformation that is already taking place bodily, both at the individual and at the social level that Paul calls the body of Christ.[272] What emerges from the seeds being sown are social relationships that correspond to the specific kinds of seeds being sown (see R. Collins 1999: 566). Thus, Paul appears to reason that God enlivens these

---

269. *Pace* Barrett, who concludes that Paul does not emphasize the necessity of death, but only transformation and revivification (1968: 370).

270. According to Ashton, '[t]he death of Christ, then, can be thought of as instrumental in the transformation of the Christian, and his risen body as the exemplar of what will eventually belong to his followers too' (2000: 137). Based on 2 Cor. 3.18–4.17, Ashton concludes that this transformation is a process that is already underway among believers as they are changed into the image of God in Christ by conforming to Christ's mould or pattern (2000: 137). Like Engberg-Pedersen, however, Ashton further concludes that much of this language is difficult for modern people to appropriate (2000: 138).

271. In connection with Paul's use of the phrase συμμορφιζόμενος τῷ θανάτῳ αὐτοῦ in Phil. 3.10, Segal observes that the language is not merely that of analogy or imitation but a process of transformation from one state of being to another as Paul becomes the same substance with Christ through his death (1990: 22). Segal further points out that Paul's use of the concept of metamorphosis was also used in the ancient world to describe the seeming decay of a seed underground before it begins new growth.

272. Thiselton notes the present tense of δίδωσιν in 15.38 (2000: 1264), but does not comment on the obvious connotation that transformation is already underway.

social relationships with enriched new life (cf. 1.5–8), shaping them into a transformed social body in connection with actions that conform to Christ's cruciform
pattern.[273] The metaphor thus parallels the construction imagery in 3.10–18,
where Paul argued that specific human actions impact the construction of the
social body, for which there will be divine accountability.

The body remains the central focus in 15.39–42. There are heavenly bodies
(σώματα ἐπουράνια) and earthly bodies (σώματα ἐπίγεια) and each has a
distinctive δόξα (15.40). Just as the sun, moon and stars have particular glories,
various believers also have different glories in their earthly bodies (see also
12.26).[274] By 'heavenly body' Paul refers to embodied existence in heaven – the
dwelling place or sphere of God and the risen Christ (Thiselton 2000: 1268). He
contrasts this with existence on earth,[275] establishing a priority for the glory of the
heavenly body over the glory of the earthly one.[276]

This does not mean, however, that Paul thereby denigrates earthly existence.
During the time of Christ's interim reign, embodied Christ-conforming actions
constitute the means by which the glory of earthly bodies becomes manifest
through the Spirit.[277] Since 15.42 expressly refers back (οὕτως καὶ) to the analo-
gies used in 15.38–41 to differentiate between the glories associated with heavenly and earthly bodies, Paul seems to incorporate the logic of his reasoning from
those verses to explain resurrection from the dead. Further, in the Greek there is
no verb in 15.42. Because the verbs that follow are expressed in the present
tense, however, it seems preferable to imply a present tense verb in this verse
also (Fee 1987: 784 n. 35).

Thus, in 15.42–44 he contrasts the glory of the individual body in its earthly
form with the glory associated with the heavenly individual *and* social body into
which it is being transformed as part of a 'progression of dynamic life-processes'
(Thiselton 2000: 1272). In 15.42 φθορά denotes 'decreasing capacities and
increasing weaknesses, issuing in exhaustion and stagnation' (Thiselton 2000:
1272). This occurs in the earthly body that is subject to decay but is being raised
to a body that constitutes decay's reversal, in other words a body where there is a
'progressive purposive flourishing in fullness of life' (Thiselton 2000: 1272).
Indeed, for Paul the body 'provides the vehicle of communicative flourishing and
identity recognition in the public, intersubjective domain of community' (Thiselton
2000: 1272).[278] Thus, in 15.42, Paul refers to more than just death/perishability
and immortality/imperishability.

273. For the correspondences between Paul's imagery and the Genesis ch. 1 creation story in
15.36–38, thereby suggesting that Paul has new creation implicitly in mind, see R. Collins 1999: 565–
67; Horsley 1998: 200–213.
274. M. Mitchell 1991: 289.
275. See also Phil. 3.20–21.
276. D. Martin argues that Paul evokes the 'cosmology of popular philosophy' by focusing on the
hierarchy of the heavenly bodies over the earthly bodies in order to ground his assertion that the
resurrected body will be much higher in the physiological hierarchy than the present earthly body
(1995: 126–27).
277. See 2.1–12; cf. 12.4–7, 26.
278. Cf. Käsemann 1969d: 135.

Paul appears to be arguing that there are different glories associated with different Christ-conforming actions taken by earthly bodies, a conclusion clearly supported by the logic underlying 12.26b.[279] Paul's reasoning also suggests that through their Christ-conforming actions these earthly bodies participate in a process of divine bodily transformation (see 2 Cor. 3.18). That process started when believers were baptized into the one body of Christ by the Spirit (see 1 Cor. 12.13). It will conclude at the consummation when transformation is complete (15.24; cf. 15.51; Phil. 3.20–21).[280]

The two contrasts in 1 Cor. 15.43 support this conclusion, showing Paul's deep sense of Christ-patterned *continuity* between the earthly and heavenly modes of bodily existence involved in this transformation process.[281] These contrasts unmistakably echo Paul's earlier characterization of his own Christ-conforming lifestyle. First, there is the contrast in 15.43 between what is sown in dishonour (ἀτιμίᾳ) in the earthly body but raised ἐν δόξῃ in the heavenly one. This recalls Paul's ironic contrast in 4.10 between his own conduct that renders him ἄτιμοι to those who apply the world's standards and the conduct of some Corinthians who are being held 'in glory' (ἔνδοξοι) by those who assess them according to those same worldly norms. Second, the antithesis between what is sown in weakness (ἀσθενείᾳ) in the earthly body but raised in power (δυνάμει) in the heavenly body recalls the way that Paul came among them in weakness (ἐν ἀσθενείᾳ) with his own embodied proclamation of Christ crucified (2.2–3).[282]

It is critical to note that this conduct led to a demonstration of Spirit and power that grounded the Corinthians' faith in the power of God manifest in their *earthly* existence.[283] This same antithesis also appears in the ironic contrasts in 4.10. In 15.43 Paul thus refers to the way that Christ-conforming conduct in an earthly body that is undergoing decay nevertheless becomes the instrument for the manifestation of God's power. To describe this pre-resurrection body as sown in weakness expresses Paul's realism about the frailty, fragility, vulnerability and constraints of human existence (Thiselton 2000: 1274). It does not, however, diminish the transformative dimension of God's power to override the process of decay by manifesting glory in connection with Christ-conforming behaviour, thereby creating new worlds of perception, projection and reality (cf. Thiselton 2000: 1274–75).

---

279. Cf. Thiselton, who finds that for Paul the meaning of δόξα lies in God's glory that becomes manifest in God's self-giving and gracious love in and through Christ (2000: 1270).

280. Cf. Thiselton, who identifies 15.42 as the start of Paul's 'theology of transformation' that does not conclude until 15.57 (2000: 1178), with Segal, who concludes that '[t]his process of transformation will end in a glorious new body, spiritual rather than material, which corresponds with the body Christ has already revealed' to Paul (1990: 23).

281. *Pace* Adams, who concludes that for Paul there is a sharp distinction between the present physical body and the future spiritual body that mirrors the discontinuity between the different worlds to which they belong (2000: 146). Adams acknowledges at another point, however, that Paul describes a greater sense of continuity between the present and future modes of bodily existence in 15.51–54 (2000: 146 n. 116).

282. For similar uses of 'weakness', see 2 Cor. 12.9–10; 13.3–4; Gal. 4.13.

283. See 1 Cor. 2.1–5; cf. 1.25, 27.

Thus, if weakness, dishonour and decay represent the decreasing crescendo of human mortality, then power, glory, and the reversal of decay denote the divinely energized crescendo of embodied capacities for unimagined tasks and service yet to come (see Thiselton 2000: 1275). Paul thus describes a process of decay's reversal through the power of God that is underway, but will not be completed until the final transformation at the end (see 15.51).

A change in terminology starting in 15.44 emphasizes that earthly life is being transformed even before it becomes fully a part of the heavenly resurrection body. What is first sown (σπείρεται) is a physical body (σῶμα ψυχικόν) that is raised a spiritual body (σῶμα πνευματικόν). The phrase σῶμα ψυχικόν represents the mode of individual bodily existence in the present world/age (see Adams 2000: 145), a conclusion supported by Paul's reference to the ψυχικὸς ἄνθρωπος in 2.14. More specifically, it refers to the individual earthly body shaped by conduct that conforms to the standards of the world (cf. 3.1–3). The σῶμα πνευματικόν, on the other hand, characterizes the spiritual body of the risen Christ (Cullmann 1953: 33). This includes the *earthly* body (individual and social) that is *even now* being transformed into new life.[284] It includes the community that is being led by the Spirit that dwells among them and is being divinely constructed in connection with conduct that conforms to Christ's cruciform pattern (cf. Rom. 6.1–11; 8.1–14). This conclusion is supported by Paul's reference to the 'spiritual person' (ὁ πνευματικὸς) in 1 Cor. 2.15 (see also 3.1; cf. Gal. 6.1) that he contrasts with the ψυχικὸς ἄνθρωπος described in the preceding verse. Indeed, as their behavioural example, Paul has already shown them the way by sowing the 'spiritual things' among them (1 Cor. 9.11). Thus, as in 6.12–20, Paul's body language in these verses involves both the individual body and the larger social body.[285]

Indeed, the adjective πνευματικός in 15.44 denotes that which pertains to the Holy Spirit sent from God, suggesting that the 'spiritual body' refers to the group whose individual members act according to 'a mode and pattern of inter-subjective life directed by the Holy Spirit' (Thiselton 2000: 1277).[286] The members of a 'spiritual body' are thereby transformed 'in accordance with the moral and theological character of the Holy Spirit' (Thiselton 2000: 1269). Paul makes his point again in 15.44b. If God can make a σῶμα ψυχικόν among all the other forms and species of earthly bodies, it is also logical to assume that God is able to make an earthly body appropriate to the realm of the Spirit – that new age that has descended upon those who still live an earthly life (see 10.11). To use the terminology of doctrinal theology, we might say that, for Paul, christology and ecclesiology become co-extensive to the extent that everyone in the social body conforms their actions to Christ's cruciform pattern and practises spiritual discernment.

---

284. Contra Pearson, who concludes that Paul uses this terminology only in an 'eschatological fashion': humans will only possess the πνευματικός element of existence in the future resurrection, since present human existence takes place *only* in the old age of sin and death (1973: 24, 26).

285. According to D. Martin, for Paul the individual body lacks meaning apart from its participation in the larger bodies of which it is merely a microcosm (1995: 129–36).

286. See also Louw and Nida 1994: 141–43; cf. Pearson 1973: 7–26.

With the phrase 'spiritual body' in 15.44, Paul refers to *earthly* life that has been reoriented to the Spirit and is characterized by what 'befits the transformation of character or pattern of existence effected by the Holy Spirit' (Thiselton 2000: 1279).[287] It would appear that for Paul this reorientation and transformation takes place among those who have been baptized by the one Spirit into the one body of Christ (see 12.13). This study has shown that, as part of this reorientation, Paul expects them to practise spiritual discernment by engaging in theo-ethical reasoning. Knowing that the Spirit dwells among them (see 3.16; 6.19), the spiritual ones are the mature ones who orient themselves to this Spirit sent from God to help them perceive the new life being given by God (see 2.12; cf. 3.1; Gal. 6.1) in connection with Christ-conforming actions (see 1 Cor. 1.6–8).[288] Indeed, says Paul in 15.45, while the 'first Adam' was a physical being (ψυχὴν ζῶσαν), the 'last Adam' (Jesus Christ) became a life-giving Spirit (πνεῦμα ζῳοποιοῦν). This is the 'same Spirit' (see 12.4; cf. 12.7, 13) that leads believers to discern experiences of new life from God that divinely confirm behaviour conforming to Christ's cruciform pattern (see 1.6, 8; 2.12; 4.3–5; cf. 2 Cor. 3.18).

The logic of Paul's reasoning suggests that Christ-conforming conduct and the practice of spiritual discernment are the means by which believers (in their earthly existence) *presently participate* in experiences of the life of the heavenly realm. This is the place where God builds up individuals, churches, and the cosmos into a spiritual body of new life by exercising the same power that raised Jesus from the dead. The one Spirit sent from God leads believers to recognize these experiences of new life in the transformed σῶμα πνευματικόν.[289] This σῶμα πνευματικόν is the community that is the body of Christ, the earthly, spiritual body of the risen Lord (Cullmann 1953: 33). It does not come only at the 'Eschaton', understood as the end of time (*pace* Fee 1987: 791).

Moreover, by emphasizing Jesus Christ as 'the last Adam' (1 Cor. 15.45), Paul re-emphasizes his earlier assertion that through a *man* has come resurrection (15.21; see also Rom. 5.18). Paul seems to argue that transformation into resurrection life *begins* as part of a person's *earthly* existence. The spiritual body originates as individual ψυχικός earthly bodies. People undergo transformation into a πνευματικός body (see 1 Cor. 15.46) as they respond to the experiences of Spirit and power that ground Christian faith in the power of God (see 2.1–5; 12.13). They respond by conforming their actions to Christ's cruciform pattern and practising spiritual discernment. God will bring to completion this process of transforming earthly life into embodied resurrection life only at the consummation (15.24). At that time all believers who inhabit the spiritual body that is the body of Christ will be fully changed into resurrection life, the heavenly and eternal dimension of God's kingdom (cf. R. Collins 1999: 569). Thus, this study concludes that in these verses where Paul is describing the divine process of

287. See also 12.4, 7, 11, 13.
288. See also Rom. 8.1–13; Gal. 5.18–25; cf. Thiselton, who cites 15.44, 45, 49–57 and concludes that '[t]he resurrection mode of existence, for Paul, is decisively shaped and directed by the Holy Spirit in accordance with the transformation into the image of Christ' (2000: 1286).
289. Cf. Dunn 1973: 132–33; *pace* Fee 1987: 789–90, including n. 12.

bodily transformation, he envisions an intermediate level of embodied existence (the 'spiritual body') lying between a person's original existence as a σῶμα ψυχικόν and a person's full and final transformation into resurrection life.[290]

In 15.47–50 Paul continues to describe this transformation process. Characterizing 'the first man' (Adam) as made of dust from the earth (15.47), Paul uses the adjective χοϊκός to describe the quality of physical bodily existence. According to 15.48, even believers have something in common with that 'first man' since they all share the same body 'made of dust from the earth' (D. Martin 1995: 132).

In 15.47 Paul also refers to Jesus Christ as the 'second man' who is ἐξ οὐρανοῦ. He thereby stresses Christ's fully human nature but divine origin (cf. Rom. 8.3; 1 Cor. 8.6; Gal. 4.4). Paul thus contrasts *qualitatively* two distinct experiences of earthly human life. The reference to Christ as the 'second man' does not refer exclusively to his resurrected bodily existence.[291] Rather, the phrase denotes the heavenly origin of the earthly human life lived by Christ before his resurrection. It is tentatively suggested that the phrase ἐξ οὐρανοῦ describes the quality or character of earthly human life that is directed by the Spirit sent by God from the heavenly realm (cf. Col. 3.1–4).[292]

It is important to observe that 15.47 directly follows the verse where Paul describes the sequence of bodily life from σῶμα ψυχικόν to σῶμα πνευματικόν. This seems to indicate that the first body (the σῶμα ψυχικόν) begins to undergo transformation into the second body (the σῶμα πνευματικόν) because there is a change of focus grounded in the experience of the Spirit and power of God (cf. 2.1–5; 12.13). Thereafter, believers should look consistently to the life-giving Spirit for behavioural direction that will transform their *earthly* existence. Through the practice of spiritual discernment, the life-giving Spirit who is the risen Lord (see 15.45; 2 Cor. 3.18) leads believers into new earthly life ἐξ οὐρανοῦ.

Thus, God's new order has already begun. It is experienced as transformation into Christ-likeness as believers are led by the Spirit, even though earthly human life remains fragile with room for fallibility and constraint prior to consummation of the resurrection.[293] All those who are 'heavenly' are like the 'second man' whose life is 'heavenly'. The correlative pronouns twice repeated in 1 Cor. 15.48

290. While this study agrees with Adams' conclusions that for Paul there is a sharp quantitative, qualitative, and material distinction between the σῶμα ψυχικόν and the σῶμα πνευματικόν and that these are two different bodies (2000: 145), it disagrees with his conclusion that this 'sharp distinction between the present body and the future body mirrors the discontinuity of the different worlds to which they belong' (2000: 146). Adams seemingly overemphasizes the 'not yet' nature of future spiritual existence in Paul's 'already/not yet' apocalyptic perspective. Paul's characterization of some as 'spiritual' people (see 1 Cor. 2.15; cf. 3.1; Gal. 6.1) because they are led by the Spirit suggests the possibility that believers experience transformed earthly life and participate in the σῶμα πνευματικόν by conforming their conduct to Christ's cruciform pattern and practising spiritual discernment.

291. *Pace* Fee 1987: 791–92; Horsley 1998: 212.

292. Contra Pearson, who concludes that in no sense can humans be said to partake of or bear the image of the man from heaven, since humans can only bear the image of Adam (1973: 24–25). In the present, concludes Pearson, they can only cling to the σῶμα πνευματικόν as 'an eschatological hope' that lies with resurrection in the future (1973: 25).

293. For this latter conclusion, see Thiselton 2000: 1288.

(οἷος…τοιοῦτοι) are pronouns of quality or character, suggesting that these verses indicate matters of moral likeness to Christ (Thiselton 2000: 1286). In this way the man 'from heaven models those who pertain to heaven'.[294]

Conversely, earthly life in a σῶμα ψυχικόν means living by the human standards of the world. It means being unable to receive the things of the Spirit sent from God because they are foolishness to those who live by worldly standards and do not practise spiritual discernment (2.14). Indeed, according to 2.14, the ψυχικὸς ἄνθρωπος is unable to know the new life being given by God in connection with Christ-conforming conduct because such things must be *spiritually discerned*.

Paul confirms in 15.49 that transformation into heavenly life requires a change of behavioural standards. He dramatically exhorts the Corinthians: 'just as we wore (εφορέσαμεν) the image of the dustly man, let us also wear (φορέσωμεν) the image of the heavenly man'.[295] With this metaphor related to putting on clothing,[296] Paul encourages the Corinthians to represent this image of the heavenly man in their own appearance and earthly life in the world.[297] He thus exhorts them to conform their behaviour to the new, divinely approved social norm of self-giving love for others manifest in the death of Jesus Christ.[298]

As he does in 15.33–34 and 15.58, Paul merges his concerns over their denial of resurrection and patently worldly conduct in 15.49 (Fee 1987: 795). 'The implication is that not only are they not fully πνευματικός now, but they will not be fully πνευματικός at all if they do not presently also "bear the likeness of the man from heaven"' (Fee 1987: 795). This is not, however, another expression of Paul's 'already/not yet' eschatological framework whereby he urges them 'to become what they are by grace'.[299] Instead, this is Paul's acknowledgment and admonition that the Corinthians will not be fully transformed into the resurrection body if they continue to live by the standards of the dustly man who will perish with the world that already stands condemned (cf. 1.18; 11.32). By refusing to practise spiritual discernment, some will remain ψυχικός rather than become πνευματικός (cf. 2.14–15; 3.1), unable to receive and know the gifts of new life being given by God that are spiritually discerned in connection with Christ-conforming actions (cf. 8.1–3).

Paul describes the heavenly mystery of the final resurrection in 15.50–57. Transformation must be completed before believers inherit the kingdom of God (15.50–51). This takes place when earthly human life is changed (15.51–52) as

294. Thiselton 2000: 1286; cf. Fee 1987: 793 n. 30; *pace* Barrett 1968: 377. See now Phil. 3.20–21.

295. In support of this textual choice for the hortatory subjunctive, see Fee 1987: 787. Similarly, R. Collins observes that in 15.34, 49 and 58, Paul concludes each of his rhetorical proofs and peroration with an exhortation (1999: 572); contra Metzger 1994: 502; Barrett 1968: 377; Thiselton 2000: 1289.

296. See also Rom. 13.12, 14; 1 Cor. 15.53–54; Gal. 3.27; cf. Eph. 4.24.

297. See Fee 1987: 794 n. 34; contra Pearson 1973: 24–25.

298. Cf. Fee, who concludes that Paul is urging the Corinthians 'to conform to the life of the "man of heaven" as those who now share his character and behavior' (1987: 795).

299. *Pace* Fee 1987: 795, who by implication adopts Bultmann's well-worn phrase (see Chapter 1, section 2).

the body puts on immortality and imperishability (15.53). This is the victory that God gives through (διά) the Lord Jesus Christ (15.57; see also 8.6). The victory is given to those who remain steadfastly committed to Christ's cruciform pattern and practise spiritual discernment so that the last Adam who became a life-giving Spirit can lead them into the new life God promises to members of the σῶμα πνευματικόν.

Paul closes this long and climactic section of the letter with another exhortation in 15.58 that emphasizes the 'ethical objective' (Koenig 1978: 169) of the chapter and the letter. Rather than constituting an afterthought, in this verse Paul articulates the whole point of the divine mystery (Koenig 1978: 169). Having asserted in 15.57 that God is presently giving (διδόντι) believers victory over death and Sin through the Lord Jesus Christ,[300] he connects the revelation of this mystery to the practice of spiritual discernment and conduct that conforms to Christ's cruciform pattern.

First, Paul encourages them to be firm (ἑδραῖοι γίνεσθε) and unmoveable (ἀμετακίνητοι), always abounding in the work of the Lord. With the phrase 'work of the Lord' Paul seems to be referring to the Corinthians' actions that conform to the self-giving pattern of the one Lord (cf. 12.5).[301] The imperative alludes to 3.10–11 and appeals to the building metaphor that Paul has used throughout the letter. It refers to the steadiness of a foundation,[302] thereby insisting that they remain solidly and unchangeably fixed to that one foundation who is Jesus Christ according to 3.10–11 (Mitchell 1991: 109–10). Thus, in 15.58 Paul exhorts the Corinthians to remain firm in their commitment to conform their behaviour to the foundation that Paul laid for them – Christ's cruciform pattern of self-giving love for others (see 3.10–11; 11.1).

In addition the Corinthians are to remain steadfastly committed to Christ's cruciform pattern, 'always perceiving (εἰδότες)[303] that their labour in the Lord is not without fruit' (15.58b; cf. Phil. 1.20). This directly links Christ-conforming actions (the 'work of the Lord') with the practice of spiritual discernment by which the Corinthians perceive how such conduct proves fruitful (see 1 Cor. 1.4–9; 2.1–5, 12–14). In 15.58 Paul once again connects the revelation of the divine mystery with these practices. The verse illuminates the nature of the victory that God is giving through the Lord Jesus Christ to believers who experience new life by conforming their actions to Christ's cruciform pattern.[304]

In summary Paul brings together in 15.58 various strands of arguments made throughout the letter. This closing exhortation highlights the important connection between experience and conduct that lies at the heart of the letter and Paul's theo-

---

300. Had this victory been a once-for-all achievement, Paul would have applied the aorist tense verb form in 15.57.

301. See Betz, who concludes that ἔργον in 15.58 refers to the Corinthians' *praxis* (1986: 33).

302. Mitchell 1991: 107; LSJ, 478; BAGD, 218.

303. Throughout the letter Paul uses this verb at critical junctures to characterize human perception or knowledge that comes through experience. See, e.g., 2.2, 12; 3.16; 6.19; 8.1; 12.2; 13.2.

304. Indeed, Koenig calls this the 'from mystery to ministry' pattern that is evident in 15.50–58 (1978: 167).

ethical reasoning. He encourages the Corinthians to understand that by conforming their actions to Christ's cruciform pattern and practising spiritual discernment they will be led by the Spirit to perceive the power of God that demonstrates the divine victory over Sin and death. Through these practices the Spirit continues to lead them into new life in the σῶμα πνευματικόν, the locus of presently transformed earthly life and the locus of the future, final, complete, and eternal transformation into heavenly, embodied resurrection life in Christ.

5. *Exhortations to Live the Cruciform Pattern and Call on the Name of the Lord in Spiritual Discernment (16.1–24)*

a. *Concluding Exhortations*
Paul closes the letter with exhortations that build on earlier themes and further illuminate the role of theo-ethical reasoning and the practice of spiritual discernment. First, he immediately follows his revelation of the divine mystery (15.50–57) and exhortation to remain steadfastly committed to Christ's cruciform pattern and the practice of spiritual discernment (15.58) with instructions about the collection for the holy ones in Jerusalem (16.1–4). As he has done throughout the letter, Paul thereby associates the mystery of divine transformation with Christ-conforming acts of self-giving love for others.[305]

Second, the short, terse exhortations at the end of the letter are characteristic of Paul's style.[306] The unusual closing emphasis on the importance of 'love' (16.14, 24; cf. 16.22), however, highlights Paul's consistent focus on the failure of the Corinthians to conform their behaviour to Christ's cruciform pattern of self-giving love for others. From the letter's opening paragraphs, Paul has been focused on the deficient practice of love by some Corinthians, a shortcoming that defines the course of action that Paul urges throughout the letter.[307]

Third, the imperative to 'keep alert' (1 Cor. 16.13) is better understood as another response to the breakdown of community spiritual discernment than as an eschatological warning concerning the Lord's *end-time* return.[308] Indeed, 'Paul diagnoses much of the problem of misperception of the resurrection as caused by an absence of alert, coherent reflection' (Thiselton 2000: 1336). Having pointed out their numerous failures to discern the Lord's confirming or disciplining presence in their midst, Paul encourages the Corinthians to be more attentive to what the Lord is doing among them (see 1.8).

Paul follows this imperative with another exhortation to 'stand firm in the faith' (16.13; cf. 15.1). The verb form στήκετε invariably has the sense of standing firm in Christ as opposed to falling out of his presence (Fee 1987: 827).[309] In the

---

305. Once again, Koenig identifies this aspect of the 'mystery to ministry' pattern (1978: 167–74).

306. See Rom. 16.17–19; 2 Cor. 13.11; Phil. 4.8–9; 1 Thess. 5.12–22.

307. As noted in Chapter 2, section 2.d above, there is the conspicuous absence of any reference in 1.5 to the Corinthians' works of love.

308. The so-called non-eschatological context is noted by Fee 1987: 827; Thiselton 2000: 1336.

309. For Paul's use of the verb in similar contexts, see Rom. 14.4; Gal. 5.1; Phil. 1.27; 4.1; 1 Thess. 3.8; cf. 2 Thess. 2.15.

context of this letter, standing firm in 'the faith' suggests that the Corinthians must remain persuaded about two things: (1) the death and resurrection of Jesus Christ manifested a new, divinely confirmed social norm of self-giving love for others (see also Phil. 2.6–11); and (2) believers' conduct conforming to this new social norm constitutes the means divinely chosen for believers to experience the same power of God that raised Jesus from the dead as their own experiences of new earthly life, so that their faith is grounded solely in the power of God (see 1.4–9; 2.1–5).

The phrase is also synonymous with standing firm in a place (i.e. God's king-dom).[310] Paul thus draws again on the imagery of spatial dualism. This is the place where God's discernible power prevails over the powers of the world to give experiences of new life in connection with Christ-conforming conduct (cf. 1.17–18; 2.1–5; 4.19–20). Thus, Paul encourages the Corinthians not to waver from the conviction that they continue to experience new life in the *earthly* mani-festation of God's kingdom. They must stand firm in this place by continuing to conform their actions to the 'more excellent way' of love that eternally endures in God's kingdom (cf. 12.31; 13.13).

Indeed, Paul confirms this in 16.14, exhorting the Corinthians to 'let all things that you do be done in love'. The parallels between this exhortation and 14.26 ('let all things be done for building up') and 8.1 ('love builds up') are significant (Mitchell 1991: 280 n. 525). Every action must be grounded in Christ's cruci-form pattern of self-giving love for others. The actions they contemplate must be discerned by taking into consideration the needs of others rather than self advan-tage.[311] Through spiritual discernment they must anticipate that the power of God will build up the community into the spiritual body of Christ through specific Christ-conforming actions. In this way the active practice of love becomes the divinely revealed antidote to their divisive factionalism.

b. *Calling on the Name of the Lord: 'May Our Lord Come!' (16.22)*
For Paul a letter's conclusion usually functions to summarize and highlight his arguments throughout the letter (R. Collins 1999: 615). This process began in 1 Cor. 16.13–15 and continues in the enigmatic but important verse at 16.22. Paul closes the letter as it began – with a reference to calling upon the name of the Lord (1.2). He petitions in Aramaic (Μαρανα θα) for the Lord to come among the gathered community to reveal his discipline and judgment.[312] Simi-larly, he invokes a curse on anyone who 'does not kindly welcome (φιλεῖ) the Lord', using a phase not otherwise found in the New Testament. Paul would normally use the verb ἀγαπάω if he wished to speak of 'loving' God (Thiselton 2000: 1351; see, e.g., 2.9; 8.3) or the risen Lord. With the unusual verb φιλέω, Paul thus alludes to the fact that there are some who are not welcoming the risen Lord for purposes of practising spiritual discernment (cf. 1.8).[313] He appears to be

310. According to Fee, the phrase means 'locative of a sphere' (1987: 828 n. 11).
311. See 8.1–13; 10.24, 33; 12.31–13.3; cf. Phil. 2.4–11.
312. See R. Collins 1999: 614; cf. Rev. 22.20.
313. In light of the fact that the verb φιλεῖ is a *hapax legomenon* in Paul and that throughout the

challenging those who are tearing the body of Christ apart (see 1.13) through their divisive factionalism and disregard for this important practice in the deliberative assembly (see 11.22). Thus, the *anathema* implies a 'summons to self-examination' (Bornkamm 1969: 171).

Consequently, with the imperative Μαρανα θα in 16.22, Paul is probably petitioning for the Lord to come among the gathered community again to reveal himself through the Spirit.[314] The purpose is to guide the community by confirming conduct that conforms to Christ's cruciform pattern (see 1.8) and help believers to distinguish the conduct of those whose actions conform to the standards of the world and lead to experiences of destruction (see 5.1–13; 6.1–11; 8.1–13; 11.17–34). Paul thus draws on earlier reminders that their conduct is still subject to the close examination of the risen Lord (see 4.5; cf. 1.8) and, potentially, to his judgment and discipline (see 11.29–32) if their actions do not faithfully declare the Lord's death by conforming to his cruciform pattern (see 11.26).[315] For Paul this should be taking place during the symposium-like period of moral dialogue that follows the Lord's Supper. It is the time when the community discerns how the Day of the Lord impinges on the present through the 'judging presence of the Lord' (see Roetzel 1972: 139).

By consistently reflecting on the Corinthians' own experience throughout the letter, Paul reminds them that they have experienced how the Lord can still come to earth, even after his resurrection appearances. Moreover, they experience it again every time they come together and fervently pray for the coming of the risen Christ (see Cullmann 1953: 14). Thus, this ancient prayer Μαρανα

---

letter Paul regularly uses ἀγάπη, some interpreters conclude that he is quoting a Christian formula. See, e.g., Barrett 1968: 396; Fee 1987: 837; Bornkamm 1969: 170. This misses Paul's point that is actually made by his use of this atypical verb.

314. Pauline interpreters are undecided about the way Paul uses the phrase Μαρανα θα. According to Kuhn, a future meaning for the phrase is excluded (1967: 466–72). Cullmann calls it a reference to Christ's 'Second Advent' (1953: 22) as well as a prayer for the coming of the Lord in the assembled community as the anticipation of his coming in revealed glory at the last day (1953: 35). For other views, see, e.g., Fee 1987: 839; Moule 1960: 307–10; Bornkamm 1969: 170–71; Robinson 1953: 38–41.

There is also debate about whether Paul deliberately incorporated this language, otherwise found in the context of celebrations of the Lord's Supper (see *Did.* 10.6; Rev. 22.20), as a transition from the public reading of his letter directly into the celebration of the Lord's Supper. Robinson (1953: 38–41), Cullmann (1953: 24), and Bornkamm (1969: 169–70) support this view, while Fee disputes the conclusion (1987: 834). Or, possibly, the phrase is intended to ban certain people from participating in the Supper. Robinson (1953: 38–41) argues for this latter function, while Fee disputes the conclusion (1987: 834) and R. Collins counsels caution before making such an assertion (1998: 615).

315. Bornkamm points out a similar construction in *Did.* 10–14. Bornkamm's conclusion and those of this study suggest that there was an important aspect of Christian worship focused on the discernment of appropriate conduct and the testing of spirits that was carried out in the presence of the Lord in the symposium-like period that followed the Lord's Supper. The practice has been referred to in this study as spiritual discernment, with theo-ethical reasoning constituting the framework for that community practice.

θα meant, for those who spoke it, both 'Lord, come at the end to establish thy kingdom' and 'Come now while we are gathered' (see Cullmann 1953: 35). Having argued consistently that the church must engage in theo-ethical reasoning by practising spiritual discernment, Paul invokes the Lord's presence to guide them to understand their dilemma. They must identify their experiences of contentious discord and division and correspondingly amend their practices that are not meeting with the Lord's approval.

6. *Conclusion*

Paul writes to the church in Corinth to point out two key aspects of Christian existence and to bring the Corinthians in line with his apocalyptic (i.e. revelatory) perspective. First, while he encourages community members to have contact with the world outside the church,[316] confessing Jesus as Lord (12.3) commits them to conform their behaviour to Christ's cruciform pattern of self-giving love for others.[317] This means that believers must 'die daily' (15.31) to the wisdom, standards and values of this world.[318] This necessarily involves a radical change in the contours of personal relationships for all believers in Corinth.

Second, Paul stresses that it is essential for the entire community to engage in theo-ethical reasoning by practising spiritual discernment. Through this dialogical process of comparative reasoning, believers practise looking for life by reflecting together on conduct and experience. In this process the Spirit leads them behaviourally by illuminating their experiences of new life from God (χαρίσματα) that are associated with conduct that conforms to Christ's cruciform pattern. Those who consistently and collectively call on the name of the confirming, judging and disciplining Lord by practising spiritual discernment grow more persuaded about the reality of the power of God that raised Jesus to resurrection life after death. By abounding in the work of the Lord through Christ-conforming conduct, believers perceive through demonstrations of Spirit and power that their labour in the Lord is not without fruit (see 2.1–5; 15.58). This discernible link between Christ-conforming conduct and their experience of new life in the spiritual body of Christ grounds their faith in the power of God and gives them hope that God will continue to transform them until they are fully changed into resurrection life at the completion.

Chapter 3 has thus shown that in 1 Corinthians 5–16 Paul implements his strategy (introduced in 1 Corinthians 1.1–4.21) to transform community perceptions by aligning them with his apocalyptic (i.e. revelatory) perspective.[319] Paul

---

316. See, e.g., 5.9–13; 7.16; 9.19–23; 10.32–33. Adams concludes that for Paul 'the world outside the church is not to be reformed; it is to be destroyed' (2000: 148–49), a finding that underestimates Paul's conviction that God is re-creating and transforming the world through Christ-conforming conduct.

317. Cf. Engberg-Pedersen 1987: 566–67; Horrell 1997a: 109.

318. Cf. 1.17–2.5; 7.29–31; Barclay 1992: 59.

319. See Brown (1995: 21) and Chapter 2, section 1 above.

consistently engages in theo-ethical reasoning, modelling the dialogical practice of spiritual discernment that seeks to link specific behaviour with community experience. Paul the pastoral theologian thereby integrates Christian living and thinking, synthesizing theology and ethics.[320]

320. According to Brown 'in 1 Corinthians Paul calls for an integration of epistemology and ethics, of knowing and acting "according to the cross" without which there can be no genuine Christian existence' (1995: 167). Chapter 3 has confirmed that aspect of Elliott's conclusion that Paul is 'engaged in the constant interplay of praxis and reflection' as the apostle engages in 'critical reflection on praxis' (1994: 83, citing Gutiérrez 1973: 300).

Chapter 4

Engaging in Theo-Ethical Reasoning:
Looking for Life in Christ and Not in Law (Galatians)

1. *Introduction*

Through exegesis of the letter to the Galatians, this chapter continues to look beneath the surface of the text to identify Paul's theo-ethical reasoning and the role of the community practice of spiritual discernment.[1] The chapter argues that reasoned reflection on the links between conduct and experience constitutes the means by which Paul theologizes, as he integrates Christian living and thinking and combines what many interpreters usually distinguish as theology and ethics. As in 1 Corinthians, we will show how Paul applies the motifs of spatial, temporal, and ethical dualism to contrast experiences of life in Christ (God's new age/new creation) with life in the present evil age/this world.[2] Paul employs this strategy to try to persuade members of his churches to reject the arguments of those who are advocating circumcision and adherence to the law as the appropriate behavioural standard in the churches. The chapter will thereby demonstrate the letter's 'interpenetration of history, theology and ethics' (Barrett 1985: 17).

There are three correlative components of Paul's theo-ethical reasoning and the practice of spiritual discernment that will be explored in Chapter 4. First, believers participate in God's cosmic war of liberation when their actions faithfully portray Christ's cruciform pattern in the context of their own lives. In Gal. 1.1–2.21 Paul reflects on conduct and experience in his own life and in other churches to establish Christ's cruciform pattern as the universal behavioural norm by which Jews and Gentiles alike are now experiencing justified life in Christ. This will be explored in section 2. Second, in Gal. 3.1–4.31 Paul reflects on conduct and experience recorded in scripture and in the churches of Galatia to try to show that believers experience new life in Christ when their actions are

---

1.   For this approach to 'New Testament ethics', see Keck 1996a: 8–10, discussed in Chapter 1, section 4.

2.   For Paul's use of the two ages theme, see Keck 1993: 29–30; Martyn 1997b: 98; Schütz 1975: 116; Burton 1921: 14; Duff 1989: 281; cf. Sampley 1990. According to B. Longenecker, the phrases 'in Christ' and 'new creation' (Gal. 6.15; 2 Cor. 5.17) are virtually synonymous for Paul (1998: 63). For a recent argument that Paul's phrase 'new creation' is primarily an anthropological term in Paul, however, see Hubbard 2002. The present study contends that the phrase 'new creation' includes individual, social, and cosmic dimensions, since Paul understands that the individual human body has no reality apart from its participation in larger bodies identified with greater cosmic realities. See D. Martin 1995: 131, 133.

discerned from faith in Christ and not law observance. This argument will be examined in section 3.

Third, while Paul models the practice of spiritual discernment by engaging in theo-ethical reasoning throughout the letter, Gal. 5.1–6.10 specifically addresses this community discipline of *looking for life* in the manifestations of the Spirit. The logic of Paul's argument in Gal. 5.1–12 (see section 4 below) suggests that some believers, by rejecting Christ's cruciform pattern and the practice of spiritual discernment in favour of law observance, have cut themselves off from Christ and fallen out of that spatial realm where God's life-giving grace/power prevails to effectuate new life. Thus, not everyone in these churches is practising spiritual discernment by engaging in theo-ethical reasoning. Paul addresses this concern in Gal. 5.5–6, where he also re-emphasizes the importance of practising self-giving love for others. By taking on law observance and abandoning Christ's cruciform pattern, some Galatians are no longer involved in the process of divine persuasion that takes place during the practice of spiritual discernment (Gal. 5.7–12).

In Gal. 5.13–6.10, Paul suggests ways in which the community may associate conduct with experience and thereby distinguish between divinely confirmed behaviour and actions that conform to the standards of the world (see section 5). Spiritually discerning these distinctions allows community members to continue walking in line with the Spirit, so that they may continue experiencing new life from faith in Christ. In this way they fulfil the law of Christ.

Paul closes the letter in 6.11–18 by summarizing the arguments. He concludes that believers experience life in God's new creation by walking in line with the 'rule' that we have characterized as Christ's cruciform pattern (see section 6). This chapter closes with a short summary (section 7).

2. *God is Creating a Discernible History in the Gospel (1.1–2.21)*

Contrary to usual approaches, this section seeks to show that Paul defends his apostleship and gospel by reflecting on experience to show how God is creating a discernible history through Paul's apostleship and gospel.[3] As in 1 Corinthians, Paul the pastoral theologian consistently focuses on the manifest power of God as his central concern, speaking 'fundamentally of what God has done, is doing, and will do' (Martyn 1988: 12–13 n. 17). Paul connects his own Christ-conforming behaviour with God's exercise of life-giving power. The apostle's earthly life becomes a paradigm of his gospel, creating a 'christomorphic historiography' (Barclay 2002: 147, 153). Moreover, Paul emphasizes that others in the church are also able to discern the manifest power of God that confirms his gospel. By implication Paul presents himself as an example for the Galatians to follow, a strategy

---

3.   Martyn concludes that Paul is describing 'the history created by the gospel' in this section (1997b: 159–61). He observes general similarities between certain sections of this letter and an earlier Hebrew literary genre that Martyn calls 'revelatory history in the form of personal memoir' (1997b: 160). The primary characteristic of these writings, says Martyn, is the consistent emphasis on the activity of God.

expressly confirmed in Gal. 4.12.[4] Paul thereby attempts to persuade the Galatians that the 'truth of the gospel' (2.14) means that Christ's cruciform pattern has become the universal behavioural norm for conduct through which both Jews and Gentiles experience new life in Christ through the power of God.

a. *The Apocalyptic (i.e. Revelatory) Scene (1.1–5)*

Paul establishes a keynote theme of the letter in the first verse (Bryant 2001: 141). God has begun the new age by raising Jesus from the dead (see Bryant 2001: 115, 144).[5] In 1.1 Paul also connects God's exercise of this life-giving power with his own apostolic status, the consequence of 'a cooperative act' (Bryant 2001: 144) by means of ($\delta\iota\grave{\alpha}$) Jesus Christ and God the Father. The verse then contrasts his own divine sending with that of other missionaries sent from and through human sources (1.1; cf. 1.8–16; 4.25–26).

In 1.4a Paul incorporates early Jewish-Christian language that identified Christ's death as an atoning sacrifice for sins.[6] He uses the existing tradition to emphasize Christ's voluntary self-giving ($\tau o\hat{u}\ \delta\acute{o}\nu\tau o\varsigma\ \dot{\epsilon}\alpha\upsilon\tau\grave{o}\nu$), a reference to his death on the cross that accomplished a once-for-all-time divine forgiveness of human sins (Martyn 1997b: 89).[7] The apparent emphasis on forgiveness of sins in 1.4a, however, is 'to a significant degree foreign' and 'partially alien' to Paul's own interpretation of 'God's apocalyptic act in Christ' (Martyn 1997b: 90, 116).[8]

Consequently, Paul adds a distinctive purpose clause in 1.4b[9] that strikes another keynote of the letter (Lightfoot 1874: 73). The clause illuminates Paul's own interpretation of the effects of Christ's voluntary self-giving death for others (see also 2.20). Christ's death on the cross occurred so that ($\acute{o}\pi\omega\varsigma$) believers might be delivered out ($\dot{\epsilon}\xi\acute{\epsilon}\lambda\eta\tau\alpha\iota$)[10] of the present evil age, where the power of worldly forces prevails.[11] This clause that contains both spatial and temporal imagery does not suggest, however, a deliverance from earthly human life.[12]

---

4. See W. Barcley 1999: 24; cf. Lyons, who concludes that Paul is only presenting himself as a model rather than also defending his apostleship (1985: 123–76).

5. See also Furnish 1993a: 112; Dunn 1993a: 35. Some interpreters mistakenly downplay this theme because resurrection is mentioned only once (1.1). See, e.g., Martyn 1997b: 85, 101; Gaventa 1991: 157; Beker 1980: 58; Sampley 1996: 120. They overlook the fact that resurrection means new life, a theme that is prominent in Galatians both directly (2.19, 20; 3.11, 12, 21; 5.25; 6.8) and by implication (4.19, 26–28; 5.2–4).

6. See Martyn 1997b: 88–90; Furnish 1993a: 113, 119; Betz 1979: 41–42; Dunn 1993a: 35; R. Longenecker 1990: 7; Bryant 2001: 129, 142; cf. Stuhlmacher 1968: 64 (a hymnic tradition).

7. In addition to 1.4, Paul only uses the plural 'sins' three other times (Rom. 7.5; 1 Cor. 15.3, 17). This strengthens the claim that this is language from an early church tradition or confession.

8. Cf. E.P. Sanders 1983: 25; *pace* Dunn 1993a: 34–35; Schütz 1975: 116.

9. R. Longenecker 1990: 8; Burton 1921: 13; S.K. Williams 1997: 35.

10. Martyn persuasively proposes that $\dot{\epsilon}\xi\acute{\epsilon}\lambda\eta\tau\alpha\iota\ \dot{\eta}\mu\hat{\alpha}\varsigma$ constitutes a synonym for God's 'rectification' (i.e. justification), as do Paul's later uses of $\zeta\omega\sigma\pi\sigma\iota\hat{\eta}\sigma\alpha\iota$ in 3.21 and $\dot{\eta}\mu\hat{\alpha}\varsigma\ \dot{\epsilon}\xi\eta\gamma\acute{o}\rho\alpha\sigma\epsilon\nu$ in 3.13 (1997b: 273 n. 176); cf. Theissen 1992: 159–86.

11. R. Longenecker 1990: 8; cf. Witherington 1998: 76–77. In Galatians, Paul understands existence in the present evil age as being subject to ($\dot{\upsilon}\pi\grave{o}$) worldly powers. See, e.g., 3.10, 22, 23, 25; 4.2–5, 9, 21a; 5.18; cf. 5.6.

12. See Gal. 2.20, where Paul uses the phrase $\dot{\epsilon}\nu\ \sigma\alpha\rho\kappa\acute{\iota}$ to refer to his earthly human life that continues even after such deliverance. See also 2 Cor. 10.3; Phil. 1.22, 24; but see Rom. 8.8.

Rather, these motifs suggest that Paul interprets this deliverance as taking place even in earthly human life when believers are relocated into God's new spatial realm/temporal age that Paul calls the 'kingdom of God';[13] life 'in Christ';[14] life 'in the Spirit';[15] life 'in the Lord';[16] and occasionally life in the 'new creation'.[17]

In 1.4 Paul does not indicate how or even when Jesus' voluntary self-giving death for others might accomplish this deliverance.[18] His language merely suggests that it is not yet complete (see also 1 Cor. 15.24–28), with Paul leaving open the possibility that some people might not be delivered (Bryant 2001: 157). He later expressly confirms this reality in Gal. 5.2–4. Paul's hearers would be right to assume at this point that the letter would later clarify how Christ's voluntary self-giving death for others becomes the means of divine deliverance from the power of worldly forces.[19]

Paul also links this same power of God with his apostleship (1.1). He almost always uses the phrase 'will of God' to characterize specific human conduct associated with the way that God carries out God's plans for the world.[20] Through the sequence in 1.1–4, Paul thus associates the manifest power of God that raised Jesus Christ from the dead with Christ's voluntary self-giving death for others 'according to the will of God' (1.4; see also Phil. 2.5–11).[21] Paul thus lays the foundation for arguing that, when he and other believers conform their actions to Christ's cruciform pattern, they mediate experiences of new life, as God delivers people out of the present evil age into God's new spatial realm/temporal age in Christ (cf. Gal. 3.1–5).[22] Paul thereby emphasizes the revelatory nature of these experiences.

b. *The Revealed Gospel Includes a Behavioural Standard (1.6–12)*
From the outset of the letter, Paul and his audience know that some members of the churches are considering circumcision or have already been circumcised and

---

13. See Rom. 14.17; 1 Cor. 6.10; 15.50; Gal. 5.21; cf. 1 Cor. 4.20; 6.9; 15.24; 1 Thess. 2.12; see also Eph. 5.5; Col. 1.13; 4.11; 2 Thess. 1.5.

14. See, e.g., Rom. 3.24; 6.11, 23; 8.1, 2, 39; 9.1; 12.5; 15.17; 16.3, 7, 9, 10; 1 Cor. 1.2, 4, 30; 3.1; 4.10, 15, 17; 15.18, 19, 31; 16.24; 2 Cor. 2.17; 3.14; 5.17, 19; 12.2, 19; Gal. 1.22; 2.4, 17; 3.14, 26, 28; Phil. 1.1, 13, 26; 2.1, 5; 3.3, 14; 4.7, 19, 21; 1 Thess. 2.14; 4.16; 5.18; Phlm. 8, 20, 23; cf. Eph. 1.1, 3; 2.6, 7, 10, 13; 3.6, 21; 4.32; Col. 1.2, 4, 28.

15. See, e.g., Rom. 2.29; 8.9; 9.1; 14.17; 15.16; 1 Cor. 12.3; 14.16; 2 Cor. 6.6; Gal. 6.1; 1 Thess. 1.5; cf. Eph. 2.22; 3.5; 5.18; 6.18; Col. 1.18.

16. See, e.g., Rom. 14.14; 1 Cor. 4.17; 7.22, 39; 9.1, 2; 15.58; Gal. 5.10; Phil. 1.14; 4.1, 2; 1 Thess. 3.8; 4.1; 5.12; Phlm. 16, 20; cf. Eph. 2.21; 4.17; 5.8; 2 Thess. 3.12.

17. See Gal. 6.15; 2 Cor. 5.17.

18. According to S.K. Williams (1997: 36), this deliverance is 'in process' or 'still in the future' since the purpose clause leaves the point uncertain (cf. Rom. 3.4; see also Rom. 9.17; 1 Cor. 1.29; 2 Cor. 8.11, 14; Phlm. 6); *pace* Martyn, who contends that deliverance has already occurred in Christ's death (1997b: 90), a reading that overemphasizes the 'already' nature of Paul's 'already-not yet' dialectic.

19. Cf. S.K. Williams 1997: 35; Bryant 2001: 165.

20. See, e.g., Rom. 1.10; 2.18; 12.2; 15.32; 1 Cor. 1.1; 2 Cor. 1.1; 8.5; 1 Thess. 4.3; 5.10; cf. Eph. 1.1, 5, 9–12; 5.15; 6.6; Col. 1.1, 9–10; 4.12.

21. According to Bryant, Gal. 1.1 and 1.4 establish the keynote themes of the letter (2001: 141–42).

22. Cf. Burton 1921: 14–15; Engberg-Pedersen 2000: 144–45; contra Witherington 1998: 77.

should be living by the Mosaic law (see 5.2–4). With this shared knowledge as background, Paul focuses in 1.6–12 on whether the Galatians will continue to live by grace – the power of God[23] that becomes manifest as God's action in history (see Barclay 2002: 154) by which believers were delivered out of the present evil age.

According to 1.6 the Galatians were first called in/by God's manifest exercise of divine power (ἐν χάριτι).[24] The aorist participle καλέσαντος in 1.6 indicates a past event when the Galatians were called by God into the new life associated with Paul's gospel (cf. 1.15; 5.8). The context of 1.6 and the rest of the letter, however, make it clear that this calling was not a once-for-all-time event.[25] Indeed, the present participle καλοῦντος in 5.8 reflects that God continues to call the same people in/by God's power.[26] Thus, the experience of God's call must be regularly discerned and continually tested in the community.

Indeed, Paul also contends in 1.6 that the Galatians are now transferring themselves from (ἀπò) God and into (εἰς) another gospel.[27] Paul's combination of ἀπò and εἰς indicates that they have now moved from one place to another through their own actions (see Martyn 1997b: 108). Further, in Paul's era the verb μετατίθημι sometimes carried behavioural overtones. It designated a defector from one philosophical school to another and, at least since the second century BCE, the verb was applied to characterize Jews who committed apostasy from the law (Bryant 2001: 197, citing 2 Macc. 4.46; 7.24).

Thus, Paul appears to reason that those who submit to circumcision and law observance are rejecting God's power that Paul associates with *another* behavioural standard.[28] Through their new commitment to law observance, these Galatians transferred themselves back into the present evil age, where the power of worldly forces still prevails (see 4.9; cf. 5.2–4). The logic of Paul's argument implies that deliverance out of the present evil age may be reversed when believers take on the law's pattern and turn away from the behavioural standard proclaimed in Paul's gospel.

Paul grounds his arguments in 1.6–7 in his understanding that there is only one gospel (εὐαγγέλιον) of Christ.[29] For Paul the noun εὐαγγέλιον refers to the 'divine event' of which 'God is both the ultimate and immediate author (*apokalypsis*)' (Martyn 1997b: 115). This *revelatory* event takes place when God comes

23. For understanding 'grace' as God's power, see Käsemann 1964c: 65; Nolland 1986: 31; Polaski 1999: 107; cf. Furnish 1968: 182.

24. The preposition ἐν is used with both its local and instrumental aspects here. *Pace* Martyn 1997b: 109 (local only).

25. Burton 1921: 20; see also Rom. 4.17; 9.12; 1 Thess. 2.12; 4.7–8.

26. See also Rom. 6.19, 22; 12.1–2; 15.16; 1 Thess. 5.23–24.

27. Martyn plausibly suggests that the outside Judaizers were also calling their message a gospel (1985b: 314).

28. See also Gal. 2.21; cf. 1 Thess. 4.7–8.

29. According to Schütz (1975: 121) and Gaventa (1991: 149), this is the 'singular gospel'. Martyn translates εὐαγγέλιον as Paul's 'glad-tiding', thereby emphasizing its singular nature. For discussions about the role that the word played in the emperor cult, see Martyn 1997b: 127–20; S.K. Williams 1997: 39.

on the scene and there is a manifestation of God's active power.[30] Indeed, the letter's opening verses pointed to this manifest power by which God raised Jesus from the dead – the 'divine event' closely associated with Christ's voluntary self-giving death for others on the cross according to the will of God (1.4).[31] Paul thus links a behavioural standard (Christ's cruciform pattern) with the revelatory 'divine event' that took place when God raised Jesus from the dead.

According to the logic of Paul's argument in Gal. 1.1–9, God is creating a 'new history' that unfolds in a 'series of gospel-events' (Martyn 1997b: 130).[32] Paul uses the verb form εὐαγγελίζομαι in 1.8–9 to characterize human participation in each of these revelatory events.[33] As already shown in connection with 1 Cor. 2.1–5, these divine events take place in connection with the embodied proclamation of Jesus Christ crucified. Through actions that conform to Christ's cruciform pattern, Paul becomes an active participant in the revelation of Jesus Christ (see Gal. 3.1–5; 4.14; cf. 1 Cor. 9.23; 11.1).[34] Moreover, he also expects members of his churches to become partners in that same gospel of Christ,[35] as these divine events continue to take place in the daily life and death (literal and metaphorical) of Christian believers.[36] Consequently, he also argues that the Judaizers were hoping to pervert (μεταστρέψαι) this gospel by advocating circumcision and, probably, law observance (1.7). Paul implies that law-observant behaviour is now blocking the revelation of other divine events from taking place (cf. Rom. 14.1–4; 1 Cor. 1.6–8).

Paul thus enters the debate with the Judaizing teachers and church members. He offers his own interpretation of God's plan. He links God's will for human conduct (i.e. conduct conforming to Christ's cruciform pattern) with the manifest power of God that raised Jesus from the dead and gives new life to believers (cf. Bryant 2001: 141–42).

Paul's rhetorical questions in the puzzling (Betz 1979: 54) and obscure (Dunn 1993a: 49), but significant[37] transitional verse at 1.10, thrust into focus a related

---

30. Martyn 1997b: 115; 1997a: 219; Winger 1994: 84; cf. Brown 1998; Schütz 1975: 53, 281; Käsemann 1969e: 168–82.

31. In 1 Cor. 2.1–5, discussed above in Chapter 2, section 2.c, Paul speaks of this divine event from another perspective. Through Paul's embodied proclamation of Christ crucified, there is a demonstration of Spirit and power that is the foundation for believers' faith in the power of God. See also Gal. 3.1–5.

32. Cf. Schütz 1975: 52.

33. Schütz emphasizes that the verb reflects the human activity relating to the visibly perceptible gospel (1975: 36), with each person merely becoming an instrument through which divine power becomes perceptibly visible (1975: 282).

34. In Galatians, Hansen concludes that Paul is a participant in the apocalypse of Jesus Christ and presents himself as 'a paradigm of the apocalypse' (1994: 194–209). Cf. Rom. 15.18–19; 1 Cor. 11.1; 2 Cor. 12.1–7; Gal. 4.14; Phil. 4.9; see also Acts 22.15. According to Gal. 1.16 and the logic underlying 4.14, Jesus Christ is being revealed in the actions of Paul.

35. See 1 Cor. 1.4–9. This includes becoming a financial partner in Paul's ministry (Phil. 1.5) or contributing to the collection for the saints in Jerusalem (2 Cor. 8.1–15).

36. Brown 1998: 282; cf. Schütz 1975: 53 (when its 'pregnant' or 'dynamic' dimension is stressed, the gospel emerges as a 'continuing element' in the life of the Christian community).

37. According to B.J. Dodd, the significance of 1.10 is often overlooked (1996: 90).

aspect of Paul's apocalyptic (i.e. revelatory) understanding of the gospel. He contrasts his role as servant of Christ – including its goals of persuading God[38] and humans[39] – with his former role as a Pharisee who tried only to please humans (cf. 1.13–14).[40] In his attempt to persuade the Galatians to remain steadfast to their original commitments, Paul contrasts himself with the Judaizing teachers who merely seek to please other humans (see also 6.12–13). They are also pressuring Paul and the Galatians to do likewise (see 2.4–5; 4.17–19; 5.2–4). He reasons that he would not be a servant of Christ if he was still pleasing humans (1.10c) by rejecting Christ's scandalous, cruciform pattern (see 5.11; 6.12).[41]

In 1.11–12 Paul offers 'a revelation of Jesus Christ' as authoritative on the behavioural matter at issue.[42] Indeed, according to 1.11 the divine event he communicated to the Galatians did not conform to human standards (οὐκ ἔστιν κατὰ ἄνθρωπον).[43] Paul neither received nor was taught this gospel by any person. Instead, he received it and was taught it through a revelation of Jesus Christ (δι᾽ ἀποκαλύψεως Ἰησοῦ Χριστοῦ).[44] Paul thereby seeks to establish the authenticity of his apostolic gospel and mission. He appeals to credentials on a par with those apostles who had actually walked with Jesus during his lifetime and seen the risen Lord.[45] Later, he also offers proof that others in the church have discerned God's approval of Paul's gospel.[46] They have discerned God's power given to Paul (2.9) and acknowledged the way that God is working in him (2.8).

With the use of the predominantly Pauline word ἀποκαλύψις,[47] Paul contrasts the heavenly source of his gospel with any other gospel taught by humans. The

38. Bryant observes that Paul is seeking the 'favor of God as a slave of Christ' (2001: 227); cf. 2.7–9. As shown by 1 Thess. 2.4–6, God continues to assess Paul's fitness to be entrusted with the gospel based on Paul's own conduct (Best 1972: 95–96; *pace* Malherbe 2000b: 141). The close linguistic parallels between Gal. 1.10 and 1 Thess. 2 (noted by Martyn 1997b: 139; Dunn 1993a: 48–49; Best 1972: 96–97) establish the critical, dual aspects of behaviour and speaking necessary for effective gospel communication.

39. Bultmann concludes that Paul's rhetorical question in 1.10a begs a response that Paul does seek to persuade humans (1968a: 1–3).

40. The first particle ἤ in 1.10a is conjunctive. *Pace* Lyons 1985: 138; Kraftchick 1996: 191 n. 34; Martyn 1997b: 139. The second particle in 1.10b is disjunctive.

41. The arguments in favour of equating πείθω and ἀρέσκειν in 1.10 should be rejected. For various attempts to avoid Paul's use of πείθω in its ordinary sense of 'persuade' (see also 2 Cor. 5.11), see, e.g., B.J. Dodd 1999: 143; Lyons 1985: 142–43; Kraftchick 1996: 191, 194; Burton 1921: 30; Esler 1998: 67, 124; R. Longenecker 1990: 18; Koptak 1990: 101; Betz 1979: 54–55; Dunn 1993a: 48–49; Martyn 1997b: 145; cf. Schütz 1975: 128–29. Bultmann (1968a: 1–3) and Malherbe (2000b: 139) correctly conclude that the verb should be given its customary meaning 'to persuade'.

42. See Winger 1994: 79; cf. Betz 1979: 62 (1.12 identifies the 'thesis' Paul defends).

43. Cf. Betz 1979: 56; Dunn 1993a: 52. See also Rom. 3.5; 1 Cor. 3.3; 9.8; 15.32; Gal. 3.15.

44. Paul speaks twice in other letters about being divinely taught in connection with specific conduct (see 1 Cor. 2.13; 1 Thess. 4.9). The verbs in the clause in Gal. 1.12b must be supplied, although commentators are divided over how this should be accomplished. Compare Betz (1979: 62), R. Longenecker (1990: 20, 25), and S.K. Williams (1997: 43) with Martyn (1997b: 144) and Dunn (1993a: 53).

45. Kelly makes this latter observation in connection with 1 Cor. 9.1 and 15.8 (1979: 112).

46. See Gal. 1.23–24; 2.7–9; Hill 1977: 130; cf. 1 Thess. 2.4–6.

47. Dunn 1993a: 53 (13 of 18 NT uses are in Paul).

noun ἀποκαλύψις suggests the action of God in Paul's life.[48] It implies that revelation unlocks the mystery of God's purpose for creation (Dunn 1993a: 53; see also 1 Cor. 2.6–16). By linking Christ's cruciform death (Gal. 1.4) with the power of God that raised him from the dead (1.1), Paul appears to be interpreting God's cosmic plan that Paul received through this revelation (see also 1 Cor. 2.1– 10). Indeed, the revelation of the risen Christ opened Paul's eyes to the way that the 'universal God' was acting in order to transcend Jewish particularity (Boyarin 1994: 39). Thus, it is tentatively suggested that from this revelation Paul understood that Christ's cruciform pattern transcended Torah and was now the new, *universal* norm for human behaviour in God's new age/spatial realm in Christ.[49]

Paul utilizes διά in Gal. 1.12b to indicate that this revelation of Jesus Christ was the means by which the gospel came to him (see R. Longenecker 1990: 24). The nature of the genitive Ἰησοῦ Χριστου in 1.12 is more difficult to determine.[50] Undoubtedly, God is the ultimate source of Paul's revelation.[51] Paul seems to assert, however, that the risen Lord Jesus Christ may be one of God's agents in this revelatory process.[52] The person of Jesus Christ – crucified and raised – may also become the content of this divinely revealed gospel.[53] Paul thus interprets the crucified and risen Christ as the expression of God's purpose for the world (Bryant 2001: 201). God is working out that purpose through Jesus Christ, as believers continue to conform their actions to his cruciform pattern. Paul explores this in the following verses.

c. *Reflecting on Conduct and Experience (1.13–2.14)*
The logic lying beneath the surface of the narrative in 1.13–2.14[54] illuminates important aspects of theo-ethical reasoning. After grounding his gospel in a revelation of Jesus Christ, Paul immediately turns to explain the effect of this

48. See Bryant 2001: 149. Paul later affirms that God continues to direct Paul's activities by means of revelation (Gal. 2.2).

49. Cf. Boyarin 1994: 39. According to Kraftchick, the Philippians knew they were to act in conformity with Christ but were unsure what shape their behaviour should take, so Paul offered the Christ hymn as a 'metaphorical hermeneutic' to provide criteria for evaluating conformity (1993a: 28, 31). The present study shows how Paul follows a similar rhetorical strategy in Galatians.

50. For the subjective genitive (a revelation from Jesus Christ), see R. Longenecker 1990: 24. For the objective reading (Jesus Christ as the content of the revelation), see Burton 1921: 39–43; Betz 1979: 82–83.

51. See 1 Cor. 2.10; Phil. 3.15; Martyn 1997b: 144; Bryant 2001: 200–201.

52. R. Longenecker 1990: 24; see also 1 Cor. 1.7–8; 4.4–5; 2 Cor. 12.1, 7; cf. Eph. 1.17; 2 Thess. 1.7. Elsewhere, Paul also understands that the Spirit (sometimes the Spirit of Christ) also plays a role in this process. See Rom. 8.1–17; 1 Cor. 2.10, 12; 12.4, 7, 11; 15.45; Gal. 4.6–7; 5.18, 22–23; 1 Thess. 4.8–9.

53. See Bryant, who observes how Paul consistently notes that Jesus Christ is the core content of the gospel, citing Rom. 1.3–4, 9; 15.19; 1 Cor. 1.23; 2.2; 2 Cor. 1.19; Gal. 3.1; Phil. 1.15, 27 (2001: 202 n. 25). Later, Paul concludes that he was commissioned to proclaim the person of Jesus Christ (Gal. 1.16), asserting that in some sense Jesus Christ becomes manifestly present through Paul's own earthly life (2.19–20; cf. 3.1; 4.14, 19).

54. Some interpreters characterize this as the autobiographical narrative. See Schütz 1975: 114– 58; Lyons 1985: 136–76; Gaventa 1986: 309–26; B.J. Dodd 1999: 133–70. Barclay calls it Paul's 'testimony' (2002: 136).

revelation on his own *behaviour*.[55] A similar pattern was also identified in 1 Cor.
15.8–10. Paul reminds the Galatians of his former Jewish pattern of conduct
(ἀναστροφήν).[56] As one zealously committed to the law's pattern of conduct
that defined Jewish identity,[57] Paul persecuted the church. He sought to destroy it
(Gal. 1.13, 23; cf. Phil. 3.6), perhaps for the implications of their stance on law
observance.[58] Because Paul's conduct pleased other humans, he advanced beyond
many of his contemporaries in Judaism (Gal. 1.14). The very phrase 'in Judaism',
used twice in 1.13–14, 'carries connotations which hint at those practices which
separated Jew from Gentile' (Räisänen 1992: 23),[59] in other words Jewish life
regulated by the *halakhah* (Dunn 1993a: 57).

Paul's life in Judaism shaped by law-observant conduct ended with the divine
revelation(s)[60] of Jesus Christ to Paul (1.11–12)[61] and in (ἐν) Paul (1.16).[62] The
revelation becomes Paul's key for understanding his own prophetic calling according to the will and purpose of God (Bryant 2001: 202).[63] In his revelatory experience, Paul comes to know Christ by personal acquaintance (see also Phil. 3.10).[64]
It constitutes an 'epistemological revolution that transforms his understanding of
himself from before birth onwards' (Barclay 2002: 139). Indeed, 'part of the
meaning of this [revelation 'in' Paul] is that God had reproduced in Paul a pattern

55. According to R. Longenecker, the force of the explanatory γάρ (1.13) extends throughout the
autobiographical section (1990: 27).

56. R. Longenecker explains that, based on inscriptions and literary uses in Koine Greek,
ἀναστροφήν became a locution for 'behaviour', 'conduct' or 'way of life' (1990: 27); cf. Dunn
1993a: 55. Similarly, Lyons (1985: 132–33) suggests that ἀναστροφήν and περιπατεῖν are synonymous (cf. 2 Cor. 4.2; 5.7; 10.2–3; 12.18; Phil. 3.17, 18; 1 Thess. 2.12; 4.1). Therefore, he concludes that the Pauline autobiographical passage is more concerned with ethics than with historical
recitation of events. This latter distinction is unnecessary. It overlooks how Paul directly associates
conduct with experience as part of theo-ethical reasoning.

57. For late Second Temple references to being a zealot for the law, see 1 Macc. 2.26, 27, 50, 54,
58; 2 Macc. 4.2.

58. Räisänen 1992: 23; cf. Fredriksen 1991: 532–64.

59. For the source of the term Ἰουδαϊσμός in the Maccabean revolt to describe those fiercely
loyal to the law, see 2 Macc. 2.21; 8.1; 14.38; *4 Macc.* 4.26; see also Räisänen 1992: 23; Dunn 1993a:
56.

60. Morray-Jones argues that Paul's apostolic commission occurred in a later revelation than
Christ's first appearance to Paul described in 2 Cor. 12.1–5 (1993: 289); cf. Betz 1979: 71. Although
highly plausible, the present study does not rely on such a finding.

61. For other references to Christ's appearance(s) to Paul, see 1 Cor. 9.1; 15.8.

62. For this translation of 1.16, see Engberg-Pedersen 2000: 146; Ashton 2000: 131; S.K.
Williams 1997: 47; Hays 1987: 281; Barclay 2002: 140–41; *pace* Martyn 1997b: 158; Bockmuehl
1990: 136 n. 136. For other references to Paul's understanding of how Christ lives 'in' him, see 2 Cor.
4.10–12; Gal. 2.20; Phil. 1.20.

63. Paul's language in 1.16 alludes to a prophetic vocation to the Gentiles reminiscent of Jer. 1.5–
6 and Isa. 49.1–5, a connection that has been frequently noted. See, e.g., Betz 1979: 70, including nn.
134, 137; S.K. Williams 1997: 46; Dunn 1993a: 63; Martyn 1997b: 156–57; Rowland 1995a: 47;
Tabor 1986: 40–41; Bryant 2001: 201 n. 23; Barclay 2002: 139; see also Chapter 3, section 3.d above
in connection with Paul's discussion of prophecy in 1 Cor. 14.1–40.

64. Engberg-Pedersen 2000: 95; S.K. Williams 1997: 47. Betz distinguishes between the
'external' visions reported in 1 Cor. 9.1 and 15.8 and the 'internal' vision of Gal. 1.16, but concludes
that they complement each other (1979: 71).

of dying and rising' (Ashton 2000: 131). Through it, God appointed Paul to a 'new way of life as an apostle' (Bryant 2001: 202).

Paul also offers his interpretation of the purpose (ἵνα) for this revelation of God's Son in him. Following his encounter with the risen Christ, Paul understood that he must become a 'bearer of God's eschatological news' (Bryant 2001: 202).[65] The content is the revealed person of Jesus Christ, who Paul proclaims by deeds and words.[66] Thus, it may be concluded that through a revelation of Jesus Christ *to* Paul and *in* Paul, he began to know Christ as he saw God exercising life-giving power in connection with conduct that conforms to Christ's cruciform pattern of voluntary self-giving love for others (cf. Gal. 2.19–20).[67]

In this critical verse 1.16 (see Engberg-Pedersen 2000: 146), Paul also characterizes the revealed Christ as the son of God.[68] He lays the groundwork for one of the letter's important themes addressing the identity of the 'sons of God'.[69] In Paul's Judaism the phrase 'sons of God' had become more than a metaphor, serving as a technical term based on God's renewed promise to Israel to make them 'sons of the living God' (see Hos. 1.10; *Jub.* 1.23–25; cf. Rom. 9.26).[70] The term was linked with law observance and faithful obedience to God's commandments (Martyn 1997b: 375 n. 248).[71] It was often used to describe the 'righteous' within Israel (Dunn 1993a: 202).[72] In the intertestamental literature the phrase similarly carried a strongly behavioural tone (Byrne 1979: 29).[73]

Although mirror-reading a text is always a tentative undertaking (Barclay 1987: 73–93), it may be reasonably hypothesized that Paul was engaged in an intra-Jewish debate about the identity of the 'sons of Abraham' (cf. 3.6–14, 29) and the 'sons of God'. Consequently, in 1.16 Paul introduces Jesus Christ as God's son, a status he affirms in 2.19–20. It would appear that Paul follows the Jewish *pattern* of defining the 'sons of God' in the context of behaviour. Paul

---

65. Cf. Gal. 3.1; 1 Cor. 1.18; 2.2.

66. See also Rom. 15.18–19; 1 Cor. 2.1–5; cf. Phil. 4.8–9. *Pace* Bryant, who characterizes Paul's proclamation simply as *preaching* activity (2001: 203).

67. Engberg-Pedersen concludes that 'it seems clear what Paul wishes to say: that through God's revelation of Christ, he came to live in Paul' (2000: 335 n. 34). Dunn also connects 1.16 with 2.20 (1993a: 64). In Phil. 3.10 Paul similarly associates conduct conforming to Christ's cruciform death with knowing Christ and the power of his resurrection.

68. See also Rom. 1.3, 4, 9; 5.10; 8.3, 14, 19, 29, 32; 1 Cor. 1.9; 15.28; 2 Cor. 1.19; Gal. 2.20; 4.4; 1 Thess. 1.10; cf. Eph. 4.13; Col. 1.13.

69. See 3.26; 4.6–7; see also Rom. 8.14, 19; cf. 9.26; 2 Cor. 6.18.

70. Eastman 2002: 270; Byrne 1979: 166; Martyn 1997b: 375 n. 248.

71. See, e.g., *Jub.* 1.24–25; cf. Gal. 6.15–16.

72. See, e.g., Wis. 2.13–18; 5.5; Sir. 4.10; *Pss. Sol.* 13.8.

73. See, e.g., Wis. 1.13–15; *Jub.* 1.23–25; *Pss. Sol.* 17.26–27. In his summary of the theme of 'adoption as sons' in the intertestamental literature, Byrne concludes: '…it is not so much a matter of what one must be, as of what one is *recognized* to be; that is, it is not so much a question of being righteous, of being obedient (to God, to the law, etc.) because one is a son of God. Rather, *because* one is *righteous*, one is *recognized* as a son of God and therefore free from any association or molestation on the grounds of unrighteousness' (1979: 29, emphasis added). Later, in 3.26–4.7 Paul employs a similar understanding of *how* God acknowledges God's recognition of a person as a 'son of God': God sends the Spirit of Christ into believers' hearts.

defines these 'sons' not in terms of law observance, however, but as those who conform their actions to Christ's cruciform pattern. Thus, he argues that Gentiles also become 'sons of God' through the faith (διὰ τῆς πίστεως) in Christ Jesus (3.26; cf. 4.4, 6, 7). By this Paul refers to believers' faith that, in the death and resurrection of Christ, God has confirmed Christ's cruciform pattern as the new behavioural standard that now defines the 'sons of God'.

As this section of the letter continues, Paul reflects on his own experience and conduct to build the Galatians' confidence in his gospel. He shows that God's action in his life is the fulcrum of his own personal history.[74] Moreover, Paul highlights the importance of community reflection on experience. He emphasizes the affirmation and proof provided when others recognize and acknowledge that God is manifestly working through Paul's embodied proclamation of Christ and 'the faith' (see 1.23–24; 2.7–9).

Thus, responding to another revelation, Paul went up to Jerusalem (2.2). He recognized that missionaries from the Jerusalem church could destroy his apostolic labours (2.2) by advocating a competing, law-observant gospel for new Gentile communities in Christ (cf. Dunn 1990a: 119). Paul's narration stresses the interdependence of both groups for the spread of the gospel.[75]

In connection with the Jerusalem leaders, Paul applies two parallel aorist participles of perception – ἰδόντες (2.7) and γνόντες (2.9) – to confirm the results of the collective discernment process initiated by revelation.[76] Through this dialogue, the Jerusalem leaders discerned that Paul had been divinely entrusted (πεπίστευμαι) with the gospel to the uncircumcised. They perceived the power that God gave him, recognizing that God worked an apostleship in both Peter and Paul.[77] They determined that Paul's success with Gentile churches proved God's favourable verdict on Paul's apostolic labours (see also 1 Cor. 9.1; 2 Cor. 3.1–3; 1 Thess. 2.1–10).[78] Thus, Paul's account of the meeting prompted by revelation is fundamentally informed by his conviction that community reflection on conduct and experience leads to vision, insight and knowledge when believers practise community discernment to identify God's manifest power working in the world (see Gal. 5.19–23; 1 Cor. 14.29–32).[79]

Paul continues to reflect on the relationship between conduct and experience in Gal. 2.11–14. His reasoning suggests that the 'truth of the gospel' involves a particular behavioural standard, but not law observance. Indeed, Paul illustrates what will become clear in 5.13–26 and 6.11–18. He associates community experiences of division and strife with law-observant conduct. Moreover, he rebukes

---

74. Gaventa 1986: 322; Martyn 1997b: 157 n. 191.

75. Martyn 1997b: 203; *pace* Holmberg 1978: 30.

76. Cf. R. Hall 1996a: 443 n. 32. For discussion of this process in 1 Corinthians, see Chapter 2, section 3.d and Chapter 3, section 3.d above.

77. See Bryant 2001: 203 n. 31; Martyn 1997b: 201. For other uses of the verb ἐνεργέω to reflect divine power at work in Paul, see 1 Cor. 12.6, 11; Gal. 3.5; 5.6; Phil. 2.13; 1 Thess. 2.13; cf. Clark 1935: 93–101.

78. Wrede 1907: 68.

79. According to Martyn, Paul's account of the meeting is fundamentally informed by the relationship between apocalyptic and new epistemology (1997b: 201).

Peter for returning to a law-observant lifestyle after having lived as a Gentile beyond the law's prescriptions (2.14).

Peter and the other Jews were not walking upright (ὀρθοποδοῦσιν) with 'the truth of the gospel' (2.14). Paul attributes their hypocrisy to a fear of persecution for failing to act in law-observant ways (2.12; cf. 5.11; 6.12). They were effectively compelling Gentiles to conform to the Jewish pattern of conduct in the law ('Ιουδαϊκῶς ζῆς) if they were to maintain relationships with Jewish-Christians. This law-observant conduct led to the kind of strife and division that Paul later identifies as some of the manifest 'works of the Flesh' (5.19–21).[80] Thus, he illustrates the adverse impact that such behaviour can have on others (see 5.9), noting that the remaining Jews (even Barnabas) joined Peter in the hypocrisy (2.13).

Throughout 1.13–2.14 Paul engages in theo-ethical reasoning. He consistently points out the important links between community experience and particular conduct, identifying the manifestations of God's power that establish the revelatory history being created by Paul's gospel. Moreover, the logic of Paul's argument underlying 2.11–14 highlights that the 'truth of the gospel' involves a behavioural standard. This conclusion follows from Paul's assertion that Peter did not conform his behaviour (ὀρθοποδοῦσιν) to the 'truth of the gospel'.

Having ruled out the law as the proper behavioural standard pursuant to the 'truth of the gospel', Paul now turns in 2.15–21 to identify the new, universal standard for conduct through which believers experience the life-giving power of God that is justifying all humanity.

d. *Paul Commends Christ's Cruciform Pattern for New Life (2.15–21)*

In this transitional and programmatic passage,[81] the logic of Paul's theo-ethical reasoning reflects how he combines ethics and theology. Pointing out that living like a Jew (2.14) 'cannot be the limiting framework in which the grace of God takes effect' (Barclay 2002: 142), Paul argues that Christ's cruciform pattern has become the universal standard for conduct through which Jews and Gentiles alike are being divinely justified.[82] This justification occurs ἐκ πίστεως Χριστοῦ (2.16).[83] Moreover, Paul also brings into sharp focus that the community must

---

80. Cf. Barclay 1988: 239; Hays 1996a: 32.

81. See Dunn 1993a: 132; R. Longenecker 1990: 80–81; Burton 1921: 117–18; B.J. Dodd 1999: 160; Barclay 1988: 76 n. 3; Betz 1979: 114. Gorman concludes these verses contain the thesis of the letter (2001: 135). Commentators have regularly noted the transitional quality of 2.15–21. See, e.g., Martyn 1997b: 246–47; Barclay 1988: 76, including n. 3; Dunn 1993a: 132; S.K. Williams 1997: 61; Gaventa 1986: 318; Witherington 1998: 169–71.

82. See also Rom. 3.29–30. Paul was not the first to think in terms of 'justification by faith' according to Hays (1985: 85) and Betz (1979: 115). For justification traditions that precede Paul, see Stuhlmacher 1966: 185–88; 217–20.

83. Different configurations of the genitives Χριστοῦ or Ἰησοῦ Χριστοῦ that govern the noun πίστις arise seven times in the authentic Pauline corpus (Rom. 3.22, 26; Gal. 2.16, 20; 3.22; Phil. 3.9). Although a number of possibilities for translation have been proposed, the present thesis is not dependent on a determination of this issue.

One common argument favours what is called the 'subjective genitive' ('faith/fulness of Christ'),

choose between Christ's cruciform pattern and the law, understood as alternative
behavioural standards. Paul affirms that he died to the law, having been crucified
with Christ (2.19). He affirms that he now intentionally conforms his own actions
to Christ's universal cruciform pattern rather than the law (2.18). Through conduct that conforms to the cruciform pattern, the crucified but risen Christ continues to become manifest in Paul (2.19–20; cf. 1.16; 4.14) and he experiences the
power of God that gives new life (see 2.20–21).

Paul opens the section by citing what is perhaps an older Jewish-Christian
atonement formula (2.16a) to appeal to the knowledge of Peter and the Judaizers.[84] This interpretation of Christ's death does not necessitate abandonment of
law observance.[85] It contends that neither Jews nor Gentiles[86] are justified by
works of the law except (ἐὰν μὴ)[87] through faith in Christ Jesus. If the traditional

where Christ's own 'faith/fulness' serves as an example or model of 'faith' that grounds and effectuates believers' 'faith'. For those advocating this position generally, see e.g., Howard 1967: 459–65;
G.M. Taylor 1966: 58–76; Donaldson 1997: 208–209; L.T. Johnson 1982: 77–90; Hays 2002: 139–
91; Hays 1997: 35–60; Hooker 1989: 321–42; R. Longenecker 1990: 87–88, 93–94, 145; Gaventa
1991: 147–59; Matera 1992: 92–104; Keck 1989a: 443–60; D. Campbell 1992b: 91–103; 1994: 265–
85; S.K. Williams 1997: 83–85; B. Longenecker 1993: 478–80; 1996: 75–97; 1998: 95–107; Gaston
1987: 12; Stowers 1989: 665–74; 1994: 194–226; Witherington 1994a: 267–72; Cousar 1990a: 39–
40; D. Hay 1989: 461–76; Wallis 1995; Foster 2002: 75–96. The 'subjective genitive' is sometimes
called the 'authorial genitive' (Martyn 1997b: 251), indicating that Christ is the author of the faith
under consideration. Martyn also finds that 'the faith of Christ' is an expression by which Paul speaks
of 'Christ's atoning faithfulness, as, on the cross, he died faithfully for human beings while looking
faithfully to God' (1997b: 270–71).
    Other interpreters argue the traditional view that the genitive is 'objective', making Christ the
object or content of human belief. For those supporting this position, see e.g. Dunn 1988: 178; 1997a:
61–81; Hultgren 1980: 248–63; Harrisville 1994: 233–41; Matlock 2003; 2000; Westerholm 1988;
Barclay 1988.
    Other genitival constructions have found less support than the two mentioned above. One bears
mention. Finding the either/or nature of the objective/subjective genitive analysis insufficient, Deissmann (1957: 161–66; see also Boers 1993: 107) advocates that these uses be characterized as a
'mystical genitive' or 'genitive of fellowship' because they indicate mystical fellowship with Christ.
Essentially, says Deissmann, 'of Christ' is 'in the main identical' with the 'in Christ' translation
(1957: 163). Wißmann rejects Deissmann's 'mystical genitive' (1926: 70) in favour of 'Christ faith'.
    Our hypothesis about Paul's theo-ethical reasoning suggests that Deissmann and Boers may be
correct in concluding that the either/or decision is unnecessary. Faith in Christ (objective genitive)
may refer to the believer's conviction that, in Christ, God has revealed a new standard for conduct
(Christ's cruciform pattern) and that, by means of conduct conforming to this pattern, believers may
experience new life through the power of God. Paul may have understood that Christ had a similar
faith: believing that God would continue to act powerfully through Christ's own acts of self-giving
love for others that conformed to the will of God. This faith in the power of God emboldened Christ
to conform to God's will, even when it meant submitting to death on the cross.
    84. Betz 1979: 115–16. According to Das, Paul's use of εἰδότες reflects an undisputed, shared
affirmation in early Jewish Christianity (2000: 537).
    85. See Schweitzer 1931: 225; Martyn 1997b: 268; Das 2000: 533.
    86. Martyn (1997b: 249) notes that Paul's use of ἄνθρωπος refers to both Jews and Gentiles;
pace Stowers (1989: 670–71) and Gaston (1987: 65–66), who both contend that ἄνθρωπος refers
only to a Gentile. The latter reading seems to ignore the rhetorical force of the emphatic 'we' in 2.15,
16 and 17.
    87. Although the thesis is not dependent on this choice, this study takes ἐὰν μη in its most natural

adversative translation of the ἐὰν μη phrase ('*but* through faith in Christ') is applied, Paul's use of the Jewish-Christian atonement formula becomes less intelligible. The adversative leads to the implausible result that Paul and the Judaizers agree to the very antithesis between justifying 'faith' and non-justifying 'works of the law'. Such a translation would render Paul's subsequent argument unnecessary (cf. 5.4).[88]

In 2.16b Paul employs the emphatic 'we' to remind Peter and other Jewish-Christians of their common ground. He also employs the ingressive aorist ἐπιστεύσαμεν.[89] The Greek construction of verb and preposition (εἰς Χριστὸν Ἰησοῦν ἐπιστεύσαμεν) indicates an act of persuasion or conviction that moved them 'into Christ Jesus' (Gorman 2001: 114 n. 45). The verb denotes the 'point of entrance' into something that has a continuing quality,[90] a moment of 'reorientation and commitment' (S.K. Williams 1997: 70). This deliberate decision distanced them from the socio-religious world of Judaism that once provided them with their identity and practices (S.K. Williams 1997: 50).

Moreover, by allowing the preposition εἰς to retain its basic sense of movement 'toward' or 'into',[91] the phrase describes that past moment when each of them took the first step for relocating 'into' God's new spatial realm/temporal age in Christ. Indeed, this is movement 'into' that 'new socio-spiritual domain where Jesus Messiah is Lord' (S.K. Williams 1997: 50).[92] Throughout the letter Paul's language about 'faith' and 'believing' includes a person's active participation in God's dawning new age/spatial realm in Christ (B. Longenecker 1996: 82). Paul thus draws on the motif of spatial dualism. By implication, he contrasts that initial movement into Christ with the recent one whereby some Galatians are removing themselves from God and placing themselves into the sphere of the power of some other 'gospel' (1.6; cf. 5.2–4). As a result, he argues later, the grace/power of God and the presence of Christ no longer benefit them (see 5.4; cf. 2.21).

This movement into Christ took place so that (ἵνα) Peter and Paul might also be justified ἐκ πίστεως Χριστοῦ ('from faith in Christ'). Paul applies the divine passive of the verb δικαιόω three times in 2.16 and a fourth time in the following verse to indicate that God is the source of this justifying power. The phrase ἐκ πίστεως Χριστου signifies the identical means by which all humanity – both Jews and Gentiles alike – will be justified (Horrell 2000: 335). Paul has already

---

grammatical sense as an exceptive rather than adversative linking conjunction. See Das 2000: 530–31; Rom. 10.15; 11.23; 1 Cor. 8.8; 9.16; 14.6, 9; 15.36. The vast majority of interpreters render the phrase as an adversative. See, e.g., Dunn 1990a: 212; 1993a: 137; Burton 1921: 120–21; Engberg-Pedersen 2000: 171; Bruce 1982: 136; Walker 1997: 515–20; R. Longenecker 1990: 83–84; Fung 1988: 115; Witherington 1998: 178.

88. Das reaches the same conclusion (2000: 537).

89. *Pace* R. Longenecker 1990: 88 (the verb is the 'historical aorist', a once-for-all response).

90. See Moule 1959: 10; cf. 1 Cor. 3.5.

91. See also 1.6; 5.4; cf. Col. 2.5; S.K. Williams 1987b: 443.

92. Similar spatial language will be examined below in connection with 5.4 (see Chapter 4, section 4.a), where Paul says that those who are being justified ἐν νόμῳ fell out of grace and cut themselves off from Christ.

shown that law-observant conduct restricts relationships between Jews and Gentiles (2.11–14; cf. 3.28). The law divides humanity by distinguishing as sinners those who consciously disregard its prescriptions (see 2.17). In effect, Paul argues that, in Christ, God is now forging a new solidarity of all humanity.[93] Jews and Gentiles, who have faith in the son that God sent to redeem humanity, experience this new solidarity through conduct that conforms to Christ's cruciform pattern. This is the new behavioural standard that Paul associates with the 'truth of the gospel'.[94] He thereby stresses the universal rather than ethnic character of this new norm.

Paul later confirms this understanding in 3.27, where he further illuminates the logic of the argument. There, he uses the parallel phrase εἰς Χριστὸν ἐβαπτίσθητε (cf. Rom. 6.3).[95] For those who were baptized into Christ and clothed themselves (ἐνεδύσασθε) with Christ (Gal. 3.27), the new cruciform pattern renders redundant all worldly social and ethnic distinctions that ground the law's prescriptions (3.28; cf. 5.6; 6.15) and lead to human division and separation (cf. 2.14; 5.19–21).[96]

In 2.15–17 Paul shapes his argument for a new behavioural norm around the law's Jew-Gentile distinction, one that characterizes Gentiles as ἁμαρτωλοί because they reject the law's pattern of conduct.[97] He responds to criticism that through his disregard for the law he has made Christ a servant of Sin (understood as a personified power in the world). Paul admits that 'we ourselves'[98] were found (εὑρέθημεν) to be ἁμαρτωλοί, a conclusion he never denies (2.17). From the perspective of Torah observance, Paul's unbounded engagement with Gentile believers (2.11–14) makes him a 'sinner' because he steps outside the boundaries of covenant loyalty centred on Torah (Horrell 2000: 336). Further, Paul uses καὶ ('also') with the reflexive plural pronoun and plural ἁμαρτωλοί to link 2.17 with 2.15. Thus, he associates law-offending conduct with the actions of Gentile 'sinners' who disregard the law (cf. 4.12).[99]

According to 2.17, Paul was found (aorist) to be a 'sinner' during a time when he was actively 'seeking (ζητοῦντες) to be justified in Christ'.[100] Paul uses the

93. See also 3.26–28; 5.6; 6.15; 1 Cor. 3.6. 9; 12.18, 24.

94. Cf. Reinmuth 1991: 99–100.

95. For the close connection between these two phrases, see S.K. Williams 1987b: 442.

96. Paul also uses the verb ἐνδύω in connection with being 'clothed' with the Lord Jesus Christ in other behavioural contexts in Rom. 13.12–14 and 1 Thess. 5.8; cf. Eph. 6.11; Oepke 1964: 320. Oepke also notes the ethical use of the word in the Septuagint (1964: 319). For further discussion of 3.27, see Chapter 4, section 3.d below.

97. For similar distinctions in late Second Temple Judaism, see *Jub.* 23.23–24; *Pss. Sol.* 2.1–2; cf. 1 Macc. 2.44–48; *Pss. Sol.* 4.8; 13.6–12; *1 En.* 5.4–7; 1QH 10.5–19; see Dunn 1993a: 133, 136; 1997b: 147–53.

98. Paul uses the plural 'we' to show again what he and Peter hold in common.

99. Burton 1921: 125; S.K. Williams 1997: 71–72.

100. Contra Lyons, who concludes that this took place before Paul was a member of the 'body of Christ' (1985: 94); cf. Martyn 1997b: 254–55; S.K. Williams 1997: 72; Dunn 1993a: 141. Other commentators overlook this aorist tense of the main verb and place the emphasis on a present or future hypothetical occurrence. See, e.g., Betz 1979: 113; Fung 1988: 118–19; R. Longenecker 1990: 88–90.

continuative present participle (ζητοῦντες) to characterize an ongoing process.[101] We suggest that the participle signifies Paul's practice of reflecting on
experience and behaviour as he seeks to embody faithfully the person of Jesus
Christ in every context (cf. 1 Cor. 9.19–23). This reflective practice takes place
as Paul engages in theo-ethical reasoning in the course of practising spiritual discernment. Paul consistently seeks to discern conduct that will conform to Christ's
cruciform pattern (i.e. God's will), anticipating that God will work through such
behaviour and exercise the power that brings the experience of justification/new
life to others.[102]

    This proposed understanding of ζητοῦντες is consistent with Paul's earlier
use of the same verb in Gal. 1.10 and in his other letters.[103] Believers reflectively
seek to identify actions that were pleasing to God, a conclusion grounded in their
identification of community experiences of new life that divinely confirm such
behaviour (see 1 Cor. 1.5–8; 2.1–5; 12.4–7). From this reflective discernment,
they imaginatively envision future actions that may conform to Christ's cruciform pattern, anticipating that the risen Lord Jesus Christ and God will provide
'vindicating commendation'[104] or 'blessing' (see Gal. 4.15) that confirms divine
approval of such conduct.[105]

    Having confidently advocated Christ's cruciform pattern as the new behav-
ioural standard in 2.16–17, Paul boldly commends himself (ἐμαυτὸν συνιστάνω)[106] as a transgressor (παραβάτην) of the law in 2.18.[107] After the crucified
but risen Christ was revealed in Paul (1.16) and the gospel came to him through a
revelation of Christ (1.11–12; cf. 1 Cor. 1.7–8), Paul intentionally turned his back
on the pattern of conduct prescribed by the law.[108] He became as a Gentile sinner

    101. Paul commonly uses the participle ζητοῦντες to describe an active, ongoing process of 'seek-
ing' a goal through specific conduct. In addition to Gal. 1.10, see Rom. 2.7; 10.3, 20; 1 Cor. 10.24,
33; 14.12; 2 Cor. 13.3; Phil. 2.21; 1 Thess. 2.6.
    102. Commentators often wrongly attempt to explain away or reject this process. See, e.g., Dunn
1993a: 141; Betz 1979: 119; Martyn 1997b: 254; Soards 1989: 237–54.
    103. See, e.g., Rom. 2.6–7; 10.3; 1 Cor. 1.22; 14.12.
    104. For use of this latter phrase, see Cosgrove 1987: 663; cf. 1 Cor. 4.4–5; 2 Cor. 10.18.
    105. This discernment process creates a parallel structure to the pattern of religion that E.P.
Sanders identified as central to the Tannaitic literature and religion of the rabbis (1977: 83). The study
of the commandments and the intent to obey them constituted appropriate behaviour within the
Jewish covenant and represented the means of reaching the goal of knowing God and adhering to
God's will. See also W.D. Davies 1972a: 310–32; Hooker 1990a: 155–64; cf. 1 Cor. 8.1–3; 15.34;
Gal. 4.8–9.
    106. For a similar translation, see Gaston 1987: 65. Paul's use of the verb elsewhere also supports
this translation. See Rom. 3.5; 5.8; 16.1; 2 Cor. 3.1; 4.2; 5.12; 6.4; 7.11; 10.12, 18; 12.11. Betz
describes the rendering of συνιστάνω in Galatians as 'difficult' (1979: 121 n. 73) because he fails to
recognize the logic of Paul's theo-ethical reasoning.
    107. For this understanding of παραβάτην, see Betz 1979: 121 n. 71; Dunn 1993a: 143; N. Young
1998: 85; *pace* Bachmann 1992; Lambrecht 1991: 228–29. See also Rom. 2.25, 27; Jas 2.9, 11; cf.
Rom. 2.23, 24, 27; 4.15; Gal. 3.19.
    108. In connection with his discussion of Gal. 3.10, N. Young observes that Paul is advocating a
conscious and purposeful abandonment of certain requirements of the law (1998: 84). For a similar
conclusion in the context of Philippians 3, see Engberg-Pedersen 2000: 92.

by seeking to act in ways that conform to Christ's cruciform pattern, without regard for the law's protective boundaries (cf. Gal. 2.11–14; 3.23–25).

Paul thus commends himself as a model for Gentile behaviour (see also 4.12).[109] As a servant of Christ (1.10), he now builds up (οἰκοδομῶ) again what he sought to destroy (κατέλυσα), referring to the church and 'the faith'.[110] Far from making Christ a servant of Sin (cf. 4.3, 9), Paul carries out his role as a servant of Christ by intentionally dying to the law's prescriptive pattern for human behaviour.

Paul continues to explain (γὰρ) his self-commendation as a sinner under the law in 2.19–21. In these three important verses,[111] Paul brings together what are normally distinguished as theology and ethics. He tells the Galatians that he died to the law, as seen in his transgression of the law, so that he might live to God (2.19). Paul thus emphasizes the death to new life sequence that represents the keynote themes of the letter introduced in 1.1–4.

Paul's assertion in 2.19 that he has been crucified with Christ means that he has become an active participant with Christ in his crucifixion. While this language is clearly metaphorical, there is no doubt that Paul refers to the complete destruction of his personal identity and former way of life in Judaism as a result of the revelation of Jesus Christ in his life (Barclay 2002: 143; see also 1.13–16). In this way Paul died to the law, voluntarily accepting the law's curse for non-compliance (see 3.13).[112] Further, the perfect passive συνεσταύρωμαι indicates a past event that carries ongoing significance in Paul's life. In fact he dies daily to the law (see 1 Cor. 15.31) by rejecting all worldly standards of conduct. Thus, through his cruciform actions he consistently re-enacts his crucifixion with Christ.

At the same time, however, Paul now lives to God (Gal. 2.19). He now lives his new earthly life in the flesh by faith (ἐν πίστει) in 'the son of God who loved me and gave himself for me' (2.20). By this Paul means that he consistently enacts 'the Christ life of self-giving love, which is the product of faith (5.6) and the fruit of the Spirit (5.22)' (Barclay 2002: 144). His reasoning suggests that when he 'believed into Christ' (2.16) he clothed himself with Christ in baptism (3.27) by committing to conform his behaviour to Christ's cruciform pattern. This reconstruction of Paul's identity fashions in him a self that is both his own self and, at the same time, 'the expression of the person of Christ' (Barclay 2002: 143). By means of Paul's embodied proclamation of Christ crucified (see 1 Cor.

109. See Harvey 1985: 85–86; cf. Engberg-Pedersen 2000: 126.
110. Gaston 1987: 71; *pace* Lambrecht 1991: 217; Räisänen 1985: 548. With one exception (1 Cor. 8.10) Paul uniformly applies the verb οἰκοδομέω (and the closely related ἐποικοδομέω and οἰκοδομῆς) in the context of encouraging conduct that conforms to Christ's cruciform pattern and leads to the divine upbuilding of the community. See Chapter 3, section 2.h.
111. According to Gaston, 2.19–20 are the two most important verses in the Pauline corpus for understanding his 'theology' (1987: 72); see also Gorman 2001: 39.
112. Paul's reference in 2.19 to dying to the law *through* the law remains enigmatic. He appears to be referring to the role of the law in the crucifixion of Christ and pointing forward to his argument in 3.13. See Barclay 1988: 80–81 n. 14; Engberg-Pedersen 2000: 348 n. 32; Tannehill 1967: 58–59; Martyn 1997b: 257.

4. *Looking for Life in Christ and Not in Law (Galatians)*

1.23; 2.2; Gal. 3.1), the living Christ continues to be presented to others.[113] Paul differentiates, however, between experiences of the new, earthly life of Christ embodied in Paul (2.20) and the experience of Christ's resurrection life after death, a life that Paul has not yet attained (see Phil. 3.11–12). Through conduct that conforms to Christ's cruciform pattern, Christ becomes manifest in Paul's bodily, earthly existence (see also Gal. 4.14; Phil. 1.20; cf. Gal. 4.19).[114]

Moreover, by implication in 2.20, Paul explains further what it means to experience Christ by personal acquaintance as Christ was revealed 'in' Paul (see Engberg-Pedersen 2000: 85). Christ comes alive in Paul as his conduct conforms to Christ's cruciform pattern of self-giving love for others, Paul's new behavioural norm.[115] In fact Paul's identification with Christ through such conduct is so intimate that it may be characterized as an embodied form of 'mystical solidarity' with Christ.[116]

Paul closes this important section in 2.21, a verse that further reflects the participatory role of Christ-conforming conduct in the deeper logic of Paul's theo-ethical reasoning. He reasons that if 'righteousness' (i.e. new life)[117] came through the law ($\delta\iota\grave{\alpha}$ νόμου), then Christ died without purpose. What he means by this compact statement is that Christ's voluntary self-giving death for others according to the will of God (1.4) has an important purpose that lies in human practice (see Engberg-Pedersen 2000: 138). Christ's death manifested that special way of actual living (Engberg-Pedersen 2000: 139) – namely, the cruciform pattern – that God has divinely confirmed by raising Christ to new life (see 1.1). Paul thus concludes that experiences of righteousness/new life no longer come through conduct conforming to the law ($\delta\iota\grave{\alpha}$ νόμου) but through conduct conforming to Christ's cruciform pattern.

Consequently, Paul asserts that he does not set aside/reject (ἀθετῶ) God's grace/power (χάριν).[118] Unlike Peter, Paul does not revert to conduct that conforms to the law's prescribed pattern. Such action would render Christ's death without effect. Instead, righteousness/new life is now experienced in connection with conduct that conforms to Christ's cruciform pattern rather than law-

---

113. Bryant refers to the new life of Christ as resurrection life (2001: 151).

114. B. Dodd wrongly contends that Paul's emphasis here is on Christ's action rather than Paul's, since it is Christ who lives in Paul (1999: 158–59). This interpretation is similar to that of Käsemann, Martyn and Gorman. They suggest that the external powers of the heavenly or earthly realms determine a person from the outside, taking possession of the person and thereby deciding into which of the two dualistically opposed spheres the person will be integrated. Their position understates the human participatory role in the complex divine–human partnership that grounds Paul's theo-ethical reasoning (cf. 1 Cor. 1.9; 12.4–7).

115. Cf. Schürmann, who concludes that Paul's reference to the 'law of Christ' in Gal. 6.2 confirms Paul's understanding that the teaching and conduct of Jesus now serve as Paul's 'external norm' (1974: 293). While his conclusion regarding the importance of Jesus' 'Wort' for Paul may be contested (cf. 1 Cor. 7.10–16; 9.14–15), Schürmann's insight that Paul viewed the 'love' manifested in the conduct of Jesus Christ as an 'external norm' correctly represents Paul's position.

116. The phrase is from Rowland 1995a: 48.

117. For this correlation of 'righteousness' and 'new life', see Theissen 1992: 159–86.

118. For Paul's understanding of 'grace' as divine power, see Käsemann 1964c: 65; Nolland 1986: 31; Polaski 1999: 107; cf. Furnish 1968: 182.

observant actions. This becomes the universal means by which all humanity experiences new life through the power of God.[119]

According to the logic underlying 2.16–21, Paul seeks to become a vehicle for the manifestation of God's power by taking actions that conform to Christ's cruciform pattern (see also 1 Cor. 2.1–5). This conviction lies at the heart of his understanding of the divine incarnation in Christ that has been the backdrop of Gal. 2.16–21.[120] We thus discover how Paul brings together theology and ethics in his theo-ethical reasoning: God's life-giving power may be experienced in connection with Christ-conforming conduct. In 3.1–5 Paul turns to clarify this connection.

3. *God Gives New Life from Faith in Christ (3.1–4.31)*

Paul introduced the key phrase ἐκ πίστεως Χριστοῦ in 2.16. It represents the source and means by which both Jews and Gentiles are being justified by God (see Horrell 2000: 335). In 3.1–4.31 Paul reflects specifically on the Galatians' own experience. He interprets it through examples from scripture to show that it is ἐκ πίστεως ('from faith') rather than law observance that they are experiencing new life from God. In this section Paul consistently employs the motifs of spatial, temporal, and ethical dualism to contrast life in the present evil age, experienced by means of law-observant conduct, with life in Christ, experienced in connection with actions that conforms to Christ's cruciform pattern.

a. *The Spirit Illuminates the Link between New Life and Christ-Conforming Conduct (3.1–5)*

Paul reflects on the link between conduct and experience by recalling his first encounter with the Galatians in the short but critical passage in 3.1–5.[121] The logic underlying Paul's argument suggests that the Galatians witnessed visible signs that Paul suffered persecution.[122] Apparently, Paul's preaching characterized this suffering as the crucifixion of Christ publicly displayed (προεγράφη) before their very eyes (3.1; cf. 2.19–20; Phil. 3.9–10).[123] In this way Paul's life becomes 'the canvas upon which the crucified Christ was publicly displayed' (B. Davis 1999: 208, also quoted by Gorman 2001: 31 n. 30). Paul became for them 'a representative, even a personification, of the crucified Christ whom he placarded' (Barclay 2002: 145).[124] Indeed, Paul was the Galatians' own 'revela-

---

119. Cf. Rom. 5.1–21; see also Eph. 2.18; 3.12.

120. Nickelsburg identifies the centrality of God's incarnation in Christ for Galatians, Romans and Philippians (1991: 348–57), concluding that the centre of Paul's theology may be found in the language of participation (1991: 355–56; cf. E.P. Sanders 1977: 522–23).

121. According to Cosgrove, 3.1–5 plays the central role in the letter (1988: 38).

122. For Paul's emphasis on persecution in the letter, see 4.13, 29; 5.11; 6.12, 17.

123. B. Davis argues that Paul's language in 3.1 is more literal than metaphorical, referring to the physical manifestations of persecution that Paul associates with Christ's crucifixion (1999: 208); cf. Hofius 1991: 384 n. 37; see also Baasland 1984: 135–50; Goddard and Cummins 1993: 93–126; cf. Cosgrove 1988: 187; Bockmuehl 1990: 143 n. 71; *pace* Martyn 1997b: 283.

124. For other references to this style of embodied proclamation in Paul, see e.g. Rom. 15.18–21; 1 Cor. 4.8–13; 2 Cor. 4.9–12; 12.6–7; Phil. 1.20–30; 4.8–9.

tion of Jesus Christ' (Barclay 2002: 145), a conclusion already suggested in Gal. 1.16 (cf. 4.14).

Paul links this embodied proclamation of Christ crucified with the Galatians' receipt of the Spirit in 3.2, a sequence that parallels 1 Cor. 2.1–16. Their receipt of the Spirit did not occur in connection with law-observant conduct (ἐξ ἔργων νόμου), but from their own 'hearing of faith' (ἐξ ἀκοῆς πίστεως).[125] Based on his background in Hebrew scripture, where the term שמע is prominent, Paul seems to understand ἀκοῆς as an active heeding. Thus, a 'hearing of faith' refers to their behavioural response to Paul's public portrayal of Christ crucified in word and deed.[126]

The Galatians responded to Paul's embodied proclamation of Christ crucified in a way that did not simply involve a number of individual human decisions to have faith in Christ. Instead, they offered their own self-giving acts of Christ-conformity to Paul in his time of need.[127] They would have torn out their eyes for him (Gal. 4.14–15). Moreover, the Galatians resisted the temptation to interpret Paul's persecution and suffering as a sign of God's disfavour (see 4.14). By receiving Paul and helping him, they, too, died to the standards and expectations that usually determine conduct in the present evil age (cf. 2.19). They, too, participated in Christ's crucifixion (cf. 2.19), portraying his cruciform pattern in their own behavioural response to Paul.[128]

In connection with their Christ-conforming hearing of faith, the Galatians received the Spirit (3.2; cf. 4.6; 5.5).[129] But some of the Galatians have now forgotten the importance of this sequence. Consequently, in 3.1 and 3.3 Paul characterizes them as ἀνόητοι ('ones without understanding'). The usual translation ('foolish'[130]) understates the important role of community spiritual discernment to which Paul alludes in the following verses and which later becomes an important focus in the letter (see 5.5–25). It has been shown already that, for Paul, practising spiritual discernment by engaging in theo-ethical reasoning is a prerequisite for properly understanding the link between community experiences of God's life-giving power and conduct that conforms to Christ's cruciform pattern (see 1 Cor. 2.1–16). Thus, Paul's emphatic use of ἀνόητοι in Gal. 3.1 and 3.3 highlights the Galatians' failure to practise this discipline.

125. Paul's use of ἀκοῆς refers to the Galatians' act of hearing (S.K. Williams 1989: 82–93), rather than Paul's 'message' or 'report', which would signify only a passive reference to the content of a message that Paul merely preached. Contra Hays 2002: 143–49; 1989: 110; Martyn 1997b: 287–89; Schlier 1971: 78–82; Kittel 1964: 221.

126. Nanos observes that there is no word 'obey' in Hebrew and that the Septuagint frequently uses the term ὑπακούω to render the Hebrew שמע, with its heritage of responding obediently to what one hears (1996: 222). Cf. S.K. Williams 1987a: 94; 1997: 91.

127. Cf. S.K. Williams 1989: 91 with Kraftchick, who concludes that the gospel understood means the gospel embodied as a living out of the mission in the service of others (1993a: 27).

128. According to Cosgrove, 'participation in the cross of Christ is the sole condition for life in the Spirit...the fundamental "ground" of life in the Spirit' (1988: 178–79, 194).

129. Cf. Martyn 1997b: 532. According to Bryant, in 3.2 Paul is describing the time when the Galatians experienced new creation existence by receiving the Spirit (2001: 230).

130. See KJV, RSV, NRSV, NAB, NKJ, NIV.

With his series of questions in 3.3–5, Paul introduces and contrasts the Spirit
and the Flesh (understood as a personified power).[131] This opposition continues
throughout the remainder of the letter. With this contrast Paul tries to address
the Galatians' lack of understanding. He directs them to the links between their
experiences and specific conduct that conforms to one of two alternative behavioural standards. He inquires of them whether, having begun by the Spirit (ἐναρξάμενοι πνεύματι), they are now perfecting themselves by the Flesh (νῦν σαρκὶ
ἐπιτελεῖσθε).[132] Since those who are reading and listening to the letter know
that some community members are now submitting to circumcision and law
observance, this second question in 3.3 implies a connection between those
behavioural practices and the Flesh. Paul thus suggests that at least some of the
Galatians are now in danger of perfecting themselves by means of conduct that
conforms to a social standard that is merely human (cf. 1.1, 10–12), since observ-
ing the law is simply a 'human way of life'.[133] This contrast points to Paul's
understanding (ignored by some Galatians according to 3.1, 3) that there is a
link between the Spirit and human behaviour. Paul further explores this ethical
dualism in 3.4–5 and 5.1–25 by connecting it with the Galatians' community
experiences.

Indeed, Paul refers to the Galatians' past experiences of suffering and asks
them whether they have been in vain (3.4–5). His underlying logic implies that
their past experiences of suffering were associated with their 'hearing of faith',
reception of the Spirit, and original acceptance of Christ's cruciform pattern as
their new behavioural standard. These experiences will be in vain, however, if
they all transfer their allegiance to certain human teachers and take on law observance (see 1.6).

In 3.5 Paul poses yet another question that calls for them to reflect collectively on the connections between their experiences and conduct. He demands
that they consider whether God is presently supplying (ἐπιχορηγῶν) them
with the Spirit (cf. 1 Thess. 4.8) and working powerful deeds among them
(ἐνεργῶν δυνάμεις ἐν ὑμῖν) in connection with their law-observant conduct
(ἐξ ἔργων νόμου) or their responsive 'hearing of faith' (ἐξ ἀκοῆς πίστεως).
In language that parallels 1 Cor. 2.1–5, Paul highlights the presence of the
Spirit and these powerful 'works of life for the community'.[134] By this latter
phrase Paul refers to experiences of transformed life that God effectuates in
association with Christ-conforming actions. Paul's *separate* references to God
continuing to supply the Spirit and to God working powerful deeds among them

131. For Paul's use of σάρξ as a personified power (thus, 'Flesh'), see also 4.23, 29; 5.13, 16, 17,
19, 24; 6.8. Other uses of σάρξ ('flesh') simply refer to earthly human life (see 1.16; 2.16, 20; 4.13,
14; 6.12, 13).

132. Paul's debate with the Judaizers may have included disagreement over the requisite conduct
for achieving 'perfection' and protection from the evil impulse of the Flesh (the יצר concept that originates in Gen. 6.5 and 8.21). See Marcus 1986: 10; Martyn 1997b: 290–94.

133. For this latter conclusion, see Barclay 1988: 209. Barclay also argues that Paul uses the phrase
'the flesh' to signify what is human in social rather than individualistic terms (1988: 209).

134. For this characterization of the phrase ἐνεργῶν δυνάμεις, see Cosgrove 1988: 175.

parallels the reasoning highlighted in 1 Cor. 1.4–9 and 12.4–7. As he has done throughout the letter, Paul emphasizes the important connection between conduct and community experience. He anticipates that the answers to his questions will be evident to those who engage in theo-ethical reasoning by reflecting together on these connections.

The contrast between Spirit and Flesh is thus set in the context of behaviour and experience. This provides an important clue for deciphering the relationship between Paul's use of the unusual phrase ἐναρξάμενοι πνεύματι in Gal. 3.3 and his emphatic assertions that the Galatians are without understanding (3.1, 3). Read together, both questions in 3.3 imply that it was by means of the Spirit rather than the Flesh (πνεύματι and σαρκί are datives of means) that the churches *first perceived* the importance of Paul's embodied proclamation of Christ crucified (see 3.1, 2; see also 1 Cor. 2.1–12). Further, their own original acceptance of this new behavioural norm and conformity thereto (i.e. their 'hearing of faith') that led to experiences of suffering (Gal. 3.4) will be in vain if they all submit to circumcision and take up law observance. By pointing out that God continues to supply the Spirit and to effectuate experiences of new life in connection with their 'hearing of faith', Paul expects them to recognize and understand the direct connection between Christ-conforming conduct and experiences of God's life-giving power.

Thus, in 3.1–5 Paul addresses the experiential, behavioural and theological components of theo-ethical reasoning. The Galatians must understand that the Spirit and the Flesh represent two exclusive, alternative forces that guide community behavioural discernment. Moreover, they must recognize the ethical dualism whereby Paul juxtaposes two parallel, but alternative, human responses to the Christ event: law observance or cruciform conduct grounded in their responsive 'hearing of faith'. Paul expects them to understand the important role played by the Spirit supplied by God to illuminate the link between Christ-conforming actions and experiences of this divine life-giving power. They must spiritually discern this connection.

In the following verses, Paul turns to Scripture and Christ's advent in the world to illuminate these distinctions more fully. In the process he will also contrast the quality of life being experienced by the community in connection with conduct that conforms to each of these two alternative behavioural standards.

b. *Contrasting Life ἐκ πίστεως with Life in the Law (3.6–14)*
Paul argues in 3.11 that it is clear that no one is being justified in/by law (ἐν νόμῳ οὐδεὶς δικαιοῦται) because 'the righteous one shall live from faith' (ὁ δίκαιος ἐκ πίστεως ζήσεται). Paul thus cites Hab. 2.4,[135] which uses the key phrase ἐκ πίστεως found throughout Paul's argument (Hooker 1989: 174). He thereby makes justification from God virtually synonymous with the *life* promised ἐκ

---

135. Most commentators agree that Paul is referring to Hab. 2.4 in Gal. 3.11b (see also Rom. 1.17). See, e.g., Dunn 1993a: 174; Martyn 1997b: 312.

πίστεως.[136] In 3.12, however, Paul contrasts the life promised ἐκ πίστεως with the life promised in the law that is not ἐκ πίστεως.[137] His quotation from Lev. 19.8 (ὁ ποιήσας αὐτὰ ζήσεται ἐν αὐτοῖς) demonstrates that he still acknowledges that the law promises some form of earthly life for those who keep its commandments.[138] This is true even though the law also promises a curse on those who fail to do them (Gal. 3.10). Nevertheless, the adversative ἀλλά in 3.12b distinguishes the experiences associated with the life promised and given ἐκ πίστεως from experiences of life among those who do the law's commandments (see also 3.21).[139] Paul thereby juxtaposes two contrasting experiences of life, each with its own distinctive means of human access.[140]

Having made this contrast, Paul turns to interpret Christ's cruciform death in 3.13–14. The two concurrent purpose clauses explain the results of Christ's redemptive act of dying and becoming a curse under the law (3.13). First, this took place so that Abraham's blessing – i.e. new life/justification (see 3.6; cf. Rom. 4.19–25) – might be extended to the Gentiles 'in Jesus Christ' (Gal. 3.14a). Second, according to 3.14b, Christ redeemed humanity by becoming a curse under the law so that through the faith believers might receive the 'Spirit's promise' (τὴν ἐπαγγελίαν τοῦ πνεύματος) – with this phrase being understood as a subjective genitive.[141] With the new word ἐπαγγελία, Paul does not simply equate the blessing of Abraham with justification[142] or receipt of the Spirit.[143]

136. As noted earlier, Theissen concludes that for Paul 'life' and 'justification' are virtually synonymous (1992: 159–86).

137. For the law's promise of life, see, e.g., Lev. 18.5; Deut. 11.26–28; 30.15; Sir. 17.11; 45.5; Bar. 4.1; *2 Bar.* 45.2; *4 Ezra* 7.21, 14.30; *Pss. Sol.* 14.2; cf. Lk. 10.28; Nickelsburg 1991: 353. Patte points out that for the Pharisees and later rabbis Torah 'cannot but be *coextensive with life*' (1983: 112, original emphasis). Similarly, Martyn observes that in Ps. 118.93 and Sir. 45.5 (cf. *m. 'Abot* 2) the law is the 'law of life', 'meaning that life is the goal which the law in fact accomplishes, having been given directly by God for that purpose' (1997b: 59 n. 19).

138. See Rom. 7.10; 10.5; Byrne 1981: 568; Beker 1980: 235.

139. See N. Young 1998: 80–81; Barclay 1988: 82 n. 18; Westerholm 1988: 120–21; Dunn 1985; 1992. These interpreters correctly observe that the phrase 'works of the law' in 3.10 is not a derogatory phrase implying legalism, but neutrally defines those who are seeking to live in accordance with the pattern of conduct prescribed by the law.

140. These distinctions are explored further in section 3.c below (3.15–25) and section 5 (5.13–6.10).

141. S.K. Williams points out that there is no consensus regarding the content of this promise (1988: 709 n. 2). He incorrectly concludes that it refers to the promise of the Spirit, since God promised innumerable descendants and the Spirit is the means by which God accomplishes this promise (1988: 712, 716). Cf. Burton 1921: 185; Betz 1979: 156–59; Hays 2002: 153.

142. Contra Burton 1921: 175; C.D. Stanley 1992: 237; Barrett 1962: 40.

143. Contra Hooker 1989: 172; Martyn 1997b: 322; Dunn 1993a: 160, 180; Bryant 2001: 178–79, 207; Cosgrove 1988: 50; Betz 1979: 152–53. These interpreters who contend that in 3.14 Paul correlates the receipt of the Spirit with fulfilment of the Abrahamic 'blessing' frequently rely on non-Pauline Christian texts to reach that conclusion. See, e.g., Lk. 24.49; Acts 1.4–5; 2.33; 26.6; Heb. 9.15, as variously cited by Martyn (1997b: 323), Dunn (1993a: 179), Cosgrove (1988: 105–106) and Burton (1921: 176). This produces an interpretation that includes a dramatic, fully 'realized eschatology' for the letter. This conclusion must be rejected. See now Harrisville (1992: 11), who points out that nowhere else in Paul is the Spirit referred to as the content of the promise.

Instead, we suggest that the 'Spirit's promise' describes another aspect of the 'blessing of Abraham' that originates in the death and resurrection of Jesus Christ, who is characterized as Abraham's singular 'seed' in 3.16.

According to the logic of Paul's argument, to 'the ones from faith' there are both present and future dimensions of the blessing of new life grounded in God's promise to Abraham and his singular 'seed' Jesus Christ. To the faithful Abraham, God gave new earthly life in the form of a son Isaac, a child of the promise (4.28) born according to promise (4.23). Just as Abraham, Sarah and Isaac experienced this new life as part of their *earthly* existence, Paul reasons that believers *now* experience this new life ἐκ πίστεως (see 3.11) in the context of *their earthly* existence.

As Paul's argument unfolds, however, it also becomes clear that he makes a distinction. Pursuant to this first aspect of the promise, God's life-giving power is experienced as part of earthly life. Believers presently experience new life ἐκ πίστεως as part of embodied human life. Paul distinguishes these earthly experiences of new and eternal life, however, from the resurrection life after death experienced by the risen Jesus Christ. 'To the ones believing' (3.22), who still live in the flesh in the world (see 2.20), the resurrection aspect of new and eternal life from God still remains only a *promise* to be fulfilled in the future after their death.

Paul thus interprets God's action in the story of Abraham and his 'singular seed' Jesus Christ as having a present and future dimension for believers. As embodied inhabitants of the world, believers experience new and eternal life as did Abraham and Sarah – as part of their earthly existence. In the future they will experience the divine blessing promised by God as new and eternal (resurrection) life after death. Indeed, those who 'belong to Christ' become part of the (singular) 'seed of Abraham', heirs according to promise (3.29; cf. 3.16).

According to the logic of the argument in 3.16 and 3.28–29, God made the promises to Abraham and his singular 'seed', who is Christ. Those who live ἐκ πίστεως presently experience the divine blessing promised and given to Abraham in the form of new earthly life. At the same time, by living ἐκ πίστεως, they also become 'one in Christ Jesus' (3.28) and share collectively the *promise* of *future* new and eternal (resurrection) life after death experienced by Christ, Abraham's singular 'seed'. Paul later confirms this interpretation in 5.5. He refers to believers' *expectation* of future resurrection life, asserting that this expectation is *presently* being experienced *only* as 'the hope of righteousness/new life'.[144]

According to the densely-packed, second purpose clause in 3.14b, believers may now receive (λάβωμεν) the Spirit's promise through the faith (διὰ τῆς πίστεως). Paul draws on the fact that church members have faith in Jesus Christ as God's revelation of a new, universal behavioural standard (the cruciform pattern) and as God's manifestation of a new and eternal (resurrection) life after death (see 1.1, 4). Thus, believers receive the *promise* of sharing in that future resurrection life after death through their faith in Christ (see also 3.22). By conforming their actions to Christ's cruciform pattern and receiving the Spirit in the

---

144. See section 4 below.

present time (3.1–5), however, they *now* experience new life through the power of God as part of their earthly existence (see 5.25). Paul later explains that the practice of being led by the Spirit from faith grounds believers' 'hope of right-eousness' (see 5.5, 18).[145] By this Paul means that their hope of experiencing new and eternal resurrection life after death in the future is *grounded* in their *present* experiences of new life/righteousness associated with Christ-conforming conduct as an aspect of embodied life in the world.

In summary, Paul argues in 3.14 that Gentile believers are *now* receiving the *blessing* of new life associated with God's fulfilled promise to Abraham as part of earthly existence. They are also receiving the *promise* that in the future they will experience new and eternal resurrection life after death associated with the *fulfilled* promise to Abraham's singular 'seed', who is Christ.

c. The Law and 'the Faith': Successive but Now Alternative Pathways to Life (3.15–3.25)

Paul continues to interpret God's action in history in 3.15–25, a section that includes what one interpreter calls some of the most difficult and obscure verses in the entire Pauline corpus (Wright 1991: 157–58). The deep logic of Paul's theo-ethical reasoning illuminates these verses, however, by showing the complex relationship between Paul's key term 'promise' (3.14),[146] the 'curious' use of the plural 'promises' in 3.16 and 3.21 (Martyn 1997b: 339), and the important new concepts involving the testator's 'will',[147] 'inheritance'[148] and 'ratification' of the 'covenant'.[149] Paul again uses the motifs of spatial, temporal, and ethical dualism to argue that the law was to bring life and protection from worldly powers only until the advent of Christ in the world. With Christ also came 'the faith destined to be revealed',[150] so that all humanity – Jews and Gentiles alike – might be justified/receive new life ἐκ πίστεως (3.23–24; cf. 2.16).

According to Paul's metaphorical reasoning in this section, the original will involved multiple promises to Abraham of progeny and land.[151] Paul's use of αἱ ἐπαγγελίαι in 3.16 is thus intentional rather than careless (cf. Rom. 9.4; 15.8). By implication, Paul later includes these items in 'the inheritance' addressed in Gal. 3.18.[152] Moreover, even before the law was given, God had already acted to ratify the original 'will', fulfilling that portion of what was promised directly to Abraham. By means of their faithful acts, God gave new life (a son, Isaac) to the

---

145. See section 4.b below.

146. See also 3.17, 22, 29; 4.23, 28.

147. See 3.15, 17. The allusion to Israel's covenant with God stands in the background, as the use of the same word διαθήκη in 4.24 confirms.

148. The noun κληρονομία appears in 3.18; cf. 3.29. For Paul's use of the related noun 'heir', see 3.29; 4.1, 7. He incorporates the verb form κληρονομέω in 4.30 and 5.21.

149. See 3.15, 17.

150. For this purposive translation of the prepositional phrase τὴν μέλλουσαν πίστιν ἀποκαλ-υφθῆναι in Gal. 3.23, see Bryant 2001: 153, including n. 37 (cf. Rom. 8.18).

151. For Paul's understanding that the promises to Abraham involved innumerable descendants and land, see S.K. Williams 1988: 716–17; Wan 1995: 7–8; Esler 1998: 194. For these promissory passages, see Gen. 12.7; 13.15, 17; 15.18; 17.8; 24.7.

152. See Betz 1979: 157; Esler 1998: 194; cf. Dunn 1993a: 183.

aged Abraham and barren Sarah in the land where God promised to bless them. Through promise (δι' ἐπαγγελίας), God exercised life-giving power to give Abraham these gifts (κεχάρισται) that constitute his inheritance (3.18).[153]

Thus, the 'will' may not be rejected (ἀθετεῖ), having been ratified (κεκυρωμ-ένην) by the subsequent action of the testator (God). Additions to it may not be made (3.15, 17). The law that came later, after God's ratifying act, cannot undo the effect (ἄκυροι) of God's prior act of ratification so as 'to cut off'[154] the original promise of life ἐκ πίστεως to Abraham and his 'seed'. Consequently, ratification does not refer to God's initial act of speaking the promises but to God's *subsequent* exercise of life-giving power that ratified the covenant by *fulfilling* Abraham's portion of what was promised to him and his 'seed'.[155]

Although Paul does not expressly include the promise of land in his interpretation of the story of Abraham, his sudden introduction of the key theme of inheritance in 3.18 (cf. 3.29; 4.1, 7, 30; 5.21) implies this material element of the Abrahamic promises recorded in Genesis.[156] In some Jewish circles during the late Second Temple period, the Abrahamic blessing of the 'inheritance' of land was being transformed into the spatial, this-worldly motif. It became associated with a new world or new age, usually identified or defined historically by law-observant conduct.[157] It often included the whole earth within its scope.[158] Moreover, the influence of the two-age motif led to the inclusion of language about life in the coming age and world within the 'inheritance' context,[159] thereby bringing the idea of eternal life within its scope.[160] In many of these late Second Temple texts, observance of the law became a paramount concern as a condition for gaining the 'inheritance'.[161] Thus, these texts frequently envision a spatial realm created by God, where God's law-observant people dwell or will dwell and receive the blessings of life that God intends for them to enjoy.[162]

153. The 'inheritance' is the implied direct object of the verb κεχάρισται in 3.18, as noted by Dunn (1993a: 187).
154. Here, Paul introduces another verb (καταργέω) that he will utilize in a double entendre involving circumcision in 5.4 and 5.11.
155. Commentators regularly (wrongly) make the 'promise' itself the content of God's gracious gift to Abraham. See, e.g., Martyn 1997b: 338–41; Hays 1989: 114; Betz 1979: 159–60. This seemingly ignores the argument's logic suggested by Paul's repeated emphasis on God's act of ratification after the promise but before the law appeared.
156. For this characterization, see Byrne 1979: 160. In connection with Rom. 8.17, Käsemann concludes that 'κληρονομία refers in a transferred sense to the eschatological occupation of the land, namely, participation in the *basileia*' (1980: 229).
157. See Byrne 1979: 68; Hester 1968: 30; Gen. 15.7; Num. 34.2; Deut. 30.5; Tob. 4.12; 1 Macc. 15.33–36; 2 Macc. 2.4, 17; *Jub.* 22.7; 49.18–19; *Pss. Sol.* 9.1–2; 17.26; 1CD 1.5–10, 15–17; 3.5–10; 4.20–25; 1QH 15.14–15; cf. *2 En.* 10.6; *Pss. Sol.* 14.9; 15.11.
158. See Sir. 44.21; *1 En.* 5.7; *Jub.* 17.3; 22.14; 32.19; cf. *4 Ezra* 6.59; 1QH 4.12–15; 1QS 4.22–24; 1CD 3.20; Byrne 1979: 68; 1996: 157.
159. See, e.g., *1 En.* 71.16; 99.14; *2 Bar.* 14.13; 44.13; 51.3; 57.1–3; *4 Ezra* 6.59; 7.9; *Pss. Sol.* 12.6; *Ps.-Philo* 32.3, 17.
160. See, e.g., *1 En.* 40.9; *2 En.* 9.1 (cf. 10.6); 50.2; 55.2; *Jos. Asen.* 12.12; *Pss. Sol.* 14.7 (cf. 15.11, 12).
161. See, e.g., *Pss. Sol.* 12.7; 14.10; cf. 2 Macc. 2.14–17; Hester 1968: 32–33.
162. See 2 Macc. 2.17–18; *2 Bar.* 44.1–13 (cf. 42.12–15; 51.3, 7–8); see also *1 En.* 37.1–5; 39.1–14;

This study suggests that Paul contributed to this discourse by integrating the motifs of spatial, temporal, and ethical dualism into his interpretation of God's action in Christ. According to Paul's gospel, people put their trust in the God who raised Jesus from the dead by 'believing into Christ Jesus' (2.16; cf. 3.22) and looking for life ἐκ πίστεως (see 3.11). By this Paul means that believers have faith in the crucified and risen Christ as God's revelation of a new and universal behavioural norm (the cruciform pattern of self-giving love for others) and that conduct associated with this norm provides the human means of access to new and eternal life from God experienced both in earthly existence and in resurrection after death. Believers experience the earthly dimension of new life in God's new spatial realm/temporal age in Christ that is identified or defined by conduct that conforms to Christ's cruciform pattern. Eternal life in this spatial/temporal realm in Christ endures even after a believer's death. Paul characterizes this as the hope associated with God's fulfilment of the promise of new life to Abraham's 'seed', who is the crucified and risen Christ.

As a consequence of having this faith in Christ, believers now seek to conform their actions to Christ's cruciform pattern. They do this by practising spiritual discernment as they engage in theo-ethical reasoning. This replaces instruction in the law as the means of discerning God's will and proving through testing the behavioural actions that matter in connection with experiences of new and eternal life in Christ (see also Rom. 2.17–18; 12.1–2; Phil. 1.9–10).[163]

Paul then explains the reason for the temporally-limited appearance of the law in Gal. 3.19–25. The law's role was to identify God's will (cf. Rom. 2.18) for conduct that leads to life. It also defined transgressions until such time as Abraham's 'seed' (Christ) comes. The law intensified consciousness of transgressions, thereby activating the law's cursing power (Gal. 3.10). Paul thereby alludes to the law's promise of death (see Deut. 30.15–20) for those intentional or deliberate violations that were not remedied by the law's atonement provisions.[164] The law thus provided a type of protective custody (ἐφρουρούμεθα) from the worldly forces that exercise power in connection with conduct that conforms to worldly standards (see Gal. 3.23; cf. Phil. 4.7).

Indeed, says Paul in Gal. 3.24, the law served as a trainer or custodian (παιδα-γωγός). The first-century παιδαγωγός was a temporary moral guide, a guardian who for protective purposes restricted a child's freedom (cf. Gal. 4.1–3) and was to be obeyed until the child reached the age of maturity.[165] At that point the

---

48.1, 7; 58.1–6; 71.16–17; 103.4; *2 En.* 9.1; 10.5–6; 50.1–2; 55.2–3; *2 Bar.* 4.1–6; 32.1–7; 44.1–15; 46.1–7; 48.22–24; 51.1–16; 54.1–5, 12–22; 59.1–12; 85.1–9; *4 Ezra* 7.17–28, 45–48, 88–100, 119–30; 9.6–13, 26–37; 12.34; 13.52–56; 14.13–17, 22, 27–36.

163. We thus affirm the conclusion of W.D. Davies that this *structure* of primitive Christianity was in some respects modelled upon or grew out of the structure of Judaism: the early church reinterpreted the moral tradition of Judaism in the light of Christ, as the person of Christ became normative for understanding morality and replaced their law (1972a: 313–15). For Paul it was Christ's cruciform pattern of self-giving love for others manifest in his death on the cross that replaced Torah as the universal behavioural norm. See now Boyarin 1994: 39.

164. For this latter conclusion, see Byrne 1979: 161 n. 98; N. Young 1998: 84; Wright 1991a: 223.

165. N. Young 1987: 150–76; cf. D.M. Stanley 1984: 138.

restrictions and curtailed freedom imposed by the παιδαγωγός were lifted. The mature person was free to 'bid farewell to the admonitions of the παιδαγωγός' and to explore a wider range of potential conduct.[166]

Paul thus provides a functional analogy between the law and the παιδαγωγός rather than making a positive or negative value judgment about the law.[167] His later introduction of the theme of behavioural freedom won by Christ (5.1; cf. 2.4) further echoes the παιδαγωγός metaphor. It implies a range of possibilities for Christ-conforming conduct that extends beyond the law's boundaries. This becomes part of Paul's broader co-operative, creative, and participatory structure for the collective discernment of faithful conduct.[168]

We suggest that the now-dominant view that Paul only attributes a negative function for the law misunderstands Paul's argument.[169] By means of the motifs of spatial, temporal, and ethical dualism, Paul interprets God's apocalyptic (i.e. revelatory) initiative in Christ. He simply contrasts the life promised by the law (3.12) with the new and eternal resurrection life that God promises ἐκ πίστεως (3.11). He makes a *qualitative* distinction between life in the present evil age (even life guarded and protected through law observance) and the new and eternal life experienced in Christ – God's new spatial realm/temporal age characterized in part in its earthly form by conduct that conforms to Christ's cruciform pattern (cf. 1.4; 2.16, 21; 5.4, 6).

This distinction becomes clear in 3.21, where Paul resoundingly rejects any contention that the law stands against God's promises of new life to Abraham and his 'seed'.[170] The logic of Paul's argument implies that the late-arriving law (3.17) never promised new and eternal earthly life and resurrection after death. It only promised life that was guarded and protected from the powers of the world during the course of the faithful person's earthly existence (cf. Phil. 3.4–8). According to Gal. 3.21, no law was given that brings life after death (ζῳοποιῆσαι).[171] This is an aspect of new life, however, that was always included in

---

166. N. Young 1987: 174; cf. Dunn 1993a: 199.

167. For the variety of positions on this issue, see, e.g., Dunn 1993a: 198; S.K. Williams 1997: 102–103; Stanton 1996: 114; Martyn 1997b: 363; N. Young 1987: 173. Paul's use of the παιδαγωγός image suggested in this study is consistent with his only other use of παιδαγωγός in 1 Cor. 4.15 (see Chapter 2, section 3.h above).

168. See, generally, Lategan 1990: 318–28; Kraftchick 1993a: 27, 30.

169. See Lull 1986: 481. For various interpretations that identify Paul's negative view of the function of the law, see Schlier 1971: 152–54; Bultmann 1951: 266; Furnish 1968: 143, 159–60; Bornkamm 1971: 120–29; Betz 1979: 145–46, 163–67, 175, 178; Beker 1980: 55, 243; E.P. Sanders 1983: 66–67; Barrett 1985: 33; Westerholm 1988: 178; Martyn 1997b: 354–55; cf. Engberg-Pedersen 2000: 350 n. 35.

170. Indeed, according to Engberg-Pedersen, 'it is astonishing…that commentators generally do not see that the sentence quoted from 3.21 constitutes a well-aimed *praise* of the law' (2000: 348 n. 34, original emphasis).

171. Paul regularly uses this verb in connection with God's power that gives life after death (whether literal or metaphorical) among those who live to God and die to the world's standards for behaviour. See Chapter 3, sections 4.c and 4.d above; see also Rom. 4.17; 8.11; 1 Cor. 15.22, 36, 45; 2 Cor. 3.6). This follows the use of the word in the Septuagint. See Judg. 21.14; 2 Kgs 5.7; Ezra 9.8, 9; Neh. 9.6; Ps. 70.20; Eccl. 7.12; Job 36.6. Contra Byrne 1979: 162 n. 103.

God's promises to Abraham and Christ, his 'seed' (see also Rom. 4.19–24). Otherwise, reasons Paul, this new life that he also calls righteousness (δικαιοσύνη)[172] would have been ἐκ νόμου rather than ἐκ πίστεως (Gal. 3.21; see also 2.21).

Paul thus reaffirms his conclusions from 2.16–21. There, he argued that new life comes not by means of the law (διὰ νόμου) but by means of faith in Christ (διὰ πίστεως Ἰησοῦ Χριστοῦ). This takes place so that believers might be justified ἐκ πίστεως Χριστοῦ. The logic underlying both climactic verses (2.21; 3.21) and the sustained arguments that precede them define Paul's understanding of the divine–human relationship.[173] Conduct conforming to Christ's cruciform pattern – manifest in his death on the cross according to God's will (1.4; 2.20) – has become the universal means of access to God's spatial realm/temporal age in Christ, where believers experience new and eternal life in its earthly dimension and the hope of resurrection life after death.

Paul pursues this argument in 3.22–25, applying the language of apocalypse to characterize his understanding of the divine–human relationship that grounds theo-ethical reasoning. He refers to the advent of Christ and 'the faith' (τὴν πίστιν) that was 'destined to be revealed' (3.23–24).[174] The logic of the argument suggests that 'the faith' was first revealed in Christ, the one who placed all his faith in the life-giving power of God, even to the point of giving himself for others by submitting to death on a cross according to the will of God.

Consequently, Paul characterizes those who are now ἐκ πίστεως as 'the ones believing' (3.22). The present indicative πιστεύουσιν points to those who continue seeking to conform their actions to Christ's cruciform pattern, believing and trusting that God will exercise life-giving power among them in connection with such conduct. These are also the ones being given the promise (3.22) of future, resurrection life after death. Indeed, by means of their Christ-conforming actions they become like Isaac, 'children of the promise' (4.28 29), whose 'mother' is the 'new Jerusalem' from above (4.26; cf. 4.19). Like Sarah the barren one, this mother from the heavenly realm is giving birth to more numerous children than the worldly Jerusalem (4.25–27). Her inhabitants are still experiencing life in the present evil age because they are conforming their actions to the law that only guarded them from the power of worldly forces until the advent of Christ and the revelation of 'the faith' (3.23–24).

Once again we find Paul employing the motifs of spatial, temporal, and ethical dualism and the language of revelation. He contrasts life in the present evil age (promised and given in association with law-observant conduct) with life in God's new spatial realm/temporal age 'in Christ Jesus' (promised in connection with conduct that faithfully conforms to Christ's cruciform pattern).[175] Given through the same power of God that raised Jesus from the dead, experiences of

---

172. Theissen concludes that δικαιοσύνη is one of Paul's metaphors for the new life of salvation (1992: 159–86).

173. See also 1 Cor. 1.4–9.

174. For this purposive translation of the prepositional phrase in Gal 3.23, see Bryant 2001: 153, including n. 37 (cf. Rom. 8.18).

175. See 3.14; cf. 2.16; 3.22; Rom. 3.30–31; see also Eph. 3.12, 17; Col. 2.12.

this new, earthly life also carry with them the promise of eternal resurrection life after death.

d. *Becoming 'Sons of God' through the Faith in Christ Jesus (3.26–29)*

In 3.26–29 Paul further explains the impact of the advent of Christ and revelation of 'the faith'. Emphasizing the universality of this revelation, Paul confirms that the Galatians are 'all (πάντες) sons of God through the faith in Christ Jesus' (3.26).[176] Now that 'the faith' has been revealed in Christ, no one should be under the law as a παιδαγωγός any longer (3.25). They must look solely to Christ Jesus and his cruciform pattern as the model for behaviour grounded in their faith in God's life-giving power (cf. 1 Cor. 2.5). This is the same faith that leads believers to anticipate that God will continue working in connection with such Christ-conforming actions so that others might also experience righteousness/ new life from God (see Gal. 2.20–21; Phil. 3.9).

Continuing to explain the consequences of the advent of Christ and revelation of 'the faith' in Gal. 3.27, Paul asserts that all the ones who were baptized into Christ clothed themselves with Christ (Χριστὸν ἐνεδύσασθε). In the ancient world the imagery of donning new clothes was widely used as a religious metaphor. It meant taking on certain characteristics or virtues or a change of lifestyle, including the assimilation of the power of a deity represented by the new garb.[177] It was also applied in the context of an actor playing a specific part in a drama (Dunn 1993a: 204). Similarly, in the Septuagint, ἐνδύω was a figure of speech meaning 'to be characterized by the named quality or attribute',[178] including righteousness and salvation. The word's Septuagint usage frequently carries the sense of the person (or deity) being recognized as manifesting the particular characteristic under consideration (S.K. Williams 1997: 105).

Paul applies this metaphor in 3.27 to emphasize that, in baptism, people become 'not merely believers in the Messiah but are in some sense clothed with the Messiah's person...they put on Christ like a garment' (Rowland 1995a: 48).[179] Paul's other uses of this verbal metaphor[180] appear as 'the epitome of ethical paraenesis' (Dunn 1993a: 204–205). These exhortations are made with a view

176. See R. Longenecker 1990: 151; Burton 1921: 202; Dunn 1993a: 201; Martyn 1997b: 374. Burton (1921: 202) argues that the phrase 'in Christ Jesus' does not limit πίστεως because Paul rarely employs ἐν after πίστις (cf. Eph. 1.15; Col. 1.4) and in this letter typically uses the genitive (Gal. 2.16, 20; 3.22). This observation may point to the possibility that 3.26–28 quotes or draws from an early baptismal liturgy, although the present study is not dependent on a determination of this issue. For discussion of this point, see Martyn 1997b: 375; S.K. Williams 1997: 104. Similarly, for purposes of the present study, a decision on the issue of the sudden shift from 'we' to the plural 'you' in 3.26 is not essential. For consideration of this issue, see, e.g., Dunn 1993a: 201; Burton 1921: 202; Betz 1979: 185; R. Longenecker 1990: 151; Martyn 1997b: 374; Bruce 1982: 183.

177. Meeks 1973: 183; cf. Dunn 1993a: 204. Meeks points out that its 'most obvious' New Testament use was in paraenesis, particularly Eph. 4.17–24 and Col. 3.8 (1973: 184).

178. S.K. Williams 1997: 105, citing, among others, Ps. 131.9, 16; Isa. 52.1; 59.17; 61.10; Job 29.14; Prov. 31.26; Wis. 5.18; Sir. 6.31.

179. Cf. J.A.T. Robinson 1952: 63; Käsemann 1964d: 111; contra Ebeling 1985: 211–12.

180. See Rom. 13.12–14; 2 Cor. 5.3; 1 Thess. 5.8; cf. Eph. 4.24; 6.11, 14; Col. 3.10, 12.

toward helping believers continue to experience new life in Christ, subject to God's life-giving power (cf. 2.21). This is the power that prevails to give new and eternal life in God's new spatial realm/temporal age in Christ. Further, as argued in connection with 2.17, this baptismal commitment leads believers into the process of 'seeking to be justified in Christ'. Paul means that they must reflect together on conduct and experience, spiritually discerning whether particular actions conform to Christ's cruciform pattern by virtue of their links to experiences of new life. Believers must live into this baptismal commitment on a regular, continuing basis (cf. 3.22).[181]

Moreover, Paul's baptismal image of putting on new clothing 'has less to do with cleansing than with equipping the baptizand for participating in apocalyptic warfare' (Martyn 1997b: 376). As the present study has argued, for Paul a believer participates in God's cosmic plan by dying regularly to the behavioural standards of the world. Believers conform their actions to Christ's cruciform pattern with the anticipation that the power of God will work in connection with such conduct to bring new life to others.[182]

Paul addresses a Jewish argument in 3.26–27, arguing that believers become 'sons of God' in earthly life 'through the faith in Christ Jesus' (3.26; cf. 2.16; 3.14, 26). Human faith in Christ Jesus thus becomes the distinctive mark of the 'sons of God'.[183] We suggest that believers actively live this faith in Christ Jesus by practising spiritual discernment as they engage in theo-ethical reasoning – seeking to conform their actions to Christ's cruciform pattern, the universal behavioural standard that reflects the will of God. Moreover, by means of such conduct, God liberates the cosmos from the worldly powers that enslave it (cf. 4.9). This occurs not just when a believer submits to the initial act of baptism itself.[184] God continues to free the world from these foreign powers in connection with spiritually-discerned conduct that conforms to Christ's cruciform pattern.

As with Paul's integrated use of the motifs of spatial, temporal, and ethical dualism throughout the letter, the prepositional phrase 'in Christ Jesus' (3.26) denotes that spatial realm where God faithfully fulfils the promise to give new life/justification. The phrase is synonymous with Paul's characteristic phrase 'in Christ', a conclusion supported by his parallel use of the latter phrase in 3.28d (Hays 2002: 169) and the reference in 3.27 to baptism 'into (εἰς) Christ' (Dunn 1993a: 203).[185]

To be 'in Christ' means that one's life and relationships cannot go on as before (Bryant 2001: 211). The baptismal commitment to conform one's actions to Christ's cruciform pattern terminates the practice of relating to other people on

---

181. This is how Paul characterizes the continuing responsibility to battle sin (see Luther 1958: 28). It may also be understood as the perpetual return to baptism, whereby a person is recalled daily to the allegiance to Christ (Käsemann 1969e: 175; Barclay 1988: 214).

182. See 1 Cor. 1.4–9; 2.2–5; 12.4–7; Gal. 2.8; 3.1–5; 2 Cor. 4.10–12; 13.1–4.

183. Cf. Dunn, who argues that 'faith' replaces the law as the 'distinctive mark' of the 'sons of God' (1993a: 202).

184. *Pace* Dunn 1993a: 205; Betz 1979: 188; Martyn 1997b: 431.

185. See also Gal. 2.16; 1 Cor. 1.13.

the basis of racial, cultural, social, economic or gender distinctions of the old world (cf. Horrell 2000: 333–40). Paul addresses this in 3.28 in the 'baptismal reunification formula' that speaks about the cosmic reunification of opposites that was part of early Christian baptismal paraenesis (Meeks 1973: 180–81). He modifies community social roles by suggesting new attitudes and altered behaviour (Meeks 1973: 180–81, 185).[186] In 3.28 Paul breaks down the three 'most profound and obvious differences' among humans that gave structure to the ancient world (Dunn 1993a: 205–206). For him these considerations have now been 'rendered redundant' in Christ (Dunn 1993a: 205). His language suggests a radically reshaped social world as believers die daily (see 1 Cor. 15.31) to the world's old behavioural standards by conforming their actions to Christ's cruciform pattern.[187] Paul thereby announces the *beginning* of the end of the cosmos.[188]

Paul uses the technical Jewish phrase 'sons of God' in Gal. 3.26 and 4.6 (cf. Rom. 8.1–25) and in 4.5 the associated concept of υἱοθεσίαν ('adoption as sons'[189]). These phrases are used within the conceptual framework of Judaism, involving Jewish categories, terminology, and scripture as a basis of proof (Byrne 1979: 220–21). Paul thus enters the broader context of a Jewish and Jewish-Christian discourse, debating the behavioural standards for God's recognition and adoption of Gentiles as 'sons of God' (cf. Byrne 1979: 222). The 'sons are made sons by being conformed to the image of the Son (Rom. 8.29; cf. Gal. 4.19)' (Martyn 1997b: 376). This takes place each time a believer's action conforms to Christ's cruciform pattern.

Finally, it is tentatively suggested that this explanation sheds further light on Paul's earlier description of the turning point in his own life when God's *son* was revealed 'in' Paul (1.16). This revelation may have taken place in connection with some action of Paul that conformed to Christ's cruciform pattern. In the action, Paul may have experienced his own profound sense of personal identification and acquaintance with Christ (see Phil. 3.10). Thereafter, this did not represent Paul's unique apostolic self-understanding but became a central concern of his gospel applicable to every believer (see Gal. 2.16; 3.14, 22, 27–29).

e. *The Spirit of God's Son Confirms 'Adoption as Sons' and Knowledge of God (4.1–11)*

The logic underlying the arguments in 4.1–11 further illuminates theo-ethical reasoning as Paul brings together theology and ethics. He interprets God's act of sending Jesus Christ into the world in human form (see 4.4).[190] This accomplishes

186. See also 1 Cor. 12.13; cf. Col. 3.11.

187. Cf. Meeks 1973: 165–208; Horrell 2000: 333; Dunn 1993a: 207. Martyn ascribes a passive role to the believer in this process, based simply on the believer's recognition of these distinctions, rather than action (1997b: 376). As Meeks points out, however, a factual claim *about* changed reality that fundamentally modifies social roles only produces the intended results when the 'novel declaration' is *put into practice* to become effective (Meeks 1973: 182, citing Geertz 1966: 4).

188. Martyn overstates the finality and completeness of God's victory in Christ, finding that it represents the 'end of the cosmos' (1997b: 376).

189. For this translation, see Martyn 1997b: 390; Scott 1992; *pace* Byrne 1979: 215.

190. This is accomplished through the two ἵνα clauses in 4.5 (cf. 3.14).

two purposes according to 4.5: (1) to redeem those subject to the law and its cursing power (see 3.10, 13); and (2) to manifest the universal means by which all humanity might receive 'adoption as sons' (υἱοθεσίαν ἀπολάβωμεν).[191]

Paul has already established that Christ's cruciform pattern is the universal behavioural standard for experiencing new life ἐκ πίστεως (see 2.16–21; 3.14, 23–27). He now seems to suggest that believers receive 'adoption as sons' when they are 'known by God' (4.9) *because* their conduct conforms to Christ's cruciform pattern rather than the law. The logic underlying Paul's argument points to his conviction that believers come to know God (4.8) when they experience God's life-giving power in connection with conduct that conforms to the cruciform pattern (see also 3.1–5; cf. 1 Cor. 2.1–5; 8.1–13).[192] Paul thus draws on the Jewish theme of 'knowing God' (Dunn 1993a: 224–25) that is frequently linked in Jewish literature to keeping God's commandments in the promised land of the inheritance.[193]

Moreover, God confirmed this divine recognition of their Christ-conforming actions. God sent (ἐξαπέστειλεν)[194] the Spirit of Christ into their hearts (Gal. 4.6–7) with a cry of recognition.[195] Indeed, God first sent the Spirit of Christ (4.6) because (ὅτι) they are 'sons' – that is, because God knew them as 'sons' by recognizing their faithful Christ-conforming conduct (cf. 1.16). It is suggested that the aorist verb ἐξαπέστειλεν refers to that first punctiliar moment of recognition when the Spirit's cry confirmed in the hearts of each believer the connection between their experience of new life and their Christ-conforming actions. Thereafter, God continues to supply the Spirit (see 3.5) to aid them in discerning other connections between experiences of new life and Christ-conforming conduct (see also 1 Cor. 2.10–16; 12.4–7). Paul thereby identifies the Spirit's external, confirming role (cf. Rom. 8.14–15).[196]

Further, Paul re-emphasizes his central concern about the appropriate behavioural standard in the churches. He contends in 4.9 that those Galatians who have taken on law observance are now turning back again (πάλιν) to the powers that prevail in the world (τὰ στοιχεῖα τοῦ κόσμου).[197] He suggests a connection between law-observant actions and the exercise of the power associated with the

---

191. See 2.16; 3.14, 23–26; see also Rom. 3.22, 25, 30, 31; 2 Cor. 5.7; Phil. 3.9; cf. Eph. 2.8; 3.12, 17; Col. 2.12.

192. B. Longenecker also observes the similarities between Gal. 4.1–11 and 1 Cor. 8.1–13 (1998: 50).

193. See, e.g., Deut. 4.38–40; cf. Hos. 8.2; Wis. 2.3.

194. This is the same verb used in connection with Christ's divine sending into the world in 4.4.

195. Based on the fact that the participle κρᾶζον in 4.9 is neuter, B. Longenecker concludes that the cry is that of the Spirit of Christ and not the individual (1998: 61).

196. In connection with Romans 8, Burke finds that God sends the Spirit to assure believers of their new sonship in Christ (1998: 323). According to Byrne, in Rom. 8.16 there is a kind of dual witness in which the divine confirms the human (1996: 251).

197. The literature interpreting Paul's use of this phase is extensive and the conclusions varied. This study follows Arnold, who concludes that the στοιχεῖα are 'demonic powers', evil spirits that are equivalent to the 'principalities and powers' (1996: 57, 75); see also B. Longenecker 1998: 46–53; Kovacs 1989: 222–23; Martyn 1997b: 407; Dunn 1993a: 213; Betz 1979: 205.

στοιχεῖα. This constitutes an enslavement once again to these 'weak and inferior' στοιχεῖα (4.9).[198]

Paul implies a contrast between these weak and inferior worldly powers and the power of God that raised Jesus from the dead, a keynote theme of the letter (1.1). He is incredulous that, after knowing God (4.9) by experiencing this life-giving power (see 3.5), they would turn back again to serve the στοιχεῖα through conduct that conforms to worldly standards (cf. 1.6–7; 5.2–4).[199] The active voice of the verb δουλεύω twice in 4.8–9 suggests that the Galatians become enslaved/ subjected to these στοιχεῖα when they conform their actions to the law rather than to Christ's cruciform pattern. According to Paul, this is not the means by which they will be known by God and recognized as 'sons' in the future.

f. *The Birth of Christ 'In/Among' Believers (4.12–20)*
Paul continues to engage in theo-ethical reasoning by emphasizing the importance of Christ-conforming conduct for individual and community formation. He focuses on his own Christ-like actions and those of the Galatians and this provides the conceptual framework for 4.12–20.[200]

In Paul's day the matter of appropriate lifestyle received much attention among philosophical groups. The philosopher's manner of life often served as the legitimating criterion of the particular philosophy.[201] Indeed, among ancient philosophers the manner of life had 'both a revelatory and a demonstrative function' (Fitzgerald 1988: 114–15). The philosopher's pattern of conduct provided a model to be imitated as part of ancient exhortation.[202] Similar guidance for distinguishing between the true and false prophet and prophecy was also an aspect of life in the early church.[203] The logic of Paul's argument throughout the letter suggests this background, but it is particularly evident in this section.

The passage opens with the letter's first imperative (4.12). Paul (a Jew) offers himself to Gentiles as a model for the commitment to conform one's actions to Christ's cruciform pattern rather than the law. As was shown in 2.17–19 and 3.1, this is a behavioural choice that Paul unhesitatingly commends to others, even though it makes him a sinner under the law and subjects him to Jewish persecution (see also 1 Cor. 4.8–13; 2 Cor. 4.8–14; 11.23).[204]

Paul concludes that it was on account of a 'weakness (ἀσθένειαν) of the flesh' that he first communicated the gospel to them (4.13; cf. 3.1). The Greek word

---

198. Most commentators acknowledge that Paul presents the law as associated with the powers of the old world and age. See, e.g., Dunn 1993a: 211; Martyn 1997b: 401.

199. According to Betz, Paul's use of ἐπιστρέφετε, a technical term belonging to the language of conversion, suggests a return to the practices of paganism (1979: 216, including n. 31).

200. Cf. B. Longenecker, who argues that 'Christian character' provides the conceptual frame for this passage (1999: 101).

201. Sumney 1993: 72–74, citing Epictetus, *Diss.* 4.8.1–33, especially 5–6; 2.1.20–29.

202. Malherbe 1989: 51–53; Sumney 1993: 74.

203. See Mt. 7.15–20; 1 Cor. 14.29–32; 1 Thess. 5.20–22; *Did.* 11.8; Hermas, *Man.* 11.7, 16.

204. B. Longenecker correctly observes that the imperative derives its force from Paul's own life presented as the 'demonstration of Christian commitment and resilience' (1999: 100).

ἀσθένεια might mean both 'weakness' and 'disease' or 'illness' (D. Martin 1995: 168). Illness was a problematic status indicator, calling into question the strength of the sufferer. In fact 'bodily' appearance was so important for rhetoricians that they studied physiognomics in order to learn how to present themselves and attack the physical characteristics of their opponents (D. Martin 1995: 53–54).

In view of Paul's references to persecution sprinkled throughout the letter, this study tentatively suggests that his 'weakness' may refer to the physical manifestations of persecution arising from his disregard for the law (cf. 2 Cor. 11.23). In light of this, Paul's real concern may be to respond to his debate opponents. They may have been pointing to Paul's condition and arguing that it was proof that he was accursed for refusing to conform his actions to the law (see Gal. 3.10; cf. 1.8–9, 23; 2.18).[205]

In fact, 'weakness' was integral to Paul's understanding of his own ministry.[206] Following the example of Christ, Paul intentionally accepted the law's judgment and characterized it as being crucified with Christ (see 2.17–19; 3.13).[207] This naturally followed from Paul's own commitment to forsake the law by conforming his conduct to Christ's cruciform pattern. Paul's body was living proof of his allegiance to Christ, his scars the present epiphany of the crucifixion of Jesus (cf. 2.19; 3.1; 6.17).[208] Paul's embodied proclamation of Jesus Christ crucified (see 3.1) was the means by which he communicated the person of Jesus Christ (see Gal. 1.16).[209] This is the heart of Paul's 'gospel of the *weakness* of God'.[210] It is the crucified Messiah who was revealed in Paul (cf. Gal. 1.16) and now lives 'in' Paul (see Gal. 2.19–20; 4.14; 2 Cor. 4.10–12).[211] Paul interpreted his 'weakness' and suffering as a constituent part of his ministry resulting from his commitment to conform his own apostolic lifestyle to Christ's cruciform pattern.[212]

Apparently, the Galatians understood and accepted Paul's explanation of his embodied 'weakness' as he communicated the person of Jesus Christ, crucified and raised. Paul lauds them for resisting temptation by refusing to reject and despise him (Gal. 4.14), as normal cultural conventions would dictate (Barclay 2002: 145). He is probably referring to their refusal to interpret his physical con-

205. Cf. B. Longenecker (1999: 101–102) and Dunn (1993a: 234), who point out that physical ailments were often thought to be the result of the influence of demonic or supra-human forces.

206. Sumney 1993: 72. See, e.g., 1 Cor. 2.3; 2 Cor. 10.1, 10–11; 11.29–30; 12.5, 9, 10; 13.3, 4, 9; cf. Rom. 8.17; 1 Cor. 4.8–13; 2 Cor. 1.5–7; 4.10–11; Phil 3.10; 1 Thess. 2.1–12. Paul also extends this understanding to members of his churches in Phil. 1.29.

207. See Harvey, who concludes that Paul thought that all Jewish-Christian followers of Christ should voluntarily be willing to submit to the penalties of the synagogue since Jesus himself submitted to sentence and death under Jewish law (1985: 85–86); cf. Engberg-Pedersen 2000: 126.

208. According to Güttgemanns, in Gal. 4.13–20 Paul uses ἀσθένεια as an 'epiphany of the crucified' (1966: 185); see also Gorman 2001: 31.

209. See also 1 Cor. 1.18, 23; 2.2; 2 Cor. 4.10–12; Phil. 3.10.

210. The phrase is from Dunn (1975: 329, original emphasis), quoted also in Gorman 2001: 18; cf. 1 Cor. 1.25.

211. According to Betz, Paul's apostolic presence is the manifestation of the crucified and risen Lord (1986: 44); see also Sumney 1993: 90; Funk 1967: 249–68.

212. Cf. Sumney 1993: 90–91; see, e.g., 1 Cor. 4.8–13; 2 Cor. 4.10–12; 6.4–10.

dition as the manifestation of a power being exercised in connection with the law's curse.[213]

Instead, the Galatians received Paul as a messenger of God, as Christ Jesus himself (4.14). Even in Paul's weakened condition, they acknowledged and received him as the presence of the crucified and risen Christ (see 2.19–20; cf. 1.16, 23). This 'revelation of Jesus Christ' and its effect on the Galatians proved to be just as dramatic as the revelation of Christ in Paul's own life (Barclay 2002: 145). Indeed, at the time of Paul's first visit, they responded with understanding (cf. 3.1, 3). They were willing to pluck out their own eyes for Paul (4.15) as part of a Christ-conforming response.[214] Paul thereby implies that the Galatians' own 'hearing of faith' (see 3.2, 5) manifested their initial understanding about the importance of conforming their own conduct to Christ's cruciform pattern.[215] By the time of the letter, however, the Judaizers had interfered and some of the Galatians no longer had that understanding (see 3.1, 5; 5.7).

The context of Paul's question in 4.15 further suggests that their own original experience of divine blessing (ὁ μακαρισμὸς ὑμῶν)[216] came in association with conduct that conformed to Christ's cruciform pattern. Rather than responding to Paul with actions that would be expected according to the world's standards (i.e. rejecting and despising Paul because of his condition),[217] they accepted him and offered to comfort and aid him in his affliction. God blessed them in connection with this Christ-conforming conduct. Paul is probably referring to their experiences of the Spirit and the powerful acts of God that gave them new life (see 3.2, 5; cf. 1 Cor. 2.1–5). These experiences confirmed them as 'sons of God', as God sent the Spirit of Christ to authenticate their 'adoption as sons' (Gal. 4.6; see also 3.26).[218]

Paul concludes this section of the letter in 4.19–20, applying the 'established connection between apocalyptic expectation and the anguish of childbirth' (Gaventa 1990b: 193). Paul describes himself metaphorically as a woman once again bearing the pains of childbirth (cf. 4.4) until 'Christ has been formed

---

213. Cf. 2.17; 3.10, 13; 4.14; B. Longenecker 1999: 101; Kraftchick 1996: 201; Güttgemanns 1966: 185; Goddard and Cummins 1993: 108, 110.

214. According to Barclay, their 'extreme generosity…was a sign of their reconstruction by the one who loved and gave himself' (2002: 145).

215. Bryant attributes an element of intentionality to the Galatians' initial response, finding that 'they had fully embraced the necessity of self-sacrificing service in the manner of Jesus Christ' (2001: 155).

216. Elsewhere, Paul uses this noun and its related adjective to speak of blessings received from God (Rom. 4.6–9; 14.22; 1 Cor. 7.40). Thus, with B. Longenecker (1999: 103–104), this study concludes that ὑμῶν is an objective genitive with God as its implied subject.

217. See B. Longenecker 1999: 103.

218. This study thus challenges the conclusion of B. Longenecker (1999: 103–104), who adopts a position very similar to that of Käsemann, Martyn, Brown, and Gorman. He argues that divine transformation occurs *first* through the invasion of an external power that *thereafter* determines a person's specific conduct, which in turn attests to the initial blessing. This study argues a different sequence: God sends the Spirit to confirm experiences of new life and to illuminate their connection with conduct that faithfully portrays Christ's cruciform pattern.

in/among you' (μορφωθῇ Χριστὸς ἐν ὑμῖν).[219] As a servant of Christ (see 1.10), Paul participates in God's apocalyptic process of 'begetting'[220] or 'giving birth' to communities in Christ[221] (cf. 4.29). Indeed, 'what counts is that Christ is formed within them, and because their lives have adopted, and continue to adopt, that pattern of death to the world and self-giving love, they carry positive significance' (Barclay 2002: 154).

Part of this birthing process thus involves working with God to persuade the Galatians (see 1.10; 5.8) that Christ's cruciform pattern is the new and universal standard for conduct through which both Jews and Gentiles may experience new life/justification together in Christ through the life-giving power of God. The Judaizers, however, have forced Paul to re-enter this important apocalyptic birthing process in the Galatian churches.[222] They have persuaded some in the churches to submit to circumcision and thereby take on law observance (see 5.7–8). This means that the ones they have persuaded have abandoned their commitment to 'clothe themselves with Christ' as their exclusive behavioural standard and no longer practise spiritual discernment to seek actions that conform to the cruciform pattern.

Paul confirms this with his metaphorical characterization of the birth of churches in 4.21–31. The metaphor effectively draws on Paul's arguments that began as early as 3.6. He correlates the birth of the churches in Galatia with the birth of Isaac, the son of Abraham and Sarah. Isaac was born according to promise rather than the Flesh (4.23, 28), according to the Spirit rather than the Flesh (4.29). The churches in Galatia were born of their mother, who is the free Jerusalem from above, rather than the earthly Jerusalem who is enslaved to the law (see 4.25–26).

Paul thus implies a contrast between the birth and life of different churches. It is a contrast clearly created by Paul's view that one group of churches has committed to the behavioural standard of the law, while a second group has committed to Christ's behavioural standard of cruciformity in lieu of law observance. A person may live in the present Jerusalem, whose inhabitants conform to the law and experience the life or curse promised by the law (see 3.10–13). Conversely, the person may dwell in the heavenly Jerusalem, whose inhabitants are free from the law's requirements and restrictions. Inhabitants of this new city from above experience life ἐκ πίστεως rather than ἐκ νόμου (see 3.6–26).

As those who are ἐκ πίστεως, they have become 'sons of Abraham' and their earthly lives are being blessed with the new life experienced by the faithful

219. The ἐν ὑμῖν is translated both as 'in' and 'among you' in recognition that Christ continues to live in each person (cf. 1.16, 23; 2.19–20) when that person's actions faithfully portray Christ's cruciform pattern *and* that God builds the community that Paul refers to as the body of Christ through such Christ-conforming conduct (cf. 1 Cor. 1.5–8; 2.2–5; 3.6–15; 12.4–7).

220. See also 1 Cor. 4.14–15; Phlm. 10; cf. Gaventa (1996b: 38), who calls attention to 1QH 7.13–15, 21. There, the one being directed in the paths of righteousness, walking in the land of the living into paths of glory and peace, has become a father to the sons of grace.

221. Martyn (1997b: 427–28) notes the connections between 4.19 and Isa. 45.7–11.

222. For the conclusion that this birthing process is ongoing, see Gaventa 1996b: 33; Martyn 1997b: 424–25; Dunn 1998c: 460; 1993a: 240.

Abraham (3.7–9, 14). Having clothed themselves with Christ in baptism – that is, having committed to conform their actions to Christ's cruciform pattern – they have become 'sons of God' διὰ τῆς πίστεως ἐν Χριστῷ Ἰησοῦ (3.26–27). They now belong to Christ and have become a 'seed' of Abraham, heirs according to promise (3.29). Paul thus argues that those who clothe themselves with Christ receive the Spirit's promise of resurrection life after death because they trust God's life-giving power that raised Jesus from the dead after he voluntarily gave himself for others on the cross (cf. 3.14, 22). Moreover, *because* they are sons of God from and through this faith, the Spirit of God's son has been sent into their hearts to *confirm* their adoption as God's sons (4.5–7).

As a result, argues Paul, the Galatians must not return to their enslavement to the powers of the cosmos that work through behaviour that conforms to the law (4.8–9). Now that the faith has been revealed in the person of Christ Jesus, believers are no longer under the law and restrained by its requirements (3.23–25). They are free from that law and the powers that work through it. They must discern appropriate behaviour *only* by seeking to be justified in Christ and not in the law (2.17; 5.4). This means they must seek only to discern actions that conform to Christ's cruciform pattern. It is through such cruciform actions that they were born as churches and continue to experience new and eternal life through the Spirit ἐκ πίστεως (3.1–5, 21; cf. 5.5–6). Paul expands on the nature of this behavioural freedom in Christ in the following sections of the letter.

4. *God Requires Christ-Conforming Conduct and the Practice of Spiritual Discernment (5.1–12)*

The association of conduct with experience has been Paul's focus throughout the letter (cf. Stowers 1986: 23). In 5.1–12 he continues to engage in theo-ethical reasoning, intensifying the behavioural and spatial imagery to contrast life in one of two distinct spatial realms. Paul also addresses more directly the practice of spiritual discernment that should be taking place in the churches of Galatia. He reminds the Galatians that divine persuasion about the truth of the gospel takes place only when the community seeks to conform their behaviour to Christ's cruciform pattern and practises spiritual discernment to connect such cruciform actions with experiences of new life through the power of God.

a. *Law Observance Cuts People Off from Christ and the Power of God (5.1–4)*
In 5.1–4, Paul again employs spatial imagery in connection with human conduct. He issues dramatic warnings to those who do not 'stand firm' in the behavioural freedom won for them by Christ (5.1; see also 2.4; 5.13). Those who are choosing circumcision[223] are thereby subjecting themselves again (πάλιν) to a ζυγῷ δουλείας (5.1). This is almost certainly an allusion to the Jewish notion of the 'yoke of the Law' (Barclay 1988: 62–63, including n. 76; cf. Mt. 11.29). As a former Pharisee who was zealous for the law (1.13–14; Phil. 3.5–6), Paul

---

223. The present participle περιτέμνησθε in 5.3 (cf. 6.13) grounds Munck's argument that the Judaizers are Gentiles (1959: 87–89), an unlikely conclusion.

bears witness again as an expert (Gal. 5.2, 3). Circumcision obligates a person
(ὀφειλέτης) to do everything the law prescribes (5.3), since the law is a '*total
way of life*' (Dunn 1993a: 267, original emphasis). Having begun by the Spirit
(3.3), this new commitment by some to 'do the whole law' (5.3) means they are
now being completed by the Flesh (see 3.3). Taking on the law's commitments
strips believers of their freedom to discern *spiritually* what constitutes appropriate Christ-conforming behaviour.[224]

Indeed, argues Paul, the risen Christ will not benefit (ὠφελήσει) those who
have obligated themselves to law observance (5.2; cf. 2.21).[225] According to 5.4,
those who are seeking life in the law (cf. 3.12) and are being justified by law
observance cut themselves off from Christ and fell out of that realm where God's
grace/power prevails (τῆς χάριτος ἐξεπέσατε).[226] By rejecting Christ's cruciform pattern in favour of law observance, some of the Galatians have rejected
God's life-giving power (see 2.21; cf. 1.6). This means that some of the Galatians
no longer benefit from the Spirit that leads believers to discern the connections
between Christ-conforming conduct and experiences of that life-giving power of
God (see 3.1–5; 5.22–25; cf. 1 Cor. 2.1–16; 12.4–7). Paul's assertions appear to
be grounded in his foundational conviction that, since God raised Jesus from the
dead (Gal. 1.1), Christ still lives actively in the lives of believers through the
Spirit (Bryant 2001: 156).

The logic of Paul's argument seems clear. By rejecting Christ's cruciform
pattern and the practice of spiritual discernment, some have fallen out of that
spatial realm where God's grace/power prevails to give new life. They are now
ὑπὸ νόμον and submitting again to powers of the world that are exercised in
connection with conduct that conforms to worldly standards, even the law (see
4.3–5, 9, 21).[227] As a result they are experiencing the manifest works of the Flesh
(5.19–21). They are once again experiencing life in the present evil age, where
they are unable to know God in the revelation of Jesus Christ and unable to
recognize the power of God that works in connection with Christ-conforming
actions (cf. 4.6–9). This defection by some (1.6) confirms that not everyone is
practising spiritual discernment by engaging in theo-ethical reasoning, a concern
to which Paul now turns.

b. *The Spirit Grounds the Hope of New Life Associated with Believers' Acts
of Love (5.5–6)*
Theo-ethical reasoning underlies the critical verses in 5.5–6, as Paul continues to
explain 5.1–4 (γὰρ introduces both 5.5 and 5.6). He indicates how the proper

224. Contra Bockmuehl, who tentatively suggests that in 5.3 Paul asserts that every Jewish Christian is obligated to obey the whole Torah (1995b: 98).

225. Aune refers to 5.2 as a 'prophetic utterance' directly relating to human conduct (1983: 258),
reflecting Paul's understanding of the role of prophecy. For the role of prophecy in 1 Corinthians, see
Chapter 3, section 3.d above.

226. Cf. *Pss. Sol.* 9.1: Israel's apostasy from the law led to their expulsion from the land of inheritance into a foreign land.

227. Martyn concludes that Paul's use of ὑπὸ throughout the letter means 'to be under the power
of' something (1997b: 495).

relationship between humans and God and the proper relationship among humans belong together. They cannot be separated by those who might otherwise distinguish theology and ethics.[228]

Although πίστις and ἀγάπη appear often in Paul's letters, they are not frequently brought into immediate association as they are in 5.6.[229] This does not make 5.6 atypical for Paul, however, but emphasizes the importance of this connection in the context of the specific issues addressed in this letter.[230] In the churches of Galatia, community members in effect disagree about whether Christ's cruciform pattern is now the universal, exclusive standard for Gentile believers' conduct. Paul writes to emphasize the intimate connection between faith and love, with ἀγάπη being understood as conduct that conforms to Christ's cruciform pattern of self-giving *love* for others (see 1.4; 2.20).[231]

In 5.5, a sentence that one interpreter finds 'almost impossible to translate' (Betz 1979: 262), Paul opens with the emphatic 'we'[232] to create an important contrast.[233] On the one hand are those who cut themselves off from Christ and fell out of the realm where God's life-giving power prevails because they are now seeking justification through circumcision and law observance. On the other hand are Paul and other members of the churches who remain steadfastly committed to: (1) Christ's cruciform pattern as the universal, exclusive standard for conduct (see 2.16, 20); and (2) the practice of spiritual discernment, by which believers are looking for life in the manifestations of the Spirit (cf. 5.16, 18, 22–23, 25) that illuminate experiences of new life that may be linked with acts of cruciform love. Although this contrast may not be apparent on the surface in 5.5–6, closer scrutiny supports this reading.

The verb ἀπεκδέχομαι is a key for unlocking the complexity encountered in 5.5. It is frequently called an 'eschatological term'.[234] It supposedly denotes the believer's eager expectation of the future return of Christ.[235] Understood in this usual way, the verb 'thus underlines the "already/not yet" character of Christian existence for Paul', with the implication that the tension of the 'confident but yet

228. See Engberg-Pedersen 2000: 177. Similarly, Cosgrove concludes that in these verses justification, the Spirit, and ethics are brought together (1988: 150).
229. See R. Longenecker 1990: 229; cf. 1 Cor. 13.1–2; 1 Thess. 5.8.
230. For the relationship between contingency and coherency in Paul's letters, see Beker 1980; 1991.
231. See Engberg-Pedersen 1987: 566–67.
232. There is no agreement about who is included in Paul's use of 'we' in 5.5. See, e.g., R. Longenecker 1990: 229; Witherington 1998: 277; Burton 1921: 277; Martyn 1997b: 472; Dunn 1993a: 269.
233. Dunn wrongly calls 5.5 a 'theological aside' (1993a: 270).
234. For this characterization using the language of doctrinal theology, see Betz 1979: 262 n. 83; cf. Witherington 1998: 369.
235. See Dunn 1993a: 269–70; Engberg-Pedersen 2000: 175; Martyn 1997b: 472; Burton 1921: 278; R. Longenecker 1990: 228–29; Witherington 1998: 369; Betz 1979: 262; Lull 1980: 99; Cosgrove 1988: 153; S.K. Williams 1997: 137. Similarly, BAGD only lists 'await' as the meaning of the verb. That the word means 'await' in many non-biblical texts is without doubt, as a check of LSJ confirms. Swetnam points out, however, that according to LSJ there is at least one more meaning in non-biblical texts: to 'understand in a certain sense', 'infer', 'understand from the context' (1967: 104, including n. 4).

unfulfilled expectation' cannot be 'resolved or reduced by seeking to make the hope more certain' through present action (Dunn 1993a: 270).

We suggest that this typical 'eschatological' understanding of ἀπεκδέχομαι distorts Paul's perspective because it fails to incorporate Paul's theo-ethical reasoning that we have identified throughout this study. This causes interpreters to overlook how the present practice of spiritual discernment does in fact make the hope of future resurrection life more certain for believers as they link present experiences of God's life-giving power with cruciform actions.

Indeed, the clear implication of the usual 'eschatological' translation and interpretation of ἀπεκδέχομαι is that Jesus Christ is now *absent* from those who eagerly await and expect his *future*, final return. This completely *contradicts* the argument Paul just concluded in 5.1–4, where he contended that by taking on circumcision and law observance some church members cut themselves off from Christ and that Christ will no longer benefit them.[236] The logic of Paul's preceding argument in 5.1–4 implies that those who still live in God's spatial realm have a *present*, beneficial relationship with the risen Christ who remains active in the community. Moreover, the so-called 'eschatological' understanding of ἀπεκδεχόμεθα in 5.5 ignores several of Paul's earlier statements about the continuing presence of the crucified but risen Christ (see 1.12, 16; 2.20; 3.1; 4.14, 19) and his Spirit (see 4.6; cf. 5.16–25). These assertions hardly betray an understanding that Christ is now absent from the community that merely awaits his future, final return.

Thus, as commonly interpreted, Paul's choice of ἀπεκδεχόμεθα in 5.5 appears to be logically ill-suited for the rhetorical context of his unfolding argument. This unlikely conclusion suggests that the so-called 'eschatological' understanding of the verb must be re-examined.

In the compound verb form ἀπεκδέχομαι, the ἀπό intensifies the force already given to the simple verb δέχομαι by the addition of ἐκ, suggesting that ἀπεκδεχόμεθα means 'to be receiving [something] from a distance' (Burton 1921: 278).[237] As a 'verb of attaining' (Burton 1921: 278), the present tense in 5.5 signifies the receipt of something being sought or expected and *being attained* by the community – the 'hope of righteousness' (ἐλπίδα δικαιοσύνης).

We suggest that this objective genitive refers to the hope that builds up among believers that they are destined for new and eternal life. The genitive has two dimensions. First, it refers to the hope of new *earthly* life among those who are 'sons of Abraham' because they live ἐκ πίστεως like Abraham (3.6–9, 14, 21–27). To live ἐκ πίστεως after the revelation of Jesus Christ and 'the faith' now means that believers clothe themselves with Christ in baptism (3.27). Consequently, their hope centres on their conviction that they will continue to experience new earthly life through God's life-giving power when they conform their

236. A similar contradiction was noted in 1 Cor. 1.7–8, where the participle ἀπεκδεχομένους leads interpreters to understand (incorrectly) the phrase τὴν ἀποκάλυψιν τοῦ κυρίου ἡμῶν Ἰησοῦ Χριστοῦ as referring only to the future, final return of Christ . See Chapter 2, section 2.b above.

237. Burton alters his final translation, however, concluding that the verb merely means 'to be intently waiting' (1921: 278).

actions to Christ's cruciform pattern. Second, the genitive also refers to the hope of resurrection life after death. This is the new and eternal life promised to Abraham's 'seed', who is Christ (see 3.4–16), and fulfilled when God raised him from the dead (1.1). For believers it is the hope of resurrection life after death promised to all the ones believing in Christ (3.22), who thereby belong to Christ (3.29). This dual-faceted hope of new and eternal life is grounded in the Galatians' past experiences of righteousness – understood as new earthly life experienced through God's life-giving power in connection with Christ-conforming actions (see 2.16–21; 3.1–5, 21).

According to 5.5, believers are expecting *and receiving* this hope – whose object is new life/righteousness from God – by means of the Spirit from faith (πνεύματι ἐκ πίστεως). Paul uses the dative πνεύματι instrumentally without the article as a 'dative of means' to limit the main 'verb of attaining' implied in his use of ἀπεκδεχόμεθα.[238] What Paul means, we contend, is that the Spirit becomes the instrument by which those who have faith receive illumination about the connections between Christ-conforming conduct and their experiences of new earthly life. In other words, practising spiritual discernment provides believers with insights into the *present* reality of the new life from God that Paul refers to at some points as δικαιοσύνη (see 2.21; 3.6, 21). These insights also ground believers' hope in the ultimate reality of future resurrection life after death.[239]

Indeed, in 5.6, another critical verse for understanding Paul's religion,[240] he once again connects Christ's cruciform pattern with God's life-giving power.[241] He concludes that 'in Christ Jesus' neither circumcision nor uncircumcision prevails with any strength (ἰσχύει).[242] Instead, what prevails with strength is faith

238. Burton 1921: 278; see also Betz 1979: 262; Cosgrove 1988: 152; Dunn 1993a: 269; Martyn 1997b: 472; cf. S.K. Williams 1997: 138; Witherington 1998: 369. Martyn (1997b: 472) *internalizes* the Spirit's work as audible rather than visible ('the Spirit whispers in the believer's ear').

239. According to Gorman, 'the Spirit forges a link between believers' present and future experience' (2001: 55). Thus, concludes Gorman, Paul also refers to the Spirit elsewhere as the 'down payment' or 'first installment' of future life with God. This is the same pattern we addressed in connection with 1 Cor. 1.4–9, 2.1–16 and 12.4–13, discussed above in Chapters 2 and 3.

Martyn finds Paul's reference to future justification surprising since he thinks that the cosmos 'has already been changed by God's rectifying deed in Christ's advent and death' (1997b: 472). Similarly, Cosgrove concludes that Paul speaks of 'two distinct justifications' in 5.5 (1988: 150). S.K. Williams points out, however, that believers can still turn their backs on God (2.21) since 'being justified' does not describe an irreversible transaction (1997: 137–38). Our discussion of 5.1–4 confirms Williams's assertion. See now, Käsemann, who concludes that justification is to be had on earth 'only as a pledged gift, always subject to attack, always to be authenticated in practice – a matter of promise and expectation' (1969e: 170).

240. According to Burton, '[f]or the disclosure of the apostle's fundamental idea of the nature of religion, there is no more important sentence in the whole epistle, if, indeed in any of Paul's epistles' than 5.6 (1921: 279).

241. Betz expressly notes the 'ethical' significance of 5.6 (1979: 262). For the importance of Paul's power language in this verse, see Dunn 1993a: 271; Kraftchick 1996: 215.

242. For this translation of ἰσχύει, see LSJ, 844; see also 6.15; 1 Cor. 7.19; cf. Phil. 4.13; Betz 1979: 263.

working through love (ἀλλὰ πίστις δι' ἀγάπης ἐνεργουμένη).[243] Throughout his letters Paul uses the noun ἀγάπη and the verb ἀγαπάω synonymously to denote conduct that conforms to Christ's cruciform pattern.[244] Later, in 5.13, Paul exhorts the Galatians to enslave themselves to one another by means of love (διὰ τῆς ἀγάπης). He thereby confirms that 'love' signifies *actions* taken to serve and benefit others. In other words, faith includes an active behavioural component (Engberg-Pedersen 2000: 176–77).[245] We suggest that this is what it means for believers to conform their behaviour to Christ's cruciform pattern of self-giving love for others (cf. 1.4; 2.20).

Paul has already asserted that 'in Christ Jesus' the social, ethnic, economic and gender distinctions that determine appropriate conduct according to worldly standards – including the law – no longer apply (3.28).[246] In 5.6, he reaffirms that one's status as a Jew or Gentile makes no difference, since all humanity may now experience new life from God in connection with conduct that conforms to Christ's universal pattern of self-giving love for others (2.16–21).[247] This does not mean, however, that these distinctions involving earthly human life are completely dissolved (cf. 1 Cor. 7.17–24).[248] Rather, in God's new spatial realm in Christ these distinctions do not serve as appropriate criteria for discerning Christ-conforming conduct.[249] Since the righteous one (ὁ δίκαιος) shall live ἐκ πίστεως (Gal. 3.11) and not from the law, community members may not rely solely on the law's prescriptions as determinative of appropriate conduct. Instead, living from faith, they must rely on the Spirit (5.5) – the Spirit of God's Son (4.6) – to lead them (see 5.18) into experiences of new life (see 5.25). The Spirit accomplishes this by illuminating the connections between Christ-conforming acts of self-giving love and the fruit of the Spirit that reflect experiences of new life from God (see 5.22–23).[250]

This study concludes that Paul's phrase 'faith working through love' characterizes an essential aspect of his theo-ethical reasoning. Those who have faith in Christ are the ones trusting in the revelation of Christ's cruciform pattern as the

---

243. Cf. 1 Thess. 1.3.

244. Cf. Furnish, who finds that 'the liberating and transforming grace of God is active as love, and Christ's death ("for us", "for our sins") is the decisive actualization of that love in history'; it is the 'new age itself, powerfully present and active in history' (1972: 92–93).

245. This same pattern is reflected throughout the letter of James.

246. *Pace* Tomson 1996: 267; Bockmuehl 1995b: 98–99; Finsterbusch 1996: 15.

247. According to Engberg-Pedersen, it is not in law observance but in this 'form of life' ('faith working through love'), the positive account of which is finally given in 5.13–26, that the 'full meaning of the Christ event' lies (2000: 177). He concludes that this 'form of life' is also the one that will give believers the 'final verdict of righteousness' if they will stick to it (2000: 177). In this way he brings together faith and ethics, highlighting Paul's synthesis of theology and ethics by showing that 'faith' includes an active behavioural component (2000: 176–77).

248. Horrell 2000: 338; *pace* Boyarin 1994: 155.

249. Horrell (2000: 333, 335, 338–39, 341–42) and B. Longenecker (1998: 67) correctly emphasize the social, community dynamic that lies at the forefront of Paul's understanding of the 'new creation' being constructed 'in Christ'; cf. Barclay 1996a: 381–95; *pace* Hubbard 2002.

250. This is the same pattern identified in connection with 1 Cor. 1.4–9, 2.1–16 and 12.4–11 in Chapters 2 and 3 above.

pathway – the means of access – to new life through the power of God. They put into practice their faith in the power of God that works in connection with acts of love that conform to Christ's cruciform pattern (see 1 Cor. 2.1–5).[251] They also expect and receive spiritual insights by means of the Spirit from faith sent by God. Those who practise spiritual discernment seek to associate their present experiences of new life with acts of cruciform love. Making these connections grounds their hope that in the future they will continue to experience this new life/righteousness in their earthly existence and, ultimately, that they will experience resurrection life after death.

c. *Divine Persuasion Takes Place in Connection with Christ-Conforming Conduct (5.7–12)*

After Paul departed the churches in Galatia, community life was disrupted (5.15; cf. 1.6–7; 2.4–5; 5.26). This study has argued that the letter attempts to persuade these churches that conduct conforming to Christ's cruciform pattern constitutes the behavioural means of access to the new life promised by God (cf. 3.11–12). This contention is supported by 5.7–12, where Paul continues to speak metaphorically about matters related to lifestyle and conduct.[252] In this section he also builds on the practice of spiritual discernment described in 5.5–6, by implication characterizing it as a process of divine persuasion (see 5.8; cf. 1.10).

Indeed, knowing that some are advocating circumcision and law observance, Paul asks in 5.7 who hindered (ἐνέκοψεν) them from 'being persuaded by the truth' (ἀληθείᾳ μὴ πείθεσθαι).[253] The Judaizers hindered this process of persuasion by convincing some to conform their actions to the law.[254] Consequently, some church members are now looking for life in the law by following its prescriptions. They are no longer seeking life ἐκ πίστεως (see 3.10–12; cf. 5.1–4) by conforming to Christ's cruciform pattern and practising spiritual discernment (cf. 5.5–6, 16–18, 22–23). According to Paul, their persuasion is no longer coming through the manifestations of the Spirit from the God who is calling them (see 5.8). They are blocking this process of *divine* persuasion from taking place because they are looking to the law for their life and conforming their actions to its pattern. Thus, we contend that these law-observant Galatians are not being persuaded by God because: (1) their conduct is not being conformed to Christ's cruciform pattern; and, being under the law, (2) they are not being led by the

---

251. Thus, this study confirms Engberg-Pedersen's conclusion that faith and 'ethical' behaviour cannot and must not be separated out from one another (2000: 176). In section 3 below, however, we challenge his broader conclusion that the 'ultimate purpose of the Christ event and faith lies in *practice*' (2000: 138, original emphasis).

252. Dunn 1993a: 273; Burton 1921: 282–83; R. Longenecker 1990: 222; Barclay 1988: 94; see also Pfitzner 1967: 135–36; cf. Martyn 1997b: 138.

253. For this translation of the infinitive πείθεσθαι, see Dunn 1993a: 274. It is signalled by Paul's application of the same verb again in 5.10 (πέποιθα) and the related noun πεισμονή ('the persuasion') in 5.8.

254. While Dunn correctly emphasizes the role of persuasion in Paul's argument (1993a: 274–75), by focusing on the intellectual persuasion of oral preaching he underestimates the role of human conduct as part of the persuasion process.

Spirit from faith (see 5.5, 18), who illuminates the links between Christ-conforming conduct and experiences of new life through the power of God.

For those practising spiritual discernment and conforming their conduct to
Christ's cruciform pattern, however, this is an ongoing persuasive process, as the
present tense of the passive infinitive πείθεσθαι in 5.7 indicates.[255] Thus, Paul
suggests that these faithful believers distance themselves from those who are now
law-observant. Indeed, in 5.9 he says 'a little yeast leavens the whole batch'. He
makes the same behavioural point raised in 1 Cor. 5.6–8, focusing on the dele-
terious community experiences associated with those whose conduct conforms to
worldly standards (even the law).[256]

Moreover, Paul expresses confidence in this process of divine persuasion. He
implies in Gal. 5.10 that if the Galatians remain steadfast in their commitment to
conform their actions to Christ's cruciform pattern and practise spiritual discernment, they will not think any differently from him (οὐδὲν ἄλλο φρονήσετε). As
they experience new life from God and associate it with conduct that conforms to
Christ's cruciform pattern, they, too, will be divinely persuaded about the 'truth
of the gospel'.[257] God sent Jesus Christ into the world to submit voluntarily to
death on the cross, revealing that Christ's cruciform pattern of self-giving love
for others has become the universal means by which believers may experience
new life from God in connection with conduct that conforms to this pattern.

5. Looking for Life: Practising Spiritual Discernment
by Associating Conduct with Experience (5.13–6.10)

This thoroughly descriptive, pastoral section[258] plays '*the* crucial role'[259] in the
letter. It is grounded in Paul's theo-ethical reasoning, the means by which he
theologizes as he integrates Christian living and thinking, combining what are
commonly distinguished as theology and ethics.[260] The section contains Paul's
most comprehensive description of Christ's cruciform pattern and the practice
of spiritual discernment that Paul offers as a positive alternative to the law-

---

255. For the latter conclusion, see R. Longenecker 1990: 230, although Longenecker adopts the
more common translation 'obey' rather than 'persuade'.
256. See Chapter 3, section 2.a above.
257. Cf. 1 Thess. 4.9; 1 Cor. 2.13.
258. For this description of 5.13–26, see Martyn 1997b: 481–82, including n. 41.
259. Engberg-Pedersen 2000: 136 (original emphasis), referring only to 5.13–26.
260. According to Engberg-Pedersen, modern scholars generally have been unable to recognize the
crucial role of Gal. 5.13–26 in the letter because they distinguish 'theology' and 'ethics' as two
separate things that are in fact two sides of the same coin (2000: 136–37). He observes that they often
characterize Gal. 5.13–26 as being about 'ethics' (something distinct from 'theology' addressed
earlier in the letter) and 'paraenesis' (something distinct from 'indicative' facts stated in preceding
sections). He contends that 'there is no new Christ-believing "identity"…which is not also a matter of
"behaviour" (or actual social *practice*)' (2000: 327, original emphasis). While the present study
shares Engberg-Pedersen's interest in identifying the underlying logical structure of Paul's presentation of the Christ-centred alternative to law observance, it rejects his almost exclusively Bultmannian
emphasis on the role of human self-understanding in his analysis (see 2000: 25).

observant life being enjoined by his opponents.[261] It spells out the pattern of community life that the Galatians should once again adopt when they turn away from the law-observant life that Paul has been arguing against from the letter's opening verses (Engberg-Pedersen 2000: 136).

In this section Paul identifies the community experiences of conflict and discord that he thinks results when, in effect, members of the churches disagree about the proper community behavioural norm or its exclusivity.[262] He provides the Galatians with revelatory criteria to recognize particular experiences that are linked to conduct that conforms to worldly standards (see 5.19–21).[263] Paul thus provides criteria to help the Galatians distinguish between experiences of life in God's new spatial realm/temporal age and life in the present evil age. He also gives them revelatory criteria for recognizing the links between experiences of new life from God and Christ-conforming actions, a connection illuminated by the Spirit in the practice of spiritual discernment. Paul thereby transforms the traditional discourse associated with lists of individual vices and virtues by shaping them into revelatory criteria for distinguishing conduct and experiences that take place in one of two distinct spatial realms/temporal ages. Paul thus provides a more comprehensive description of freedom in Christ – the positive alternative to law observance.[264]

According to 5.13, conduct directed towards the needs of others constitutes the essence of the cruciform pattern that represents Paul's alternative to law observance. He warns the Galatians, however, that this new behavioural freedom in Christ must not become a 'base of operations for the Flesh' (Martyn 1997b: 485). His reasoning implies that this personified power (the Flesh) works certain effects in association with particular human actions that conform to worldly standards rather than the divinely revealed standard of cruciform love. To avoid this result, Paul exhorts them to 'be enslaved to one another through love' (5.13). His use of the phrase διὰ τῆς ἀγάπης echoes its use in 5.6 (Barclay 1988: 109), where Paul contended that the only conduct that now manifests God's power is 'faith working through love'. The reciprocal, reflexive pronoun ἀλλήλοις in 5.13 (cf. 5.15, 17, 26; 6.2) emphasizes the other-directedness that lies at the heart of Christ's cruciform pattern of self-giving love for others (see 2.20).[265]

Paul concludes that the whole law (cf. 5.3) has been brought to completion (πεπλήρωται) in Christ's one embodied message: love your neighbour as your-

261. Cf. Engberg-Pedersen, who concludes that in 5.13–26 Paul provides the 'most comprehensive description of the form of life that Paul aims to present to his Galatian addressees as the true, positive alternative to the kind of life enjoined by his opponents' (2000: 136, without original emphasis).

262. According to Martyn, the Galatians are 'double-minded' because they are trying to direct their allegiance to both Christ and the Mosaic law (1997b: 540); cf. Schürmann 1974: 293; Hays 1987: 288.

263. See Chapter 1, section 3.e above for a discussion of the broad first-century 'discourse of revelatory authority' in which Paul participates.

264. Engberg-Pedersen 2000: 136; 329 n. 10. Similarly, says Engberg-Pedersen, Rom. 6.1–8.13 describes what 'Christ faith means for actual practice' (2000: 255).

265. Cf. Hays 1987: 288–89; Engberg-Pedersen 2000: 327 n. 6; Dunn 1993a: 295.

self (5.14).[266] The law with its promise of life[267] was thus brought to completion when God raised Jesus to new life after he gave himself for others through his death on the cross according to God's will (cf. 1.1, 4; Phil. 2.5–11).

Thus, according to the logic of Paul's theo-ethical reasoning, it is both God and the human Christ who have worked together in the divine–human partnership[268] to bring the law to completion.[269] The perfect passive πεπλήρωται signifies that God continues to bring the law to completion by exercising God's life-giving power in connection with believers' conduct that conforms to Christ's cruciform pattern. Thus, believers now participate in that same divine–human partnership by dying to the behavioural standards of the present evil age and faithfully portraying Christ's cruciform pattern in the context of their own lives.[270]

In Gal. 5.16–6.10 Paul vigorously tries to persuade the Galatians about the moral sufficiency of Christ's cruciform pattern and the importance of the practice of spiritual discernment.[271] According to 5.16, he promises the Galatians that any person who walks by the Spirit will never carry out the impulsive desire of the Flesh.[272] With the phrase πνεύματι περιπατεῖτε Paul asserts that the Spirit serves as a community resource.[273] As in 5.5–6 (see also 5.18), the dative πνεύματι signifies that the Spirit is the instrument or means of behavioural discernment in the community. The Spirit illuminates the connections between Christ-conforming actions and experiences of new life. Paul promises those who are being led by the Spirit because they practise spiritual discernment that they will never walk in ways that respond to the lures of the Flesh (see 5.18).

Through the motifs of ethical and spatial dualism in 5.17–18, Paul starkly contrasts the alternative sources of behavioural discernment that present believers with a choice between life and death. In the problematic 5.17, he uses the verb ἐπιθυμεῖ with κατά to draw on the imagery of warfare.[274] He designates the Spirit and Flesh as two warring forces (cf. 3.3; 4.29), invoking the motif of

266. For this translation of πεπλήρωται, see Martyn 1997b: 488; cf. Dunn 1993a: 289; see also 6.2; cf. Rom. 15.19; Mt. 1.22; Jn 13.18.

267. See Rom. 7.10; Gal. 3.12; Lev. 18.5; Deut. 30.15–16.

268. For this partnership, see 1 Cor. 1.9, discussed in Chapter 2, section 2.b above.

269. Cf. B. Longenecker, who finds that 'Paul considered the character of Christ-like self-giving to be the manifestation of God's eschatological in-breaking…and this same eschatological character is also the means whereby the law is fulfilled' (1998: 83). For discussions that primarily emphasize the human role of Jesus Christ or other believers in bringing the law to completion, see Martyn 1997b: 489–90; Betz 1979: 275; Barclay 1988: 139–41; R. Longenecker 1990: 242–43; Westerholm 1988: 203; Thielman 1989: 140.

270. Martyn observes that Paul's exhortation in 5.13 presupposes the Galatians' active engagement in the Spirit's war of liberation (1997b: 531).

271. See Chapter 4, section 2.b above for discussion of Gal. 1.10, where Paul implies that he is trying to persuade both God and humans at the same time.

272. For the 'emphatic promissory future' rendering of οὐ μὴ τελέσητε rather than the imperative (as in RSV and NRSV), see Burton 1921: 299; Barclay 1988: 111; Dunn 1993a: 294 n. 1; Martyn 1997b: 492.

273. See Barclay 1988: 113 n. 15, 115; Dunn 1993a: 295; *pace* Martyn 1997b: 535.

274. Cf. Martyn 1997b: 493; Barclay 1988: 112.

spatial dualism to suggest that each reigns with power in different spatial realms that are 'set opposite to one another' (ἀλλήλοις ἀντίκειται).[275] This language suggests a radical juxtaposition of human experiences. On the one hand, a person may be walking by the Spirit, seeking to conform to Christ's cruciform pattern (cf. 3.3; 5.16, 25) and anticipating the experience of new life in God's spatial realm/temporal age in Christ. On the other hand, one may be walking by the Flesh (cf. 3.3; 5.13, 17), conforming to the behavioural standards of the world (including the law) and experiencing life in the present evil age that is 'set opposite' to God's new realm in Christ.[276] According to 5.17, freedom does not present a licence to do whatever one wants (ἃ ἐάν θέλητε ταῦτα ποιῆτε).[277] Being enslaved to one another and loving one's neighbour according to Christ's cruciform pattern (5.13–14) demands that one's actions be other-directed rather than self-focused (see also 1 Cor. 10.24, 33; Phil. 2.2–5).

In Gal. 5.18 Paul continues to juxtapose these two warring forces that prevail with power in either of two opposing spatial realms (cf. 6.14–15). Those who are presently being led by the Spirit are not under the law. Once again he uses the non-articular dative πνεύματι, pointing to the Spirit as the instrument by which believers are presently being divinely led (ἄγεσθε). Just as in 5.5 and 5.16, this dative signifies the divine means chosen to illuminate the connection between Christ-conforming conduct (i.e. 'faith working through love') and experiences of new life during the community practice of spiritual discernment (cf. Rom. 8.1– 25; 1 Cor. 1.4–9; 2.12–16).

According to the reasoning of the argument up through Gal. 5.18, anyone who is 'under law' looks for the life promised in connection with conduct that conforms to the law's prescriptions and prohibitions (see 3.12). Conversely, those who are being led by the Spirit as they practise spiritual discernment are looking for life ἐκ πίστεως (see 3.11) by means of the Spirit ἐκ πίστεως (5.5). They put their faith in Christ and the life-giving power of God exercised in connection with actions that conform to Christ's cruciform pattern of self-giving love for others (cf. 2.19–20; 5.5–6; 1 Cor. 2.1–5).[278] In other words, by means of the Spirit

275. For the possibility of this translation, see LSJ, 156. The position taken in this study opposes that of Dunn, who seems to characterize the battle as one taking place *exclusively inside* each Christian, as the Spirit creates an internal tension and exacerbates an 'inward contradiction' between a person's 'higher or deeper' spiritual level and the fleshly 'level of animal appetites' (1993a: 298). While there is undoubtedly an internal aspect to the war raging between the Flesh and the Spirit, it is not just internal to each person but also takes place at the community level.
276. Cf. Barclay, who concludes that the mutual opposition of Flesh and Spirit implies mutual exclusion (1988: 112), thus satisfactorily explaining why those who walk in the Spirit will not carry out the desire of the Flesh.
277. Barclay concludes: 'this clause is generally acknowledged to be one of the most difficult in the whole letter' (1988: 112). He concisely summarizes the various positions (1988: 110–15) before reaching his own conclusion on the meaning ('doing whatever you want'); cf. Martyn 1997b: 494–95.
278. The exegesis presented bears certain similarities to that of B. Longenecker, who concludes that Paul consistently envisaged that relationships between Christians constitute the 'sphere in which the eschatological power of God is [to be] evident, manifesting Christ-like relationships and social character' (1998: 161). According to Longenecker, Paul associates certain 'spiritual forces' with certain 'forms of character' (1999: 93, 99–100); cf. Barclay 1988: 231–32; Fowl 1994: 78, 91. Longe-

from faith, believers are expecting and receiving the Spirit's illumination of the
links between their experiences of new life and Christ-conforming actions. Seeing
these connections also grounds their hope that future resurrection life after death
will become a reality (see Gal. 5.5). The Spirit empowers believers who collectively practise spiritual discernment to recognize experiences of the power of
God that gives new life in connection with Christ-conforming conduct (see 4.6–
9; 5.5–6, 22–25).

Paul immediately turns in 5.19–23 to provide specific criteria to aid in this
community practice of spiritual discernment. He characterizes experiences of life
in each of the two, alternative spatial realms/temporal ages that are 'set opposite'
to one another. He thereby transforms traditional lists of individual virtues and
vices into *evidentiary manifestations* of community life.[279]

He contrasts the manifest (φανερά) 'works of the Flesh' (5.19–21) with the
'fruit of the Spirit' (5.22–23). Paul emphatically places φανερά in the sentence
to remind the Galatians that what is wrought by these external powers – whether
divine or worldly – is *discernible* as community experience (see also 3.1–5; 1 Cor.
2.1–5; 3.3). Thus, reflection on the association between conduct and experience
is essential if the Galatians are to discern whether they are experiencing life in
the present evil age or life in God's new spatial realm. Indeed, the community
members 'practising' (πράσσοντες) such things set out in Gal. 5.19–21 will not
inherit the kingdom of God (5.21; see also 1 Cor. 6.10; cf. Gal. 3.18, 29; 4.1, 7,
30).

This reflects an aspect of theo-ethical reasoning that lies beneath the surface of
the text. By implication, God will give the promised 'inheritance' of resurrection
life after death (cf. 6.8) to those who, at the end, are still resident in God's new
spatial realm/temporal age. Paul thereby emphasizes the importance of regularly
practising spiritual discernment so that believers may continue to conform their
actions to Christ's cruciform pattern (cf. 1 Cor. 4.1–2) and continue to be recognized as 'sons of God' (cf. 3.26; 4.6). The disciplined practice of this discipline
thereby provides continuing divine confirmation that believers remain resident in
God's new spatial realm/temporal age in Christ (cf. 1 Cor. 1.7–8).

Paul's use of ἔργα in 5.19 recalls his repeated use of the phrase 'works of the
law' earlier in the letter (see 2.16; 3.2, 5, 10). He thus reasons that the personified
force that he calls Flesh effectuates particular community experiences in connec-

---

necker concludes from this that much of Paul's case in Galatians depends on the connection Paul
establishes between a person's pattern of life and the 'suprahuman powers with which one is inevita-
bly aligned and the respective "worlds" in which those powers operate' (1999: 100).

The present study suggests that, according to Paul's theo-ethical reasoning, these 'suprahuman
powers' – divine and worldly – work certain effects in connection with particular human actions
rather than through a specific person's 'character' (see 1 Cor. 12.4–7). Thus, it is by means of Paul's
faithful portrayal of Christ's cruciform pattern in his own life that God's power works to provide
discernible credibility for Paul's apostleship and gospel.

279. See Martyn (1997b: 532–33), who calls them 'marks of community character', communal
evidence of the effects of the Flesh or of the Spirit's own activity. Betz (1979: 281) and Barclay (1988:
231–32) characterize them simply as lists of virtues and vices, thereby understating the role of
community experience in this discernment process.

tion with conduct that conforms to the law's prescriptions (cf. 4.3, 9). This produces disruption, division and ill-feelings among community members (cf. 2.11–14; 5.26).[280]

On the other hand, the phrase 'fruit of the Spirit' in 5.22 describes aspects of new life in God's spatial realm that dawned with the death and resurrection of Christ. This characterizes new earthly life being effected in connection with Christ-conforming behaviour when God exercises the same power that raised Jesus from the dead (cf. 3.1–5; 1 Cor. 2.1–5; 12.4–7; 2 Cor. 3.3; 4.5; 1 Thess. 1.4–10).[281] These manifestations of new life are the experiences that may be associated with walking by the Spirit (see Gal. 5.25). They are spiritually discerned by those who are being led by the Spirit (see 5.18).[282] The 'fruit' metaphor implies the cooperation between the Spirit and believers in this community practice that is focused on identifying the links between experiences of new life and Christ-conforming acts of love.[283]

Not surprisingly, then, Paul includes πίστις and ἀγάπη as 'fruit of the Spirit' in 5.22, a verse that raises problems for interpreters who overlook theo-ethical reasoning and the role of spiritual discernment in Paul's religion.[284] In the first-century Graeco-Roman world, the terms πίστις and πιστεύω often carried connotations associated with persuasion.[285] Thus, it is quite possible that for Paul and his churches the verb denoted the status of 'being convinced or persuaded'.[286] Against this background, πίστις is properly characterized as 'fruit of the Spirit'.

We suggest that believers who are led by the Spirit in the practice of spiritual discernment grow in faith.[287] This takes place over time as they consistently recognize the connections between their experiences of new life from God and

280. Barclay notes that ἔχθραι, ἔρις, ζῆλος, θυμοί, ἐριθεῖαι, διχοστασίαι, αἱρέσεις and φθόνοι specifically relate to matters of community dissension (1988: 153–54). He thus points to *experiences* of community discord directly related to some law-observant behaviour by church members.

281. According to Gorman, Paul refers metaphorically to the Spirit's 'fruit' that represents the divine transformation that is taking place in the present as effected by the Spirit (2001: 55).

282. Cf. W. Barclay, who concludes that the Spirit produces growth and its fruit is the 'natural outcome of living by the Spirit' (1999: 30).

283. Cf. Betz, who observes that the 'fruit of the Spirit' presupposes active human involvement (1979: 287); see also 1 Cor. 2.10–16.

284. For instance, R. Longenecker translates πίστις in this verse as the 'ethical virtue' of 'faithfulness', expressly rejecting the translation of the word as 'faith' which, he says, conforms to Paul's use elsewhere in the letter and means a person's response of trust regarding God's salvation provided in Christ Jesus (1990: 262). Others take similar positions to avoid aligning 'justifying faith' with ethics. See, e.g., Betz 1979: 288; Bruce 1982: 254; Burton 1921: 316. More correctly, Barclay (1988: 236) and Engberg-Pedersen (2000: 177) find that, for Paul, 'faith' has very definite moral aspects that may be exercised through love as believers seek to 'walk in/by the Spirit'.

285. This is one of the main conclusions of Kinneavy's 1987 study that focuses on the Greek rhetorical origins of Christian faith.

286. S.K. Williams (1997: 65–66), generally citing Kinneavy 1987.

287. For Paul's understanding of 'faith' as fluid and subject to growth as a function of reflection on the relationship between human behaviour and God's life-giving power, see Phil. 1.25–30; 1 Thess. 3.1–10. The observations made above confirm Paul's polysemous use of the πίστις word group in Galatians and suggest that an either/or choice need not be made between translating πίστις as 'faith' or 'faithfulness'. See now Boers 1993: 91–108.

specific actions that conform to Christ's cruciform pattern.[288] By means of the Spirit's illumination of these links, believers grow more and more persuaded (i.e. they grow in faith) that specific acts of ἀγάπη constitute the means of human access to experiences of God's life-giving power.[289] This also leads believers to envision imaginatively what *future* actions might also conform to Christ's cruciform pattern, allowing them to anticipate other experiences of new life through the power of God (cf. 1 Cor. 1.8; 2.12–16). In this way, it may be said that future acts of ἀγάπη are the fruit of the Spirit's *present* revelatory activity that takes place during the community practice of spiritual discernment.

As Paul winds down this portion of the letter, he restates certain fundamentals of theo-ethical reasoning. Those who 'belong to Christ' crucified (ἐσταύρωσαν) the Flesh (Gal. 5.24; cf. Rom. 8.1–13). This probably alludes to baptism, when believers clothed themselves with Christ (Gal. 3.27). By this Paul means that in baptism believers committed to seek life ἐκ πίστεως (3.11) in their daily existence by crucifying the Flesh – understood as that personified, external force that works in conjunction with behaviour that conforms to the behavioural standards of the world (including the law).[290]

This does not mean, however, that the Flesh has disappeared as a power on the historical scene. It continues to pose a significant threat and tempting reality (Barclay 1988: 206). This conclusion necessarily follows from the logic of Paul's argument in 5.1–4. There, Paul seems to speak about previously baptized Christians who fell out of God's spatial realm and rejected God's power (cf. 2.21). This occurred because they submitted to circumcision and took on law observance, abandoning their baptismal commitment to conform their actions to Christ's cruciform pattern.[291] They began looking for life in the law (see 3.11–12) rather than in the manifestations of the Spirit from faith in the practice of spiritual discernment (see 3.11; 5.5).[292] Thus, the warfare between the Spirit and the

288. We suggest that this is what Paul means in Rom. 1.16–17 when he says that the gospel is the power of God for salvation to everyone believing, as the righteousness of God is *being revealed* from faith for faith (ἐκ πίστεως εἰς πίστιν). What Paul means is that the gospel is that 'divine event' (Martyn 1997b: 115) that takes place each time there is a revelation of God's life-giving power, experienced by believers as new earthly life and characterized by Paul as salvation from God. These experiences are revealed ἐκ πίστεως – i.e. by means of cruciform actions grounded in a believer's faith in the revelation of God in Jesus Christ (cf. Rom. 4.16; 14.23). This takes place so that believers may grow in faith as they become even more persuaded that conduct conforming to Christ's cruciform pattern constitutes their means of access to God's life-giving power for salvation (see also Rom. 5.1–21; cf. 1 Cor. 1.23–25; 2.1–5). Moreover, this revelation of God's power leads believers to envision imaginatively other future actions to be taken in faith, through which they may anticipate other experiences of new earthly life from God. See also Chapter 3, section 3.d above.

289. Thus, Burton correctly concludes that the word πίστις represents either 'faithfulness' (fidelity) or 'faith in the specific form of belief in the power and willingness of God to work through men' (1921: 316).

290. Within these stated parameters, this study thus affirms Käsemann's conclusion that the Christian life is a 'perpetual return to baptism' (1969e: 176); see also 1 Cor. 15.31.

291. Within these stated parameters, this study thus affirms the language of E.P. Sanders about the importance for Paul of 'getting in' and 'staying in' (1983: 6–10). Moreover, it also affirms the importance of Paul's use of spatial dualism.

292. Cf. Barclay 1988: 207.

Flesh continues, even though Christ's resurrection represents the beginning of the end of the reign of the powers of the world, including the Flesh.[293]

Paul continues his pastoral advice to the Galatians in the important transitional verse at 5.25. The Spirit, as God's agent,[294] leads believers into new life in God's new spatial realm.[295] It illuminates the links between Christ-conforming conduct and the experiences of new earthly life that divinely confirm such conduct.[296] Paul thus implies the critical role of reflecting on conduct and experience, as guided by the revelatory criteria characterized as 'fruit of the Spirit'.[297] He thus amplifies what it means for believers to walk by the Spirit (5.16) and to be led by the Spirit (5.18). He also lays the groundwork for 6.1–10, where he describes more specifically what it means to walk in line with the Spirit (5.25).

Paul concludes the first portion of this descriptive section in 5.25, highlighting the indicative-imperative structure in his thought.[298] In the indicative clause (ζῶμεν πνεύματι), Paul again employs πνεύματι as a non-articular dative of means.[299] He thus emphasizes the role of the Spirit in the practice of spiritual discernment for confirming the links between new life and Christ-conforming conduct. The indicative clause does not signify, however, fully-conferred eschatological life among the baptized.[300] Rather, it describes the Spirit's *conditional* but *continuing* role in the community practice of spiritual discernment. Paul uses a real condition (Martyn 1997b: 545) to remind the Galatians that the Spirit leads them to recognize experiences of new life associated with Christ-conforming actions *only* when they practise spiritual discernment.

Consequently, in the imperative clause of 5.25b, Paul renews his call to walk by the Spirit. Rather than using the more common verb περιπατεῖτε as he did in 5.16, however, he uses the third-person plural verb form στοιχῶμεν. The verb στοιχέω can be translated as 'walk in line with' the Spirit.[301] Thus, Paul insists that believers should *imaginatively* align their future actions with the insights gleaned from the Spirit, who illuminates the *past* connections between experiences of new life and Christ-conforming conduct. Paul thus emphasizes that

293. Cosgrove correctly asserts that 'the cross itself is the beginning of new creation and life in the Spirit, which means that life in the Spirit belongs to those who are crucified with Christ' (1988: 193).

294. See 3.5; 4.6; 5.5; cf. 1 Cor. 2.12; 12.4, 7.

295. Cf. Rom. 8.11; 1 Cor. 15.45; 2 Cor. 3.6.

296. Barclay concludes that the Spirit is the 'standard of obedience' and that Paul is concerned that 'the Spirit be applied to concrete moral behaviour' in the community (1988: 155). This study shows more specifically how the Spirit constitutes a 'standard for obedience' according to theo-ethical reasoning as it is 'applied' to community behavioural issues in the practice of spiritual discernment.

297. Betz (1979: 291–92) and Kuck (1994: 290) argue that the theme of self-examination holds the section 5.25–6.10 together. We suggest that the theme of *community* spiritual discernment accomplishes this goal.

298. See Bultmann 1924: 123–40; Barclay 1988: 155.

299. Burton 1921: 322; cf. 3.3; 5.5, 16, 18.

300. *Pace* Martyn, whose interpretation separates Paul's theology from his ethics. For Martyn the 'walk' according to the Spirit (5.16) becomes merely derivative of the once-for-all-time, previously given life. Thus, 'ethics' become merely a celebration of what already has taken place with finality. As this study has shown, 5.1–4 belies Martyn's interpretation.

301. See LSJ, 1647–48.

behavioural discernment is grounded in the collective practice of spiritual discernment by those who engage in theo-ethical reasoning.

In fact, he uses the same verb στοιχέω in 6.16, suggesting that the Galatians are to 'walk in line with this rule'. We suggest that this behavioural 'rule' (κανών) to which he refers in 6.16 is Christ's cruciform pattern that has become the universal standard for the conduct of Jews and Gentiles in God's new creation. Thus, in 5.25 and 6.16, Paul brings together once again the motifs of spatial and ethical dualism. He conjoins them to establish that life in God's new creation is being divinely wrought in connection with conduct that conforms to the pattern of the cross, Christ's cruciform pattern of self-giving love for others.

In 5.26–6.10 Paul then turns to describe in greater detail the appearance of conduct that conforms to Christ's cruciform pattern. Throughout these verses, Paul's theo-ethical reasoning dominates the logic of his argument and exhortation that has a specific application in the churches of Galatia.[302]

Without becoming expressly prescriptive, Paul hypothetically addresses the issue of a community member who might be detected (προλημφθῇ) in some transgression (6.1). As shown in connection with 1 Corinthians 14, this may occur during the community practice of spiritual discernment.[303] Paul's characterization of some Galatians as 'spiritual ones' (οἱ πνευματικοί) parallels the use of this terminology in 1 Cor. 2.15 and 3.1, another passage involving the practice of spiritual discernment to determine the connections between conduct and experience.[304] In Gal. 6.1 Paul encourages the 'spiritual ones' to restore the transgressor to a right mind (καταρτίζετε)[305] by a 'spirit of gentleness'. It is suggested that the phrase 'spiritual ones' refers to those members of the Galatian churches who remain committed to Christ's cruciform pattern as their exclusive standard for behaviour and are still practising spiritual discernment.[306] Paul thus implies a collective community process for admonishing a transgressor. The goal of this process – restoring the person to a right mind – is to help the person grow in faith by achieving a more confident understanding that Christ-conforming conduct proves to be a believer's means of access to experiences of new life through the power of God (cf. 1 Cor. 1.10; 14.20–25; 1 Thess. 3.10).

Paul exhorts them in Gal. 6.2 to 'bear one another's burdens', another phrase that characterizes conduct conforming to Christ's cruciform pattern. The emphatic placement of ἀλλήλων at the beginning of the verse highlights once again the

302. For this latter conclusion, see Barclay 1988: 153–54.

303. Indeed, Martyn implies that 6.1 involves discernment of specific transgressions according to the Spirit, who provides criteria for identifying actions that destroy community life (1997b: 546).

304. See Chapter 2, sections 3.d and 3.e above.

305. For this translation, see LSJ, 910; see also Burton 1921: 327–28; Martyn 1997b: 546. Paul employs this verb in the context of restoring community agreement on matters relating to conduct. See 1 Cor. 1.10; 2 Cor. 13.11; 1 Thess. 3.10. In 1 Thess. 3.10, Paul specifically tells the church that he wishes to come to them again to restore what is lacking in their faith. By this he means that he wants to restore their faith by giving them greater confidence as he persuades them about the essential link between their experiences of new life and conduct that conforms to Christ's cruciform pattern.

306. For a discussion of many of the different permutations of what Paul might mean by the phrase, see Dunn 1993a: 318–20.

other-directedness of such conduct (see 1.4; 2.20; 5.13–14). This establishes a stark contrast with 5.26, where Paul uses the same word twice in connection with conduct that is destroying community cohesion and manifesting the 'works of the Flesh'.

In 6.2 Paul concludes that bearing one another's burdens will fulfil (ἀναπλη-ρώσετε) the law of Christ. In 6.2, as well as 5.14, he probably refers to the behavioural law associated with the new and eternal life that has been revealed through the crucified and risen Christ (see also Rom. 8.2).[307] He reinterprets the Jewish conviction that God promises life through law observance (cf. Rom. 7.10; 10.5; Gal. 3.12). According to Paul's reasoning, Christ's cruciform pattern of self-giving love for others has now become universal law – the universal norm for conduct associated with experiences of new life from God. 'No wonder this love can be described as "the law of Christ" (6:2): mutual burden bearing is precisely to *be Christ* to one another' (Barclay 2002: 144, original emphasis). Paul thus emphasizes the revelation of Jesus Christ that takes place from time to time in connection with conduct that conforms to his cruciform pattern (cf. 4.14; 1 Cor. 1.7–8).

In Gal. 6.1 and 6.3 Paul also includes an element of warning to those practising spiritual discernment. The participants must be attentive to the way they seek to restore the transgressor, lest they might be tempted to act in a way that does not faithfully portray the cruciform pattern (cf. Martyn 1997b: 547). This begins a series of such warnings that persist throughout the remainder of the section. Paul emphasizes the need to reflect consistently on all aspects of community life.[308] In 6.3 he amplifies his concern for maintaining Christ-conforming humility at all times, cautioning 'the spiritual ones' not to deceive themselves by thinking they are important.

In 6.4–5 Paul makes explicit what has only been strongly implied to this point. A person must reflect on conduct and experience and, where necessary, modify future behaviour in order to conform to Christ's cruciform pattern. He exhorts the Galatians to let each person prove his or her own conduct through testing (δοκιμαζέτω ἕκαστος).[309] Paul thus alludes to the practice of spiritual discernment that involves reflecting on conduct and experience to identify whether one is experiencing life in the present evil age or life in God's kingdom (see 5.19–23). With this discipline, believers prove through testing what actions conform to God's will because they faithfully portray Christ's cruciform pattern. Continuing to experience new life from God is thereby linked with doing good to all people according to Christ's cruciform pattern. It is proven through testing by those who practise spiritual discernment to identify the experiences of new life that divinely confirm such actions (cf. 6.8–10).

The imperative in 6.6 (κοινωνείτω) suggests that the Galatians should continue as partners in the gospel (see also 1 Cor. 1.9; 9.23; Phil. 1.5; 4.15). As the

---

307. See Barclay 1988: 134; Martyn 1997b: 549; cf. Dunn 1993a: 322.

308. Cf. Betz 1979: 291–92; Kuck 1994: 290.

309. See LSJ, 442. Paul consistently uses the verb δοκιμάζω in the context of proving through reflective testing that one's conduct conforms to the will of God. See, e.g., Rom. 1.18; 12.2; 14.22; 1 Cor. 3.13; 11.28; 2 Cor. 8.8, 22; 13.5; Phil. 1.10; 1 Thess. 2.4; 5.21.

ones being instructed about Christ's embodied message of cruciformity (ὁ κατηχούμενος τὸν λόγον), they are encouraged to provide material support for those who Paul left behind.[310] It seems that Paul left behind teachers to help guide the Galatians in their practice of spiritual discernment (cf. 1 Cor. 4.17). Such action further exemplifies the mutual support (see Gal. 6.1–2) and service (see 5.13–14, 22) that Paul has been advocating. Paul uses κατηχέω in 6.6, a verb he usually employs to characterize the means by which a person articulates the links between experiences of new life and divinely confirmed actions that conform to Christ's cruciform pattern.[311]

Applying the common imagery of sowing and reaping that he also uses in 1 Cor. 15.36–46, Paul offers an eschatological warning in Gal. 6.7 grounded in God's just dealings with humanity.[312] He exhorts them not to be led astray (see also 1 Cor. 6.9; 15.33). He implies that by following the Judaizing teachers and refusing to support the catechetical instructors he left behind, the Galatians' own conduct (i.e. the seed that is sowed)[313] will reflect contempt for God (cf. Gal. 1.6; 2.21). Such conduct will not be tolerated by God and will be repaid in the final judgment (the harvest).

Paul shifts the focus of the metaphorical imagery in 6.8 from the seed representing the Galatians' own conduct to the two different types of soil into which that seed might be sown (Martyn 1997b: 553). In this case the soil metaphorically signifies the spatial realm where a particular power works in connection with specific conduct that conforms to the standards of that particular realm. Paul skilfully exploits the semantic ambiguity of σάρξ[314] as he weaves together four threads: (1) his exegetical work (see 4.23, 29; 5.13–14); (2) his reinterpretation through Ps. 142.2 of the Jewish-Christian atonement formula, whereby Jews and Gentiles will be justified from faith and experience new life in connection with conduct that conforms to Christ's cruciform pattern; (3) the Judaizing teachers' stress on physical circumcision of the flesh (see 5.11; 6.12–13); and (4) Paul's own reflections on the manifestations of power associated with the Flesh (cf. 5.19–21) and the Spirit (5.22–23). He warns the person who is sowing into the soil of a person's own flesh, seemingly referring to those who abandoned Christ's cruciform pattern by submitting to circumcision with its commitment to conform entirely to the law's pattern of behaviour. This person shall reap corruption and experience life in the present evil age when the powers associated with the Flesh work their manifest effects in connection with such worldly conduct.

Conversely, says Paul in 6.8, the one sowing into (εἰς) the soil of the Spirit will reap 'eternal life' from the Spirit. The phrase 'sowing into the Spirit' constitutes the metaphorical equivalent of the imperatives in 5.16 and 5.25b, where Paul encourages the Galatians to take specific actions that are imaginatively

---

310. According to Martyn, Gal. 6.6 refers to those who Paul left behind, whose material existence may be threatened by the Judaizers (1997b: 551–52).

311. See, e.g., 1 Cor. 14.19; cf. Rom. 2.18; Acts 18.25.

312. For the latter conclusion, see Betz 1979: 307; Barclay 1988: 164, including n. 63.

313. See Chapter 3, section 4.e above for a similar discussion in the context of 1 Cor. 15.35–58.

314. Barclay 1988: 212; Martyn 1997b: 553.

envisioned by means of the Spirit who is active in the practice of spiritual dis-cernment.[315] The phrase denotes behaviour that believers *anticipate* will conform to Christ's cruciform pattern because the Spirit has illuminated for them the *past* links between such behaviour and their experiences of new life. The phrase 'eter-nal life' signifies Paul's conviction that God faithfully gives new life perpetually to those who continue to inhabit God's new spatial realm/temporal age in Christ. This 'eternal life' is presently experienced in earthly life in connection with Christ-conforming actions and experienced in the future as resurrection life after death.

Paul continues to use the agricultural imagery of the harvest in 6.9–10. He exhorts the Galatians not to lose heart but to continue 'doing the good' and to 'work the good' for which there will be a harvest in God's time. He echoes his discussion in 4.18 (cf. 5.22), where he encouraged the Galatians to remain zealous in a 'good thing', whether or not he was present with them. Thus, he encourages them to continue portraying Christ's cruciform pattern (cf. 3.27) as they are led by the Spirit, with the assurance that God continues to effectuate new life in connection with such conduct in order to build up and give growth to the community.

Moreover, in 6.10, Paul exhorts them to 'work the good to everyone', but especially to the members of the family of 'the faith'. While Paul reinforces their commitment of mutual service to one another in the churches (cf. 5.13–14), he also implies that they should model Christ's cruciform pattern in relationships with those outside the churches. In this way others might receive a 'revelation of Jesus Christ', just as Paul and the Galatians have also experienced (cf. 1.16; 3.1). Through such behaviour, believers may participate with the Spirit to help illumi-nate for others these experiences of new life in God's new spatial realm in Christ. By doing so, they follow the example that Paul set for them (see 3.1–5; 4.12–20).

Paul's reference to the members of the family of 'the faith' further emphasizes the central role of Christ's cruciform pattern in the churches (see 1.22–23). Members of the household of 'the faith' are those who continue to believe in the life-giving power of God that raised Christ from the dead and that gives them new earthly life in connection with conduct that conforms to Christ's cruciform pattern. Moreover, those in the household of 'the faith' know that these experi-ences of new earthly life ground their hope in the reality of future resurrection life after death.

6. The Letter's Closing Suggests Its Purpose (6.11–18)

Paul closes the letter in 6.11–18 by integrating once again the three motifs of spatial, temporal, and ethical dualism. He recapitulates the letter's weightier argu-ments and makes a final statement about the letter's central purpose and message that were introduced in the opening paragraph (Bryant 2001: 226, including n. 1).

---

315. Barclay concludes that 'the choice of sowing to the Spirit or Flesh is the choice of a person's basic direction in life', since 'Paul can admit only these two possibilities which signify, for him, the choice between obeying and disobeying the truth' (1988: 165).

Throughout the letter, Paul has contrasted alternative responses to the gospel of Christ – distinguishing between the responses of the Judaizing teachers and his own response to the God who called him through power according to 1.15 (Bryant 2001: 227). Paul contrasts the focus by some Galatians on circumcision and law-observant behaviour with his own gospel that proclaims God's apocalyptic (i.e. revelatory) act in Jesus Christ. God sent Christ into the world to act in ways that conform to God's will – including his voluntary self-giving love for others manifest in his death on the cross – and to be raised to new life through the power of God. As a consequence, Christ's cruciform pattern of self-giving love for others has become the universal and exclusive standard for conduct by which humanity may experience this life-giving power of God.

By attributing to the Judaizing teachers the desire to avoid persecution for the cross of Christ (6.12), Paul contrasts their merely human, worldly perspective (cf. 1.1, 10; 1 Cor. 1.18, 23–24) with his own steadfast commitment to conform to Christ's cruciform pattern even in the face of persecution. He thereby links the Judaizer's cause to that of the 'false brothers' in Jerusalem (see Gal. 2.4–5). He associates their motives with the same fear that drove Peter's destructive law-observant actions in Antioch (see 2.11–14). Those who compel Gentiles to be circumcised and to live as Jews according to the law (2.3, 14) pervert the gospel of Christ (1.7). They fail to conduct themselves according to the truth of the gospel – that divine event that takes place in the revelation of Jesus Christ, who manifests the life-giving power of God in connection with cruciform actions.

Paul reasserts the Judaizers' commitment to a worldly pattern of conduct in 6.13. He accuses them of boasting in the Galatians' flesh rather than in the cross of Christ (cf. 6.4), through which Paul and the old cosmos have been crucified to one another (6.14). Every person who belongs to Christ 'crucified the Flesh' (5.24) by dying intentionally to the standards and practices of the present order (see 2.17–18; 1 Cor. 15.31).[316] Paul and all those who crucified the Flesh have been 'crucified with Christ' (see Gal. 2.19), making a commitment to conform their actions to Christ's cruciform pattern rather than any of the behavioural standards of the world. This commitment carries ongoing significance for their lives. The inaugurating Christ event becomes an existentially-present event that happens anew in 'the revelation of Jesus Christ' that takes place in the world from time to time (see Barclay 2002: 146). Indeed, these revelations of Jesus Christ and the 'identity-defining story of Christ' completely redefine the lives of Paul and other believers, who are now 'dead to any other sphere of influence (6.14)' (Horrell 2002: 171).

Thus, Paul declares in 6.15 that all the worldly standards for conduct no longer carry power (cf. 5.6). Instead (ἀλλά), the only thing that now reflects any power is 'new creation'. His terminology highlights how he integrates the three motifs of spatial, temporal, and ethical dualism to create a contrast. On the one hand is life in the new creation. This new life is divinely wrought and experienced in connection with conduct that conforms to Christ's cruciform pattern. On

---

316. Cf. Martyn 1997b: 564.

the other hand is life in the old world (cf. 6.14), the present evil age that continues to be shaped by the power of worldly forces (cf. 4.3, 9) working in conjunction with actions that conform to the behavioural standards of the world.

Based on this contrast of power in 6.15, the phrase καινὴ κτίσις probably refers to the new, creative activity of God (see Bryant 2001: 160).[317] Paul correlates the cross, the supreme symbol of Christ's cruciform pattern of self-giving love for others, with the power of God, who raised Jesus from the dead to inaugurate the new age (see 1.1, 4; cf. 3.22–25). The people of God are invited to participate in God's new creation in Christ – God's new spatial realm/temporal age – by conforming their own actions to Christ's cruciform pattern and experiencing new life through the power of God. According to our interpretation of the letter, believers spiritually discern this behavioural and experiential participation in the new creation by practising spiritual discernment, engaging in theo-ethical reasoning to look for life in the manifestations of the Spirit (cf. Bryant 2001: 161).

Paul pronounces a blessing in 6.16 upon all those who walk in line with (στοιχήσουσιν) this 'rule' of cruciformity. He thereby refers once again to the links between experiences of God's life-giving power and conduct that conforms to this 'rule' – that is, Christ's cruciform pattern.[318] By means of conduct conforming to the cruciform 'rule' – that is, to the 'law of Christ' (6.2) – believers experience new life in God's new creation in Christ.[319]

Paul probably uses the phrase 'Israel of God' in the blessing, a phrase often alluding to the Jewish understanding of the 'remnant', because the Judaizers first introduced the concept in the course of their argument for law observance.[320] Paul entered the debate, however, contending that the remnant (the 'Israel of God') is now being divinely constituted in connection with conduct that conforms to Christ's cruciform pattern rather than the law.[321]

---

317. For this concept in the Septuagint, see Isa. 42.9; 43.18–19; 65.17; 66.22; cf. Rom. 5.17–21.

318. Cf. 2 Cor. 10.15. According to Barclay, this κανών governs the existence of every person in Christ (2002: 138).

319. Hubbard has recently concluded that Paul's own experience of the crucified and risen Christ grounds his understanding of new creation as an anthropological matter of personal conversion (2002: 240–41). While Paul's language of new creation certainly *includes* this element of personal conversion – emphasized in this study as the believer's commitment to conform to Christ's cruciform pattern – this does not exclude the possibility that Paul *also* includes community and cosmic components in his understanding of God's new creation. We contend that the phrase 'new creation' for Paul includes individual, social, and cosmic dimensions, since Paul understood that the individual human body has no reality apart from its participation in larger bodies identified with greater cosmic realities. See now D. Martin (1995: 131, 133), discussed above at n. 2. Hubbard does not acknowledge or respond to Martin's work or these particular conclusions in the context of Paul's 'new creation'.

320. For this latter suggestion, see R. Longenecker 1990: 298; Bryant 2001: 221.

321. As E.P. Sanders has concluded, no group within late Second Temple Judaism boldly proclaimed itself *exclusively* as 'Israel' or as the remnant of Israel (1977: 250, including n. 35). They simply recognized that the 'remnant' existed and protected Israel from complete annihilation. While Paul was certainly aware of the 'remnant' tradition (cf. Rom. 9.27; 11.5), he never associated it directly with the church and certainly not with the Gentile churches. As with all other sectarian Jewish groups of the period that were participants in the discourse of revelatory authority (see Polaski

7. Conclusion

Throughout the letter, Paul has reflected on conduct and experience to illustrate theo-ethical reasoning. He consistently makes the connection between conduct that conforms to Christ's cruciform pattern and the experiences of new life being wrought through the power of God that raised Jesus from the dead. Paul uses the phrase 'new creation' in 6.15 to characterize God's apocalyptic activity that inaugurated the new age. Jesus was sent into the world (4.4) to give himself voluntarily for others on the cross according to the will of God and to be raised from the dead – central themes that Paul asserted in the letter's opening at 1.1 and 1.4 (cf. Bryant 2001: 229). This divine event established the new and universal cruciform pattern for conduct by Gentiles and Jews through which God is working to carry out God's cosmic plan that gives new and eternal life to all believers, even resurrection life after death.

Paul's central focus has been to encourage the Galatians to remain committed to the 'rule' of cruciformity, even in the face of persecution (3.4; 6.17). They must walk in line with the Spirit to continue experiencing new and eternal life (see 5.25) through the power of God that prevails in God's new spatial realm/ temporal age in Christ. In this realm of new creation, believers were delivered out of the present evil age. Moreover, if they are to continue as residents in God's new creation, they must remain steadfastly committed to being led by the Spirit in the practice of spiritual discernment. They must continue to engage in theo-ethical reasoning to look for life in the manifestations of the Spirit that confirm actions conforming to Christ's cruciform pattern. This practice of reflecting on the links between conduct and experience leads to growth in the faith, as believers are divinely persuaded that Christ-conforming conduct is the exclusive pathway to experiences of new and eternal life through the power of God that prevails in God's new creation in Christ.

1999: 43), Paul never made the claim that his own interpretation of what God was doing in the world was the exclusive definition of 'Israel'.

Chapter 5

CONCLUSION

1. *Introduction*

Through historical reconstruction this study has challenged the adequacy of three interrelated foci of twentieth-century Protestant Pauline interpretation: (1) the separation of Paul's theology from his ethics; (2) the overemphasis on his oral preaching as the primary means of gospel proclamation and divine revelation; and (3) the denial that Paul engages in reasoned ethical reflection. Following Keck's proposal, this study has looked beneath the surface of 1 Corinthians and Galatians and focused on the logic of Paul's arguments and reasoning (see Keck 1996a: 3–16). We identified Paul's consistent pattern of reasoning by which he analyses and responds to behavioural issues. This confirmed the hypothesis that Paul theologizes by combining theology and ethics as he engages in theo-ethical reasoning, effectively integrating Christian living and thinking. We have depicted Paul as an active participant in the divine–human partnership in Jesus Christ, a pastoral theologian who builds Christian communities by working with God to persuade people that conduct conforming to Christ's cruciform pattern constitutes the pathway to experiences of new earthly life and the hope of eternal resurrection life after death.

The study developed this approach through exegesis of 1 Corinthians and Galatians. In Chapter 5, section 2 we summarize our findings. Implications for contemporary scholarship are reviewed in section 3. We show certain connections between the contemporary theory of discourse (communicative) ethics and Paul's theo-ethical reasoning that shapes the practice of spiritual discernment in section 4, tentatively confirming the heuristic benefits of exploring these similarities.[1] The study closes with a short conclusion in section 5.

2. *Summary*

Chapter 2 identified Paul's theo-ethical reasoning and the practice of spiritual discernment in 1 Corinthians 1.1–4.21. It highlighted how Paul's conduct and speech interpret to others what God has done and is doing in the world through the death and resurrection of Jesus Christ. The chapter established that, for Paul, the revelation of Christ's cruciform pattern of self-giving love for others has become the universal behavioural standard for both Jews and Greeks. Believers

---

1. For this proposal, see Horrell 1999: 321–25, discussed in Chapter 1, section 3.

experience new life in God's new age in connection with conduct that conforms to this new norm. Moreover, we showed how Paul directs the Corinthians' attention to the link between his own Christ-conforming conduct and that demonstration of Spirit and power that first grounded their faith in the power of God.

Chapter 2 also illuminated how believers are to practise spiritual discernment by engaging in theo-ethical reasoning. This process of comparing spiritual experiences emphasizes the central role of the Spirit for community behavioural discernment in the deliberative assembly. Paul presents the Spirit as the divine agent who guides church members to perceive their experiences of new life, manifesting where God's life-giving power may be linked to specific conduct that conforms to Christ's cruciform pattern.

It was further shown in Chapter 2 that Paul uses the motifs of temporal, spatial, and ethical dualism to contrast these experiences of new and eternal life in God's new age/spatial realm in Christ with experiences of life in the world that is perishing. For instance, Paul uses the phrase τοῦ αἰῶνος τούτου (1 Cor. 1.20; 2.6, 8; see also 2 Cor. 4.4) to imply a contrast with God's new age inaugurated with the death and resurrection of Jesus Christ. Similarly, he uses the phase τοῦ κόσμου τούτου (1 Cor. 3.19; see also 5.10; 7.31; cf. Eph. 2.2) to imply a contrast with the spatial realm he calls the kingdom of God (see 1 Cor. 4.20), where believers experience new and eternal life 'in Christ' through the power of God (see 1.4, 29–30; cf. 4.20). With this terminology, Paul constructs an alternative social world, pressing the distinction between earthly life in Christ – where the new and old ages and worlds overlap   and life in the wider society and world (see Adams 2000: 114). For Paul, this realm outside of Christ remains subject to destruction because its inhabitants continue to conform to its behavioural standards rather than the universal standard of cruciformity. This new behavioural norm manifest in Christ's death on the cross for others – the cruciform pattern – now governs new and eternal life in God's new age/spatial realm in Christ.[2]

Through exegesis of 1 Cor. 5.1–16.24, Chapter 3 highlighted two key aspects of Christian existence for Paul. First, the chapter showed how he consistently argues in a variety of contexts that believers must conform their behaviour to Christ's cruciform pattern of self-giving love for others. Second, it established how Paul consistently practises spiritual discernment, engaging in theo-ethical reasoning to link specific actions to community experiences. The chapter illuminated how God's life-giving power experienced in connection with Christ-conforming conduct grounds believers' hope in the future reality of embodied resurrection life after death. Paul thereby integrates Christian living and thinking, bringing together theology and ethics as he tries to transform community perceptions by aligning them with his cosmic, apocalyptic (i.e. revelatory) perspective.

Chapter 4 demonstrated that in Galatians Paul practises spiritual discernment by engaging in theo-ethical reasoning to associate conduct with experience. It established how Paul sets Christ's cruciform pattern as the new and universal

---

2.   Cf. Adams (2000: 148–49), who concludes that for Paul the apocalyptic event of the cross overthrew the values and ordering structures of 'this world', as Paul embraces alternative forms of sociality, patterns of living, and community ideals.

behavioural norm by which both Jews and Gentiles alike become 'one in Christ Jesus' (Gal. 3.28). He encourages the Galatians to remain like him, committed to this 'rule' of cruciformity, even in the face of persecution from those advocating circumcision and law observance. The chapter showed how Paul uses spatial, temporal, and ethical dualism to contrast life in God's new spatial realm/temporal age in Christ, lived according to the 'rule' of cruciformity, with temporally-limited life in 'the present evil age', lived according to the world's behavioural norms that include the law.

The chapter once again pointed to the central role of the Spirit and the related practice of spiritual discernment for behavioural guidance in Paul's communities. Believers must walk in line with the Spirit if they are to continue experiencing new life in God's new creation in Christ. The chapter concluded that, for Paul, it is critical for his churches to identify these connections between Christ-conforming conduct and experiences of God's life-giving power. By spiritually discerning these connections with Paul's help, believers are persuaded by God that conduct conforming to Christ's cruciform pattern is the pathway to new life in God's new creation in Christ. Thus, acting with faith in Christ by conforming one's actions to his cruciform pattern becomes the human means of access to experiences of new and eternal life from God. These experiences, in turn, ground believers' hope in future resurrection life after death.

These exegetical results show the fruitfulness of Keck's proposal. The interpreter attempting to do 'New Testament ethics' must bring to the surface the rationale or moral reasoning that undergirds enjoined morality in biblical texts, even when that rationale is not apparent on the surface of the texts.[3] Substantively, our results suggest that for Paul there is a consistent pattern of reasoning that underlies his evaluation of behavioural issues and discernment of the will of God. Paul's theo-ethical reasoning reflects his understanding of the divine–human partnership in Jesus Christ and the role of Spirit-led, Christ-conforming conduct in God's plan for transforming the world into the new creation in Christ. As believers practise spiritual discernment by engaging in theo-ethical reasoning, they regularly make the discernible connections between Christ-conforming human conduct and experiences of God's life-giving power. By consistently looking for life in one or more revelations/manifestations of the Spirit, believers grow more persuaded (i.e. they grow in faith) that conduct conforming to Christ's cruciform pattern constitutes the human means of access to other experiences of new life in God's kingdom. This association grounds their faith in the power of God and their hope of eternal resurrection life after death.

3. *Implications for Contemporary Scholarship*

If these contentions are accepted, then there are a number of implications for Pauline scholarship. First, the study confirms the general conclusion of Sally Baker Purvis that Paul's apostolic ministry did not find completion in his oral

---

3. See Keck 1996a: 8, discussed in Chapter 1, section 4.

proclamation, despite the fact that preaching was foundational and central to Paul's mission (Purvis 1993: 70). We have shown that Paul's gospel demanded that it be enacted in the lives of the persons who heard and saw it lived out in Paul's own Christ-conforming actions (cf. Purvis 1993: 70).

Similarly, we have shown that for Paul there is a discernible link between Christ-conforming conduct and the experience of new life through the power of God. We concluded that this connection lies at the heart of theo-ethical reasoning and the practice of spiritual discernment. These findings confirm two observations made by Neil Elliott. First, Paul engages in the constant interplay of praxis and reflection – 'critical reflection on praxis' (Elliott 1994: 83, citing Gutiérrez 1973: 300).[4] Second, Paul's so-called 'theology' does not establish a system of doctrinal beliefs, but emphasizes the importance of applied theology in practical behavioural situations (Elliott 1994: 83; see also Hurtado 2000: 185). Paul thereby combines what are commonly distinguished as theology and ethics in the context of his ministry as a pastoral theologian. His ministry focuses on working with God to build Christian communities through God's life-giving power associated with Christ-conforming conduct.

Moreover, the link we found Paul making between Christ-conforming conduct and experiences of God's life-giving power confirms Schütz's important thesis that Paul interprets the power of God to others (see Schütz 1975). Our exegesis has shown, however, that Schütz over-emphasizes Paul's oral preaching as the exclusive or primary vehicle by which Paul communicated the power of God to others. Rather, we have shown that Paul's behavioural interpretation of Christ crucified constitutes a central component in the way that he communicates and mediates God's life-giving power to others. Paul and other believers participate in the divine event that Paul calls gospel by means of their own Christ-conforming conduct. Through that conduct, the revelation of Jesus Christ takes place as God's life-giving power becomes manifest as the lives of others in the community are enriched (see 1 Cor. 1.4–9). In this way the power of God is active and recognizable in history in the experiences of Paul and other believers, whose actions conform to the pattern of Christ crucified (see Horrell 2002: 156–60).

This study also illuminates Engberg-Pedersen's conclusion that Paul comes to know Christ by 'personal acquaintance' in the context of revelation (Engberg-Pedersen 2000: 95), as we showed in connection with Gal. 1.16 (cf. Phil. 3.10). We have not only confirmed his conclusion, but shown how Paul attempts to bring all believers to this same relationship with Christ by helping them associate their experiences of God's life-giving power with the embodied proclamation of Christ crucified.

Two related conclusions of this study affirm and build on aspects of the recent work of Engberg-Pedersen. First, Paul advocates that Christ's cruciform pattern has become the universal behavioural norm by which believers experience new life as they are divinely justified by means of their faith in Christ. Second, God is building up the spiritual, social body of Christ in connection with conduct that

4. Elliott adds the phrase 'in light of the word of God', which may differentiate his finding from the one in this study, although he does not elaborate.

conforms to this cruciform pattern. These conclusions thereby amplify Engberg-Pedersen's findings that: (1) Paul theologizes by describing a general scheme for a Christian 'form of human living' (see Engberg-Pedersen 2000: 47); and (2) Paul creates congregations engaged in this shared form of life grounded in Christ's death and resurrection (see Engberg-Pedersen 2000: 37).

On the other hand, this study challenges Engberg-Pedersen's additional conclusion that Christian practice is the ultimate goal of Paul's theologizing (Engberg-Pedersen 2000: 295). We have shown that Paul's ultimate goal is for all believers, by means of Christ-conforming actions, to become active participants in God's plan to carry through to completion the new creation that became a present reality in the death and resurrection of Jesus Christ. Paul structures community life to facilitate this objective. By engaging in theo-ethical reasoning in the practice of spiritual discernment, believers recognize experiences of God's life-giving power associated with Christ-conforming conduct. They are thereby led by the Spirit into new life as they walk by the κανών of Christ's cruciform pattern, as God shapes community life in God's new creation in Christ in connection with such conduct.

Thus, the present study incorporates Paul's theological/moral reasoning as an essential component of our historical reconstruction. His theo-ethical reasoning is the means by which Paul aligns theology with ethics and integrates aspects of Christian thinking and living. Unlike Engberg-Pedersen, who would probably deem this reasoning process inaccessible to modern readers, the interpreter must incorporate this reasoning in order to present an adequate historical reconstruction rather than fashioning an accessible contemporary theology.

Further, we suggest that this association between conduct and experience may also constitute that 'new category of perception' sought by E.P. Sanders to explain Paul's language about participation in Christ (1977: 522–23). We have shown that, for Paul, demonstrations of Spirit and power ground believers' faith in the power of God. It has also been established that believers who practise spiritual discernment by engaging in theo-ethical reasoning are led by the Spirit to perceive these gifts of new life being experienced in connection with Christ-conforming conduct. This is the means by which all believers come to know Christ and the power of his resurrection, sharing in his suffering and being conformed to his death (see Phil. 3.10). Thus, we tentatively conclude that this reflected integration of conduct and experience constitutes that 'category of reality – real participation in Christ, real possession of the Spirit' that lies 'between naïve cosmological speculation and belief in magical transference on the one hand' and simply a revised self-understanding on the other (see E.P. Sanders 1977: 522–23).

In a related context, the present study also shows why other scholars have recently agreed that 'Pauline theology' is better understood as an activity called theologizing than as a set of theological propositions or presuppositions about how Paul understands God.[5] The present study has shown that the centre of Paul's theology does not lie in propositional or doctrinal terms. Instead, Paul

---

5. See Bassler 1993: 10–11; Kraftchick 1993b: 23; Engberg-Pedersen 2000: 15, 47, 79; Hays 1996a: 56 n. 7.

theologizes by consistently practising spiritual discernment as he engages in theo-ethical reasoning to associate Christ-conforming conduct with experiences of God's life-giving power. Through this practice, Paul the pastoral theologian continues to identify where God is manifestly effecting new life in the world in connection with Christ-conforming conduct.

These conclusions also suggest that Gorman makes an artificial and unnecessary distinction when he asserts that Paul's letters are less theological than 'pastoral or spiritual' since Gorman claims the letters focus on what he calls 'spiritual formation' (Gorman 2001: 4). This study has shown that the letters incorporate Paul's theo-ethical reasoning and are indeed pastoral and spiritual. Paul helps believers recognize and understand the important links between Christ-conforming conduct and experiences of new life from God as part of Spirit-led discernment. The letters and Paul's theo-ethical reasoning are also theological, however, since they focus on discernible experiences of God's life-giving power and it is God who sends the Spirit to illuminate these experiences associated with divinely approved, Christ-conforming behaviour.

Thus, this study provides a corrective to those interpreters who conclude that Paul is convinced that humans and their actions are controlled by the invasion of powers from outside the person. It has concluded that, for Paul, these external powers bring about certain community/relational *experiences* in connection with specific human behaviour. We conclude that humans participate in the power of God or with worldly powers by virtue of their specific actions. The study thereby highlights Paul's understanding that there is a divine–human partnership in Jesus Christ in which God and humans work together to realize God's cosmic plan to redeem the world from the powers that enslave it. In this cosmic warfare, believers become participants with God by conforming their behaviour to Christ's cruciform pattern. Thus, as Paul shows in his own lifestyle and as he exhorts others to follow, imitating Christ is not an impossibility (contra Gorman 2001: 49, 299, 400). Instead, it is constitutive of believers' participation in God's new creation in Christ.

The study further confirms that, for Paul, divine justification/sinlessness involves moral transformation, is recognizable as behaviour, and perceptible as human experience (contra Bultmann 1924: 136, 140). Indeed, we have concluded that, for Paul, the revelation of Jesus Christ takes place in connection with Christ-conforming conduct that may be linked to demonstrations of Spirit and power that ground believers' faith in the power of God. Spiritually discerning these manifest links between conduct and experience becomes the means by which believers prove through testing the divine confirmation of behaviour that is pleasing to God.

Moreover, as we suggested in connection with Paul's discussion of prophecy in 1 Corinthians 14 (see Chapter 3, section 3.d), these Spirit-illuminated connections between experience and conduct also point the way forward for believers' behaviour. Extrapolating from Paul's discussion of prophecy in 1 Corinthians 14, we tentatively conclude that, for him, prophecy is grounded in these *past* associations between Christ-conforming conduct and experiences of new life. These connections lead believers to envisage imaginatively *future* actions that they *anticipate* will conform to Christ's cruciform pattern and be divinely confirmed through other experiences of God's life-giving power that represent the fruit of such behaviour.

We thus affirm Furnish's conclusion that Paul insisted on the urgency of discerning God's will in his churches and presupposed that it was a practical possibility (1968: 233). Unlike Furnish, however, the study has also identified how this was taking place in Paul's churches, as believers practise spiritual discernment by engaging in theo-ethical reasoning. This means that Paul consistently practised critical reflection on the relationship between his behavioural concerns and his theological convictions about the discernible power of God.[6]

Moreover, our focus on the *external* role of the Spirit as the divine revelatory agent in the community practice of spiritual discernment establishes that the Spirit plays a direct role in practical human decisions and actions (contra Furnish 1968: 232). By following the Spirit's lead in the practice of spiritual discernment, believers come to know God and Christ when they identify God's demonstrated power associated with Christ-conforming behaviour. This establishes a link for Paul between what Martyn calls 'epistemology' and Christ-conforming human conduct. It also means that this knowledge is not just about human self-understanding and identity – that is, it is not wholly cognitive, a state of mind (contra Engberg-Pedersen 2000: 128). Instead, this knowledge derives from the collective community recognition of God's life-giving power that becomes manifest in connection with conduct that conforms to Christ's cruciform pattern.

This latter point also emphasizes the important role of community experience for Paul, thereby affirming certain conclusions of Hurtado (2000: 184), L.T. Johnson (1998: 4), Ashton (2000: 23, 26–27, 78) and Gorman (2001: 3–4). Moreover, it highlights that God in Jesus Christ becomes presently and actively manifest in the lives and experiences of believers. This occurs not just in oral proclamation but also in Christ-conforming behaviour in which the reality of Jesus Christ becomes experientially present among believers (contra Bultmann 1951: 302, 305). This also means that, for Paul, the salvation occurrence is not confined to oral preaching but involves the experiences of new life through the power of God in the context of interpersonal human relationships (see L.T. Johnson 1993: 520–36). This study has shown that, according to Paul, God's power breaks into the world and is demonstrated by means of the Spirit, who illuminates experiences of new life in the community in connection with Christ-conforming actions (contra Furnish 1968: 215). We have established that in Paul's understanding of gospel proclamation, oral preaching associates these community experiences of new life with Christ-conforming conduct, thereby proclaiming the revelation of Jesus Christ in the world.

Paul's uses of the motifs of spatial, temporal, and ethical dualism in theo-ethical reasoning illuminate several issues in Pauline interpretation. For instance,

---

6. Both Furnish (1968: 211–12) and Martyn (1997b: 502) deny that Paul engages in critical reflection on this relationship.

they shed light on Paul's locative uses of the distinctive phrase 'in Christ'.[7] The phrase seems to describe existence in that new spatial realm and temporal age that Paul characterizes as being 'in Christ'. This is the place where God's new age has descended to overlap the old age (see 1 Cor. 10.11). It is the place where earthly life is now lived according to the cruciform standard associated with the revelation in the world of Jesus Christ and 'the faith'. In this place believers experience new life through the power of God in connection with Christ-conforming conduct (see 1 Cor. 12.4–7). It is the place where the Spirit dwells among believers to guide them behaviourally by illuminating moments of new life associated with divinely confirmed, Christ-conforming conduct that serves the common good of the community.[8] This guidance takes place frequently in the deliberative assembly, where believers practise spiritual discernment by reasoning together with the mind of Christ to reflect on conduct and experience.[9]

As shown in connection with Gal. 5.2–4, however, believers may fall out of this spatial realm when they conform their actions to a behavioural standard of the world (including – astonishingly – the Mosaic law) rather than to Christ's cruciform pattern. In that case, they cut themselves off from Christ and he is no longer of any benefit to them. This suggests that, outside this new spatial realm, the risen Christ who closely examines and judges believers' conduct (1 Cor. 4.1–5) and will confirm Christ-conforming actions until the end (1 Cor. 1.8) no longer leads believers through the Spirit in their behavioural discernment. Indeed, those who are not 'in Christ' experience life that is shaped by the powers that prevail in this world in connection with conduct that conforms to the world's standards. We showed how Paul makes this contrast in passages such as 1 Cor. 3.1–4 and Gal. 5.16–25.

Paul's conviction that believers can fall out of the spatial realm 'in Christ' by virtue of their conduct underscores how important it is for believers to practise spiritual discernment by engaging in theo-ethical reasoning in the deliberative assembly. As we have shown, Paul anticipates that those who practise this discipline may be able to identify their experiences that illuminate how they participate with the power of worldly forces in conjunction with behaviour that conforms to worldly standards.[10] According to Paul, such experiences occur because believers are not adequately declaring the death of the Lord in their interactions with one another (see 1 Cor. 11.26). In that case they are being shaped into a community that mirrors the world rather than the kingdom of God 'in Christ'.

Conversely, we have established that believers who practise spiritual discernment by engaging in theo-ethical reasoning may also identify experiences of new

7. For discussions of Paul's use of 'in Christ' in 1 Corinthians and Galatians, see Chapter 1, section 3.b, Chapter 2, section 2.a, and Chapter 4, sections 2.a and 3.d. The present study does not deny that some occurrences of the phrase represent its so-called instrumental use.
8. See 1 Cor. 3.16; 6.19; 12.4–7; Gal. 5.18, 25.
9. See 1 Cor. 2.1–16; 14.1–40; Gal. 5.19–25. Paul also describes this practice in Rom. 8.1–17. He distinguishes those who walk by the Spirit by setting their minds on things of the Spirit from those who walk according to the standards of the world and set their minds on the things of the flesh.
10. See 1 Cor. 1.11; 3.3; 5.1–13; 6.1–11; 11.27–32; Gal. 5.19–21.

life in God's kingdom, where the power of God prevails in connection with Christ-conforming behaviour. Recognizing these experiences enables believers to envisage imaginatively future actions that they anticipate will conform to Christ's cruciform pattern and lead to further experiences of new life 'in Christ'. Thus, we may conclude that believers maintain their place 'in Christ' as they reflect together on conduct and experience under the leadership of the Spirit. Through this discipline, they maintain their embodied human existence in that place where God's new age has dawned in the life, death and resurrection of Jesus Christ and overlaps with life in the world. Those who practise spiritual discernment by engaging in theo-ethical reasoning maintain their existence in the body of Christ, where they experience God's life-giving power in connection with conduct that conforms to Christ's cruciform pattern.

Paul spells this out in Rom. 8.1–17, a critical passage for understanding how Paul does ethics theologically. In this passage he makes one of his most important contributions to ethical reflection.[11] The relevance of this passage for Paul's ethics is not clear, since it suggests no specific behaviour for believers. But, in the passage, the underlying logic of Paul's theo-ethical reasoning establishes the foundation for how he combines theology and ethics. Although space limitations prevent exegetical scrutiny of these verses, we will review briefly how theo-ethical reasoning may potentially illuminate difficult aspects of the passage. This will further confirm the validity of the present thesis.

In Rom. 8.1–2 Paul concludes that now there is no condemnation for those who are 'in Christ Jesus' because the 'law of the Spirit of life in Christ Jesus' freed believers from the law of sin and death.[12] In the context of Paul's theo-ethical reasoning, this refers to the way that believers experience 'life in Christ Jesus' (by means of the power of God) when they follow the 'law of the Spirit' that Paul elsewhere calls the 'the law of Christ' (Gal. 6.2; cf. 1 Cor. 9.21). By this, Paul means that those who are 'in Christ' conform their actions to Christ's cruciform pattern and experience new life through the power of God. This takes place so that the law's 'just decree' for life might be fulfilled among those walking κατὰ πνεῦμα rather than κατὰ σάρκα (Rom. 8.4).[13] Following the pattern we have already identified in theo-ethical reasoning, Paul thereby associates the new and eternal life promised by God with those who walk according to the Spirit rather than the flesh – conforming their actions to Christ's cruciform pattern rather than to the behavioural standards of the world.

Moreover, in 8.5–17, Paul describes how believers practise spiritual discernment by engaging in theo-ethical reasoning, so that they might walk κατὰ πνεῦμα. He depicts a *structure* for community life that is characteristic of his religion as

---

11. Keck observes that 'Rom. 8.1–4 is foundational for Paul's ethics, no less than for his theology' since key terms such as law, Spirit, flesh, sin and death are all used (1980: 41). In these verses, says Keck, Paul makes one of his most important contributions to ethical reflection (1980: 54). According to Beker, 'Rom 8 constitutes the crown of Paul's theological achievement' (1980: 290).

12. Of course, there is much disagreement over Paul's use of the terminology of 'law' in these verses. A determination of this issue is not necessary for the broad points addressed here.

13. For this translation and interpretation of the phrase τὸ δικαίωμα τοῦ νόμου in 8.4, see Wright 1991b: 203; cf. Keck 1980: 41–57.

we have portrayed it in this study. Believers must set their minds on the Spirit rather than the flesh if they are to experience *life* and peace rather than death (8.5–8, 13; cf. Col. 3.1–4). Addressing an issue also present in Galatians, Paul identifies the 'sons of God' as those who are being led by the Spirit of God (Rom. 8.14; cf. Gal. 3.26). The 'sons of God' are the ones who follow the Spirit in order to spiritually discern specific actions to take in faith – confidently believing that the actions will be Christ-conforming and anticipating the divine confirmation that such actions are pleasing to God and proving to be divinely fruitful through enriched life in the community.

In other words, believers must practise spiritual discernment by looking for life in the manifestations of the Spirit associated with Christ-conforming behaviour. This leads them to envision imaginatively those appropriate future actions through which they may anticipate that the same power of God that raised Jesus from the dead will also give new life to their mortal bodies (Rom. 8.11, 13; cf. 6.4). By putting to death the practices of the body that conform to worldly standards and conforming them to Christ's cruciform pattern, believers may rightly expect to experience new life from God (see 8.13; cf. Gal. 5.24; 6.14). Indeed, says Paul in Rom. 8.17, it is necessary for believers to suffer with Christ if they expect to be glorified with him (see also Phil. 3.10).

Paul's uses of the motifs of spatial, temporal, and ethical dualism in his theo-ethical reasoning confirm certain claims made by E.P. Sanders: Paul focuses on believers 'getting in and staying in' the place of divine salvation and this is somehow directly connected to believers' actions (1983: 6–10). We have shown that believers identify Christ-conforming behaviour by spiritually discerning their experiences of new life 'in Christ'. This practice confirms their standing in that place of divine salvation: God's new spatial realm and temporal age in Christ that has descended upon and overlaps with embodied human existence in the world (see 1 Cor. 10.11). By practising spiritual discernment as they engage in theo-ethical reasoning, believers associate these divinely wrought experiences of new life 'in Christ' with conduct that conforms to Christ's cruciform pattern.

Thus, our exegesis suggests that believers 'get in' and 'stay in' this place of salvation when, in their faith response to the gospel: (1) they recognize and accept the discernible links between Christ-conforming conduct and their experiences of Spirit and power that ground their faith in the power of God (see 1 Cor. 2.1–5); (2) they commit to clothe themselves with Christ (Gal. 3.28) by conforming their actions to Christ's cruciform pattern; and (3) they collectively practise spiritual discernment by engaging in theo-ethical reasoning in the deliberative assembly. This means that believers' actions may not always succeed in conforming to Christ's cruciform pattern. They practise spiritual discernment, however, in order to discern the divine confirmation of their witness of Christ (see 1 Cor. 1.5–8) or the Lord's judgment on conduct that does not conform (see 1 Cor. 11.29–32). In the latter case, they may act differently in the future in order to avoid future condemnation with the world that is doomed to destruction.

Paul's uses of these motifs of spatial, temporal, and ethical dualism also challenge certain traditional understandings of Luther's doctrine of *simul iustus et peccator* applied in connection with Pauline studies. Some interpreters find a

tension in Paul's already-not yet perspective that gives rise to the problem of
ethics in Paul. They perceive a contradiction when Paul offers moral exhortation
to sinners who are already justified. The 'problem of ethics in Paul' then arises
because some interpreters fail to recognize that, from Paul's perspective, believers may later fall out of God's new spatial realm 'in Christ' when they seek to
conform their actions to any behavioural standard other than Christ's cruciform
pattern.

Indeed, Paul's regular use of these motifs suggests that in fact he may *juxtapose* the experiences of new life from God (associated with Christ-conforming
conduct) against experiences linked to conduct that conforms to standards of
the world. In other words, a person or community may experience life in God's
kingdom or experience life outside the spatial realm 'in Christ', but cannot
experience life in both places *at the same time*.

This sheds light on Paul's understanding of what it means for believers to live
an embodied human existence 'in Christ' in the overlap of the two ages. It also
emphasizes how important it is in the structure of Paul's religion for believers to
practise spiritual discernment by engaging in theo-ethical reasoning. Believers
who practise looking for life in the manifestations of the Spirit may recognize
experiences of new life from God associated with Christ-conforming conduct.
This divinely confirms for them that they continue to live in the overlap of the
ages, where inhabitants are destined to experience the final consummation and
transformation into eternal (resurrection) life after death. It also empowers believers to envisage imaginatively future conduct through which they may anticipate
other experiences of new life wrought by God 'in Christ'. In this way believers
may keep finding in their own lives – understood as paradigms – the presence
and continuance of the Christ story, as well as God's grace/power that 'keeps
puncturing the folds of time to reenact the new creation' (Barclay 2002: 156).

Therefore, we conclude that Paul's so-called theological indicative refers to
the new and eternal resurrection life after death first made manifest when God
raised Christ from the dead to inaugurate God's new creation/new age. It also
refers to the new earthly life effected by God among those who are newly-
oriented to the Spirit and seek to walk by the Spirit in that new spatial realm 'in
Christ', where the Spirit dwells. The indicative characterizes new embodied life
in the overlap of the ages, where believers, whose bodily conduct conforms to
Christ's cruciform pattern, experience new earthly life through the same power
of God that raised Jesus from the dead.

Paul uses the imperative to suggest that believers must consistently conform
their actions to Christ's cruciform pattern if they expect to continue experiencing
new life through the power of God. By implication, he points out the direct and
discernible links between Christ-conforming human conduct and the experiences
of God's life-giving power. This power effects the edification and enrichment of
life in the community – the deliberative assembly of those who are set apart 'in
Christ' and conform their actions to his cruciform pattern.

If accepted, these conclusions would also mean that for Paul the baptismal
'victory' is *not decisive*, but must be constantly re-enacted in the daily lives of

believers.[14] We thereby affirm Luther's conclusion that believers must have some form of ongoing practice by which they unceasingly battle sin (Luther 1958: 28). This also highlights the importance of Käsemann's related insight that Christian life is 'a perpetual return to baptism' (Käsemann 1969e: 175). Believers must 'keep on the pilgrim way' and allow themselves 'to be recalled daily to the allegiance of Christ' (Käsemann 1969e: 175).

We conclude that this takes place as believers practise spiritual discernment by engaging in theo-ethical reasoning. By spiritually discerning experiences of new life that confirm Christ-conforming conduct or by spiritually discerning the manifestations of divine judgment so that their behaviour may be amended, believers remain confident that there is no condemnation 'in Christ Jesus' (see Rom. 8.1–4). By comparing spiritual experiences with spiritual experiences (1 Cor. 2.13), believers discern the will of God. They reflect together on conduct and experience to prove through testing what actions conform to the will of God (see Rom. 12.2). As they seek to be led by the Spirit in order to walk in ways that conform to Christ's cruciform pattern, believers anticipate future experiences of new life effected through the power of God in connection with such conduct (see 1 Cor. 12.4–7).

These conclusions raise a question about the adequacy of Bultmann's time-worn phrase 'become what you are' in connection with Paul's indicative/imperative, 'already/not yet' scheme. As we have shown, Paul dualistically *juxtaposes* two alternative experiential realities that are humanly discernible and shaped by observable behaviour that conforms to different norms. Bultmann's phrase effectively spiritualizes new life from God and strips it of its experiential reality.

Moreover, Bultmann denies that a believer's moral transformation in Christ is recognizable by behaviour. Conversely, he fails to acknowledge that, for Paul, this new life in God's kingdom/spatial realm 'in Christ' will not be experienced in connection with conduct that conforms to worldly standards. He fails to account adequately for the central role of the 'revelation of Jesus Christ' in Paul's religion. He underestimates Paul's language about the *manifest* power of God that gives new life in connection with Christ-conforming conduct and grounds believers' faith in the power of God (see 1 Cor. 2.1–5). Thus, 'become what you are' should more accurately be stated in terms of 'be transformed into the image of Christ by practising spiritual discernment and seeking to conform your behaviour to Christ's cruciform pattern'.

Indeed, Paul suggests how believers participate in this unceasing battle against sin in Rom. 12.1–2, two verses that further encapsulate the goal of theo-ethical reasoning and the practice of spiritual discernment (cf. Eph. 5.7–20; Col. 1.9–12; 3.1–4). Believers are to offer their body as a living sacrifice, holy and acceptable to God. According to 12.1 this constitutes their 'logical/reasoned' service/worship (λογικὴν λατρείαν) in everyday life.[15] He exhorts believers to be trans-

---

14. Contra Martyn 1997b: 501 ('That victory was decisive, but it is paradoxically incomplete').

15. For the conclusion that Paul is referring to embodied actions as rational worship in Rom. 12.1–2, see Stowers 2001: 94. Stowers also asserts that the central practices of Pauline Christianity

formed by the renewal of their minds, so that they might prove through testing (δοκιμάζειν) what is the will of God in a variety of daily contexts. As we have previously shown, Paul's idea of proof through testing suggests a *reflective* practice of looking back on the connections between conduct and experience.

In connection with Rom. 12.1–2, Käsemann concludes that λογικός and πνευματικός are interchangeable, such that 'spiritual worship' becomes the guiding theme of the passage (1980: 328–29). On the other hand, he also *contrasts* what he calls the 'eschatological decision' and the 'ethical decision' in these verses (1980: 331). He implies that, for Paul, human reason *cannot* be applied to make the so-called 'eschatological decision'. His analysis (rather than his conclusion) and the results of our exegesis in connection with 1 Corinthians and Galatians suggest otherwise. The point deserves a brief elaboration.

Käsemann emphasizes Paul's use of νοῦς in this passage as the exercise of 'critical judgment', the ability to test and differentiate (δοκιμάζειν), according to the applicable standard of the 'will of God' rather than the standards of ethics that may apply in the world (1980: 330–31). He concedes, in light of 1 Corinthians 14, that '[f]aith does not rule out reason' (1980: 330). He concludes that Paul's emphasis in Rom. 12.1–2 is 'undoubtedly on the critical faculty' as the sign of the renewed mind and the gift of the Spirit. Thus, he concludes with the claim that, in light of the new age, 'Christians can do a better job with reason than the world in general', precisely at the point where 'corresponding to God's will, they oppose the trend of this world and do what seems to be irrational, as God himself did in sending his Son to the cross' (1980: 331). This is because 'Christian reason is not self-evidently oriented to the standards which apply elsewhere' in the world (1980: 331). Thus, Käsemann suggests that human reason informs the 'ethical decision' addressed in 12.1–2.

The present study confirms Käsemann's analysis and conclusion about the *interchangeable* nature of the terms λογικός and πνευματικός in Paul's theo-ethical reasoning. We have shown that for Paul human reason must be applied to discern what conduct conforms to the 'will of God' because it faithfully embodies Christ's cruciform pattern. Behaviour conforming to this new and universal standard for human action in God's new age does in fact 'oppose the trend of this world'. As we have also shown, this use of human reason to discern the will of God takes place in the practice of *spiritual* discernment – that process of comparing spiritual things with spiritual things whereby believers perceive their experiences of God's life-giving power (1 Cor. 2.12–13) associated with actions that conform to Christ's cruciform pattern (see 1 Cor. 1.6–8; 2.1–5; 12.4–7). Thus, for Paul, the application of human reason is a critical aspect of the practice of spiritual discernment.

We suggest that this same practice also informs, however, what Käsemann calls the 'eschatological decision', since Paul synthesizes theology and ethics in his theo-ethical reasoning. The reasoned 'ethical decision' to conform actions to

---

were intellectual practices that made reference to the mind (2001: 93, 95), a conclusion confirmed by our proposed understanding of Paul's theo-ethical reasoning.

Christ's cruciform pattern also constitutes what Käsemann may mean by the 'eschatological decision'. We have shown that community members grow in faith that Christ's cruciform pattern has become the universal pathway to experiences of new life when they discern the links between Christ-conforming actions and the demonstrations of Spirit and power that ground their faith in the power of God (see 1 Cor. 2.1–5). This faith decision continues to be encouraged, informed and renewed *each time* believers make the connections between conduct and experience while engaging in theo-ethical reasoning in the community practice of spiritual discernment.

Therefore, we contend that what Paul means in Rom. 12.1–2 is that Jewish and Gentile believers, for whom Christ's cruciform pattern has become the universal standard of behaviour, must reflect on their conduct and experience and reason together as they spiritually discern what actions are pleasing to God. This is the same process we detected in 1 Cor. 1.4–9 (cf. 2 Cor. 13.5; Phil. 1.9–11; 1 Thess. 2.4; 5.19–21; see also Eph. 5.1–20). Experiences of God's life-giving power divinely confirm conduct that conforms to Christ's cruciform pattern. Thus, God's will may be spiritually discerned when believers practise spiritual discernment collectively by engaging in theo-ethical reasoning to relate experiences of new life with Christ-conforming conduct.[16] Paul thereby brings together theology and ethics, integrating Christian living and thinking by connecting believers' knowledge of God and the transformation of their minds with their collective and reasoned refection on conduct and experience as illuminated by the Spirit.

We have thus shown through our exegesis that believers' consistent participation in Christ's cruciform death – metaphorical, but nonetheless a participation with 'utmost reality' (Bornkamm 1969: 74) through Christ-conforming ways of thinking and acting – leads to other experiences of new life from God. Believers who reason together by looking for life identify these experiences, even though they remain partial and incomplete in the believer's earthly life (see 1 Cor. 13.8–12). As believers reason together, they correlate the manifestations of the Spirit that illuminate this new life with specific actions that faithfully conform to Christ's cruciform pattern. This association provides greater knowledge of God and insight about the divinely confirmed fruitfulness of Christ-conforming conduct.[17] It grounds believers' faith in the power of God (see 1 Cor. 2.1–5), building their confidence that the faithful God will continue to exercise power to give new life in connection with conduct that conforms to Christ's cruciform pattern.[18]

---

16. By implication this practice of community spiritual discernment underlies Paul's exhortation in a number of passages. See, e.g., Rom. 2.26; 12.2; 14.18–19; 1 Cor. 1.26; 2.12–16; 3.10; 8.9; 10.12, 18; 11.28; 14.1–33; 2 Cor. 2.9; 9.13; 10.7; Gal. 5.15; 6.4; Phil. 1.9–11; 1 Thess. 5.19–21; cf. Eph. 5.10, 15; Col. 2.8.

17. See 2 Cor. 13.5; Gal. 5.22–23; Phil. 1.9–11; 1 Thess. 5.19–21; cf. 1 Cor. 8.1–3.

18. Meeks finds that, for Paul, a robust ethical life requires moral confidence that is based on social phenomena. Through a social process Paul was instilling moral confidence in the members of his communities and was forming moral communities by admonishing, instructing, cajoling, reminding,

Thus, what Keck calls the 'event-oriented' focus of Paul's ethics actually identifies an important aspect of theo-ethical reasoning. As we have shown, in the community practice of spiritual discernment in Paul's religion, the Spirit leads believers into new life by illuminating the links between specific actions and particular community experiences. Making these connections leads to progress in believers' faith and produces hope for future resurrection life after death.[19]

Consequently, in the context of Paul's letters, Cullmann correctly concludes that this process of seeking proof through testing – δοκιμάζειν – is 'the key to all Christian ethics' (1964: 228). Cullmann wrongly finds, however, that this process takes place at the individual rather than at the community level. He contends that the capacity for forming the correct moral judgment at any given moment proceeds from the certainty of moral judgment that is the 'one great fruit' of the Holy Spirit produced in the *individual* person (1964: 228). Similarly, Dunn underestimates the community nature of this testing process. He finds that the testing denotes a spontaneous awareness or inner compulsion of God's Spirit as to what is God's will in the concrete situation, a recognition and approval of that will as good, acceptable and perfect (1975: 223–24).

While behavioural discernment always begins at the individual level, since revelation first occurs as the insight of an individual community member (see 1 Cor. 14.30), this study nevertheless calls into question all conclusions that emphasize the individual nature of spiritual, behavioural discernment in Paul's letters. According to Paul, individual revelation and insight must always be tested and evaluated through a collective reasoning process in the deliberative assembly where everyone participates (see 1 Cor. 14.29–32). Indeed, Cullmann and Dunn seem to underestimate the centrality of the *community* nature of this reflective, collective process of proving through testing what conduct is pleasing to God – the product of the community reasoning together to identify faithful cruciform acts that are divinely confirmed by experiences of new life in the community.

In this light, we may finally take up briefly the parallels between Paul's dialogical, community practice of spiritual discernment and the contemporary theory of discourse (communicative) ethics alluded to in Chapter 1, section 3.a above.

4. *Theo-Ethical Reasoning, the Practice of Spiritual Discernment, and Discourse (Communicative) Ethics*

In Chapter 1, section 3.a we noted that this study would explore further the exegetical basis of Horrell's tentative finding that Paul structures community life so

---

rebuking, reforming and arguing new converts into ways of acting that were worthy of the God who called them. Through this process of forming and reforming moral intuitions, says Meeks, Paul was creating confidence when the worldview of the community matched group ethos. See Meeks 1988: 17.

19. Keck finds that Paul's ethics, like Old Testament ethics, are 'event-oriented' (1996a: 10, 15); see also Deissmann 1957: 192. For the concept of progress in the faith, see 1 Cor. 16.18; Phil. 1.25; 1 Thess. 3.10. For references and allusions to the hope of future resurrection life, see Rom. 5.4–5; 8.18–25; 1 Cor. 1.4–9; 8.1–3; 13.8–12; 2 Cor. 1.7; 1 Thess. 1.3; cf. 2 Thess. 1.4. We have shown how this progress takes place as persuasion, as believers reflect on discernible events that manifest God's life-giving power in connection with Christ-conforming behaviour.

that effective moral discourse can take place. Horrell also proposed that certain insights from the discipline of contemporary moral philosophy might provide an effective heuristic tool for understanding Paul's structure of community life in this regard (1999: 321–25).

We conclude from our exegetical study that what we call theo-ethical reasoning and its role in the community practice of spiritual discernment illuminate and confirm Horrell's findings and proposal. We have shown how Paul's structure for community life directly involves a common pattern of reasoning to be applied in a collective, dialogical discourse focused on moral discernment. In Paul's churches, the community must discern and interpret the applicability and propriety of specific behavioural injunctions, even those proposed by Paul himself. Any proposed moral action must be evaluated exclusively against the behavioural standard of Christ's cruciform pattern and the experiential criterion of community edification. In other words, the group must agree that a proposed action appears to be one that is being taken to serve the common good and they must anticipate that the community will be divinely edified with enriched life by means of the proposed action.

Thus, we have found exegetical support for Horrell's preliminary findings about the heuristic value of the works of Jürgen Habermas (see 1984–88; 1990) and Seyla Benhabib (see 1986; 1989; 1990; 1992).[20] Their work involving the linguistic-pragmatic theory of communicative action and the related theory of discourse (communicative) ethics offers a contemporary account of the structure of community life proposed in our historical suggestions about Paul's churches. These modern philosophers attempt to bridge the gap between communicative theory and praxis, concluding that speech and behaviour must be integrated for effective communication to take place.

The procedural model associated with discourse ethics provides an argumentative, dialogical praxis that replaces the silent thought experiment enjoined by the Kantian universalizability test and implied in some accounts of Paul's ethics. It reflects a shift away from Kant's solitary, reflecting moral consciousness, where the individual moral agent is free to act on norms accepted as binding by the individual based on that single person's own insight and assessment of the common good. Discourse ethics shifts the focus to the community of moral agents and their collective dialogue.

This study has shown Paul advocating a very similar position. All worldly social status and hierarchy are set aside 'in Christ'. Conduct affecting human relationships must thereafter be grounded in Christ's cruciform pattern of self-giving love for others supremely manifest in his death on the cross. In the community where all the members have the same care for one another (1 Cor. 12.25), social relationships will not be shaped by worldly standards of power and coercion (cf. 1 Cor. 1.26–31). Every member will be able to communicate freely their own positions and feelings, so that potentially the common advantage might be discerned after taking all positions into consideration.[21]

---

20. The work of William Rehg (1994) should also be considered in this assessment.
21. These conclusions about the structure of community life in Paul's churches and the collective

This intersubjective approach to human knowledge and insight may help illuminate the relational nature of Paul's own moral discourse and the practice of spiritual discernment that we have shown Paul to be modelling to his churches. Benhabib identifies these discourses as 'moral-transformative processes', constituting 'an ethics of practical transformation through participation' (1986: 313, 315). She concludes that the validity and moral worth of discourse ethics lies more in the process itself than in its results. She concludes that participation in this dialogical process, rather than the necessity for always reaching rational agreement on issues, is what helps sustain moral relationships (cf. Rom. 7.15–8.4). Within such a setting, reasoned agreement as a way of life can flourish.

Benhabib favours a social epistemology that does justice to the description and explanation of human action and interaction. She stresses the importance of moral experience as support for the justification of the intersubjective nature of discourse ethics. For her, moral judgment rests on potential agreement with others, resulting not from pure individual reasoning, but from an actual or imagined and simulated dialogue with others. For Benhabib, speech and action are fundamentally related, having a revelatory quality. Only if someone is able to understand the meaning of a person's words as well as the 'what-ness' of the person's actions can a person's self-identity emerge. Therefore, the consequences of action and speech constitute the essence of human interaction. Similarly, Rehg also speaks of the importance of the intersubjective quality of arriving at practical insight through a process of community dialogue (1994: 78).

This study has shown how Paul adopts a similar perspective on the nature of revelation that takes place during the symposium-like period of moral dialogue that perhaps followed the Lord's Supper. He insists on the intelligibility of prophetic speech so that revelation might take place in connection with behavioural issues. Paul insists that the gospel – in other words, that divine event that takes place each time God's power is revealed in the world – does not occur except when there is integration of conduct and speech. Thus, according to Paul, effective communication of the gospel requires congruence between a person's Christ-conforming actions and the speech by which one identifies experiences of new life that build up the community in connection with conduct that conforms to Christ's cruciform pattern. Through theo-ethical reasoning and the practice of spiritual discernment, Paul thereby correlates community ethos with each believer's new identity in Christ.[22]

---

dialogue in which all members must participate challenge the arguments made by Shaw (1983), who concludes (wrongly) that Paul exercises power and incorporates devious strategies of control to manipulate his audiences to accept his specific moral injunctions.

22. Thus, we challenge the findings of Wolter (1997: 439–40; cf. Barclay 2001: 151) that Paul detaches the discriminating function of ethos from the level of practice and transfers it to the level of faith, resulting in the additional conclusion that believers are thereby freed from the burden of distinguishing themselves from outsiders through habitual practices. Our discussion of 1 Cor. 6.1–11 in Chapter 1, section 2.b suggested that this is not correct. More generally, we have also shown that believers who practise spiritual discernment by engaging in theo-ethical reasoning associate conduct with experience, effectively correlating ethos and identity.

5. *Conclusion*

We have shown how Paul theologizes by practising spiritual discernment, engaging in theo-ethical reasoning to associate divinely confirmed, Christ-conforming actions with community-building experiences of God's life-giving power. Paul thereby combines what are commonly called theology and ethics as he engages in reasoned reflection on conduct and experience. He thereby theologizes as a pastoral theologian with an apocalyptic (i.e. revelatory) perspective, whose mission focuses on building Christian communities through the power of God that gives new life in connection with Christ-conforming behaviour.

This conduct must be spiritually discerned by the community. Paul assesses the divine approval of all actions in light of the new, universal standard of Christ's cruciform pattern of self-giving love for others established in his death on the cross and resurrection to new embodied life in God's eternal kingdom – that new age and new creation that has descended upon the world (see 1 Cor. 10.11). Paul evaluates all human experiences according to the new criterion of community edification, the goal of Christ-conforming behaviour. This assessment takes place in the comparative and dialogical process of spiritual discernment, as Paul and believers engage in theo-ethical reasoning by comparing spiritual things with spiritual things. They distinguish experiences of life in this world – lived according to worldly behavioural standards and doomed to destruction – from experiences of new and eternal life being given by God and illuminated by the Spirit in connection with conduct that conforms to Christ's cruciform pattern.

Paul has looked at life from both sides now. Grounded in the life-changing appearance of the risen Lord in his own life, he distinguishes worldly illusions about life and its related behavioural standards from the enduring reality of new and eternal life that comes from God and is associated with acts of self-giving love for others. Through his behaviour and preaching, Paul mediates to all believers the revelation of Jesus Christ and experiences of the life-giving power of God that grounds their faith and their hope of resurrection life after death. He teaches his communities to reason together to look for life in Christ – to look for life in the manifestations of the Spirit that illuminate experiences of new earthly life that is linked to acts that conform to Christ's cruciform pattern of self-giving love for others. Thus, we may conclude that Paul's theo-ethical reasoning and the practice of spiritual discernment lie at the centre of his religion.

BIBLIOGRAPHY

1. *Primary Sources*

Aland, B., K. Aland, J. Karavidopoulos, C. Martini and B. Metzger (eds.)
    1994   *The Greek New Testament* (Stuttgart: Deutsche Bibelgesellschaft, 4th rev. edn).
Brenton, L.C.L.
    1851   *The Septuagint with Apocrypha: Greek and English* (Peabody, MA: Hendrickson, 5th edn).
Charlesworth, James H. (ed.)
    1983, 1985   *The Old Testament Pseudepigrapha* (2 vols.; New York: Doubleday).
De Jonge, M., in cooperation with H.W. Hollander, H.J. de Jonge and T. Korteweg
    1978   *The Testaments of the Twelve Patriarchs* (Leiden: E.J. Brill).
Elliott, J.K.
    1993   *The Apocryphal New Testament: A Collection of Apocryphal Christian Literature in an English Translation* (Oxford: Clarendon Press).
Hipparchus
    1894   *Commentary on the 'Phenomena' of Aratus and Eudoxus* (trans. C. Manitius; Lipsiae: Bibliotheca Teubneriana).
Josephus, Flavius
    1926–65   *Josephus* (LCL; London: Heinemann).
Lake, K.
    1959   *The Apostolic Fathers* (2 vols.; LCL; London: Heinemann).
Long, A.A., and D.N. Sedley (eds.)
    1987   *The Hellenistic Philosophers* (2 vols.; Cambridge: Cambridge University Press).
Luther, Martin
    1958   'The Second Article', in G.W. Forell and H.T. Lehman (eds.), *Luther's Works*, XXXII (Philadelphia: Muhlenberg Press): 19–29.
Nestle, E., and K. Aland *et al.* (eds.)
    1993   *Novum Testamentum Graece* (Stuttgart: Deutsche Bibelgesellschaft, 27th edn).
Rahlfs, Alfred (ed.)
    1993   *Septauginta* (Stuttgart: Deutsche Bibelgesellschaft).
Thackery, H.
    1961   *Josephus, Jewish Antiquities, Books I–IV* (Cambridge, MA: Harvard University Press).
Vermes, Geza
    1995   *The Dead Sea Scrolls in English: Revised and Extended Fourth Edition* (New York: Penguin Books).
Wilson, William
    1882   *The Writings of Clement of Alexandria*, II (Ante-Nicene Christian Library: Translations of the Writings of the Fathers Down to A.D. 325; ed. Alexander Roberts and James Donaldson; Edinburgh: T&T Clark).
Yonge, C.D.
    1993   *The Works of Philo: Complete and Unabridged* (Peabody, MA: Hendrickson).

2. *Reference Works*

Bauer, W., W.F. Arndt, F.W. Gingrich and F.W. Danker (eds.)
1958	*A Greek-English Lexicon of the New Testament and Other Early Christian Literature* (Chicago: University of Chicago Press, 2nd edn).
Brenton, L.C.L.
1995	*The Septuagint with Apocrypha: Greek and English* (Peabody, MA: Hendrickson).
Brown, F., with S.R. Driver and C.A. Briggs
1979	*The New Brown-Driver-Briggs-Gesenius Hebrew and English Lexicon* (Peabody, MA: Hendrickson).
Chamberlain, William Douglas
1941	*An Exegetical Grammar of the Greek New Testament* (Grand Rapids, MI: Baker Book House).
Hatch, E., and H. Redpath (eds.)
1991	*A Concordance to the Septuagint* (5th reprint, with addenda and corrigenda; Grand Rapids: Baker Book House).
Kittel, G., and G. Friedrich (eds.)
1964–76	*The Theological Dictionary of the New Testament* (10 vols.; trans. G. Bromily; Grand Rapids: Eerdmans).
Kohlenberger, J.R., and E.L. Goodrick
1995	*The Greek-English Concordance to the New Testament* (Grand Rapids: Zondervan).
Liddell, H.G., R. Scott, H.S. Jones and R. McKenzie (eds.)
1968	*A Greek-English Lexicon, with Revised Supplement* (Oxford: Clarendon Press, 9th edn).
Louw, J.P., and E.A. Nida
1994	*Greek-English Lexicon of the New Testament: Based on Semantic Domains* (Philadelphia: Fortress Press, 2nd edn).
Metzger, B.M.
1994	*A Textual Commentary on the Greek New Testament* (New York: United Bible Societies, 2nd edn).
Moule, C.F.D.
1959	*An Idiom Book of New Testament Greek* (Cambridge: Cambridge University Press).
Strack, H.L., and P. Billerbeck
1924–26	*Kommentar zum Neuen Testament aus Talmud und Midrasch* (2 vols.; München: C.H. Becksche Verlagsbuchhandlung).
Van Ness Goetchius, E.
1965	*The Language of the New Testament* (New York: Charles Scribner's Sons).

3. *Secondary Literature*

Achtemeier, P.J.
1991	'Finding the Way to Paul's Theology', in Bassler 1991: 25–36.
1996	'The Continuing Quest for Coherence in St Paul: An Experiment in Thought', in Lovering and Sumney 1996: 132–45.
Adams, E.
1997	'Abraham's Faith and Gentile Disobedience: Textual Links Between Romans 1 and 4', *JSNT* 65: 47–66.

2000   *Constructing the World: A Study in Paul's Cosmological Language* (SNTW;
            Edinburgh: T&T Clark).
2002   'Paul's Story of God and Creation: The Story of How God Fulfils His Purposes
            in Creation', in B. Longenecker 2002: 19–43.

Alexander, L.
1994   'Paul and the Hellenistic Schools: The Evidence of Galen', in Engberg-
            Pedersen 1994b: 60–83.

Andrews, E.
1952   'Heart of Christianity: The Meaning and Implications for Life of the Pauline
            Expression "in Christ"', *Int* 6: 62–77.

Arnold, C.E.
1996   'Returning to the Domain of the Powers: *Stoicheia* as Evil Spirits in Galatians
            4:3, 9', *NovT* 38: 55–76.

Ashton, J.
2000   *The Religion of Paul the Apostle* (New Haven: Yale University Press).

Aune, D.E.
1978   'Septem sapientum convivium (Moralia 146B–164D)', in Betz 1978: 51–105.
1983   *Prophecy in Early Christianity and the Ancient Mediterranean World* (Grand
            Rapids, MI: Eerdmans).
1986   'The Apocalypse of John and the Problem of Genre', *Semeia* 36: 65–96.
1991   'Romans as a *Logos Protreptikos*', in Donfried 1991: 278–96.
1994   'Human Nature and Ethics in Hellenistic Philosophical Traditions and Paul:
            Some Issues and Problems', in Engberg-Pedersen 1994b: 291–312.

Avemarie, F.
1999   'Erwählung und Vergeltung. Zur Optionale Struktur Rabbinischer Soteriolo-
            gie', *NTS* 45: 108–26.

Baarda, T.
1992   'ΤΙ ΕΤΙ ΔΙΩΚΟΜΑΙ in Gal. 5:11: *Apodosis* or *Parenthesis?*', *NovT* 34: 250–
            56.

Baasland, E.
1984   'Persecution: A Neglected Feature in the Letter to the Galatians', *ST* 38: 135–
            50.

Bachmann, M.
1992   *Sünder oder Übertreter. Studien zur Argumentation in Gal 2.15ff.* (Tübingen:
            J.C.B. Mohr [Paul Siebeck]).

Badenas, R.
1985   *Christ, the End of the Law: Romans 10:4 in Pauline Perspective* (Sheffield:
            JSOT Press).

Baird, W.R.
1957   'What is the Kerygma?: A Study of 1 Corinthians 15:3–8', *JBL* 16: 181–91.
1959   'Among the Mature: The Idea of Wisdom in I Corinthians 2:6', *Int* 13: 425–32.
1971   'Pauline Eschatology in Hermeneutical Perspective', *NTS* 17: 314–27.
1985   'Visions, Revelation, and Ministry: Reflections on 2 Cor 12:1–5 and Gal 1:11–
            17', *JBL* 104: 651–62.
1990   '"One Against the Other": Intra-Church Conflict in 1 Corinthians', in Fortna
            and Gaventa 1990: 116–36.

Baker, D.L.
1974   The Interpretation of 1 Corinthians 12–14', *EvQ* 46: 224–34.
1983   '1 Cor 7:32–35 and Stoic Debates about Marriage, Anxiety, and Distraction',
            JBL 102: 429–39.

Balch, D.L., E. Ferguson and W.A. Meeks (eds.)
    1990   *Greeks, Romans, and Christians* (Minneapolis: Fortress Press).
Bammel, E.
    1968   'Galater 1,23', *ZNW* 59: 108–12.
Banks, R.
    1987   ' "Walking" as a Metaphor of the Christian Life: The Origins of a Significant
                Pauline Usage', in E.W. Conrad and E.G. Newing (eds.), *Perspectives on Language and Text* (Winona Lake, IN: Eisenbrauns): 303–13.
    1994   *Paul's Idea of Community: The Early House Churches in their Historical Setting* (Peabody, MA: Hendrickson, 2nd edn).
Banks, R. (ed.)
    1974   *Reconciliation and Hope: New Testament Essays on Atonement and Eschatology Presented to L.L. Morris* (Grand Rapids, MI: Eerdmans).
Barclay, J.M.G.
    1987   'Mirror-Reading a Polemical Letter: Galatians as a Test Case', *JSNT* 31: 73–93.
    1988   *Obeying the Truth: A Study of Paul's Ethics in Galatians* (Minneapolis: Fortress Press).
    1992   'Thessalonica and Corinth: Social Contrasts in Pauline Christianity', *JSNT* 47: 49–74.
    1995a   'Paul Among Diaspora Jews: Anomaly or Apostate?', *JSNT* 60: 89–120.
    1995b   'Deviance and Apostasy', in Esler 1995: 114–27.
    1996a   *Jews in the Mediterranean Diaspora* (Edinburgh: T&T Clark).
    1996b   ' "Neither Jew Nor Greek": Multiculturalism and the New Perspective on Paul', in M. Brett (ed.), *Ethnicity and the Bible* (Leiden: E.J. Brill): 197–214.
    1996c   ' "Do We Undermine the Law?": A Study of Romans 14.1–15.1', in Dunn 1996: 287–308.
    2001   'Matching Theory and Practice: Josephus's Constitutional Ideal and Paul's Strategy in Corinth', in Engberg-Pedersen 2001: 139–64.
    2002   'Paul's Story: Theology as Testimony', in B. Longenecker 2002: 133–56.
Barclay, J., and J. Sweet (eds.)
    1996   *Early Christian Thought in its Jewish Context* (Cambridge: Cambridge University Press).
Barcley, W.B.
    1999   *'Christ in You': A Study in Paul's Theology and Ethics* (Lanham, MD: University Press of America).
Barré, M.L.
    1975   'Paul as "Eschatologic" Person: A New Look at 2 Cor 11:29', *CBQ* 37: 500–26.
    1980   'Qumran and the Weakness of Paul', *CBQ* 42: 216–27.
Barrett, C.K.
    1957   *The Epistle to the Romans* (New York: Harper & Row).
    1962   *From First Adam to Last* (New York: Charles Scribner's Sons).
    1968   *A Commentary on the First Epistle to the Corinthians* (Harper's NT Commentaries; New York: Harper & Row).
    1973   *The Second Epistle to the Corinthians* (Harper's NT Commentaries; New York: Harper & Row).
    1979   'Ethics and Eschatology', in L. de Lorenzi (ed.), *Dimensions de la vie Chrétienne* (Série Monographique de Benedictina, 4; Rome: Abbaye de S. Paul): 221–35.
    1982   *Essays on Paul* (London: SPCK).

1985	*Freedom and Obligation* (London: SPCK).
1986	'Boasting (καυχᾶσθαι κτλ.)', in Vanhoye 1986: 363–67.
1988	'The Gentile Mission as an Eschatological Phenomenon', in W.H. Gloer (ed.), *Eschatology and the New Testament* (Peabody, MA: Hendrickson): 65–75.

Barth, G.
1982	'Pistis in hellenistischer Religiosität', *ZNW* 73: 110–26.

Barth, K.
1933	*The Resurrection of the Dead* (New York: Fleming H. Revell).
1952	*The Epistle to the Romans* (trans. E.C. Hoskins; Oxford: Oxford University Press, 6th edn).
1956	*Church Dogmatics, Vol I/1: The Doctrine of the Word of God* (Edinburgh: T&T Clark); trans. G.T. Tomson and Harold Knight of *Die Kirchliche Dogmatik, I:1 Die Lehre vom Worte Gottes* (Zürich: Evangelischer Verlag A.G.).
1961	'Gospel and Law', in H. Schrey (ed.), *Faith and Action* (Edinburgh: Oliver & Boyd): 105–23.

Barton, J.
1986	*The Oracles of God* (London: Darton, Longman & Todd).

Barton, S.C.
1982	'Paul and the Cross: A Sociological Approach', *Theology* 85: 13–19.
1986	'Paul's Sense of Place: An Anthropological Approach to Community Formation in Corinth', *NTS* 32: 225–46.
1992	'The Communal Dimension of Earliest Christianity: A Critical Survey in the Field', *JTS* 43.2: 399–427.
1996	' "All Things to All People": Paul and the Law in the Light of 1 Corinthians 9:19–23', in Dunn 1996b: 271–85.
1999	'New Testament Interpretation as Performance', *SJT* 52: 179–208.

Barton, S.C. (ed.)
1999	*Where Shall Wisdom Be Found?* (Edinburgh: T&T Clark).

Bassler, J.
1982a	*Divine Impartiality: Paul and a Theologial Axiom* (SBLDS, 59; Chico, CA: Scholars Press).
1982b	'1 Cor 12:3 – Curse and Confession in Context', *JBL* 101: 415–21.
1993	'Paul's Theology: Whence and Whither?', in Hay 1993b: 3–17.

Bassler, J. (ed.)
1991	*Pauline Theology, Vol 1: Thessalonians, Philippians, Galatians, Philemon* (Minneapolis: Fortress Press).

Baumert, N.
1973	*Täglich Sterben und Auferstehen: Der Literalsinn von 2 Kor 4,12–5,10* (München: Kösel-Verlag).
1994	'Leben im Geist in paulinischer Sicht', *Internationale Katholische Zeitschrift* 23: 202–16.
1996	'ΚΟΙΝΩΝΙΑ ΤΟΥ ΑΙΜΑΤΟΣ ΤΟΥ ΧΡΙΣΤΟΥ (1 Kor 10,14–22)', in Bieringer 1996: 617–22.

Baumgarten, A.I.
1983	'The Name of the Pharisees', *JBL* 102: 411–28.
1987	'The Pharisaic *Paradosis*', *HTR* 80: 3–77.

Baumgarten, J.
1975	*Paulus und die Apokalyptik* (WMANT, 44; Neukirchen–Vluyn: Neukirchener Verlag).

Beale, G.K.
1989	'The Old Testament Background of Reconciliation in 2 Corinthians 5:7 and Its Bearing on the Literary Problem of 2 Corinthians 6.14–7.1', *NTS* 35: 550–81.

Becker, J.
1993   *Paul, Apostle to the Gentiles* (Louisville, KY: John Knox Press; trans. O.C.
            Dean, Jr. of *Paulus, der Apostel der Völker*; Tübingen: J.C.B. Mohr [Paul
            Siebeck]).
Behm, T., and E. Würthwein
1967   'νοέω, κτλ.', in *TDNT* IV: 948–1022.
Behm, T., and F. Baumgärtel
1965   'καρδία, κτλ.', in *TDNT* III: 605–14.
Beker, J.C.
1980   *Paul the Apostle* (Philadelphia: Fortress Press).
1982   *Paul's Apocalyptic Gospel* (Philadelphia: Fortress Press).
1986   'The Faithfulness of God and the Priority of Israel in Paul's Letter to the
            Romans', *HTR* 79: 10–16.
1991   'Recasting Pauline Theology', in Bassler 1991: 15–24.
1993   'The Promise of Paul's Apocalyptic for our Times', in Malherbe and Meeks
            1993: 152–59.
Bell, R.H.
2002   'Sacrifice and Christology in Paul', *JTS* 53.1: 1–27.
Belleville, L.
1994   'Gospel and Kerygma in 2 Corinthians', in Jervis and Richardson 1994: 134–
            64.
1996   ' "Imitate Me, Just as I Imitate Christ": Discipleship in the Corinthian Corre-
            spondence', in R. Longenecker 1996: 120–42.
Benhabib, S.
1986   'Toward a Communicative Ethics and Autonomy', in S. Benhabib, *Critique,
            Norm and Utopia: A Study of the Foundations of Critical Theory* (New York:
            Columbia University Press): 279–410.
1989   'Autonomy, Modernity and Community: Communitarianism and Critical Social
            Theory in Dialogue', in Axel Honneth *et al.* (eds.), *Zwischenbetrachtungen im
            Prozess der Aufklärung: Jürgen Habermas zum 60. Geburtstag* (Frankfurt:
            Suhrkamp, 2nd edn): 173–98.
1990   'Afterword: Communicative Ethics and Current Controversies in Practical Phi-
            losophy', in S. Benhabib and F. Dahlmyer (eds.), *The Communicative Ethics
            Controversy* (Cambridge, MA: MIT Press): 330–69.
1992   *Situating the Self* (Cambridge: Polity Press).
Berger, P., and T. Luckmann
1967   *The Social Construction of Reality: A Treatise in the Sociology of Knowledge*
            (Hammondsworth: Penguin Books).
Bertram, Georg.
1964   'ἔργον, κτλ.', in *TDNT* II: 635–54.
Best, Ernest
1955   *One Body in Christ* (London: SPCK).
1972   *A Commentary on the First and Second Epistles to the Thessalonians* (BNTC;
            London: A. & C. Black).
1986   'Paul's Apostolic Authority – ?', *JSNT* 27: 3–25.
1988   *Paul and His Converts* (Edinburgh: T&T Clark).
Betz, H.D.
1967   *Nachfolge und Nachahmung Jesu Christi im Neuen Testament* (Tübingen:
            J.C.B. Mohr [Paul Siebeck]).
1976   'In Defense of the Spirit: Paul's Letter to the Galatians as a Document of Early
            Christian Apologetics', in E. Schüssler Fiorenza (ed.), *Aspects of Religious*

Propaganda in Judaism and Early Christianity (Notre Dame, IN: University of Notre Dame Press): 99–114.

1979   *Galatians* (Philadelphia: Fortress Press).

1986   'The Problem of Rhetoric and Theology According to the Apostle Paul', in Vanhoye 1986: 16–48.

1988   'Das Problem der Grundlagen der paulinischen Ethik (Rom 12:1–2)', *ZTK* 85: 199–218.

Betz, H.D. (ed.)

1978   *Plutarch's Ethical Writings and Early Christian Literature* (Leiden: E.J. Brill).

Bieringer, R. (ed.)

1996   *The Corinthian Correspondence* (Leuven: Leuven University Press).

Bilde, P.

1993   'Deification and Ethics: A Comparative Religio-Historical Investigation of Paul on the Aims and Methods of Salvation in Christ', *Temenos* 29: 9–36.

Bittlinger, A.

1967   *Gifts and Graces: A Commentary on 1 Corinthians 12–14* (trans. H. Klassen; London: Hodder & Stoughton).

1973   *Gifts and Graces: A Commentary on 1 Corinthians 12–14* (trans. Herbert Klassen; Grand Rapids: Eerdmans).

Black, D.A.

1984   *Paul, Apostle of Weakness* (New York: Peter Lang).

Bloomquist, L.G.

1993   *The Function of Suffering in Philippians* (JSNTSup, 78; Sheffield: JSOT Press).

Bockmuehl, M.

1988   'Das verb φανερόω im Neuen Testament: Versuch einer Neuauswertung', *BZ* 32: 87–99.

1990   *Revelation and Mystery in Ancient Judaism and Pauline Christianity* (Tubingen: J.C.B. Mohr [Paul Siebeck]).

1995a   'A Commentator's Approach to the "Effective History" of Philippians', *JSNT* 60: 57–88.

1995b   'The Noachide Commandments and New Testament Ethics: With Special Reference to Acts 15 and Pauline Halakah', *RB* 102: 72–101.

1996   'Halakhah and Ethics in the Jesus Tradition', in Barclay and Sweet 1996: 264–78; reprinted in M. Bockmuehl, *Jewish Law and Gentile Churches* (Edinburgh: T&T Clark, 2000): 1–16.

1997   ' "The Form of God" (Phil 2:6): Variations on a Theme of Jewish Mysticism', *JTS* 48: 1–23.

2000   *Jewish Law and Gentile Churches* (Edinburgh: T&T Clark).

Boers, H.

1979   *What is New Testament Theology? The Rise of Criticism and the Problem of a Theology of the New Testament* (Philadelphia: Fortress Press).

1982   'The Problem of Jews and Gentiles in the Macro-Structure of Romans', *SEÅ* 47: 184–96.

1992   ' "We who are by Inheritance Jews; Not From the Gentiles Sinners" ', *JBL* 111.2: 273–81.

1993   'Polysemy in Paul's Use of Christological Expressions', in Malherbe and Meeks 1993: 91–108.

1994   *The Justification of the Gentiles: Paul's Letters to the Galatians and the Romans* (Peabody, MA: Hendrickson).

1997   'Ἀγάπη and χάρις in Paul's Thought', *CBQ* 59: 693–713.

Boomershine, T.E.
1989   'Epistemology at the Turn of the Ages in Paul, Jesus, and Mark: Rhetoric and
        Dialectic in Apocalyptic and the New Testament', in Marcus and Soards 1989:
        147–67.
Borgen, P.
2000   'Openly Portrayed as Crucified: Some Observations on Gal 3:1–14', in Horrell
        and Tuckett 2000: 345–53.
Bornkamm, G.
1969   *Early Christian Experience* (New York: Harper & Row); trans. P. Hammer of
        selections from *Studien zu Antike und Urchristentum*, 2nd edn, 1963 and *Das
        Ende des Gesetzes*, 5th edn, 1966 (München: Christian Kaiser Verlag).
1971   *Paul* (London: Hodder and Stoughton); trans. D. Stalker of *Paulus* (Stuttgart:
        W. Kohlhammer, 1969).
Bornkamm, G.
1967   'μυστήριον, κτλ.', in *TDNT* IV: 802–28.
Bousset, W.
1970   *Kyrios Christos* (Nashville: Abingdon Press); trans. J. Steely of *Kyrios Chris-
        tos: Geschichte des Christusglaubens von den Anfängen des Christentums bis
        Irenaeus* (Göttingen: Vandenhoeck und Ruprecht, 1913, 1921²).
Bouttier, M.
1966   *Christianity according to Paul* (London: SCM Press); trans. F. Clarke of *La
        condition chrétienne selon saint Paul* (Geneva: Labor et Fides, 1964).
Boyarin, D.
1994   *A Radical Jew: Paul and the Politics of Identity* (London: University of Cali-
        fornia Press).
Braaten, C.E.
1974   *Eschatology and Ethics* (Minneapolis: Augsburg).
Branick, V.
1982   'Source and Redaction Analysis of 1 Corinthians 1–3', *JBL* 101: 251–69.
1985   'Apocalyptic Paul?', *CBQ* 47: 664–75.
Brinsmead, B.H.
1982   *Galatians: A Dialogical Response to Opponents* (SBLDS, 65; Chico, CA:
        Scholars Press).
Brondos, D.
2001   'The Cross and the Curse: Galatians 3.13 and Paul's Doctrine of Redemption',
        JSNT 81: 3–32.
Brown, A.R.
1995   *The Cross and Human Transformation* (Minneapolis: Fortress Press).
1996   'Apocalyptic Transformation in Paul's Discourse of the Cross', *Word and
        World* 16: 427–36.
1997   'The Cross and Moral Discernment', *Doctrine and Life* 47: 196–203.
1998   'The Gospel Takes Place', *Int* 52: 271–85.
Bruce, F.F.
1971   *1 and 2 Corinthians* (NCBC; London: Oliphants).
1982   *The Epistle to the Galatians: A Commentary on the Greek Text* (NIGTC; Grand
        Rapids, MI: Eerdmans).
Bryant, R.A.
2001   *The Risen Crucified Christ in Galatians* (SBLDS, 185; Atlanta: Society of Bib-
        lical Literature).
Büchsel, F., and V. Herntrich
1965   'κρίνω, κτλ.', in *TDNT* III: 921–54.

Bultmann, R.
1924 'Das Problem der Ethik bei Paulus', *ZNW* 23: 123–40; ET Rosner 1995: 195–216, trans. C.W. Stenschke).
1951, 1955 *Theology of the New Testament* (trans. Kendrick Grobel; 2 vols.; New York: Charles Scribner's Sons).
1958 *Jesus Christ and Mythology* (New York: Charles Scribner's Sons).
1961 'New Testament and Mythology', in H. Bartsch (ed.) *Kerygma and Myth* (New York: Harper & Row): 1–45.
1964a 'The Primitive Christian Kerygma and the Historical Jesus', in C. Braaten and R. Harrisville (eds.), *The Historical Jesus and the Kerymatic Christ* (New York: Abingdon Press): 15–42.
1964b 'γινώσκω, κτλ.', in *TDNT* I: 689–719.
1967 'Zur Auslegung von Gal. 2.15–18', in E. Dinkler (ed.), *Exegetica: Aufsätze zur Erforschung des Neuen Testaments* (Tübingen: J.C.B. Mohr).
1969 'The Significance of the Historical Jesus for the Theology of Paul', in Robert W. Funk (ed.), *Faith and Understanding*, I (trans. L. Pettibone Smith; New York: Harper & Row): 220–46.
1985 *The Second Letter to the Corinthians* (Minneapolis: Augsburg Publishing House).
Bultmann, R.
1968a 'πείθω, κτλ.', in *TDNT* VI: 1–11.
Bultmann, R., and A. Weiser
1968b 'πιστεύω, κτλ.', in *TDNT* VI: 174–228.
Bultmann, R., and D. Lührmann
1974 'φαίνω, κτλ.', in *TDNT* IX: 1–10.
Burke, T.
1998 'Adoption and the Spirit in Romans 8', *EvQ* 70: 311–24.
Burton, E. De Witt
1921 *The Epistle to the Galatians* (ICC; Edinburgh: T&T Clark).
Byrne, B.
1979 *'Sons of God' – 'Seed of Abraham': A Study of the Idea of the Sonship of God of All Christians in Paul Against the Jewish Background* (Rome: Biblical Institute Press).
1981 'Living Out the Righteousness of God: The Contribution of Rom 6:1–8:13 to an Understanding of Paul's Ethical Presuppositions', *CBQ* 43: 557–81.
1983 'Sinning Against One's Own Body: Paul's Understanding of the Sexual Relationship in 1 Corinthians 6:18', *CBQ* 45: 608–16.
1986 *Reckoning With Romans* (Wilmington, DE: Michael Glazier).
1996 *Romans* (Sacra Pagina; Collegeville, MN: Liturgical Press).
Caird, G.
1994 *New Testament Theology* (Oxford: Clarendon Press, completed and edited by L. Hurst).
Callan, T.
1985 'Prophecy and Ecstasy in Greco-Roman Religion and in 1 Corinthians', *NovT* 27: 125–40.
Callow, K.
1992 'Patterns of Thematic Development in 1 Corinthians 5:1–13', in D. Black (ed.), *Linguistics and NT Interpretation* (Nashville: Broadman): 194–206.
Campbell, D.
1992a *The Righteousness of God in Romans* (JSNTSup, 65; Sheffield: JSOT Press).

1992b 'The Meaning of ΠΙΣΤΙΣ and ΝΟΜΟΣ in Paul: A Linguistic and Structural Perspective', *JBL* 111: 91–103.

1994 'Romans 1:17 – A *Crux Interpretum* for the ΠΙΣΤΙΣ ΧΡΙΣΤΟΥ Debate', *JBL* 113: 265–85.

Campbell, R.

1991 'Does Paul Acquiesce in Divisions at the Lord's Supper?', *NovT* 22: 61–70.

Carey, G.

1998 'Apocalyptic *Ethos*', in *1998 SBL Seminar Papers* (Atlanta: Scholars Press): 731–61.

Carlson, R.

1993 'The Role of Baptism in Paul's Thought', *Int* 47: 255–66.

Carr, W.

1976 'The Rulers of this Age – I Corinthians II.6–8', *NTS* 23: 20–35.

1981 *Angels and Principalities: The Background, Meaning and Development of the Pauline Phrase 'ἅι αρχαι και ἅι εξουσιαι'* (SNTSMS, 42; Cambridge: Cambridge University Press).

Carras, G.

1990 'Jewish Ethics and Gentile Converts: Remarks on 1 Thessalonians 4, 3–8', in R. Collins 1990: 306–15.

Carroll, J., and J. Green

1995 ' "Nothing but Christ and Him Crucified": Paul's Theology of the Cross', in J. Carroll and J. Green (eds.), *The Death of Jesus in Early Christianity* (Peabody, MA: Hendricksen): 113–32.

Carroll, J., C. Cosgrove and E. Johnson (eds.)

1990 *Faith and History: Essays in Honor of Paul W. Meyer* (Atlanta: Scholars Press).

Carter, T.L.

2002 *Paul and the Power of Sin: Redefining 'Beyond the Pale'* (SNTSMS, 115; Cambridge: Cambridge University Press).

Casey, P.M.

1999 'Monotheism, Worship and Christological Development in the Pauline Churches', in Newman, Davila and Lewis 1999: 314–33.

Castelli, E.

1991a *Imitating Paul* (Louisville, KY: Westminster/John Knox Press).

1991b 'Interpretations of Power in 1 Corinthians', *Semeia* 54: 197–222.

Cavallin, H.

1978 ' "The Righteous Shall Live by Faith" ', *ST* 32: 33–43.

Chapman, M.

1995 'Ideology, Theology and Sociology: From Kautsky to Meeks', in Rogerson, Davies, and Carroll 1995: 41–65.

Charlesworth, J.

1993 'In the Crucible', in J. Charlesworth and C. Evans (eds.), *The Pseudepigrapha and Early Biblical Interpretation* (JSPSup, 14; Sheffield: JSOT Press): 20–43.

Charry, E.

1997 *By the Renewing of Your Minds* (Oxford: Oxford University Press).

Chester, A.

1991 'Jewish Messianic Expectations and Mediatorial Figures in Pauline Christology', in M. Hengel and U. Heckel (eds.), *Paulus und antike Judentum* (Tübingen: J.C.B. Mohr [Paul Siebeck]): 17–90.

Cheung, A.
1999   *Idol Food in Corinth: Jewish Background and Pauline Legacy* (JSNTSup, 176; Sheffield: Sheffield Academic Press).
Chow, J.
1992   *Patronage and Power: A Study of Social Networks in Corinth* (JSNTSup, 75; Sheffield: Sheffield Academic Press).
Clark, K.
1935   'The Meaning of ΕΝΕΡΓΕΩ and ΚΑΤΑΡΓΕΩ in the New Testament', *JBL* 54: 93–101.
Clarke, A.
1993   *Secular and Christian Leadership in Corinth: A Socio-Historical and Exegetical Study of 1 Corinthians 1–6* (Leiden: E.J. Brill).
Clements, R.
1980   '"A Remnant Chosen by Grace" (Romans 11:5): The Old Testament Background and Origin of the Remnant Concept', in D. Hagner and M. Harris (eds.), *Pauline Studies: Essays Presented to Professor F.F. Bruce* (Exeter: Paternoster Press): 106–21.
Collins, A.Y.
1980   'The Function of "Excommunication" in Paul', *HTR* 73: 251–63.
Collins, J.
1979   'Toward the Morphology of a Genre: Introduction', *Semeia* 14: 1–20.
1984   *The Apocalyptic Imagination* (New York: Crossroad).
1986   *Between Athens and Jerusalem* (New York: Crossroad).
1993   'Wisdom, Apocalypticism, and Generic Compatability', in L. Perdue, B. Scott and W. Wiseman (eds.), *In Search of Wisdom: Essays in Memory of John Gammie* (Lousville, KY: Westminster/John Knox Press): 165–85.
Collins, R.
1983   'The Unity of Paul's Paraenesis in 1 Thess. 4.3–8, 1 Cor. 7.1–7, a Significant Parallel', *NTS* 29: 420–29.
1984   *Studies on the First Letter to the Thessalonians* (Leuven: Leuven University Press).
1984b   'The Theology of Paul's First Letter to the Thessalonians', in R. Collins (ed.), *Studies on the First Letter to the Thessalonians* (Leuven: Leuven University Press): 230–52.
1999   *First Corinthians* (Sacra Pagina; Collegeville, MN: Liturgical Press).
Collins, R. (ed.)
1990   *The Thessalonian Correspondence* (Leuven: Leuven University Press).
Conzelmann, H.
1975   *1 Corinthians: A Commentary on the First Epistle to the Corinthians* (Hermeneia; Philadelphia: Fortress Press); trans. J. Leitch of *Der erste Brief an die Korinther* (Göttingen: Vandenhoeck & Ruprecht, 1969).
Conzelmann, H., and W. Zimmerli
1974   'χαίρω, κτλ.', in *TDNT* IX: 359–415.
Corsani, B.
1984   'ΕΚ ΠΙΣΤΕΩΣ in the Letters of Paul', in W. Weinrich (ed.), *The New Testament Age: Essays in Honor of Bo Reicke, Vol 1* (Macon, GA: Mercer Press): 87–93.
Cosgrove, C.
1987   'Justification in Paul: A Linguistic and Theological Reflection', *JBL* 106.4: 653–70.
1988   *The Cross and the Spirit* (Macon, GA: Mercer University Press).

Cousar, C.
  1982   *Galatians* (Interpretation; Louisville, KY: John Knox Press).
  1990a *A Theology of the Cross: The Death of Jesus in the Pauline Letters* (Minneapolis: Fortress Press).
  1990b '1 Corinthians 2:1–13', *Int* 44: 169–73.
  1993   'The Theological Task of 1 Corinthians', in Hay 1993b: 90–102.
  1996   *The Letters of Paul* (Nashville: Abingdon Press).
  1998   'Paul and the Death of Jesus', *Int* 52: 38–52.
Cullmann, O.
  1953   *Early Christian Worship* (SBT, 10; London: SCM Press).
  1954   'Zur neuesten Diskussion über die ΕΞΟΥΣΙΑΙ in Röm. 13,1', *TZ* 10: 21–36.
  1964   *Christ and Time* (Philadelphia: Westminster Press); trans. F. Filson of *Christus und die Zeit* (Zollikon-Zürich: Evangelischer Verlag).
Culpepper, R.
  1980   'Co-Workers in Suffering: Philippians 2:19–20', *RevExp* 77: 349–58.
Cuming, G.
  1981   'ἐποτίσθημεν (1 Cor 12.13)', *NTS* 27: 283–85.
Cummins, S.
  2001   *Paul and the Crucified Christ in Antioch* (SNTSMS, 114; Cambridge: Cambridge University Press).
Dabourne, W.
  1999   *Purpose and Cause in Pauline Exegesis: Romans 1.16–4.25 and a New Approach to the Letters* (SNTSMS, 104; Cambridge: Cambridge University Press).
Dahl, N.
  1967   'Paul and the Church at Corinth According to 1 Corinthians 1:10–4:21', in Farmer *et al.* 1967: 313–35.
  1976a *Jesus in the Memory of the Early Church* (Minneapolis: Augsburg).
  1976b 'Anamnesis: Memory and Commemoration in the Early Church', in Dahl 1976a: 11–29.
  1976c 'Form Critical Observations on Early Christian Preaching', in Dahl 1976a: 30–37.
  1977a *Studies in Paul: Theology for the Early Christian Mission* (Minneapolis: Augsburg Publishing).
  1977b 'The Missionary Theology in the Epistle to the Romans', in Dahl 1977a: 70–94.
  1977c 'The Doctrine of Justification: Its Social Function and Implications', in Dahl 1977a: 95–120.
  1977d 'Contradictions in Scripture', in Dahl 1997a: 159–77.
  1977e 'The One God of Jews and Gentiles', in Dahl 1977a: 178–91.
Das, A.
  2000   'Another Look at in Galatians 2:16', *JBL* 119.3: 529–39.
Dautzenberg, G.
  1974   *Urchristliche Prophetie. Ihre Erforschung ihre Voraussetzungen im Judentum und ihre Struktur im ersten Korintherbrief* (Stuttgart: W. Kohlhammer).
Davies, W.D.
  1962   *Paul and Rabbinic Judaism: Some Rabbinic Elements in Pauline Theology* (London: SPCK, 2nd edn).
  1969   'The Relevance of the Moral Teaching of the Early Church', in E. Ellis and M. Wilcox (eds.), *Neotestamentica et Semitica* (Edinburgh: T&T Clark): 30–49.

1972a	'The Moral Teaching of the Early Church', in Efird 1972: 310–32.
1972b	*The Gospel and the Land* (Berkeley: University of California Press).
1978	'Paul and the People of Israel', *NTS* 24: 4–39.

Davis, B.
| 1999 | 'The Meaning of ΠΡΟΕΓΡΑΦΗ in the Context of Galatians 3:1', *NTS* 45: 194–212. |

De Boer, Martinus C.
1988	*The Defeat of Death: Apocalyptic Eschatology in 1 Corinthians 15 and Romans* (JSNTSup, 22; Sheffield: JSOT Press).
1989	'Paul and Jewish Apocalyptic', in Marcus and Soards 1989: 169–90.
1996	'Paul's Use of a Resurrection Tradition in 1 Cor 15,20–28', in Bieringer 1996: 639–51.

Debrunner, A., H. Kleinknecht, O. Procksch, G. Kittel, G. Quell and G. Schrenk
| 1967 | 'λέγω, κτλ.', in *TDNT* IV: 69–192. |

Deidun, T.
| 1981 | *New Covenant Morality in Paul* (Rome: Biblical Institute Press). |

Deissmann, A.
| 1892 | *Die Neutestamentliche Formel 'en Christo Jesu'* (Marburg: Elwert). |
| 1957 | *Paul: A Study in Social and Religious History* (trans. W. Wilson; New York: Harper & Brothers, 2nd edn). |

Delling, G.
1967	'λαμβάνω, κτλ.', in *TDNT* IV: 5–15.
1971	'στοιχέω', in *TDNT* VII: 666–87.
1972	'τασσω, κτλ.', in *TDNT* VIII: 27–48.
1972	'τέλος, κτλ.', in *TDNT* VIII: 49–87.

Dennison, W.
| 1979 | 'Indicative and Imperative: The Basic Structure of Pauline Ethics', *Calvin Theologial Journal* 14: 55–78. |

Dietzfelbinger, C.
| 1985 | *Die Berufung des Paulus als Ursprung seiner Theologie* (WMANT, 58; Neukirchlen–Vluyn: Neukirchener Verlag). |

Dodd, B.J.
| 1996 | 'Christ's Slave, People Pleasers and Galatians 1:10', *NTS* 42: 90–104. |
| 1999 | *Paul's Paradigmatic 'I': Personal Example as Literary Strategy* (JSNTSup, 177; Sheffield: Sheffield Academic Press). |

Dodd, C.H.
1936, 1944	*The Apostolic Preaching and its Developments* (London: Hodder & Stoughton).
1959	'The Primitive Catechism', in A. Higgins (ed.), *New Testament Essays: Studies in Memory of Thomas Walter Manson* (Manchester: Manchester University Press): 106–18.
1969	'*Ennomos Christou*', in C. Dodd, *More New Testament Studies* (Manchester: Manchester University Press): 134–48.

Donaldson, T.
| 1986 | 'The "Curse of the Law" and the Inclusion of the Gentiles: Galatians 3.13–14', *NTS* 32: 94–112. |
| 1997 | *Paul and the Gentiles: Remapping the Apostle's Convictional World* (Minneapolis: Fortress Press). |

Donfried, K.
| 1976 | 'Justification and Last Judgment in Paul', *ZNW* 67: 90–110. |

Donfried, K. (ed.)
| 1991 | *The Romans Debate* (Edinburgh: T&T Clark, 2nd edn). |

Donfried, K., and J. Beutler (eds.)
   2000   *The Thessalonian Debate: Methodological Discord or Methodological Synthe-sis?* (Grand Rapids, MI: Eerdmans).

Doty, W.
   1973   *Letters in Primitive Christianity* (Philadelphia: Fortress Press).

Doughty, D.
   1975   'The Presence and Future of Salvation in Corinth', *ZNW* 66: 61–90.

Douglas, M.
   1973   *Natural Symbols* (London: Barrie & Jenkins, 2nd edn).
   1984   *Purity and Danger: An Analysis of the Concepts of Pollution and Taboo* (London: ARK Paperbacks).

Downing, F.G.
   2001   'Paul and the Stoics: An Essay in Interpretation', *JTS* 52.1: 278–80.

Duff, N.
   1989   'The Significance of Pauline Apocalyptic for Theological Ethics', in Marcus and Soards 1989: 279–96.

Dunn, J.D.G.
   1970   *Baptism in the Holy Spirit* (London: SCM Press).
   1973   '1 Corinthians 15:45 – Last Adam, Life-giving Spirit', in B. Lindars and S. Smalley (eds.), *Christ and Spirit in the New Testament, Studies in Honour of Charles Frances Digby Moule* (Cambridge: Cambridge University Press): 127–41.
   1975   *Jesus and the Spirit: A Study of the Religious and Charismatic Experience of Jesus and the First Christians as Reflected in the New Testament* (London: SCM Press).
   1983   'The New Perspective on Paul', *BJRL* 65: 95–122; reprinted in Dunn 1990a: 183–214 (all page references to Dunn 1983).
   1985   'Works of the Law and the Curse of the Law (Gal. 3.10–14)', *NTS* 31: 523–42; reprinted with new addendum in Dunn 1990a: 215–41 (all page references to Dunn 1990b).
   1987a   '"A Light to the Gentiles": The Significance of the Damascus Road Chris-tophany for Paul', in L. Hurst and N. Wright (eds.), *The Glory of Christ in the New Testament* (Oxford: Clarendon Press): 251–66.
   1987b   '"Righteousness from the Law" and "Righteousness from Faith": Paul's Inter-pretation of Scripture in Romans 10:1–10', in Hawthorne and Betz 1987: 216–28.
   1988   *Romans* (2 vols.; Dallas: Word Books).
   1990a   *Paul and the Law* (London: SPCK).
   1990b   'Works of the Law and the Curse of the Law (Gal. 3.10–14)', in Dunn 1990a: 215–41.
   1992   'Yet Once More – "The Works of the Law": A Response', *JSNT* 46: 99–117.
   1993a   *The Epistle to the Galatians* (BNTC; London: A. & C. Black).
   1993b   'Echoes of Intra-Jewish Polemic in Paul's Letter to the Galatians', *JBL* 112: 459–77.
   1993c   *The Theology of Paul's Letter to the Galatians* (Cambridge: Cambridge Uni-versity Press).
   1993d   'Pauline Christology: Shaping the Fundamental Structures', in R. Berkey and S. Edwards (eds.), *Christology in Dialogue* (Cleveland, OH: The Pilgrim Press): 96–107.
   1993e   'How Controversial was Paul's Christology?', in M. de Boer (ed.), *From Jesus to John: Essays on Jesus and New Testament Christology in Honour of Marinus de Jonge* (JSNTSup, 84; Sheffield: JSOT Press): 148–67.

1995	*1 Corinthians* (Sheffield: Sheffield Academic Press).
1996a	'"The Law of Faith," "the Law of the Spirit" and "the Law of Christ"', in Lovering and Sumney 1996: 62–82.
1997a	'Once More, ΠΙΣΤΙΣ ΧΡΙΣΤΟΥ', in Johnson and Hay 1997: 61–81.
1997b	'4QMMT and Galatians', *NTS* 43: 147–53.
1998a	'Discernment of Spirits – A Neglected Gift', in Dunn 1998e: 311–27, originally published in W. Harrington (ed.) 79–96: *Witness to the Spirit: Essays on Revelation, Spirit, Redemption* (Manchester: Koinonia Press, 1979).
1998b	'Paul's Understanding of the Death of Jesus as Sacrifice', in J. Dunn, *The Christ and the Spirit: Collected Essays of James D.G. Dunn, Vol 1 (Christology)* (Grand Rapids, MI: Eerdmans); originally published in S. Sykes (ed.), *Sacrifice and Redemption* (Cambridge University Press, 1991): 35–56, 190–211.
1998c	*The Theology of the Apostle Paul* (Edinburgh: T&T Clark).
1998d	'The Responsible Congregation (1 Corinthians 14:26–40)', in Dunn 1998e: 260–90; originally published in L. De Lorenzi (ed.), *Charisma und Agape (1 Kor 12–14)* (Rome: Abtei von St. Paul vor den Mauern, 1983: 201–36).
1998e	*The Christ and the Spirit: Collected Essays of James D.G. Dunn, Vol 2 (Pneumatology)* (Edinburgh: T&T Clark).
1999	'Who Did Paul Think He Was? A Study of Jewish-Christian Identity', *NTS* 45: 174–93.

Dunn, J.D.G. (ed.)

1996b	*Paul and the Mosaic Law* (WUNT 89; Tübingen: J.C.B. Mohr [Paul Siebeck]).

Eastman, S.

2002	'Whose Apocalypse? The Identity of the Sons of God in Rom 8:19', *JBL* 121.2: 263–77.

Ebeling, G.

1961	*The Nature of Faith* (ET London: Collins); trans. R. Smith of *Das Wesen des christlichen Glaubens* (Tübingen: J.C.B. Mohr [Paul Siebeck], 1959), all page references to ET.
1963	'The Meaning of Biblical Theology', in *Word and Faith* (ET London: SCM Press; trans. James W. Leitch of *Wort und Glaube*; J.C.B. Mohr [Paul Siebeck], 1960) (all page references to ET).
1985	*The Truth of the Gospel* (ET Philadelphia: Fortress Press; trans. D. Green of *Die Wahrheit des Evangeliums*, Tübingen: J.C.B. Mohr [Paul Siebeck], 1981 (all page references to ET).

Eckstein, H-J.

1996	*Verheißung und Gesetz: Eine exegetische Untersuchung zu Galater 2,15–4,7* (WUNT, 86; Tübingen: Mohr-Siebeck).

Edwards, T.C.

1885	*A Commentary on the First Epistle to the Corinthians* (London: Hodder & Stoughton, 2nd edn).

Efird, J.

1972	*The Use of the Old Testament in the New and Other Essays: Studies in Honor of William Franklin Stinespring* (Durham, NC: Duke University Press): 3–65.

Elliott, N.

1990	*The Rhetoric of Romans* (JSNTSup, 45; Sheffield: JSOT Press).
1994	*Liberating Paul* (Maryknoll, NY: Orbis Books).
1997	'The Anti-Imperial Message of the Cross', in Horsley 1997: 167–83.
2000	'Paul and the Politics of Empire', in Horsley 2000: 17–39.

Ellis, E.

1974a	'"Spiritual" Gifts in Pauline Community', *NTS* 20: 128–44.

1974b   '"Christ Crucified"', in Banks 1974: 7–75.

1990   '*Sōma* in First Corinthians', *Int* 44: 132–44.

Engberg-Pedersen, T.

1987   'The Gospel and Social Practice According to 1 Corinthians', *NTS* 33: 557–84.

1991   '1 Corinthians 11:16 and the Character of Pauline Exhortation', *JBL* 110: 679–89.

1993   'Proclaiming the Lord's Death: 1 Corinthians 11:17–34 and the Forms of Paul's Theological Arguments', in Hay 1993b: 103–32.

1994a   'Stoicism in Philippians', in Engberg-Pedersen 1994b: 256–90.

1995   'Galatians in Romans 5–8 and Paul's Construction of the Identity of Christ Believers', in Fornberg and Hellholm 1996: 477–505.

2000   *Paul and the Stoics* (Edinburgh: T&T Clark).

2002   'Response to Martyn', *JSNT* 86: 103–14.

Engberg-Pedersen, T. (ed.)

1994b   *Paul in His Hellenistic Context* (Edinburgh: T&T Clark).

2001   *Paul Beyond the Judaism/Hellenism Divide* (Louisville, KY: Westminster/John Knox Press).

Enslin, M.

1925   *The Ethics of Paul* (Nashville: Abingdon Press, repr. 1957) (all page references to 1957).

Epp, E.

1986   'Jewish-Gentile Continuity in Paul: Torah and/or Faith? (Romans 9:1–5)', *HTR* 79: 80–90.

Esler, P.

1998   *Galatians* (London: Routledge).

Esler, P. (ed.)

1995   *Modelling Early Christianity* (London: Routledge).

Evans, C.

1984   'Paul and the Hermeneutics of "True Prophecy": A Study in Romans 9–11', *Bib* 65: 560–70.

Farmer, W., J. Knox, C. Moule and R. Niebuhr (eds.)

1967   *Christian History and Interpretation: Studies Presented to John Knox* (Cambridge: Cambridge University Press).

Fee, G.

1987   *The First Epistle to the Corinthians* (NICNT; Grand Rapids: Eerdmans).

1994a   *God's Empowering Presence: The Holy Spirit in the Letters of Paul* (Peabody, MA: Hendrickson).

1994b   '"Another Gospel Which you did not Embrace": 2 Corinthians 11.4 and the Theology of 1 and 2 Corinthians', in Jervis and Richardson 1994: 111–33.

1995   *Paul's Letter to the Philippians* (NICNT; Grand Rapids, MI: Eerdmans).

Finsterbusch, K.

1996   *Die Thora als Lebensweissung für Heidenchristen Studien zur Bedeutung der Thora für die Paulinische Ethik* (Göttingen: Vandenhoeck & Ruprecht).

Fiore, B.

1985   '"Covert Allusion" in 1 Corinthians 1–4', *CBQ* 47: 85–102.

1986   *The Function of Personal Example in the Socratic and Pastoral Epistles* (AnBib, 105; Rome: Biblical Institute Press).

Fitzgerald, J.

1988   *Cracks in an Earthen Vessel: An Examination of the Catalogues of Hardships in the Corinthian Correspondence* (SBLDS, 99; Atlanta: Scholars Press).

1990   'Paul, the Ancient Epistolary Theorists, and 2 Corinthians 10–13: The Purpose

and Literary Genre of a Pauline Letter', in Balch, Ferguson and Meeks (eds.)
1990: 190–200.

Fitzmyer, J.
1979   'The Gospel in the Theology of Paul', *Int* 33: 339–50; repr. in *To Advance the Gospel* (Grand Rapids, MI: Eerdmans, 1998), 149–61 (all page references to 1979).

Foerster, W., and J. Herrmann
1965   'κληρονόμος', in *TDNT* III: 758–85.

Foerster, W. and G. Fohrer
1971   'σῴζω, κτλ.', in *TDNT* VII: 965–1024.

Forbes, C.
1995   *Prophecy and Inspired Speech in Early Christianity and its Hellenistic Environment* (WUNT, 75; Tübingen: J.C.B. Mohr [Paul Siebeck]).

Fornberg, T., and D. Hellholm (eds.)
1996   *Texts and Contexts: Biblical Texts in their Textual and Situational Contexts* (Oslo: Scandinavian University Press).

Fortna, Robert T., and Beverly R. Gaventa (eds.)
1990   *The Conversation Continues: Studies in Paul & John in Honor of J. Louis Martyn* (Nashville: Abingdon Press).

Foster, P.
2002   'The First Contribution to the ΠΙΣΤΙΣ ΞΡΙΣΤΟΥ Debate: A Study of Ephesians 3:12', *JSNT* 85: 75–96.

Fowl, S.
1988   'Some Uses of Story in Moral Discourse: Reflections on Paul's Moral Discourse and Our Own', *Modern Theology* 4: 293–308.
1990   *The Story of Christ in the Ethics of Paul* (Sheffield: JSOT Press).
1994   'Who Can Read Abraham's Story? Allegory and Interpretive Power in Galatians', *JSNT* 55: 77–95.
1998   'Christology and Ethics in Philippians 2:5–11', in R. Martin and B. Dodd (eds.), *Where Christology Began* (Louisville, KY: John Knox Press): 140–53.
1999   'Learning to Narrate Our Lives in Christ', in C. Seitz and K. Greene-McCreight (eds.), *Theological Exegesis: Essays in Honor of Brevard S. Childs* (Grand Rapids, MI: Eerdmans): 339–54.

Francis, J.
1980   ' "As Babes in Christ" – Some Proposals Regarding 1 Corinthians 3.1–3', *JSNT* 7: 41–60.

Fredriksen, P.
1991   'Judaism, The Circumcision of Gentiles, and Apocalyptic Hope: Another Look at Galatians 1 and 2', *JTS* 42: 532–64.

Frey, J.
1999   'Die paulinische Antithese von »Fleisch« und »Geist« und die paulinisch-jüdische Weisheitstradition', *ZNW* 90: 45–77.

Friedrich, G.
1970   'Freiheit und Liebe im ersten Korintherbrief', *TZ* 26: 81–98.

Friedrich, G.
1964   'εὐαγγελίζομαι, κτλ.', in *TDNT* II: 707–37.
1965   'κῆρυξ, κτλ.', in *TDNT* III: 683–718.

Frör, H.
1995   *You Wretched Corinthians!* (London: SCM Press); trans. J. Bowker of *Ach Ihr Korinther Der Briefwechsel der Gemeinde in Korinth mit Paulus* (Gütersloher: Christian Kaiser Verlag/Gütersloher Verlagshaus, 1994).

Fung, R.
  1988   *The Epistle to the Galatians* (NICNT; Grand Rapids, MI: Eerdmans).
Funk, R.
  1966   *Language, Hermeneutic and Word of God: The Problem of Language in the New Testament and Contemporary Theology* (New York: Harper & Row).
  1967   'Apostolic Parousia: Form and Significance', in Farmer *et al.* 1967: 249–68.
Furnish, V.
  1961   ' "Fellow Workers in God's Service" ', *JBL* 80: 364–70.
  1968   *Theology and Ethics in Paul* (Nashville, TN: Abingdon).
  1972   *The Love Command in the New Testament* (Nashville: Abingdon).
  1984   *II Corinthians* (AB; New York: Doubleday).
  1989a   'Theology in 1 Corinthians: Initial Soundings', in D. Lull (ed.), *1989 SBL Seminar Papers* (Atlanta: Scholars Press): 246–64.
  1989b   'Paul the Μαρτυς', in P. Devenish and G. Goodwin (eds.), *Witness and Existence* (London: University of Chicago Press): 73–88.
  1990a   'Paul the Theologian', in Fortna and Gaventa 1990: 19–34.
  1990b   'Belonging to Christ: Paradigm for Ethics', *Int.* 44: 145–57.
  1993a   ' "He Gave Himself [Was Given] Up…": Paul's Use of a Christological Assertion', in Malherbe and Meeks 1993: 109–21.
  1993b   'Theology in 1 Corinthians', in Hay 1993b: 59–89.
  1994   'On Putting Paul in His Place', *JBL* 113.1: 3–17.
  1997   'Where is "the Truth" in Paul's Gospel?', in Johnson and Hay 1997: 161–77.
  1999   *The Theology of the First Letter to the Corinthians* (Cambridge: Cambridge University Press).
Gagnon, R.
  1993   'Heart of Wax and a Teaching That Stamps: ΤΥΠΟΣ ΔΙΔΑΧΗΣ (Rom 6:17b) Once More', *JBL* 112: 667–87.
Gammie, J.
  1974   'Spatial and Ethical Dualism in Jewish Wisdom and Apocalyptic Literature', *JBL* 93: 356–85.
  1990   'Paraenetic Literature: Toward the Morphology of a Secondary Genre', *Semeia* 50: 41–77.
Gardner, P.
  1994   *The Gifts of God and the Authentification of a Christian: An Exegetical Study of 1 Corinthians 8–11:1* (New York: University Press of America).
Garrett, S.
  1990   'The God of this World and the Affliction of Paul: 2 Cor 4:1–12', in Balch, Ferguson and Meeks 1990: 99–117.
Gärtner, B.
  1965   *The Temple and the Community in Qumran and the New Testament* (Cambridge: Cambridge University Press).
  1968   'The Pauline and Johannine Idea of "To Know God" Against the Hellenistic Background', *NTS* 14: 209–31.
Gaston, L.
  1987   *Paul and the Torah* (Vancouver: University of British Columbia Press).
Gaventa, B.
  1982   ' "You Proclaim The Lord's Death": 1 Corinthians 11:26 and Paul's Understanding of Worship', *RevExp* 80: 377–87.
  1986   'Galatians 1 and 2: Autobiography as Paradigm', *NovT* 28: 309–26.
  1990a   'Apostles as Babes and Nurses in 1 Thessalonians 2:7', in Carroll, Cosgrove and Johnson 1990: 93–207.

1990b	'The Maternity of Paul: An Exegetical Study of Galatians 4:19', in Fortna and Gaventa 1990: 189–201.
1991	'The Singularity of the Gospel', in Bassler 1991: 147–59.
1993	'Apostle and Church in 2 Corinthians', in Hay 1993b: 182–99.
1996a	'Mother's Milk and Ministry in 1 Corinthians 3', in Lovering and Sumney 1996: 101–13.
1996b	'Our Mother St Paul: Toward the Recovery of a Neglected Theme', *Princeton Seminary Bulletin* 17: 29–44.

Geertz, C.
1966	'Religion as a Cultural System', in M. Banton (ed.), *Anthropological Approaches to the Study of Religion* (New York: Frederick R. Prager), reprinted in C. Geertz, *The Interpretation of Cultures: Selected Essays by Clifford Geertz* (London: Hutchinson, 1975): 87–125 (all page references to 1973).
1973	*The Interpretation of Cultures: Selected Essays* (New York: Basic Books, Inc.).
1975	'Ethos, World View, and the Analysis of Sacred Symbols', in C. Gertz, *The Interpretation of Cultures: Selected Essays by Clifford Geertz* (London: Hutchinson): 126–41.

Georgi, D.
| 1986 | *The Opponents of Paul in Second Corinthians* (Philadelphia: Fortress Press); trans. H. Attridge of *Die Gegner des Paulus im 2. Korintherbrief. Studien zur Religiösen Propaganda in der Spätantike* (WMANT, 11; Neukirchen–Vluyn: Neukirchener Verlag, 1964). |

Getty, M.
| 1990 | 'The Imitation of Paul in the Letters to the Thessalonians', in R. Collins 1990: 277–83. |

Gillespie, T.
| 1978 | 'A Pattern of Prophetic Speech in First Corinthians', *JBL* 97.1: 74–95. |
| 1994 | *The First Theologians: A Study in Early Christian Prophecy* (Grand Rapids, MI: Eerdmans). |

Gillman, J.
| 1990 | 'Paul's ΕΙΣΟΔΟΣ: The Proclaimed and the Proclaimer (1 Thess 2:8)', in R. Collins 1990: 62–70. |

Glad, C.
| 1995 | *Paul and Philodemus: Adaptability in Epicurean and Early Christian Psychagogy* (NovTSup, 81; Leiden: E.J. Brill). |

Glancy, J.
| 1998 | 'Obstacles to Slaves' Participation in the Corinthian Church', *JBL* 117: 481–501. |

Goddard, A., and S. Cummins
| 1993 | 'Ill or Ill-Treated? Conflict and Persecution as the Context of Paul's Original Ministry in Galatia', *JSNT* 52: 93–126. |

Gooch, P.
| 1987 | *Partial Knowledge: Philosophical Studies in Paul* (Notre Dame, IN: University of Notre Dame Press). |

Goppelt, L.
| 1968 | *Christologie und Ethik: Aufsätze zum Neuen Testament* (Göttingen: Vandenhoeck & Ruprecht). |

Gorman, M.
| 2001 | *Cruciformity: Paul's Narrative Spirituality of the Cross* (Grand Rapids, MI: Eerdmans). |

Goulder, M.
1991   'Σοφια in 1 Corinthians', *NTS* 37: 516–34.
1994   'Vision and Knowledge', *JSNT* 56: 53–71.
Gräbe, P.
1992   'Δύναμις (in the Sense of Power) as a Pneumatological Concept in the Main
            Pauline Letters', *BZ* 36: 226–34.
Gray, R.
1993   *Prophetic Figures in Late Second Temple Jewish Palestine: The Evidence from
            Josephus* (Oxford: Oxford University Press).
Greeven, D.
1952–53   'Propheten, Lehrer, Vorsteher bei Paulus', *ZNW* 44: 1–43.
Grindheim, S.
2002   'Wisdom For the Perfect: Paul's Challenge to the Corinthian Church (1 Corin-
            thians 2:6–16)', *JBL* 121.4: 689–709.
Grudem, W.
1982   *The Gift of Prophecy in 1 Corinthians* (Lanham, MD: University Press of
            America).
1978   'A Response to Gerhard Dautzenberg on 1 Cor. 12.10', *BZ* 22: 253–70.
Grundmann, W.
1964   'ἀγαθός, κτλ.', in *TDNT* I: 10–18.
1964   'δέχομαι, κτλ.', in *TDNT* II: 50–59.
1964   'δόκιμος, κτλ.', in *TDNT* II: 255–60.
1965   'καλος', in *TDNT* III: 536–56.
Gundry, R.
1976   *Soma in Biblical Theology* (Cambridge: Cambridge University Press).
1985   'Grace, Works, and Staying Saved in Paul', *Bib* 66: 1–38.
Gundry-Volf, J.
1990   *Paul and Perseverance: Staying In and Falling Away* (Louisville, KY: West-
            minster/John Knox Press).
Gunkel, H.
1978   *The Influence of the Holy Spirit: The Popular View of the Apostolic Age and the
            Teaching of the Apostle Paul* (Philadelphia: Fortress Press); trans. R. Harrisville
            and P. Quanbeck of *Die Wirkungen des heiligen Geistes, nach der populären
            Anschauung der apostolischen Zeit und nach der Lehre des Apostels Paulus:
            Eine biblische-theologische Studie* (Göttingen, 1888).
Gunton, C.
1999   'Christ, the Wisdom of God: A Study in Divine and Human Action', in
            S. Barton 1999: 249–61.
Gutiérrez, G.
1973   *A Theology of Liberation* (Maryknoll, NY: Orbis Books).
Güttgemanns, E.
1966   *Der leidende Apostel und sein Herr. Studien zur paulinische Christologie*
            (FRLANT, 90; Göttingen: Vandenhoeck & Ruprecht).
Habermas, J.
1984–88   *The Theory of Communicative Action, Vol 1 (Reason and the Rationalization of
            Society) and Vol 2 (Lifeworld and System)* (Boston: Beacon Press).
1990   *Moral Consciousness and Communicative Action* (Cambridge, MA: Polity
            Press); trans. C. Lenhardt and S. Nicholsen of *Moralbewusstein und kommuni-
            katives Handeln* (Frankfurt: Suhrkamp, 1979).
Hafemann, S.
1990   *Suffering and Ministry in the Spirit: Paul's Defense of His Ministry in II Corin-
            thians 2:13–3:3* (Grand Rapids, MI: Eerdmans).

1995   *Paul, Moses and the History of Israel: The Letter/Spirit Contrast and the Argument from Scripture in 2 Corinthians 3* (WUNT, 81; Tübingen: J.C.B. Mohr [Paul Siebeck]).

1996   'The "Temple of the Spirit" as the Inaugural Fulfillment of the New Covenant within the Corinthian Correspondence', *Ex Auditu* 12: 29–42.

2000   'The Role of Suffering in the Mission of Paul', in J. Ådna and H. Kvalbein (eds.), *The Mission of the Early Church to Jews and Gentiles* (WUNT, 127; Tübingen: J.C.B. Mohr [Paul Siebeck]): 165–84.

Hall, B.

1990   'All Things to All People: A Study of 1 Corinthians 9:19–23', in Fortna and Gaventa 1990: 137–57.

Hall, D.

1994   'A Disguise for the Wise: ΜΕΤΑΣΞΗΜΑΤΙΣΜΟΣ in 1 Corinthians 4.6', *NTS* 40: 143–49.

Hall, R.

1987   'The Rhetorical Outline for Galatians: A Reconsideration', *JBL* 106: 277–87.

1991   'Historical Inference and Rhetorical Effect: Another Look at Galatians 1 and 2', in D. Watson (ed.), *Persuasive Artistry* (JSNTSup, 50; Sheffield: JSOT Press): 308–20.

1996   'Arguing Like an Apocalypse: Galatians and an Ancient *Topos* Outside the Greco-Roman Rhetorical Tradition', *NTS* 42: 434–53.

Hamerton-Kelly, R.

1985   'A Girardian Interpretation of Paul: Rivalry, Mimesis and Victimage in the Corinthian Correspondence', *Semeia* 33: 65–81.

Hanges, J.

1998   '1 Corinthians 4:6 and the Possibility of Written Bylaws in the Corinthian Church', *JBL* 117: 275–98.

Hansen, G.W.

1989   *Abraham in Galatians: Epistolary and Rhetorical Contexts* (JSNTSup, 29; Sheffield: JSOT Press).

1994   'A Paradigm of the Apocalypse: The Gospel in the Light of Epistolary Analysis', in Jervis and Richardson 1994: 194–209.

Hanson, A.T.

1980   'The Midrash in II Corinthians 3: A Reconsideration', *JSNT* 9: 2–28.

1983   *The Living Utterances of God: The NT Exegesis of the Old* (London: Darton, Longman & Todd).

1987   *The Paradox of the Cross in the Thought of St Paul* (JSNTSup, 17; Sheffield: JSOT Press).

Hanson, P.

1975   *The Dawn of Apocalyptic: The Historical and Sociological Roots of Jewish Apocalyptic Eschatology* (Philadelphia: Fortress Press).

1976   'Apocalypticism', *IDBSup* 28–34.

1986   *The People Called: The Growth of Community in the Bible* (San Francisco: Harper & Row).

Harrill, J.A.

2002   'Coming of Age and Putting on Christ: The *Toga Virilis* Ceremony, its Paraenesis, and Paul's Interpretation of Baptism in Galatians', *NovT* XLIV/3: 252–77.

Harrisville, Roy A.

1992   *The Figure of Abraham in the Epistles of St. Paul: In the Footsteps of Abraham* (San Francisco: Mellen Research University Press).

1994   'ΠΙΣΤΙΣ ΞΡΙΣΤΙΟΥ: Witness of the Fathers', *NovT* 36: 233–41.

Hartman, L.
  1997   *'Into the Name of the Lord Jesus': Baptism in the Early Church* (Edinburgh:
                T&T Clark).
Harvey, A.
  1985   'Forty Strokes Save One: Social Aspects of Judaizing and Apostasy', in
                A. Harvey, *Alternative Approaches to New Testament Studies* (London:
                SPCK): 79–96.
Hauerwas, S.
  1981   *A Community of Character: Toward a Constructive Christian Social Ethic*
                (Notre Dame, IN: University of Notre Dame Press).
  1983   *The Peaceable Kingdom* (Notre Dame, IN: University of Notre Dame Press).
  1989   *Resident Aliens* (Nashville: Abingdon Press).
  1994   *Character and the Christian Life* (Notre Dame, IN: University of Notre Dame
                Press, 2nd edn).
  1995   *In Good Company: The Church as Polis* (Notre Dame, IN: University of Notre
                Dame Press).
Hawthorne, G., and O. Betz (eds.)
  1987   *Tradition and Interpretation in the New Testament: Essays in Honor of E. Earle
                Ellis* (Grand Rapids, MI: Eerdmans).
Hay, D.
  1969   'Paul's Indifference to Authority', *JBL* 88: 36–44.
  1989   *'Pistis* as "Ground for Faith" in Hellenized Judaism and Paul', *JBL* 108: 461–
                76.
  1993a   'The Shaping of Theology in 2 Corinthians', in Hay 1993b: 135–55.
Hay, D. (ed.)
  1993b   *Pauline Theology Vol II: 1 and 2 Corinthians* (Minneapolis: Fortress Press).
Hay, D., and E. Johnson (eds.)
  1995   *Pauline Theology, Vol III: Romans* (Minneapolis: Fortress Press).
Hays, R.
  1985   ' "Have We Found Abraham to be Our Forefather According to the Flesh?" A
                Reconsideration of Rom 4:1', *NovT* 27: 76–98.
  1987   'Christology and Ethics in Galatians: The Law of Christ', *CBQ* 49: 268–90.
  1989   *Echoes of Scripture in the Letters of Paul* (New Haven: Yale University
                Press).
  1990   'The Church as a Scripture-Shaped Community: The Problem of Method in
                New Testament Ethics', *Int* 44: 42–55.
  1991   'ΠΙΣΤΙΣ and Pauline Christology', in E. Lovering (ed.), *1991 SBL Seminar
                Papers* (Atlanta: Scholars Press): 714–29.
  1994   'Ecclesiology and Ethics in 1 Corinthians', *Ex Auditu* 10: 31–43.
  1996a   *The Moral Vision of the New Testament* (San Francisco: Harper).
  1996b   'Three Dramatic Roles: The Law in Romans 3–4', in Dunn 1996b: 151–64.
  1997a   'ΠΙΣΤΙΣ and Pauline Christology: What is at Stake?', in Johnson and Hay
                1997: 35–60.
  1997b   *First Corinthians* (Interpretation; Louisville, KY: John Knox Press).
  1999   'The Conversion of the Imagination: Scripture and Eschatology in 1 Corin-
                thians', *NTS* 45: 391–412.
  2002   *The Faith of Jesus Christ: The Narrative Substructure of Galatians 3:1–4:11*
                (Grand Rapids, MI: Eerdmans, 2nd edn [1983]).
Hendel, R.
  1998   'The Law in the Gospel: The Law is an Essential Precondition for the Gospel',
                BR 14: 20.

Henderson, S.
2002   ' "If Anyone Hungers…": An Integrated Reading of 1 Cor 11.17–34', *NTS*
            48.2: 195–208.
Hengel, M.
1974   *Judaism and Hellenism* (London: SCM Press); trans. J. Bowden of *Judentum
            und Hellenismus, Studien zu ihrer Begegnung unter besonderer Berücksichti-
            gung Palästinas bis zur Mitte des 2 Jh.s v. Chr.* (Tübingen: J.C.B. Mohr [Paul
            Siebeck], 1969).
Héring, J.
1962   *The First Epistle of Saint Paul to the Corinthians* (London: Epworth Press);
            trans. A. Heathcote and P. Allcock of *La première épitre de saint Paul aux
            Corinthiens* (Neuchâtel: Delachaux & Niestlé, 1949).
Hester, J.
1968   *Paul's Concept of Inheritance* (Edinburgh: Oliver & Boyd).
Hill, C.
1988   'Paul's Understanding of Christ's Kingdom in 1 Corinthians 15:20–28', *NovT*
            4: 297–320.
Hill, D.
1977   'Christian Prophets as Teachers or Instructors', in J. Panogopolous (ed.), *Pro-
            phetic Vocation in the New Testament* (Leiden: E.J. Brill): 108–30.
1979   *New Testament Prophecy* (London: Marshall, Morgan & Scott).
Hock, R.
1980   *The Social Context of Paul's Ministry* (Philadelphia: Fortress Press).
Hofius, O.
1988   'Herrenmahl und Herrenmahlsparadosis: Erwägungen zu 1 Kor 11,23b–25',
            ZTK 85: 371–408.
1991   'Wort Gottes und Glaube bei Paulus', in M. Hengel and U. Heckel (eds.),
            Paulus und das antike Judentum (WUNT, 58; Tübingen: J.C.B. Mohr [Paul
            Siebeck]): 379–408.
Holladay, C.
1990   '1 Corinthians 13: Paul as Apostolic Paradigm', in Balch, Ferguson and Meeks
            1990: 80–98.
Hollander, H.
1994   'The Testing By Fire of the Builders' Works: 1 Corinthians 3.10–15', *NTS* 40:
            89–104.
Hollemann, J.
1996   *Resurrection and Parousia: A Traditio-Historical Study of Paul's Eschatology
            in 1 Corinthians 15* (NovTSup, 84; Leiden: E.J. Brill).
Holmberg, B.
1978   *Paul and Power: The Structure of Authority in the Primitive Church as
            Reflected in the Pauline Epistles* (Sweden: Studentlitteratur AB, Lund).
Holtz, T.
1971–72   'Das Kennzeichen des Geistes (1 Kor 12:1–3)', *NTS* 18: 365–76.
Holtzmann, H.
1911   *Lehrbuch der Neutestamentlichen Theologie, Band II* (Tübingen: J.C.B. Mohr,
            2nd edn).
Hooker, M.
1963–64   'Beyond the Things that are Written? St Paul's Use of Scripture', *NTS* 10: 295–
            301 (reprinted in Hooker 1990a, all page references to 1990a).
1971   'Interchange in Christ', *JTS* 22: 349–61 (reprinted in Hooker 1990a, all page
            references to 1990a).

1981	'Interchange and Suffering', in Hooker 1990a: 42–55.

1982   'Paul and "Covenantal Nomism"', in M. Hooker and S. Wilson (eds.), *Paul and Paulinism: Essays in Honour of C.K. Barrett* (London: SPCK): 102–14; reprinted in Hooker 1990a: 155–64 (all page references to 1990a).

1985   'Interchange in Christ and Ethics', *JSNT* 25: 3–17; reprinted in Hooker 1990a: 56–69 (all page references to 1990a).

1989   'Pistis Christou', *NTS* 35.3: 321–42.

1990a   *From Adam to Christ: Essays on Paul* (Cambridge: Cambridge University Press).

1990b   'Interchange and Atonement', in Hooker 1990a: 26–41.

1990c   'ΠΙΣΤΙΣ ΞΡΙΣΤΟΥ', in Hooker 1990a: 165–86; reprinted from *NTS* 35 (1989): 321–42 (all page references to 1990c).

1996   'A Partner in the Gospel: Paul's Understanding of His Ministry', in Lovering and Sumney 1996: 83–100.

Horbury, W.

1996   'Land, Sanctuary and Worship', in Barclay and Sweet 1996: 207–24.

Horrell, D.

1995a   'The Development of Theological Ideology in Pauline Christianity', in Esler 1995: 224–36.

1995b   'Paul's Collection: Resources for a Materialist Theology', *Epworth Review* 22: 74–83.

1996   *The Social Ethos of the Corinthian Correspondence* (Edinburgh: T&T Clark).

1997a   'Theological Principle or Christological Praxis? Pauline Ethics in 1 Corinthians 8.1–11.1', *JSNT* 67: 83–114.

1997b   ' "The Lord Commanded…But I Have Not Used": Exegetical and Hermeneutical Reflections on 1 Cor 9.14–15', *NTS* 43: 587–603.

1997c   'Whose Faith(fullness) is it in 1 Peter 1:5?', *JTS* 48: 110–15.

1999   'Restructuring Human Relationships: Paul's Corinthian Letters and Habermas' Discourse Ethics', *ExpTim* 110.10: 321–25.

2000   ' "No Longer Jew or Greek": Paul's Corporate Christology and the Construction of Christian Community', in Horrell and Tuckett 2000: 321–44.

2001   'From ἀδελφοὶ το οἶκος θεοῦ: Social Transformation in Pauline Christianity', *JBL* 120: 293–311.

2002   'Paul's Narratives or Narrative Substructure? The Significance of "Paul's Story"', in B. Longenecker 2002: 157–71.

Horrell, D., and C. Tuckett (eds.)

2000   *Christology, Controversy, and Community: New Testament Essays in Honour of David R. Catchpole* (NovTSup, 99; Leiden: Brill).

Horsley, R.

1976   'Pneumatikos vs. Psychikos Distinctions of Spiritual Status Among the Corinthians', *HTR* 69: 269–88.

1977   'Wisdom of Word and Words of Wisdom in Corinth', *CBQ* 39: 224–39.

1980   'Gnosis in Corinth: 1 Corinthians 8:1–6', *NTS* 27: 32–51.

1997a   'Introduction: Building an Alternative Society', in Horsley 1997c: 206–14.

1997b   '1 Corinthians: A Case Study of Paul's Assembly as an Alternative Society', in Horsley 1997c: 242–52.

1998   *1 Corinthians* (Nashville: Abingdon Press).

Horsley, R. (ed.)

1997c   *Paul and Empire* (Harrisburg, PA: Trinity Press International).

2000   *Paul and Politics: Ekklesia, Israel, Imperium, Interpretation* (Harrisburg, PA: Trinity Press International).

Howard, G.
   1967   'On the "Faith of Christ"', *HTR* 60: 459–65.
   1970   'Romans 3:21–31 and the Inclusion of the Gentiles', *HTR* 63: 223–33.
   1974   '"The Faith of Christ"', *ExpTim* 85: 212–15.
   1990   *Paul: Crisis in Galatia. A Study in Early Christian Theology* (SNTSMS, 85; Cambridge: Cambridge University Press, 2nd edn).

Howell, D.
   1994   'The Center of Pauline Theology', *Biblioteca Sacra* 151: 50–70.

Hubbard, M.
   2002   *New Creation in Paul's Letters and Thought* (SNTSMS, 119; Cambridge: Cambridge University Press).

Hughes, M.
   1908   *The Ethics of Jewish Apocyphal Literature* (London: Robert Cully)

Hultgren, A.
   1976   'Paul's Pre-Christian Persecutions of the Church: Their Purpose, Locale, and Nature', *JBL* 95: 97–111.
   1980   'The *Pistis Christou* Formulation in Paul', *NovT* 22: 248–63.
   1985   *Paul's Gospel and Mission: The Outlook From His Letter to the Romans* (Philadelphia: Fortress Press).

Hurd, J.
   1965   *The Origin of 1 Corinthians* (New York: Seabury).

Hurtado, L.
   1984   'Jesus as Lordly Example in Philippians 2:5–11', in P. Richardson and J. Hurd (eds.), *From Jesus to Paul* (Waterloo, ON: Wilfrid Laurier University Press): 113–26.
   1999a   'Pre-70 Jewish Opposition to Christ-Devotion', *JTS* 50.1: 35–58.
   1999b   'The Binitarian Shape of Early Christian Worship', in Newman, Davila and Lewis 1999: 187–213.
   2000   'Religious Experience and Religious Innovation in the New Testament', *JR* 80.2: 183–205.

Iber, G.
   1963   'Zum Verständnis von 1 Cor 12,31', *ZNW* 54: 43–52.

Jaquette, J.
   1995   *Discerning What Counts: The Function of the Adiaphora Topos in Paul's Letters* (SBLDS, 146; Atlanta: Scholars Press).
   1996   'Life and Death, *Adiaphora*, and Paul's Rhetorical Strategies', *NovT* 38: 30–54.

Jeanrond, W.
   1989   'Community and Authority: The Nature and Implications of the Authority of Christian Community', in Colin E. Gunton and Daniel W. Hardy (eds.), *On Being the Church: Essays on the Christian Community* (Edinburgh: T&T Clark): 81–109.

Jervell, J., and W. Meeks (eds.)
   1977   *God's Christ and His People: Studies in Honour of Nils Alstrup Dahl* (Oslo: Universitetsforlaget).

Jervis, A., and P. Richardson
   1994   *Gospel in Paul: Studies on Corinthians, Galatians and Romans for Richard N. Longenecker* (JSNTSup, 108; Sheffield: Sheffield Academic Press).

Jewett, R.
   1971   *Paul's Anthropological Terms: A Study of Their Use in Conflict Settings* (AGJU, 10; Leiden: E.J. Brill).

Johnson, E.E.
1989 *The Function of Apocalyptic and Wisdom Traditions in Romans 9–11* (SBLDS, 109; Atlanta: Scholars Press).
1990 'The Wisdom of God as Apocalyptic Power', in Carroll, *et al.* 1990: 137–48.
1993 'Wisdom and Apocalyptic in Paul', in Perdue, Scott and Wiseman 1993: 263–83.
Johnson, E.E., and D. Hay (eds.)
1997 *Pauline Theology, Vol IV: Looking Back, Pressing On* (Atlanta: Scholars Press).
Johnson, L.T.
1982 'Romans 3:21–26 and the Faith of Jesus', *CBQ* 44: 77–90.
1989 'The New Testament's Anti-Jewish Slander and the Conventions of Ancient Polemic', *JBL* 108: 419–41.
1993 'The Social Dimensions of *Soteria* in Luke–Acts and Paul', in E. Lovering (ed.), *1993 SBL Seminar Papers* (Atlanta: Scholars Press): 520–36.
1995 *The Letter of James* (AB; New York: Doubleday).
1996 *Scripture and Discernment: Decision-Making in the Church* (Nashville: Abingdon Press, 2nd edn).
1998 *Religious Experience in Earliest Christianity* (Minneapolis: Fortress Press).
1999 *Living Jesus: Learning the Heart of the Gospel* (New York: HarperSanFrancisco).
Johnston, G.
1984 ' "Kingdom of God" Sayings in Paul's Letters', in Richardson and Hurd 1984: 143–56.
Kammer, C.
1988 *Ethics and Liberation* (London: SCM Press).
Käsemann, E.
1933 *Leib und Leib Christi. Eine Untersuchung zur paulinischen Begrifflichkeit* (BHTh, 9; Tübingen: Mohr).
1942 'Die Legitimität des Apostels: Eine Untersuchung zu II Korinther 10–13', *ZNW* 35: 33–70.
1964a *Essays on New Testament Themes* (London: SCM Press); trans. W. Montague of selections from *Exegetische Versuche und Besinnungen*, Erster Band (Göttingen: Vandenhoeck & Ruprecht, 2nd edn, 1960).
1964b 'Is the Gospel Objective?', in Käsemann 1964a: 48–62.
1964c 'Ministry and Community in the New Testament', in Käsemann 1964a: 63–94.
1964d 'The Pauline Doctrine of the Lord's Supper', in Käsemann 1964a: 108–35.
1969a *New Testament Questions of Today* (London: SCM Press); trans. W. Montague of selections from *Exegetische Versuche und Besinnungen*, Zweiter Band (Göttingen: Vandenhoeck & Ruprecht, 1965).
1969b 'Sentences of Holy Law in the New Testament', in Käsemann 1969a: 66–81.
1969c 'The Beginnings of Christian Theology', in Käsemann 1969a: 82–107.
1969d 'On the Subject of Primitive Christian Apocalyptic', in Käsemann 1969a: 108–37.
1969e ' "The Righteousness of God" in Paul', in Käsemann 1969a: 168–82.
1969f 'Worship in Everyday Life', in Käsemann 1969a: 188–95.
1971a *Perspectives on Paul* (London: SCM Press); trans. M. Kohl of *Paulinische Perspektiven* (Tübingen: J.C.B. Mohr [Paul Siebeck], 1969).
1971b 'On Paul's Anthropology', in Käsemann 1971a: 1–31.
1971c 'The Saving Significance of the Death of Jesus in Paul', in Käsemann 1971a: 32–59.
1971d 'The Faith of Abraham in Romans 4', in Käsemann 1971a: 79–101.

1971e	'The Theological Problem Presented by the Motif of the Body of Christ', in Käsemann 1971a: 102–21.
1971f	'The Cry for Liberty in the Worship of the Church', in Käsemann 1971a: 122–37.
1971g	'The Spirit and the Letter', in Käsemann 1971a: 138–68.
1980	*Commentary on Romans* (Grand Rapids, MI: Eerdmans); trans. G. Bromily of *An die Römer* (Tübingen: J.C.B. Mohr [Paul Siebeck], 4th edn, 1980).

Katz, S.
1984	'Issues in the Separation of Judaism and Christianity After 70 C.E.: A Reconsideration', *JBL* 103: 43–76.

Kaye, B.
1975	'Eschatology and Ethics in 1 and 2 Thessalonians', *NovT* 17: 46–57.

Keck, L.
1974	'On the Ethos of Early Christians', *JAAR* 42: 435–52.
1976	'Justification of the Ungodly and Ethics', in J. Friedrich, W. Pölmann and P. Stuhlmacher (eds.), *Rechtfertigung* (Tübingen: J.C.B. Mohr [Paul Siebeck]): 199–209.
1980	'The Law and "The Law of Sin and Death" (Rom 8:1–4): Reflections on the Spirit and Ethics in Paul', in J. Crenshaw, L. Silberman and S. Sandmel (eds.), *The Divine Helmsman* (New York: Katv): 41–57.
1984	'Paul and Apocalyptic Theology', *Int* 38: 229–41.
1986	'Toward the Renewal of New Testament Christology', *NTS* 32: 362–77.
1988	*Paul and His Letters* (Philadelphia: Fortress Press, 2nd edn).
1989a	' "Jesus" in Romans', *JBL* 108: 443–60.
1989b	'The Quest for Paul's Pharisaism: Some Reflections', in D. Knight and P. Paris (eds.), *Justice and the Holy* (Atlanta: Scholars Press): 163–75.
1990	'Christology, Soteriology, and the Praise of God (Romans 15:7–13)', in Fortna and Gaventa 1990: 85–97.
1993	'Paul as Thinker', *Int* 47: 27–38.
1996a	'Rethinking New Testament Ethics', *JBL* 115: 3–16.
1996b	'The Accountable Self', in Lovering and Sumney 1996: 1–13.
1997	'Searchable Judgments and Scrutable Ways', in Johnson and Hay 1997: 22–32.

Kelber, W.
1983	*The Oral and the Written Gospel* (Bloomington, IN: University of Indiana Press).

Kelly, G.
1979	' "He Appeared to Me": 1 Cor 15:8 as Paul's Religious Experience of the "End Time" ', in Ryan 1979: 108–35.

Kertelge, K.
1974	'Apokalypsis Jesou Christou (Gal 1,12)', in J. Gnilka (ed.), *Neues Testament und Kirche* (Freiburg: Herder): 266–81.

Kim, S.
1984	*The Origins of Paul's Gospel* (Tübingen: J.C.B. Mohr [Paul Siebeck], 2nd edn).

Kinneavy, J.
1987	*Greek Rhetorical Origins of Christian Faith* (Oxford: Oxford University Press).

Kittel, G.
1906	'πίστις Ἰησοῦ Χριστοῦ bei Paulus', *Theol. Stud. u. Krit.* III: 79: 419–36.
1964	'ἀκούω, κτλ.', in *TDNT* I: 216–25.

Kittredge, C.
1998	*Community and Authority* (Harrisburg, PA: Trinity Press International).

Kitzberger, I.
1986   *Bau der Gemeinde: Das paulinische Wortfeld* οἰκοδομή/(ε π)οἰκοδομειν (Forschung zur Bibel; Würzburg: Echter Verlag).
Kleinknecht, H., F. Baumgärtel, W. Bieder, E. Sjöberg and E. Schweizer
1968   'πνεῦμα, κτλ.', in *TDNT* VI: 332–455.
Knox, J.
1961   *Life in Christ Jesus: Reflections on Romans 5–8* (Greenwich, CT: Seabury).
Koenig, J.
1978   'From Mystery to Ministry: Paul as Interpreter of Charismatic Gifts', *USQR* 33: 167–74.
1990a   'The Knowing of Glory and Its Consequences', in Fortna and Gaventa 1990: 158–69.
1990b   'Christ and the Hierarchies in First Corinthians', in A. Hultgren and B. Hall (eds.), *Christ and His Communities: Essays in Honor of Reginald H. Fuller* (Cincinnati, OH: Forward Movement Publications): 99–113.
Koperski, V.
1996   'Knowledge of Christ and Knowledge of God in the Corinthian Correspondence', in Bieringer 1996: 377–96.
Koptak, P.
1990   'Rhetorical Identification in Paul's Autobiographical Narrative', *JSNT* 40: 97–115.
Köster, H.
1972   'τόπος, κτλ.', in *TDNT* VIII: 187–208.
Kovacs, J.
1989   'The Archons, The Spirit and the Death of Christ: Do We Need the Hypothesis of Gnostic Opponents to Explain 1 Cor. 2.6–16?', in Marcus and Soards 1989: 217–36.
Kraftchick, S.
1990   'Why Do the Rhetoricians Rage?', in T. Jennings (ed.), *Text and Logos: The Humanistic Tradition of the New Testament* (Atlanta: Scholars Press): 55–79.
1993a   'A Necessary Detour: Paul's Metaphorical Understanding of the Christ Hymn', *HBT* 15: 1–37.
1993b   'Seeking a More Fluid Model', in Hay 1993b: 18–34.
1993c   'Death in Us, Life in You', in Hay 1993b: 156–81.
1996   'The Appeal of Character: Illustrations of Ethos and Pathos Argumentation in Galatians' (Unpublished revision of 'Ethos and Pathos Appeals in Galatians 5 and 6: A Rhetorical Analaysis', PhD dissertation, Emory University, 1985).
Kraftchick, S., C. Myers and B. Ollenburger (eds.)
1995   *Biblical Theology: Problems and Perspectives: In Honor of J. Christiaan Beker* (Nashville: Abingdon Press).
Kramer, W.
1966   *Christ, Lord, Son of God* (London: SCM Press); trans. B. Hardy of *Christos Kyrios Gottessohn* (Zürich: Zwingli-Verlag, 1963).
Kreitzer, L.J.
1987   *Jesus and God in Paul's Eschatology* (JSNTSup, 19; Sheffield: JSOT Press).
Krodel, G.
1967   'Gospel According to Paul', *Dialog* 6: 95–107.
Kuck, D.
1992   *Judgment and Community Conflict: Paul's Use of Apocalyptic Judgment Language in 1 Corinthians 3:5–4:5* (NovTSup, 66; Leiden: E.J. Brill).

1994	' "Each Will Bear His Own Burden": Paul's Creative Use of An Apocalyptic Motif', *NTS* 40: 289–97.

Kuhn, H.-W.
1991	'The Impact of the Qumran Scrolls on the Understanding of Paul', in D. Dimant and U. Rappaport (eds.), *The Dead Sea Scrolls* (Leiden: E.J. Brill): 327–39.

Kuhn, K.
1967	'Μαραναθά', in *TDNT* IV: 466–72.

Kümmel, W.
1965	'Πάρεσις und ἔνδειξις: Ein Beitrag zum Verständis der paulinischen Rechtfertigungslehre', in E. Grässer, O. Merk and A. Fritz (eds.), *Heilsgeschehen und Geschichte* (Marburg: N.G. Elwert): 260–70.

Lakeland, P.
1990	*Theology and Critical Theory* (Nashville: Abingdon Press).

Lambrecht, J.
1978	'The Line of Thought in Gal. 2.14b-21', *NTS* 24: 484–95.
1983	'Transformation in 2 Cor 3, 18', *Bib* 64: 243–54.
1991	'Transgressor by Nullifying God's Grace: A Study of Galatians 2,18–21', *Bib* 72: 217–36.
1994	'The Universalistic Will of God: The True Gospel in Galatians', in J. Lambrecht, *Pauline Studies* (Leuven: Leuven University Press): 299–306.

Lampe, P.
1990	'Theological Wisdom and the "Word About the Cross": The Rhetorical Scheme in 1 Corinthians 1–4', *Int* 44: 117–31.
1991a	'Das korinthische Herrenmahl im Schnittpunkt hellenistisch-römischer Mahlpraxis und paulinischer Theologia Crucis (1 Kor 11, 17 –34)', *ZNW* 82: 183–213.
1991b	'The Corinthian Eucharistic Dinner Party: Exegesis of a Cultural Context (1 Cor. 11:17–34)', *Affirmation* 4.2: 1–16.
1991c	'The Christian Worship Services in Corinth and the Corinthian Enthusiasm (1 Cor. 12–14)', *Affirmation* 4.2: 17–26.
1994	'The Eucharist: Identifying with Christ on the Cross', *Int* 48: 36–49.

Lane, W.
1982	'Covenant: The Key to Paul's Conflict with Corinth', *TynBul* 33: 3–29.

Lang, F.
1986	*Die Briefe an die Korinther* (NTD, 7; Göttingen: Vandenhoeck & Ruprecht).

Langkammer, P.
1970–71	'Literarische und theologische Einzelstücke in 1 Kor VIII:6', *NTS* 17: 195–202.

Larsson, E.
1962	*Christus als Vorbild* (Uppsala: Almsquist & Wiksells).

Lategan, B.
1988	'Is Paul Defending His Apostleship in Galatians?', *NTS* 34: 411–30.
1989	'Levels of Reader Instructions in the Text of Galatians', *Semeia* 48: 171–84.
1990	'Is Paul Developing a Specifically Christian Ethics in Galatians?', in Balch, Ferguson and Meeks 1990: 318–28.

Lessing, G.
1956	*Lessing's Theological Writings*, trans. and introduction by Henry Chadwick (London: A. & C. Black).

Lietzmann, H.
1949	*An Die Korinther I/II* (Tübingen: J.C.B. Mohr [Paul Siebeck]).
1971	*An die Galater* (HNT 9; Tübingen: J.C.B. Mohr, 4th edn).

Lightfoot, J.
1874   *Paul's Epistle to the Galatians* (London: Macmillan).
Lim, T.
1987   ' "Not in Persuasive Words of Wisdom, But in the Demonstration of the Spirit and Power" ', *NovT* 29: 137–49.
1997   *Holy Scripture in the Qumran Commentaries and the Pauline Letters* (Oxford: Clarendon Press).
Lincoln, A.
1979   'Paul the Visionary: The Setting and Significance of the Rapture to Paradise in II Corinthians 12:1–10', *NTS* 25: 204–20.
1981   *Paradise Now and Not Yet: Studies in the Role of the Heavenly Dimension in Paul's Thought with Special Reference to His Eschatology* (Cambridge: Cambridge University Press).
1983   'Ephesians 2:8–10: A Summary of Paul's Gospel?', *CBQ* 45: 617–27.
1995   'Liberation from the Powers: Supernatural Spirits or Societal Structures', in R. Carroll, M. Daniel, and D. Clines (eds.), *The Bible in Human Society* (JSOTSup, 200; Sheffield: Sheffield Academic Press): 335–54.
2002   'The Stories of Predecessors and Inheritors in Galatians and Romans', in B. Longenecker 2002: 172–203.
Lindars, B.
1985   'The Sound of the Trumpet: Paul and Eschatology', *BJRL* 67: 66–82.
Lindars, B., and S. Smalley (eds.)
1973   *Christ and the Spirit in the New Testament: Studies in Honour of C.F.D. Moule* (Cambridge: Cambridge University Press).
Lindemann, A.
1996   'Die Paulinische Ekklesiologie Angesichts der Lebenswirklichkeit der Christlichen Gemeinde in Korinth', in Bieringer 1996: 63–86.
Litfin, D.
1994   *St. Paul's Theology of Proclamation: 1 Corinthians 1–4 and Graeco-Roman Rhetoric* (SNTSMS, 79; Cambridge: Cambridge University Press).
Lohse, E.
1977   'Emuna und Pistis – Jüdisches und urchristliches Verständnis des Glaubens', *ZNW* 68: 147–633.
Longenecker, B.
1993   'ΠΙΣΤΙΣ in Romans 3:25: Neglected Evidence for the "Faithfulness of Christ"?', *NTS* 39: 478–80.
1996   'Defining the Faithful Character of the Covenant Community: Galatians 2.15–21 and Beyond: A Response to Jan Lambrecht', in Dunn 1996b: 75–98.
1997   'Contours of Covenant Theology in the Post-Conversion Paul', in R. Longenecker 1997: 125–46.
1998   *The Triumph of Abraham's God* (Edinburgh: T&T Clark).
1999   ' "Until Christ is Formed in You": Suprahuman Forces and Moral Character in Galatians', *CBQ* 61: 92–108.
Longenecker, B. (ed.)
2002   *Narrative Dynamics in Paul: A Critical Assessment* (Louisville, KY: Westminster/John Knox Press).
Longenecker, R.
1985   'The Nature of Paul's Early Eschatology', *NTS* 31: 85–95.
1990   *Galatians* (WBC; Dallas: Word Books).
Longenecker, R. (ed.)
1996   *Patterns of Discipleship in the New Testament* (Grand Rapids, MI: Eerdmans).

1997   *The Road From Damascus: The Impact of Paul's Conversion on His Life, Throught and Ministry* (Grand Rapids, MI: Eerdmans).

Lovering, E., and J. Sumney (eds.)

1996   *Theology and Ethics in Paul and His Interpreters: Essays in Honor of Victor Paul Furnish* (Nashville: Abingdon Press).

Lührmann, D.

1965   *Das Offenbarungsverständnis bei Paulus und in Paulinischen Gemeinden* (Neukirchlichener–Vluyn: Neukirchener Verlag).

1973   'Pistis im Judentum', *ZNW* 64: 19–38.

1974   *Glaube im frühen Christentum* (Gütersloh: Gütersloh Verlagshaus [G. Mohn]).

1978   *Der Brief an die Galater* (Zürich: Theologischer Verlag).

1989   'Paul and the Pharisaic Tradition', *JSNT* 36: 75–94.

1990   'The Beginnings of the Church at Thessalonica', in Balch, Ferguson and Meeks 1990: 237–49.

Lull, D.

1979   'The Spirit and the Creative Transformation of Human Existence', *JAAR* 47: 39–55.

1980   *The Spirit in Galatia: Paul's Interpretation of Pneuma as Divine Power* (SBLDS, 49; Chico, CA: Scholars Press).

1986   ' "The Law was Our Pedagogue": A Study in Gal 3:19–25', *JBL* 105: 481–98.

1991   'Salvation History. Theology in 1 Thessalonians, Philemon, Philippians, and Galatians: A Response to N.T. Wright, R.B. Hays, and R. Scroggs', in Bassler 1991: 247–65.

Lyons, G.

1985   *Pauline Autobiography: Toward a New Understanding* (Atlanta: Scholars Press).

1995   'Modeling the Holiness Ethos: A Study Based on First Thessalonians', *Wesley Theological Journal* 30: 187–211.

MacDonald, M.

1988   *The Pauline Churches: A Socio-Historical Study of Institutionalization in the Pauline and Deutero-Pauline Writings* (SNTSMS, 60; Cambridge: Cambridge University Press).

MacIntyre, A.

1985   *After Virtue: A Study in Moral Theology* (London: Gerald Duckworth, 2nd edn).

1967   *A Short History of Ethics* (London: Routledge & Kegan Paul).

Malan, F.

1981   'The Use of the Old Testament in 1 Corinthians', *Neot* 14: 134–70.

Malherbe, A.

1970   'Gentle as a Nurse: The Cynic Background to I Thess ii', *NovT* 12: 203–17.

1983a   *Social Aspects of Early Christianity* (Philadelphia: Fortress Press).

1983b   'Exhortation in First Thessalonians', *NovT* 25: 238–56.

1986a   *Moral Exhortation: A Greco-Roman Sourcebook* (Philadelphia: Westminster Press).

1986b   'Paul: Hellenistic Philosopher or Christian Pastor?', *ATR* 68: 3–13.

1987   *Paul and the Thesslonians* (Philadelphia: Fortress Press).

1989   *Paul and the Popular Philosophers* (Philadelphia: Fortress Press).

1990   ' "Pastoral Care" in the Thessalonian Church', *NTS* 36: 375–91.

1992   'Hellenistic Moralists and the New Testament', in W. Haase (ed.), *Principat* 26.1: *Religion* (Berlin: W. de Gruyter): 267–333.

1994   'Determinism and Free Will in Paul: The Argument of 1 Cor 8 and 9', in Engberg-Pedersen 1994b: 231–55.

2000a 'The Apostle Paul as Pastor', in Lo Lung-kwon (ed.), *Jesus, Paul and John* (Hong Kong: The Chinese University): 98–138.

2000b *The Letters to the Thessalonians* (AB; New York: Doubleday).

Malherbe, A., and W. Meeks (eds.)

1993 *The Future of Christology: Essays in Honor of Leander E. Keck* (Minneapolis: Fortress Press).

Malina, B.

1993 *The New Testament World: Insights from Cultural Anthropology* (Louisville, KY: Westminster/John Knox Press).

1995 'Early Christian Groups: Using Small Group Formation Theory to Explain Christian Organizations', in Esler 1995: 96–113.

Marcus, J.

1982 'The Evil Inclination in the Epistle of James', *CBQ* 44: 606–21.

1986 'The Evil Inclination in the Letters of Paul', *IBS* 8: 8–21.

1988 'Entering into the Kingly Power of God', *JBL* 107: 663–75.

1996 'Modern and Ancient Jewish Apocalypticism', *JR* 76: 1–27.

Marcus, J., and M. Soards (eds.)

1989 *Apocalyptic and the New Testament* (JSNTSup, 24; Sheffield: JSOT Press).

Marshall, I.

1978 'The Meaning of "Reconciliation"', in R. Guelich (ed.), *Unity and Diversity in New Testament Theology* (Grand Rapids, MI: Eerdmans): 117–32.

1983 'The Death of Jesus in the New Testament', *Word and World* 3: 12–21.

1997 'A New Understanding of the Present and the Future: Paul and Eschatology', in R. Longenecker 1997: 43–61.

Marshall, P.

1987 *Enmity in Corinth: Social Conventions in Paul's Relations with the Corinthians* (WUNT, 2.23; Tübingen: J.C.B. Mohr [Paul Siebeck]).

Martin, D.

1990 *Slavery as Salvation: The Metaphor of Slavery in Pauline Christianity* (New Haven: Yale University Press).

1995 *The Corinthian Body* (New Haven: Yale University Press).

2001 'Paul and the Judaism/Hellenism Dichotomy: Toward a Social History of the Question', in Engberg-Pedersen 2001: 29–62.

Martin, R.

1981 *Reconciliation: A Study of Paul's Theology* (Atlanta: John Knox Press).

1984 *The Spirit and the Congregation: Studies in 1 Corinthians 12–15* (Grand Rapids, MI: Eerdmans).

Martin, T.

1999 'Whose Flesh? What Temptation? (Galatians 4.13–14)', *JSNT* 74: 65–91.

Martyn, J.

1967 'Epistemology at the Turn of the Ages', in Farmer, Moule and Niebuhr 1967: 269–87.

1985a 'Apocalyptic Antinomies in Paul's Letter to the Galatians', *NTS* 31: 410–24.

1985b 'A Law-Observant Mission to the Gentiles: The Background of Galatians', *SJT* 38: 307–24.

1988 'Paul and His Jewish-Christian Interpreters', *USQR* 42: 1–15.

1991 'Events in Galatia', in Bassler 1991: 160–79.

1992 'Listening to John and Paul on Gospel and Scripture', *Word & World* 12: 68–81.

1993 'Covenant, Christ, and Church in Galatians', in Malherbe and Meeks 1993: 137–59.

1997a	*Theological Issues in the Letters of Paul* (Edinburgh: T&T Clark).
1997b	*Galatians* (AB; New York: Doubleday).
2002	'De-apocalypticizing Paul: An Essay Focused on *Paul and the Stoics* by Troels Engberg-Pedersen', *JSNT* 86: 61–102.

Marxsen, W.

1993	*New Testament Foundations for Christian Ethics* (Edinburgh: T&T Clark); trans. O. Dean of *'Christliche' und Christliche Ethik in Neuen Testamant* (Gerdhohm: Güterslöher Verlagshaus, 1989).

Mason, S.

1994	' "For I am Not Ashamed of the Gospel" (Rom. 1.16): The Gospel and the First Readers of Romans', in Jervis and Richardson 1994: 254–87.

Matera, F.

1988	'The Culmination of Paul's Argument to the Galatians: Gal. 5.1–6.17', *JSNT* 32: 79–91.
1992	*Galatians* (Sacra Pagina; Collegeville, MN: Liturgical Press).
1996	*New Testament Ethics: The Legacies of Jesus and Paul* (Louisville, KY: Westminster John Knox Press).

Matlock, R.B.

1996	*Unveiling the Apocalyptic Paul: Paul's Interpreters and the Rhetoric of Criticism* (JSNTSup, 127; Sheffield: Sheffield Academic Press).
2000	'Detheologizing the ΠΙΣΤΙΣ ΞΡΙΣΤΟΥ Debate: Cautionary Remarks from a Lexical Semantic Perspective', *NovT* 42: 1–23.
2003	'ΠΙΣΤΙΣ in Galatians 3:26: Neglected Evidence for "Faith in Christ"?', *NTS* 49: 433–39.

Maurer, C.

1971	'σύνοιδα συνείδησις', in *TDNT* VII: 898–919.

McDonald, J.

1993	*Biblical Interpretation and Christian Ethics* (Cambridge: Cambridge University Press).

McKelvey, R.

1969	*The New Temple: The Church in the New Testament* (Oxford: Oxford University Press).

McLean, B.

1992	'The Absence of an Atoning Sacrifice in Paul's Soteriology', *NTS* 38: 531–53.

Mearns, C.

1981	'Early Eschatological Development in Paul: The Evidence of 1 and 2 Thessalonians', *NTS* 27: 137–57.
1984	'Early Eschatological Developments in Paul: The Evidence of 1 Corinthians', *JSNT* 22: 1–35.

Meeks, W.

1973	'The Image of the Androgyne: Some Uses of a Symbol in Earliest Christianity', *History of Religions* 13: 165–208.
1977	'In One Body: The Unity of Humankind in Colossians and Ephesians', in Jervell and Meeks 1977: 209–21.
1979	' "Since Then You Would Need to Go Out of the World": Group Boundaries', in Ryan 1979: 4–29.
1980	'Toward a Social Description of Pauline Christianity', in W. Green, J. Neusner and E. Frerichs (eds.), *Approaches to Ancient Judaism, Vol 2* (Missoula, MT: Scholars Press): 27–41.
1982a	'The Social Context of Pauline Theology', *Int* 36: 266–77.

1982b   'Social Functions of Apocalyptic Language in Pauline Christianity', in
           D. Hellholm (ed.), *Apocalypticism in the Mediterranean World and the Near
           East: Proceedings of the International Colloquium on Apocalypticism,
           Uppsala, August 12–17, 1979* (Tübingen: J.C.B. Mohr [Paul Siebeck]): 687–
           705.
1983   *The First Urban Christians* (New Haven, CT: Yale University Press).
1985   'Breaking Away: Three New Testament Pictures of Christianity's Separation
           from the Jewish Communities', in Neusner and Frerichs 1985: 93–115.
1986a   *The Moral World of the First Christians* (Philadelphia: Westminster Press)
1986b   'A Hermeneutics of Social Embodiment', *HTR* 79: 176–86.
1986c   'Understanding Early Christian Ethics', *JBL* 105: 3–11.
1987   'Judgment and the Brother: Romans 14:1–15:13', in Hawthorne and Betz
           1987: 290–300.
1988   'The Polyphonic Ethics of the Apostle Paul', in D. Yeager (ed.), *The Annual of
           the Society of Christian Ethics* (Washington, DC: Georgetown University
           Press): 17–30.
1990   'The Circle of Reference in Pauline Morality', in Balch, Ferguson and Meeks
           1990: 305–17.
1991   'The Man From Heaven in Paul's Letter to the Philippians', in Pearson 1991:
           329–36.
1993a   *The Origins of Christian Morality* (New Haven, CT: Yale University Press).
1993b   ' "To Walk Worthily of the Lord": Moral Formation in the Pauline School
           Exemplified by the Letter to the Colossians', in E. Stump and T. Flint (eds.),
           Hermes and Athena (Notre Dame, IN: University of Notre Dame Press): 37–58
           (response 71–74).
1996   'The Temporary Reign of the Son: 1 Cor 15:23–28', in Fornberg and Hellholm
           1996: 801–11.
2001a   'Judaism, Hellenism, and the Birth of Christianity', in Engberg-Pedersen 2001:
           17–28.
2001b   'Corinthian Christians as Artificial Aliens', in Engberg-Pedersen 2001: 129–
           38.
Meeks, W.A., A.R. Hilton and H. Snyder (eds.)
2002   *In Search of the Early Christians: Selected Essays* (New Haven: Yale Univer-
           sity Press).
Merk, O.
1989   'Nachahmung Christi: zu ethischen Perspektiven in der paulinischen
           Theologie', in Merklein 1989: 172–206.
1998   'Der Beginn der Paränese im Galaterbrief', in R. Bebauer, M. Karrer und
           M. Meiser (eds.), *Wissenschaftsgeschichte und Exegese* (Berlin: W. de Gruyter):
           238–59; reprinted from *ZNW* 60 (1969): 83–104.
Merklein, H.
1985   'Entstehung und Gehalt des paulinischen Leib-Christi Gedankens', in W. Bre-
           uning (ed.), *Im Gespräch mit dem dreieinen Gott* (Düsseldorf: Patmos Verlag):
           115–40.
1992   *Der Erste Brief an die Korinther: Kapitel 1–4* (Würzburg: Echter).
1993   ' "Nicht Aus Werken des Gesetzes" – Eine Auslegung von Gal 2,15–21', in
           H. Merklein, *et al.* (eds.), *Bibel in jüdischen und christlichen Tradition*
           (Frankfurt am Main: Hain): 121–36.
Merklein, H. (ed.)
1989   *Neues Testament und Ethik* (Freiburg: Herden).

Michaelis, W.
1967a   'μιμέομαι, κτλ.', in *TDNT* IV: 659–74.
1967b   'ὁράω, κτλ.', in *TDNT* V: 315–82.
1967c   'ὁδός, κτλ.', in *TDNT* V: 42–114.
Miller, E.
1982   'Πολιτεύεσθε in Philippians 1.27: Some Philological and Thematic Observa-
         tions', *JSNT* 15: 86–96.
Minear, P.
1983   'Christ and the Congregation: 1 Corinthians 5–6', *RevExp* 80: 341–50.
Mitchell, A.
1993   'Rich and Poor in the Courts of Corinth: Litigiousness and Status in 1 Corin-
         thians 6:1–11', *NTS* 39: 562–86.
Mitchell, M.
1989   'Concerning ΠΕΡΙ ΔΕ in 1 Corinthians', *NovT* 31: 229–56.
1991   *Paul and the Rhetoric of Reconciliation* (Louisville, KY: Westminster/John
         Knox Press).
1992   'New Testament Envoys in the Context of Greco-Roman Diplomatic and Epis-
         tolary Conventions: The Example of Timothy and Titus', *JBL* 111: 641–62.
1994   'Rhetorical Shorthand in Pauline Argumentation: The Functions of "the Gos-
         pel" in the Corinthian Correspondence', in Jervis and Richardson 1994: 63–88.
2001   'Pauline Accommodation and "Condescension" (συγκατάβασις): 1 Cor 9:19–
         23 and the History of Influence', in Engberg-Pedersen 2001: 197–214.
Moore, R.
1996   '2 Cor 5:21: The Interpretive Key to Paul's Use of δικαιοσύνη θεοῦ?', in
         Bieringer 1996: 707–15.
Morgan, R. (ed., trans. and introduction)
1973   *The Nature of New Testament Theology: The Contribution of William Wrede
         and Adolf Schlatter* (London: SCM Press).
1992   'Theology (NT)', *ABD* 6: 473–83.
1995a   'New Testament Theology', in Kraftchick, Myers and Ollenburger 1995: 104–
         30.
1995b   *Romans* (Sheffield: Sheffield Academic Press).
1998   'Incarnation, Myth, and Theology', in R. Martin and B. Dodd (eds.), *Where
         Christology Began* (Louisville, KY: John Knox Press): 43–73.
2000   'Towards a Critical Appropriation of the Sermon on the Mount: Christology
         and Discipleship', in Horrell and Tuckett 2000: 157–91.
Morland, K.
1995   *The Rhetoric of Curse in Galatians: Paul Confronts Another Gospel* (Atlanta:
         Scholars Press).
Morgan, R., and J. Barton
1988   *Biblical Interpretation* (Oxford: Oxford University Press).
Morray-Jones, C.
1992   'Transformational Mysticism in the Apocalyptic-Merkabah Tradition', *JJS* 43:
         1–31.
1993   'Paradise Revisited (2 Cor 12:1–12): The Jewish Mystical Background of Paul's
         Apostolate', *HTR* 86: 177–217 (Part 1) and 86: 265–92 (Part 2).
Moule, C.F.D.
1960   'Reconsideration of the Context of Maranatha', *NTS* 6: 307–10.
1967   'Obligation in the Ethic of Paul', in *idem* (ed.), *Essays in New Testament Inter-
         pretation* (Cambridge: Cambridge University Press): 261–77.
1967–68 'Fulfillment-Words in the New Testament: Use and Abuse', *NTS* 14: 293–320.
1977   *The Origin of Christology* (Cambridge: Cambridge University Press).

Mouton, E.
2002 *Reading a New Testament Document Ethically* (Academia Biblica, 1; Atlanta: SBL).

Moxnes, H.
1980 *Theology in Conflict: Studies in Paul's Understanding of God in Romans* (NovTSup, 53; Leiden: E.J. Brill).
1994 'The Quest for Honor and the Unity of the Community in Romans 12 and in the Orations of Dio Chrysostom', in Engberg-Pedersen 1994b: 203–30.

Munck, J.
1959 *Paul and the Salvation of Mankind* (Richmond: John Knox Press); trans. F. Clarke of *Paulus und Die Heilsgeschichte* (Copenhagen: Universitetsforlaget, Aarhus, Ejnar Munksgaard, 1954).

Murphy, J.J.
1993 'Early Christianity as a "Persuasive Campaign": Evidence from the Acts of the Apostles and the Letters of Paul', in S. Porter and T. Olbricht (eds.), *Rhetoric and the New Testament* (JSNTSup, 90; Sheffield: JSOT Press): 90–99.

Murphy-O'Connor, J.
1977a '1 Corinthians, V, 3–5', *RB* 84: 239–45.
1977b 'Works Without Faith in 1 Cor., VII, 14', *RB* 84: 349–61.

Murphy-O'Connor, J. (ed.)
1968 *Paul and Qumran: Studies in New Testament Exegesis* (Chicago: The Priory Press).

Nanos, M.
1996 *The Mystery of Romans: The Jewish Context of Paul's Letter* (Minneapolis: Fortress Press).

Neufeld, D.
1994 *Reconceiving Texts as Speech Acts: An Analysis of 1 John* (Biblical Interpretation, 7; Leiden: E.J. Brill).

Neugebauer, F.
1957–58 'Das Paulinische "In Christ"', *NTS* 4: 124–38.
1961 *In Christus: Eine Untersuchung zum paulinischen Glaubensverständnis* (Göttingen: Vandenhoeck & Ruprecht).

Neusner, J., and E. Frerichs (eds.)
1985 *'To See Ourselves As Others See Us': Christians, Jews, 'Others', in Late Antiquity* (Chico, CA: Scholars Press).

Newman, C.
1992 *Paul's Glory Christology: Tradition and Rhetoric* (NovTSup, 49; Leiden: E.J. Brill).

Newman, C., J. Davila and G. Lewis (eds.)
1999 *The Jewish Roots of Christological Monotheism: Papers from the St Andrews Conference on the Historical Origins of the Worship of Jesus* (Leiden: E.J. Brill).

Newton, D.
1998 *Deity and Diet: The Dilemma of Sacrificial Food at Corinth* (JSNTSup, 169; Sheffield: Sheffield Academic Press).

Newton, M.
1985 *The Concept of Purity at Qumran and in the Letters of Paul* (Cambridge: Cambridge University Press).

Nickelsburg, G.
1985 'Revealed Wisdom as a Criterion for Inclusion and Exclusion: From Jewish Sectarianism to Early Christianity', in Neusner and Frerichs 1985: 73–91.

1991   'The Incarnation: Paul's Solution to the Universal Human Predicament', in
            Pearson 1991: 348–57.
Niebuhr, K.-W.
1992   *Heidenapostel aus Israel: Die jüdische Identität des Paulus nach ihrer
            Darstellung in seinen Briefen* (Tübingen: J.C.B. Mohr [Paul Siebeck]).
Niederwimmer, K.
1998   *The Didache* (Hermeneia; Minneapolis: Fortress Press); trans. L. Maloney from
            Die Didache (Göttingen: Vandenhoeck & Ruprecht, 1989).
Nolland, J.
1986   'Grace as Power', *NovT* 28: 26–31.
Oepke, A.
1964   'δύω, κτλ.', in *TDNT* II: 318–21.
1967   'παρουσία, κτλ.', in *TDNT* V: 858–71.
Oke, C.
1955   'Paul's Method Not a Demonstration But an Exhibition of the Spirit', *ExpTim*
            67: 35–36.
1957   'A Suggestion with Regard to Romans 8:23', *Int* 11: 455–60.
Ollrog, W.-H.
1979   *Paulus und seine Mitarbeiter: Untersuchungen zu Theorie und Praxis der
            paulinischen Mission* (WMANT, 50; Neukirchen–Vluyn: Neukirchener Verlag).
Olson, S.
1984   'Epistolary Uses of Expressions of Self-Confidence', *JBL* 103: 585–97.
Outka, G.
1987   'Following at a Distance: Ethics and the Identity of Jesus', in G. Green (ed.),
            Scriptural Authority and Narrative Interpretation (Philadelphia: Fortress Press):
            144–60.
Paget, J.
1994   *The Epistle of Barnabas: Outlook and Background* (Tübingen: J.C.B. Mohr
            [Paul Siebeck]).
Parsons, M.
1988   '"In Christ" in Paul', *Vox Evangelica* 18: 25–44.
1995   'Being Precedes Act: Indicative and Imperative in Paul's Writing', in Rosner
            1995: 217–47; reprinted from *EvQ* 60: 99–127 (all page references to Rosner
            1995).
Pascuzzi, M.
1997   *Ethics, Ecclesiology and Church Discipline: A Rhetorical Analysis of 1 Corin-
            thians 5* (Tesi Gregoriana Serie Teologia, 32; Rome: Editrice Pontifica Univer-
            sità Gregoriana).
Patte, D.
1983   *Paul's Faith and the Power of the Gospel: A Structural Introduction to the
            Pauline Letters* (Philadelphia: Fortress).
1988   'Speech Act Theory and Biblical Exegesis', *Semeia* 41: 85–102.
Pearson, B.
1973   *The Pneumatikos-Psychikos Terminology in 1 Corinthians: A Study in the
            Theology of the Corinthian Opponents of Paul and its Relation to Gnosticism*
            (SBLDS, 12; Missoula, MT: Scholars Press).
Pearson, B. (ed.)
1991   *The Future of Early Christianity* (Minneapolis: Fortress Press).
Pedersen, S.
2002   'Paul's Understanding of the Biblical Law', *NovT* 44.1: 1–34.

Penner, T.
1996   *The Epistle of James and Eschatology* (JSNTSup, 121; Sheffield: Sheffield
           Academic Press).
Perdue, L.
1990   'The Social Character of Paranesis and Paraenetic Literature', *Semeia* 50: 5–
           39.
Perdue, L., B. Scott and W. Wiseman
1993   *In Search of Wisdom: Essays in Memory of John G. Grammie* (Louisville, KY:
           Westminster/John Knox Press).
Peri, I.
1989   '*Ecclesia* und *synagoga* in der lateinischen Übersetzung des Alten Testa-
           mentes', *BZ* 2: 245–51.
Perriman, A.
1989   'Paul and the Parousia: 1 Corinthians 15.50–57 and 2 Corinthians 5.1–5', *NTS*
           35: 512–21.
Petersen, N.
1985   *Rediscovering Paul: Philemon and the Sociology of Paul's Narrative World*
           (Philadelphia: Fortress Press).
Pfitzner, V.
1967   *Paul and the Agon Motif: Traditional Imagery in the Pauline Literature*
           (NovTSup, 16; Leiden: E.J. Brill).
Pfleiderer, O.
1877   *Paulinism: A Contribution to the History of Primitive Christianity, Vol 1:
           Paul's Doctrine* (trans. E. Peters; London: William & Norgate,).
Pickett, R.
1997   *The Cross in Corinth: The Social Significance of the Death of Jesus* (JSNTSup,
           143; Sheffield: JSOT Press).
Pierce, C.
1955   *Conscience in the New Testament* (London: SCM Press).
Plevnik, J.
1989   'The Center of Pauline Theology', *CBQ* 51: 461–78.
1997   *Paul and the Parousia: An Exegetical and Theological Investigation* (Peabody,
           MA: Hendrickson).
Pogoloff, S.
1992   *Logos and Sophia: The Rhetorical Situation of 1 Corinthians* (SBLDS, 134;
           Atlanta: Scholars Press).
Polaski, S.
1999   *Paul and the Discourse of Power* (Gender, Culture, Theory, 8; Biblical Semi-
           nar, 62; Sheffield: Sheffield Academic Press).
Proudfoot, C.M.
1963   'Imitation or Realistic Participation: Paul's Concept of Suffering With Christ',
           Int 17: 140–60.
Purvis, S.
1993   *The Power of the Cross: Foundations for a Christian Feminist Ethic of Com-
           munity* (Nashville: Abingdon Press).
1996   'Following Paul: Some Notes on Ethics Then and Now', *Word & World* 16.4:
           413–19.
Räisänen, H.
1983   *Paul and the Law* (Tübingen: J.C.B. Mohr [Paul Siebeck]).
1985   'Galatians 2.16 and Paul's Break with Judaism', *NTS* 31: 543–53.
1987   'Paul's Conversion and the Development of His View of the Law', *NTS* 33:
           404–19.

1992   'Paul's Call Experience and His Later View of the Law', in *Jesus, Paul and Torah: Collected Essays* (Sheffield: JSOT Press): 15–47.

2000   *Beyond New Testament Theology* (London: SCM Press, 2nd edn).

Rehg, W.
1994   *Insight & Solidarity: The Discourse Ethics of Jürgen Habermas* (Berkeley, CA: University of California Press).

Reiling, J.
1973   *Hermas and Christian Prophecy: A Study of the Eleventh Mandate* (NovTSup, 37; Leiden: E.J. Brill).

1977   'Prophecy, the Spirit and the Church', in J. Panagopoulos (ed.), *Prophetic Vocation in the New Testament and Today* (Leiden: E.J. Brill): 58–76.

Reinmuth, E.
1991   ' "Nicht vergeblich" bei Paulus und Pseudo-Philo, Liber antiquitatum biblicarum', *NovT* 33: 97–123.

1995   'Narratio und argumentatio – zur Auslegung der Jesus – Christus – Geschichte im Ersten Korintherbrief: Ein Beitrag zur mimetischen Kompetenz des Paulus', *ZTK* 92: 13–27.

Reitzenstein, R.
1978   *Hellenistic Mystery-Religions: Their Basic Ideas and Significance* (Pittsburgh: Pickwick Press); trans. J. Steely of *Die Hellenistischen Mysterienreligionen: nach ihren Grundgedanken und Wirkungen* (Leipzig: B.G. Teubner, 1920).

Rengstorf, K.
1972   'ὑπηρέτης, κτλ.', in *TDNT* VIII: 530–44.

Renwick, D.
1991   *Paul, the Temple, and the Presence of God* (Atlanta: Scholars Press).

Reumann, J.
1966–67   'OIKONOMIA-Terms in Paul in Comparison with Lucan *Heilsgeschichte*', *NTS* 13: 147–67.

Richard, E.
1981   'Polemics, Old Testament, and Theology: A Study of II Cor., III, 1–IV, 6', *RB* 88: 340–67.

1995   *First and Second Thessalonians* (Sacra Pagina; Collegeville, MN: Liturgical Press).

Richardson, N.
1994   *Paul's Language About God* (JSNTSup, 99; Sheffield: Sheffield Academic Press).

Richardson, P., and J. Hurd (eds.)
1984   *From Jesus to Paul: Studies in Honour of Francis Wright Beare* (Waterloo, ON: Wilfrid Laurier University Press).

Riches, J.
1998   'Readings of Augustine on Paul: Their Impact on Critical Studies of Paul', in *1998 SBL Seminar Papers* (Atlanta: Scholars Press): 943–67.

Robertson, A., and A. Plummer
1914   *A Critical and Exegetical Commentary on the First Epistle of St Paul to the Corinthians* (ICC; Edinburgh: T&T Clark, 2nd edn).

Robinson, J.A.T.
1952   *The Body: A Study in Pauline Theology* (London: SCM Press).

1953   'Traces of a Liturgical Sequence in 1 Cor 16:20–24', *JTS* 4: 38–41.

Roetzel, C.
1972   *Judgement in the Community: A Study of the Relationship Between Eschatology and Ecclesiology in Paul* (Leiden: E.J. Brill).

1986   'Theodidaktoi and Handwork in Philo and 1 Thessalonians', in Vanhoye 1986: 324–31.
1999   *Paul, The Man and the Myth* (Edinburgh: T&T Clark).
Rogers, E.
1983   'ΕΠΟΤΙΣΘΗΜΕΝ Again', *NTS* 29: 139–42.
Rogerson, J.
1995   'Discourse Ethics and Biblical Ethics', in Rogerson, Davies and Carroll 1995: 17–26.
Rogerson, J., M. Davies, and M. Carroll (eds.)
1995   *The Bible in Ethics* (JSNTSup, 207; Sheffield: Sheffield Academic Press): 17–26.
Rollins, W.
1987   'Greco-Roman Slave Terminology and Pauline Metaphors for Salvation', in K. Richards (ed.), *1987 SBL Seminar Papers* (Atlanta: Scholars Press): 100–10.
Rosner, B.
1991a   'Temple and Holiness in 1 Corinthians 5', *TynBul* 42: 137–45.
1991b   'Moses Appointing Judges: An Antecedent to 1 Cor 6:1–6?', *ZNW* 82: 275–78.
1992a   'A Possible Quotation of Test. Reuben 5:5 in 1 Corinthians 6:18a', *JTS* 43: 123–27.
1992b   'ΟΥΧΙ ΜΑΛΛΟΝ ΕΠΕΝΘΗΣΑΤΗ': Corporate Responsibility in 1 Corinthians 5', *NTS* 38: 470–73.
1994   *Paul, Scripture and Ethics: A Study of 1 Corinthians 5–7* (Leiden: E.J. Brill).
Rosner, B. (ed.)
1995   *Understanding Paul's Ethics* (Grand Rapids, MI: Eerdmans).
Rowland, C.
1982   *The Open Heaven* (New York: Crossroad).
1983   'Apocalyptic Visions and the Exaltation of Christ in the Letter to the Colossians', *JSNT* 19: 73–83.
1988a   'Apocalyptic Literature', in D. Carson and H. Williamson (eds.), *It is Written: Scripture Citing Scripture* (Cambridge: Cambridge University Press): 170–89.
1988b   'The Inter-Testamental Literature', in P. Avis (ed.), *The History of Christian Theology, Vol 2: The Study and Use of the Bible* (Grand Rapids, MI: Eerdmans; Basingstoke: Marshall Pickering): 151–259.
1995a   '"Upon Whom the Ends of the Ages have Come": Apocalyptic and the Interpretation of the New Testament', in M. Bull (ed.), *Apocalypse Theory and the End of the World* (Oxford: Basil Blackwell): 38–57.
1995b   'Moses and Patmos: Reflections on the Jewish Background of Early Christianity', in J. Davies, G. Harvey and W. Watson (eds.), *Words Remembered, Texts Renewed: Essays in Honour of John F.A. Sawyer* (JSNTSup, 195; Sheffield: Sheffield Academic Press): 280–99.
1996a   'Apocalyptic, God and the World. Appearance and Reality: Early Christianity's Debt to the Jewish Apocalyptic Tradition', in Barclay and Sweet 1996: 238–49.
1996b   'Apocalyptic, Mysticism, and the New Testament', in Peter Schäfer (ed.), *Geshichte Tradition – Reflexion: Festschrift für Martin Hengel, Band 1* (Tübingen: J.C.B. Mohr [Paul Siebeck]): 405–30.
1999   '"Sweet Science Reigns": Divine and Human Wisdom in the Apocalyptic Tradition', in S. Barton 1999: 61–73.
2002   *Christian Origins: An Account of the Setting and Character of the Most Important Messianic Sect of Judaism* (London: SPCK, 2nd edn).

Ruef, J.
    1971   *Paul's First Letter to Corinth* (Pelican NT Commentaries; Harmondsworth: Penguin Books).
Ryan, T. (ed.)
    1979   *Critical History and Biblical Faith* (Villanova, PA: The College Theology Society).
Sampley, J.P.
    1990   'Faith and its Moral Life: A Study of Individuation in the Thought World of the Apostle Paul', in Carroll, Cosgrove and Johnson 1990: 222–38.
    1991a   *Walking Between the Times* (Minneapolis: Augsburg-Fortress).
    1991b   'From Text to Thought World: The Route to Paul's Ways', in Bassler 1991: 3–14.
    1996   'Reasoning from the Horizons of Paul's Thought World: A Comparison of Galatians and Philippians', in Lovering and Sumney 1996: 114–31.
Sanday, W., and A. Headlam
    1914   *The Epistle to the Romans* (ICC; Edinburgh: T&T Clark, 5th edn).
Sanday, W., and A. Headlam
    1902   *A Critical and Exegetical Commentary on the Epistle to the Romans* (ICC; Edinburgh: T&T Clark).
Sanders, B.
    1981   'Imitating Paul: 1 Cor 4:16', *HTR* 74: 353–63.
Sanders, E.P.
    1977   *Paul and Palestinian Judaism* (London: SCM Press).
    1983   *Paul, the Law and the Jewish People* (Minneapolis: Fortress Press).
    1990   'Jewish Associations with Gentiles and Galatians 2:11–14', in Fortna and Gaventa 1990: 170–88.
    1991   *Paul* (Past Masters; Oxford: Oxford University Press).
    1992   *Judaism: Belief and Practice 63 BCE–66 CE* (London: SCM Press).
    1996   'Paul', in Barclay and Sweet 1996: 112–29.
Sanders, J.A.
    1975   'Torah and Christ', *Int* 29: 373–90.
    1977   'Torah and Paul', in Jervell and Meeks 1977: 132–40.
Sanders, J.T.
    1986   *Ethics in the New Testament: Change and Development* (London: SCM Press).
Sandnes, K.
    1991   *Paul – One of the Prophets? A Contribution to the Apostle's Self Understanding* (WUNT II.43; Tübingen: J.C.B. Mohr).
Savage, T.
    1996   *Power Through Weakness: Paul's Understanding of the Christian Ministry in 2 Corinthians* (SNTSMS; Cambridge: Cambridge University Press).
Schäfer, P.
    1974   'Die Torah der messianischen Zeit', *ZNW* 65: 27–42.
Schiffman, L.
    1989   *The Eschatological Community of the Dead Sea Scrolls* (Atlanta: Scholars Press).
Schlatter, A.
    1956   *Paulus Der Bote Jesu: Eine Deutung Seiner Briefe an die Korinther* (Stuttgart: Calwer Verlag, 2nd edn).
    1997   *The History of the Christ* (Grand Rapids, MI: Baker Book House); trans. A. Köstenberger of *Die Geschichte des Christus* (Stuttgart: Calwer Vereinsbuchhandlung, 1923).

1999   *The Theology of the Apostles* (Grand Rapids, MI: Baker Book House); trans.
            A. Köstenberger of *Die Theologie der Apostel* (Stuttgart: Calwer Vereinsbuch-
            handlung, 1922).

Schlier, H.
1971   *Der Brief an die Galater* (Göttingen: Vandenhoeck & Ruprecht).

Schlier, H.
1964a   'βέβαιος, κτλ.', in *TDNT* I: 600–603.
1964b   'δεικινυμι, κτλ.', in *TDNT* II: 25–33.

Schmithals, W.
1971   *Gnosticism in Corinth: An Investigation of the Letters to the Corinthians* (Nash-
            ville: Abingdon Press).

Schmitz, O., and G. Stählin
1967   'παρακαλέω, κτλ.', in *TDNT* V: 773–99.

Schnabel, E.
1992   'Wie hat Paulus seine Ethik entwickel? Motivationen, Normen, und Kriterein
            Paulinischer Ethik', *European Journal of Theology* 1.1: 63–81.

Schoedel, W.
1985   *Ignatius of Antioch: A Commentary on the Letters of Ignatius of Antioch*
            (Hermeneia; Philadelphia: Fortress Press).

Schoeps, H.
1961   *Paul: The Theology of the Apostle in the Light of Jewish Religious History*
            (Philadelphia: The Westminster Press); trans. H. Knight of *Paulus: Die Theolo-
            gie des Apostels im Lichte der jüdischen Religionsgeschichte* (Tübingen: J.C.B.
            Mohr, 1959).

Schrage, W.
1960   'Zur formalethischen Deutung der paulinischen Paränese', *Zeitschrift für
            evangelische Ethik* 4: 207–33.

1961   *Die konkreten Einzelgebote in der paulinischen Paränese* (Gütersloh: Güter-
            sloher Verlagshaus [Gerd Mohn]).

1964   'Die Stellung zur Welt bei Paulus, Epiktet und in der Apokalyptik', *ZTK* 61:
            125–54.

1986   'Das Apostolische Amt des Paulus Nach 1 Kor 4,14–17', in Vanhoye 1986:
            103–19.

1988   *The Ethics of the New Testament* (Edinburgh: T&T Clark), trans. by D. Green
            of *Ethik des Neuen Testaments* (Göttingen: Vandenhoeck & Ruprecht, 1982).

1991   *Der Erste Brief an die Korinther, 1 Teilband, 1 Kor 1,1–6,11* (Zurich: Benziger
            Verlag; Neukirchener–Vluyn: Neukirchener Verlage).

1995   *Der Erste Brief an die Korinther, 2 Teilband, 1 Kor 6,12–11, 16* (Zurich:
            Benziger Verlag; Neukirchener–Vluyn: Neukirchener Verlag).

1999   *Der Erste Brief an die Korinther, 3 Teilband, 1 Kor 11, 17–14,40* (Zürich/
            Düsseldorf: Benziger Verlag; Neukirchener–Vluyn: Neukirchener Verlage).

Schreiner, T.
1989   'The Abolition and Fulfillment of the Law in Paul', *JSNT* 35: 47–74.

Schubert, P.
1939   *Form and Function of the Pauline Thanksgivings* (BZNW, 20; Berlin: Alfred
            Töpelmann).

Schulz, A.
1962   *Nachfolgen und Nachahmen. Studien Über das Verhältnis der Neuetesta-
            mentlichen Jüngerschaft zur Urchristlichen Vorbild Ethik* (München: Kösel-
            Verlag).

Schürer, E.
1973   *The History of the Jewish People in the Age of Jesus Christ (175 B.C.–A.D. 135)* (4 vols.; Edinburgh: T&T Clark, rev. and ed. Geza Vermes, Fergus Millar and Martin Goodman).

Schürmann, H.
1970   'Die Geistlichen Gnadengaben in den paulinischen Gemeinden', in *idem* (ed.), *Ursprung und Gestalt: Erörterungen und Besinnungen zum Neuen Testament* (Düsseldorf: Patmos-Verlag): 236–67.
1974   ' "Das Gesetz des Christus" (Gal 6,2). Jesu Verhalten und Wort als letzgültige sittliche Norm nach Paulus', in J. Gnilka (ed.), *Neues Testament und Kirche* (Freiburg: Herder): 282–300.

Schüssler-Fiorenza, E.
1983   *In Memory of Her: A Feminist Theological Reconstruction of Christian Origins* (New York: Crossroad).
1984   *Bread Not Stone: The Challenge of Feminist Biblical Interpretation* (Boston: Beacon Press).
1987   'Rhetorical Situation and Historical Reconstruction in 1 Corinthians', *NTS* 33: 386–403.
1994   'The Rhetoricity of Historical Knowledge: Pauline Discourse and its Contextualizations', in L. Bormann, *et al.* (eds.), *Religious Propaganda and Missionary Competition in the New Testament World* (NovTSup, 74; Leiden: E.J. Brill): 443–69.

Schütz, J.H.
1969   'Apostolic Authority and the Control of Tradition', *NTS* 15: 439–57.
1974   'Charisma and Social Reality', *JR* 54: 51–70.
1975   *Paul and the Anatomy of Apostolic Authority* (SNTSMS, 26; Cambridge: Cambridge University Press).

Schweitzer, A.
1931   *The Mysticism of the Apostle Paul* (London: A. & C. Black); trans. W. Montgomery of *Die Mystik des Apostels Paulus* [Tübingen: Mohr, 1930]).

Schweizer, E.
1967–68 'Dying and Rising with Christ', *NTS* 14: 1–14.
Schweizer, E., and F. Baumgärtel
1967   'σῶμα, κτλ.', in *TDNT* VII: 1024–94.

Scott, J.
1992   *Adoption as Sons of God: An Exegetical Investigation into the Background of* υἱοθεσία *in the Pauline Corpus* (WUNT, 2.48; Tübingen: J.C.B. Mohr [Paul Siebeck]).

Scroggs, R.
1966   *The Last Adam: A Study in Pauline Anthropology* (Philadelphia: Fortress Press).
1967–68 'Paul: ΣΟΦΟΣ and ΠΝΕΥΜΑΤΙΚΟΣ', *NTS* 14: 33–55.
1989   'Eschatological Existence in Matthew and Paul *Coincidentia Oppositorium*', in Marcus and Soards 1989: 125–46.
1993a   'New Being: Renewed Mind: New Perception. Paul's View of the Source of Ethical Insight', in *The Text and the Times* (Minneapolis: Fortress Press): 167–83.
1993b   'The New Testament and Ethics: How Do We Get There From Here?', in *The Text and the Times* (Minneapolis: Fortress Press): 192–211.
1996   'Paul and the Eschatological Body', in Lovering and Sumney 1996: 14–29.
Segal, A.
1990   *Paul the Convert* (New Haven, CT: Yale University Press).

| 1998 | 'Paul's Thinking about Resurrection in its Jewish Context', *NTS* 44: 400–19. |
| 1999 | 'Paul's "*Soma Pneumatikon*" and the Worship of Jesus', in Newman, Davila and Lewis 1999: 258–76. |

Shaw, G.
| 1983 | *The Cost of Authority: Manipulation and Freedom in the New Testament* (London: SCM Press). |

Silva, M.
| 1994 | 'Eschatological Structures in Galatians', in M. Silva and T. Schmidt (eds.), *To Tell the Mystery* (JSNTSup, 100; Sheffield: JSOT Press): 140–62. |

Smit, J.
| 1989 | 'The Letter of Paul to the Galatians: A Deliberative Speech', *NTS* 35: 1–26. |
| 2002 | ' "What is Apollos? What is Paul?" In Search for the Coherence of First Corinthians 1:10–4:21', *NovT* 44.3: 231–51. |

Smith, D.E.
| 1981 | 'Meals and Morality in Paul and His World', in K. Richards (ed.), *1981 SBL Seminar Papers* (Chico, CA: Scholars Press): 319–39. |
| 2003 | *From Symposium to Eucharist: The Banquet in the Early Christian World* (Minneapolis: Fortress Press). |

Smith, D.M.
1967	'*Ho de dikaios ek pisteôs zêsetai*', in B. Daniels and M.J. Suggs (eds.), *Studies on the History of the New Testament in Honor of Kenneth Willis Clark, PhD* (Salt Lake City: University of Utah Press): 13–25.
1972	'The Use of the OT in the New', in Efird 1972: 3–65.
1988	'The Pauline Literature', in D. Carson and H. Williamson (eds.), *It Is Written: Scripture Citing Scripture. Essays in Honour of Barnabas Lindars* (Cambridge: Cambridge University Press): 265–91.

Snodgrass, K.
| 1988 | 'Spheres of Influence: A Possible Solution to the Problem of Paul and the Law', *JSNT* 32: 93–113. |
| 1994 | 'The Gospel in Romans: A Theology of Revelation', in Jervis and Richardson 1994: 288–314. |

Soards, M.
| 1989 | 'Seeking (*Zētein*) and Sinning (*Hamartōlos*) According to Galatians 2.17', in Marcus and Soards 1989: 237–54. |

Soden, H. von
| 1892 | 'Die Ethik des Paulus', *ZTK*, 1: 109–45. |
| 1951 | 'Sakrament und Ethik bei Paulus', in *Urchristentum und Geschichte, I* (Tübingen: J.C.B. Mohr [Paul Siebeck]): 239–75. |

Spencer, W.D.
| 1989 | 'The Power in Paul's Teaching (1 Cor 4:9–20)', *JETS* 32: 51–61. |

Stählin, G.
| 1964 | 'ασθενής, ασθένεια, ασθενέω', *TDNT* I: 490–93. |

Stanley, C.D.
1992	*Paul and the Language of Scripture* (Cambridge: Cambridge University Press).
1990	' "Under a Curse": A Fresh Reading of Galatians 3.10–14', *NTS* 36: 481–511.
1999	' "Pearls Before Swine": Did Paul's Audiences Understand His Biblical Quotations?', *NovT* 41: 124–44.

Stanley, D.M.
| 1959 | ' "Become Imitators of Me": The Pauline Conception of Apostolic Tradition', *Bib* 40: 859–77. |
| 1984 | 'Imitation in Paul's Letters: Its Significance for His Relationship to Jesus and to His Own Christian Foundations', in Richardson and Hurd 1984: 127–41. |

Stanley, J.
1984   'The Sociology of Knowledge and New Testament Interpretation', in B. Hargrove (ed.), *Religion and the Sociology of Knowledge* (New York: Edwin Mellen Press): 123–52.

Stanton, G.
1985   'Aspects of Early Christian-Jewish Polemic and Apologetic', *NTS* 31: 377–92.
1996   'The Law of Moses and the Law of Christ: Galatians 3:1–6:2', in Dunn 1996b: 99–116.
2000   '*Galatians: A New Translation with Introduction and Commentary*', *JTS* 51.1 264–70.

Stendahl, K.
1976   *Paul Among Jews and Gentiles* (Philadelphia: Fortress Press).
1984   *Meanings* (Philadelphia: Fortress Press).

Sterling, G.
1995   'Wisdom Among the Perfect: Creation Traditions in Alexandrian Judaism and Corinthian Christiainity', *NovT* 37: 355–84.

Steyn, G.
1996   'Reflections on ΤΟ ΟΝΟΜΑ ΤΟΥ ΚΥΡΙΟΥ in 1 Corinthians', in Bieringer 1996: 479–90.

Stone, M.
1984   'Apocalyptic Literature', in M. Stone (ed.), *Jewish Writings of the Second Temple Period: Apocrypha, Pseudepigrapha, Qumran Sectarian Writings, Philo, Josephus* (Assen: von Gorcum): 383–441.

Story, C.
1976   'The Nature of Paul's Stewardship', *EvQ* 48: 212–29.

Stowers, S.
1984   'Social Status, Public Speaking and Private Teaching: The Circumstances of Paul's Preaching Activity', *NovT* 26: 59–82.
1986   *Letter Writing in Greco-Roman Antiquity* (Philadelphia: Westminster Press).
1989   'ἐκ πίστεως and διὰ τῆς πίστεως in Romans 3:30', *JBL* 108: 665–74.
1990   'Paul on the Use and Abuse of Reason', in Balch, Ferguson and Meeks 1990: 253–86.
1991   'Friends and Enemies in the Politics of Heaven', in Bassler 1991: 105–21.
1994   *A Rereading of Romans* (New Haven: Yale University Press).
2001   'Does Pauline Christianity Resemble a Hellenistic Philosophy?', in Engberg-Pedersen 2001: 81–102.

Strathman, H.
1967   'μάρτυς, κτλ.', in *TDNT* IV: 474–514.

Strecker, G.
1972   *Handlungsorientierter Glaube: Vorstudien zu einer Ethik des Neuen Testaments* (Stuttgart: Kreuz Verlag).
1987   'Indicative and Imperative According to Paul', *AusBR* 35: 60–72.

Stuhlmacher, P.
1966   *Gerechtigkeit Gottes bei Paulus* (Göttingen: Vandenhoeck & Ruprecht).
1968   *Das paulinische Evangelium, Vol I. Vorgeschichte* (Göttingen: Vandenhoeck & Ruprecht).
1980   'The Gospel of Reconciliation in Christ – Basic Features and Issues of a Biblical Theology of the New Testament', *HBT* 1: 161–91.
1987   'The Hermeneutical Significance of 1 Cor 2:6–16', in Hawthorne and Betz 1987: 328–43.

1991 'The Pauline Gospel', in P. Stuhlmacher (ed.), *The Gospel and the Gospels* (Grand Rapids, MI: Eerdmans): 149–72.

1992 *Biblische Theologie des Neuen Testaments, I Band. Grundlegung von Jesus zu Paulus* (Göttingen: Vandenhoeck & Ruprecht).

Stumpf, A.
1964 'ζῆλος, κτλ.', in *TDNT* II: 877–87.

Sturm, R.
1989 'Defining the Word "Apocalyptic": A Problem in Biblical Criticism', in Marcus and Soards 1989: 17–48.

Styler, G.
1973 'The Basis of Obligation in Paul's Christology and Ethics', in Lindars and Smalley 1973: 175–87.

Suggs, M.J.
1967 'The Word is Near You: Rom 10:6–10 Within the Purpose of the Letter', in Farmer *et al.* 1967: 289–312.

1994 'Koinonia in the New Testament', *Mid-Stream* 23: 351–62.

Sullivan, K.
2004 *Wrestling with Angels: A Study of the Relationship Between Angels and Humans in Ancient Jewish Literature and the New Testament* (Leiden: E.J. Brill).

Sumney, J.
1993 'Paul's "Weakness": An Integral Part of His Conception of Apostleship', *JSNT* 52: 71–91.

Swetnam, J.
1967 'On Romans 8,23 and the "Expectation of Sonship"', *Bib* 48: 102–108.

Tabor, J.
1986 *Things Unutterable: Paul's Ascent to Paradise in its Greco-Roman, Judaic, and Early Christian Contexts* (Lanham, MD: University Press of America).

Talbert, C.
2001 'Paul, Judaism and the Revisionists', *CBQ* 63.1: 1–22.

Talmon, S.
1991 'Oral Tradition and Written Transmission, or the Heard and Seen Word in Judaism of the Second Temple Period', in H. Wansbrough (ed.), *Jesus and the Oral Gospel Tradition* (Sheffield: Sheffield Academic Press): 121–58.

Tannehill, R.
1967 *Dying and Rising with Christ* (Berlin: Alfred Töpelman).

Taylor, G.M.
1966 'The Function of ΠΙΣΤΙΣ ΧΡΙΣΤΟΥ in Galatians', *JBL* 85: 58–76.

Taylor, N.H.
1995 'The Social Nature of Conversion in the Early Christian World', in Esler 1995: 128–36.

Theissen, G.
1978 *Sociology of Early Palestinian Christianity* (Philadelphia: Fortress Press); trans. J. Bowden of *Soziologie der Jesusbewegung* (München: Chr. Kaiser Verlag, 1977).

1982 *The Social Setting of Pauline Christianity: Essays on Corinth* (trans. J. Schütz; Philadelphia: Fortress Press).

1987 *Psychological Aspects of Pauline Theology* (Edinburgh: T&T Clark); trans. J. Galvin of *Psychologische Aspekte paulinischen Theologie* (Göttingen: Vandenhoeck & Ruprecht, 1983).

1992	'Soteriological Symbolism in the Pauline Writings', in *Social Reality and the Early Christians* (trans. M. Kohl; Edinburgh: T&T Clark): 159–86.
1999	*A Theory of Primitive Christian Religion* (London: SCM Press; trans. J. Bowden of *Theorie der urchristlichen Religion*; Gütersloh: Gütersloher Verlagshaus, 1999).

Thielman, F.
1989	*From Plight to Solution: A Jewish Framework to Understanding Paul's View of the Law in Galatians and Romans* (Leiden: E.J. Brill).

Thiselton, A.
1977–78	'Realized Eschatology at Corinth', *NTS* 24: 510–26.
1994	'Christology in Luke, Speech-Act Theory, and the Problem of Dualism in Christology After Kant', in J. Green and M. Turner (eds.), *Jesus of Nazareth: Lord and Christ* (Grand Rapids, MI: Eerdmans): 453–72.
2000	*The First Epistle to the Corinthians: A Commentary on the Greek Text* (NIGTC; Carlisle: Paternoster Press).

Thompson, M.
1991	*Clothed With Christ: The Example and Teaching of Jesus in Romans 12:1–15:13* (JSNTSup, 59; Sheffield: JSOT Press).

Thrall, M.
1967	'The Pauline Use of ΣΥΝΕΙΔΗΣΙΣ', *NTS* 14: 118–25.
1994–2000	*A Critical Exegetical Commentary on the Second Epistle to the Corinthians* (ICC; 2 vols.; Edinburgh: T&T Clark).

Thurén, L.
2000	*Derhetoricizing Paul* (WUNT, 124; Tübingen: J.C.B. Mohr [Paul Siebeck]).

Tinsley, E.
1960	*The Imitation of God in Christ* (London: SCM Press).

Tobin, T.
1995	'What Shall We Say that Abraham Found? The Controversy behind Romans 4', *HTR* 88: 437–52.

Tomlin, G.
1999	*The Power of the Cross: Theology and the Death of Christ in Paul, Luther and Pascal* (Carlisle: Paternoster Press).

Tomson, P.
1990	*Paul and the Jewish Law: Halakha in the Letters of the Apostle to the Gentiles* (Assen/Maastricht: Van Gorcum).
1996	'Paul's Jewish Background in View of His Law Teaching in 1 Corinthians 7', in Dunn 1996b: 251–70.

Tronier, H.
2001	'The Corinthian Correspondence between Philosophical Idealism and Apocalypticism', in Engberg-Pedersen 2001: 165–98.

Tuckett, C.
1983	'1 Corinthians and Q', *JBL* 102: 607–19.
1986	'Dt 21,35 and Paul's Conversion', in Vanhoye 1986: 345–50.
1988	'Q, the Law and Judaism', in B. Lindars (ed.), *Law and Religion* (Cambridge: James Clarke & Co.): 90–101.
1991	'Paul, Tradition and Freedom', *TZ* 47: 307–25.
1994	'Jewish Christian Wisdom in 1 Corinthians?', in S. Porter, *et al.* (eds.), *Crossing the Boundaries: Essays in Biblical Interpretation in Honour of M.D. Goulder* (Leiden: E.J. Brill): 201–19.
1996	'The Corinthians Who Say "There is No Resurrection of the Dead" (1 Cor 15,12)', in Bieringer 1996: 247–75.

2000   'Paul, Scripture and Ethics: Some Reflections', *NTS* 46.3: 403–24.
Turner, M.
1996   *The Holy Spirit and Spiritual Gifts, Then and Now* (Carlisle: Paternoster Press).
Uprichard, R.
1981   'The Person and Work of Christ in 1 Thessalonians', *EvQ* 53: 108–14.
Van der Watt, J.
1990   'The Use of *za* ✱ in 1 Thessalonians: A Comparison with *za* ✱/*z* ✱● in the Gospel of John', in R. Collins 1990: 356–69.
Vanhoye, A.
1986   *L'Apôtre Paul:Personnalité, style et conception du ministère* (BETL, 73; Leuven: Leuven University Press).
Van Spanje, T.
1999   *Inconsistency in Paul? A Critique of the Work of Heikki Räisänen* (WUNT, 110; J.C.B. Mohr [Paul Siebeck]).
van Unnik, W.C.
1973   'Jesus: Anathema or Kurios (I Cor. 12:3)', in Lindars and Smalley 1973: 113–26.
1984   'With All Those Who Call On the Name of the Lord', in William C. Weinrich (ed.), *New Testament Age* (Macon, GA: Mercer University Press): 533–51.
1993   'The Meaning of 1 Corinthians 12:31', *NovT* 35: 142–59.
Verhey, A.
1984a   'Ethics: NT Ethics', *ISBE* 2: 173–83.
1984b   *The Great Reversal: Ethics and the New Testament* (Grand Rapids, MI: Eerdmans).
Via, D.
1997   *The Revelation of God and/as Human Reception in the New Testament* (Harrisburg, PA: Trinity Press International).
Vielhauer, P.
1940   *Oikodomē: Das Bild vom Bau in der christlichen Literatur vom Neuen Testament bis Clemens Alexandrinus* (Karlsruhe: Harrassowitz).
Von Lips, H.
1985   'Der Apostolat des Paulus – ein Charisma? Semantische Aspekte zu χάρισμ-χάρισμα und anderen Wortpaaran im Sprachgebrauch des Paulus', *Bib* 66: 305–43.
Von Rad, G., G. Bertram and R. Bultmann
1964   'ζάω, κτλ.', in *TDNT* II: 832–74.
Wagner, J.
1998   'Not Beyond the Things Which are Written: A Call to Boast Only in the Lord (1 Cor 4.6)', *NTS* 44: 279–87.
Walker, W.
1992   '1 Cor 2:6–16: A Non-Pauline Interpolation?', *JSNT* 47: 75–94.
1997   'Translation and Interpretation of ἐὰν μη in Galatians 2:16', *JBL* 116: 515–20.
Wallis, I.
1995   *The Faith of Jesus Christ in the Early Christian Traditions* (SNTSMS, 84; Cambridge: Cambridge University Press).
Walter, N.
1985   'Paulus und die urchristliche Jesustradition', *NTS* 31: 498–522.
Wan, Sze-kar
1995   'Abraham and the Promise of the Spirit: Galatians and the Hellenistic-Jewish Mysticism of Philo', in E. Lovering (ed.), *1995 SBL Seminar Papers* (Atlanta: Scholars Press): 6–22.

Wanamaker, C.
1990   *The Epistle to the Thessalonians: A Commentary on the Greek Text* (NIGTC; Grand Rapids, MI: Eerdmans).
Watson, F.
1986   *Paul, Judaism and Gentiles* (Cambridge: Cambridge University Press).
1992   'Christ, Community, and the Critique of Ideology: A Theological Reading of 1 Corinthians 1:18–31', *NedTTs* 46: 132–49.
Way, D.
1991   *The Lordship of Christ* (Oxford: Clarendon Press).
Webster, J.
1986a   'Imitation of Christ', *TynBul* 37: 95–120.
1986b   'Christology, Imitability, Ethics', *SJT* 39: 309–26.
Wedderburn, A.
1985   'Some Observations on Paul's Use of the Phrases "in Christ" and "with Christ"', *JSNT* 25: 83–97.
1987   *Baptism and Resurrection: Studies in Pauline Theology Against its Graeco-Roman Background* (Tübingen: J.C.B. Mohr [Paul Siebeck]).
1988   *The Reasons for Romans* (SNTW; Edinburgh: T&T Clark).
Weima, J.
1994   *Neglected Endings: The Significance of the Pauline Letter Closings* (JSNTSup, 101; Sheffield: JSOT Press).
1996   ' "How You Must Walk to Please God": Holiness and Discipleship in 1 Thessalonians', in R. Longenecker 1996: 98–119.
Weiss, J.
1970   *Earliest Christianity*, II (Gloucester, MA: Peter Smith); trans. F. Grant of *Das Urchristentum* (Göttingen: Vandenhoeck & Ruprecht, 1937).
1977   *Der Erste Korintherbrief* (Göttingen: Vandenhoeck & Ruprecht [Zweiter Neudruck], originally published 1910).
Welborn, L.
1987   'A Conciliatory Principle in 1 Cor. 4:6', *NovT* 39: 320–46.
Wernle, P.
1897   *Der Christ und die Sünde bei Paulus* (Freiburg i. B. und Leipzip: Akademische Verlagsbuchhandlung von J.C.B. Mohr [Paul Siebeck]).
Westerholm, S.
1984   'Letter and Spirit: The Foundation of Paul's Ethics', *NTS* 30: 229–48.
1988   *Israel's Law and the Church's Faith: Paul and His Recent Interpreters* (Grand Rapids, MI: Eerdmans).
White, H.C.
1988   'Speech Act Theory and Literary Criticism', *Semeia* 41: 1–24.
White, L.M.
1990   'Morality Between Two Worlds: A Paradigm of Friendship in Philippians', in Balch, Ferguson and Meeks 1990: 201–15.
Whiteley, D.
1974   *The Theology of St Paul* (Oxford: Oxford University Press).
Wickert, U.
1959   'Einheit und Eintracht der Kirche im Präskript des ersten Korintherbriefes', *ZNW* 50: 73–82.
Wilckens, U.
1971   *Weisheit und Torheit: Eine exegetisch-religions geschichtliche Untersuchung zu 1 Kor. 1 und 2* (BHTh, 26; Tubingen: J.C.B. Mohr).
1978   *Der Brief an die Römer*, I (Zurich: Benziger Verlag; Neukirchen–Vluyn: Neukirchener Verlag).

Williams, R.
1989   'Does it Make Sense to Speak of Pre-Nicene Orthodoxy?', in R. Williams
            (ed.), *The Making of Orthodoxy: Essays in Honour of Henry Chadwick* (Cambridge: Cambridge University Press): 1–23.
1997   'Interiority and Epiphany: A Reading in New Testament Ethics', *Modern Theology* 13.1: 29–51.
Williams, S.K.
1975   *Jesus' Death as Saving Event: The Background and Origin of a Concept* (HDR, 2; Missoula, MT: Scholars Press).
1980   'The "Righteousness of God" in Romans', *JBL* 99: 241–90.
1987a   'Justification and the Spirit in Galatians', *JSNT* 29: 91–100.
1987b   'Again *Pistis Christou*', *CBQ* 49: 431–47.
1988   '*Promise* in Galatians: A Reading of Paul's Reading of Scripture', *JBL* 107: 709–20.
1989   'The Hearing of Faith: ΑΚΟΗ ΠΙΣΤΕΟΣ in Galatians 3', *NTS* 35: 82–93.
1997   *Galatians* (Nashville: Abingdon Press).
Williamson, H.
1989   'The Concept of Israel in Transition', in R. Clements (ed.), *The World of Ancient Israel* (Cambridge: Cambridge University Press): 141–61.
Willis, W.
1989   'The "Mind of Christ" in 1 Corinthians 2, 16', *Bib* 70: 110–22.
1996   'Pauline Ethics 1964–1994', in Lovering and Sumney 1996: 306–19.
Wimbush, V.
1987   *Paul the Worldly Ascetic: Response to the World and Self Understanding According to 1 Corinthians 7* (Macon, GA: Mercer University Press).
Windisch, H.
1924   'Das Problem des paulinischen Imperativs', *ZNW* 23: 265–81.
Winger, M.
1986   'Unreal Conditions in the Letters of Paul', *JBL* 105.1: 110–12.
1994   'Tradition, Revelation and Gospel: A Study in Galatians', *JSNT* 53: 65–86.
1998   'Meaning and Law (Paul's Use of Nomos)', *JBL* 117: 105–10.
1999   'From Grace to Sin: Names and Abstractions in Paul's Letters', *NovT* 41: 145–75.
Wink, W.
1992   *Engaging the Powers: Discernment and Resistance in a World of Domination* (Minneapolis: Fortress Press).
Winter, B.
1991   'Civil Litigation in Secular Corinth and the Church: The Forensic Background to 1 Corinthians 6:1–8', *NTS* 37: 559–72.
2001   *After Paul Left Corinth: The Influence of Secular Ethics and Social Change* (Grand Rapids, MI: Eerdmans).
Wire, A.
1990   *The Corinthian Women Prophets* (Minneapolis: Fortress Press).
Wißmann, E.
1926   *Das Verhältnis von ΠΙΣΤΙΣ und Christusfrömmigkeit bei Paulus* (Göttingen: Vandenhoeck & Ruprecht).
Witherington, B.
1994a   *Paul's Narrative Thought World: The Tapestry of Tragedy and Triumph* (Louisville, KY: Westminster/John Knox Press).
1994b   *Conflict and Community in Corinth: A Socio-Rhetorical Commentary on 1 and 2 Corinthians* (Grand Rapids, MI: Eerdmans).

1998   *Grace in Galatia: A Commentary on St Paul's Letter to the Galatians* (Edinburgh: T&T Clark).

Wolter, M.
1997   'Ethos und Identität in Paulinischen Gemeinden', *NTS* 43: 430–44.
2003   'Der Brief des so genannten Unzuchtsünders', in M. Gielen and J. Kügler (eds.), *Liebe, Macht und Religion: Interdisziplinäre Studien zu Grunddimensionen menschlicher Existenz* (Stuttgart: Verlag Katholisches Bibelwerk): 323–37.

Wong, E.
2002   'The Deradicalization of Jesus' Ethical Sayings in 1 Corinthians', *NTS* 48.2: 181–94.

Wood, C.
1985   *Vision and Discernment: An Orientation in Theological Study* (Atlanta: Scholars Press).

Wrede, W.
1907   *Paul* (London: Philip Green); trans. E. Lummis of *Paulus* (Halle: Gebauer-Schwetschke, 1904).
1973   'The Task and Methods of New Testament Theology', in Morgan 1973: 68–116; trans. of *Über Aufgabe und Methode der sogenannten neutestamentliche Theologie* (Göttingen: Vandenhoeck and Ruprecht, 1897).

Wright, N.T.
1991a   *The Climax of the Covenant* (Edinburgh: T&T Clark).
1991b   'Putting Paul Together Again', in Bassler 1991: 183–211.

Yarbrough, O.L.
1995   'Parents and Children in the Letters of Paul', in L.M. White and O.L. Yarbrough (eds.), *The Social World of the First Christians* (Minneapolis: Fortress Press): 126–41.

Yim, H.
1985   'Preaching God's Word "In Demonstration of the Spirit and Power"', in P. Elbert (ed.), *Essays on Apostolic Themes* (Peabody, MA: Hendrickson), pp. 71–81.

Yinger, K.
1999   *Paul, Judaism and Judgment According to Deeds* (Cambridge: Cambridge University Press).

Yoder, J.H.
1984   *The Priestly Kingdom: Social Ethics as Gospel* (Notre Dame, IN: University of Notre Dame Press).

Young, F.
1993   'Paul and the Kingdom of God', in R. Barbour (ed.), *The Kingdom of God and Human Society* (Edinburgh: T&T Clark): 242–55.

Young, F., and D. Ford
1987   *Meaning and Truth in 2 Corinthians* (London: SPCK).

Young, N.H.
1987   '*Paidagogos*: The Social Setting of a Pauline Metaphor', *NovT* 29: 150–76.
1998   'Who's Cursed – And Why? (Galatians 3:10–14)', *JBL* 117: 79–92.

Ziesler, J.
1972   *The Meaning of Righteousness in Paul* (Cambridge: Cambridge University Press).
1987   'The Just Requirement of the Law', *AusBR* 35: 77–82.
1990   *Pauline Christianity* (Oxford: Oxford University Press).

INDEXES

INDEX OF REFERENCES

OLD TESTAMENT

278   *Looking for Life*

1 Corinthians (cont.)

1.18–20	25
1.18	43, 54–56, 62, 63, 66, 74, 79, 105, 127, 139, 155, 180, 202
1.19–25	56
1.19	77
1.20–21	56
1.20	17, 55, 206
1.21	51, 54, 57, 58, 74, 78, 86, 115, 125
1.22	57, 161
1.23–25	196
1.23–24	202
1.23	39, 43, 57, 60, 74, 105, 153, 163, 180
1.24	25, 56, 57, 90
1.25	74, 78, 135, 180
1.26–2.5	58
1.26–31	96, 109, 128, 220
1.26–30	90
1.26	58, 218
1.27	74, 78, 135
1.29–31	51, 59
1.29–30	206
1.29	50, 149
1.30	25, 40, 41, 56, 57, 149
1.31	50, 77
2.1–3.3	8
2.1–16	12, 51, 54, 59, 83, 93, 129, 132, 165, 184, 187, 188, 212
2.1–12	134, 167
2.1–10	153
2.1–5	2–4, 6, 12, 15, 18, 36, 43, 46, 48, 53, 54, 57, 59, 63, 64, 77, 78, 80, 81, 86, 88, 89, 93, 95–97, 107–109, 112, 113, 121–23, 127, 128, 135, 137, 138, 140, 142, 144, 151, 155, 161, 164, 166, 178, 181, 189, 193–96, 214, 216–18
2.1–2	60
2.1	59–61, 124
2.2–5	77, 176, 182
2.2–3	135
2.2	39, 43, 44, 51, 57, 59–61, 78–80, 126, 140, 153, 155, 163, 180
2.3	61, 78, 180
2.4–5	3, 45, 78, 86, 108
2.4	42, 61
2.5	62, 175
2.6–16	3, 44, 62, 63, 70, 75, 153
2.6–8	65
2.6	17, 25, 55, 63, 206
2.7–8	111
2.7	59, 63, 64, 124
2.8	17, 55, 65, 70, 206
2.9–10	65
2.9	42, 77, 120, 142
2.10–16	100, 178, 195
2.10–12	124
2.10	21, 41, 51, 59, 74, 78, 91, 107, 108, 153
2.11	93
2.12–16	66, 68, 88, 108, 121, 193
2.12–14	140
2.12–13	106, 217
2.12	3, 41, 44, 61, 63, 65, 66, 68, 71, 74, 78, 88, 89, 91, 93, 106, 107, 109, 137, 140, 153, 197
2.13–16	54, 76, 124
2.13	3, 63, 66–69, 100, 124, 152, 190, 216
2.14–15	69, 74, 139
2.14	66, 69, 72, 74, 75, 78, 93, 107, 136, 139
2.15–16	68
2.15	69, 75, 76, 78, 136, 138, 198
2.16	51, 69, 77, 93, 102, 113
3–4	71
3.1–4	42, 71, 74, 78, 212
3.1–3	119, 120, 136
3.1–2	72
3.1	66, 72, 74, 115, 136–39, 149, 198

OTHER ANCIENT REFERENCES

INDEX OF AUTHORS